WORKBOOK FOR

Mastering Medical Coding

Fourth Edition

Marsha S. Diamond, CPC, CPC-H, CCS
Instructor, Former Department Chair
Health Information Technology
Central Florida College
Orlando, Florida

Past National Advisory Board Member
American Academy of Professional Coders
Salt Lake City, Utah

Senior Consultant/Auditor
Medical Audit Resource Services, Inc.
Orlando, Florida

D1736541

SAUNDERS

ELSEVIER

SAUNDERS
ELSEVIER

3251 Riverport Lane
Maryland Heights, Missouri 63043

Workbook for
MASTERING MEDICAL CODING, FOURTH EDITION
Copyright © 2010, 2006, 2003, 2001 by Saunders, an imprint of Elsevier Inc.

ISBN: 978-1-4160-5036-0

CPT only Copyright © 2009. Current Procedural Terminology,
American Medical Association.

Notice

Knowledge and best practice in this field are constantly changing. As new research and experience broaden
our knowledge, changes in practice, treatment and drug therapy may become necessary or appropriate.
Readers are advised to check the most current information provided (i) on procedures featured or (ii) by the
manufacturer of each product to be administered, to verify the recommended dose or formula, the method
and duration of administration, and contraindications. It is the responsibility of the practitioner, relying on
their own experience and knowledge of the patient, to make diagnoses, to determine dosages and the best
treatment for each individual patient, and to take all appropriate safety precautions. To the fullest extent of
the law, neither the Publisher nor the Author assumes any liability for any injury and/or damage to persons
or property arising out of or related to any use of the material contained in this book.

ISBN: 978-1-4160-5036-0

Vice President and Publisher, Health Professions: Andrew M. Allen
Executive Editor: Susan Cole
Developmental Editor: Beth LoGiudice
Publishing Services Manager: Patricia Tannian
Project Manager: Carrie Stetz

Printed in the United States of America

Last digit is the print number: 9 8 7 6 5 4 3 2 1

Working together to grow
libraries in developing countries

www.elsevier.com | www.bookaid.org | www.sabre.org

ELSEVIER   BOOK AID International   Sabre Foundation

CONTENTS

INTRODUCTION

Godfrey Regional Hospital Providers and Facilities

As discussed in **Mastering Medical Coding**, a number of forms and formats may be used for record keeping and reimbursement purposes. These forms and formats may also occur in different locations. The textbook and the workbook have adapted a real-life-scenario approach to help students understand the coding process. To this end, the following providers from various locations are represented throughout the textbook and its ancillaries.

Some charts are dictated and typed, whereas others are handwritten, sometimes bordering on illegible. A list of these providers and facilities is included in Table 1.

Providers and locations have been established so that students may practice the multitude of skills required in medical coding. A signature log is required so that office personnel may identify signatures of individual physicians providing the various services. Table 2 contains the signature log for the medical groups.

Table 1. Godfrey Regional Health Facilities and Providers	
Godfrey Regional Outpatient Clinic 3122 Shannon Avenue Aldon, FL 77712 (407) 555-7654	Godfrey Clinical Laboratories 465 Dogwood Court Aldon, FL 77712 (407) 555-9876
Godfrey Regional Hospital 123 Main Street Aldon, FL 77714 (407) 555-1234	Godfrey Medical Associates 1532 Third Avenue, Suite 120 Aldon, FL 77713 (407) 555-4000

Provider Names	Specialty	Location(S) of Service
Patrick Adams, MD	Gastroenterologist	Godfrey Regional Hospital Godfrey Medical Associates
Nathan Brady, MD	Internal Medicine/Cardiology	Godfrey Regional Hospital Godfrey Regional Outpatient Clinic Godfrey Medical Associates
Maria Callaway, MD	Surgical Pathologist	Godfrey Regional Hospital Godfrey Regional Outpatient Clinic
Patrick Chung, MD	Surgeon/Orthopedics	Godfrey Regional Hospital Godfrey Regional Outpatient Clinic Godfrey Medical Associates
Nancy Connelly, MD	Emergency Department	Godfrey Regional Hospital
Jay Corman, MD	Internal Medicine	Godfrey Regional Hospital Godfrey Medical Associates

Continued

Provider Names	Specialty	Location(S) of Service
Vincent DiMarco, MD	Neurologist	Godfrey Regional Hospital Godfrey Regional Outpatient Clinic
Maurice Doates, MD	Internal Medicine	Godfrey Regional Hospital Godfrey Regional Outpatient Clinic Godfrey Medical Associates
James Ellicott, MD	Otolaryngologist	Godfrey Regional Hospital Godfrey Regional Outpatient Clinic
Stanley Krosette, MD	Internal Medicine	Godfrey Regional Hospital Godfrey Regional Outpatient Clinic Godfrey Medical Associates
William Obert, MD	Family Medicine	Godfrey Regional Hospital Godfrey Medical Associates
John Parker, MD	Internal Medicine	Godfrey Regional Hospital Godfrey Regional Outpatient Clinic Godfrey Medical Associates
Linda Patrick, MD	Ophthalmologist	Godfrey Regional Hospital Godfrey Medical Associates
Luis Perez, MD	Anesthesiologist	Godfrey Regional Hospital Godfrey Regional Outpatient Clinic
Rachel Perez, MD	Surgeon/General	Godfrey Regional Hospital Godfrey Regional Outpatient Clinic Godfrey Medical Associates
Robert Rais, MD	Emergency Department	Godfrey Regional Hospital
Steven Speller, MD	Pathologist	Godfrey Clinical Laboratories
Lisa Valhas, MD	Radiologist	Godfrey Regional Hospital Godfrey Regional Outpatient Clinic
Felix Washington, MD	Family Medicine	Godfrey Regional Hospital Godfrey Medical Associates
Adam Westgate, MD	Surgeon/General	Godfrey Regional Hospital Godfrey Regional Outpatient Clinic Godfrey Medical Associates

Table 1. Godfrey Regional Health Facilities and Providers—Cont'd

Table 2. Godfrey Regional Medical Signature Log

Provider	Signature
Maurice Doates, MD	*Maurice Doates, MD*
Robert Rais, MD	*Robert Rais MD*
Stanley Krosette, MD	*Stanley Krosette, MD*
William Obert, MD	*William Obert MD*
Felix Washington, MD	*Felix Washington MD*
Jay Corman, MD	*Jay Corman MD*
Nancy Connelly, MD	*Nancy Connelly MD*
Adam Westgate, MD	*Adam Westgate MD*
Patrick Chung, MD	*Patrick Chung MD*
Rachel Perez, MD	*Rachel Perez MD*
Lisa Valhas, MD	*Lisa Valhas MD*
John Parker, MD	*John Parker MD*
Nathan Brady, MD	*Nathan Brady MD*
Luis Perez, MD	*Luis Perez MD*
Steven Speller, MD	*Steven Speller MD*
Maria Callaway, MD	*Maria Callaway MD*
Patrick Adams, MD	*Patrick Adams MD*
James Ellicott, MD	*James Ellicott MD*
Linda Patrick, MD	*Linda Patrick MD*
Vincent DiMarco, MD	*Vincent DiMarco MD*

Additional Forms

Use the following formatted worksheets to complete exercises:

Diagnostic Documentation Worksheet	ICD-9-CM codes
Evaluation and Management Level Worksheet	E & M codes
Surgery Documentation Worksheet	Surgery CPT-4 codes
Hospital Inpatient Coding Worksheet	Hospital Codes

DIAGNOSTIC DOCUMENTATION WORKSHEET

Chart#/Patient Name:

WHAT (Service/Procedure)	WHY (MEDICAL NECESSITY) (Diagnostic Information)

Step 1 Select all words for possible use as diagnosis/diagnostic statement from the document

Step 2 Determine which words are appropriate for inclusion: (Carry these forward) Diagnosis vs. signs/symptoms

Step 3 Based on each service performed, determine the appropriate order of diagnosis for each service performed

Step 4 Look up/assign the proper dx codes

EVALUATION AND MANAGEMENT LEVEL WORKSHEET

History	1	2	3	4	5
HPI:					
PMH:					
SH/FH:					
ROS					
Level History Assigned:					

Examination	1	2	3	4	5
Body Organ(s):					
Organ System(s):					
Level Exam Assigned:					

Medical Decision Making	1	2	3	4	5
Diagnosis/Management Options:					
Amount/Complexity Data:					
Risk/Morbidity/Mortality:					
Level Medical Decision Making Assigned:					

Other Factors Documented (Time, Counseling):

LOCATION OF SERVICE (CIRCLE ONE)

Office/Outpatient	Critical Care	Prolonged	Newborn Care
Hospital	Neonatal ICU	Services	Special E&M
Observation	Nursing Facility	Case Management	Service
Hospital Inpatient	Domiciliary, Rest	Care Plan	
Consultations	Home	Oversight	
Emergency	Home Services	Preventative	
Department		Medicine	

TYPE OF SERVICE (CIRCLE ONE)

New Patient   Established Patient

Patient Name:_____ **Level Assigned:**_____

Date: _____ **Coder:** _____

Surgery Documentation Worksheet

Patient Name:_____Date of Procedure:_____

Pre-Operative Information	Documented	Not Documented	Comments
Surgeon			
Resident			
Assistant			
Date of surgery			
Pre-operative diagnosis			
Post-operative diagnosis			
Procedures			

Intra-Operative Information	Documented	Not Documented	Comments
Position			
Pre/drape			
Dissection/mode of entry			
Names of structures removed/repaired			
Materials removed/inserted			
Findings			
Bilateral structures addressed/repaired			
Sponge count			
Blood loss			
Pert path findings			
Unusual findings			
Problems/complications			

Post-Operative Information	Documented	Not Documented	Comments
Post-operative findings			
Post-operative complications			

HOSPITAL INPATIENT DRG CODING WORKSHEET

Chart#/Patient Name:

List Components Here		Assign Codes Here	
Step 1 - Principal/Secondary Diagnosis 1A - List diagnosis 1B - Determine primary diagnosis "Condition established after study to be chie y responsible for admission to hospital for care" Number diagnoses in appropriate order			
Step 2 - Significant Procedures			
Step 3 - Determine whether surgical procedure performed Yes/No			
Step 4 - Assign the MDC Based on principal diagnosis			
Step 5 - Determine whether medical or surgical partition Med/Surg			
Step 6 - Check for Contributing Factors Age Sex Discharge status Presence/absence of complications or comorbidities Birthweight for neonates			
ASSIGNMENT	**DRG:** Principal Dx: Addtl Dx:		

1 Anatomy, Physiology, and Medical Terminology Review

EXERCISES 1-20

Define the following terms.

1. Blepharoplasty _____

2. OS _____

3. OD _____

4. OU _____

5. Hyperopia _____

6. OM _____

7. Otitis externa _____

8. Mastoid/o _____

9. Tympan/o _____

10. Acou/o _____

11. Tonsillectomy _____

12. Laryngectomy _____

13. Adenoidectomy _____

14. Appendectomy _____

15. Cholecystectomy _____

16. Cholecystectomy, laparoscopic _____

17. Umbilical hernia _____

18. TURP _____

19. ORIF _____

20. Rhinoplasty _____

EXERCISES 21-30

Define the **bolded** terms in the following reports.

21. This 54-year-old female known to this practice returns for the first time since 2000 for abdominal pain, primarily mid-abdominal and **epigastric** in nature. Symptoms have been present for approximately 2 weeks. Patient reports nausea, vomiting, and diarrhea as well. No chest pain, **SOB**, rectal bleeding. Patient has been treated by this practice for **arthritis** and hypertension.

    Vital signs, BP 184/94, pulse 104. Heart unremarkable, chest clear. Abdomen, soft, tender in epigastric area. Laboratory shows hematocrit of 43, WBC of 7100.

    Acute abdominal pain, cannot rule out appendicitis or gallbladder disease. Will send for abdominal ultrasound for further evaluation. Return to office following completion of studies.

    _____

    _____

    _____

    _____

22. 25-year-old male with severe **cephalgia** that began 2 weeks ago, went away for a few days, and returned even more severe approximately 2 days ago. Experiences vomiting when upright, no diarrhea. No abdominal pain, rashes, numbness, or back pain. No urinary symptoms and no allergies per the patient.

    On exam, neck was supple, no cervical **adenopathy**, oral mucosa pink, moist. Heart is regular rate and rhythm. Abdomen is nontender and soft with no guarding.

    Migraine headaches; will refer to **neurologist** for further evaluation and treatment because this problem has plagued the patient for some time.

_____

_____

_____

_____

23. Patient with abdominal pain and history of Crohn's disease. Patient presents **tachycardic**. Believe patient is going through drug withdrawal at this time. Recommended admission to drug rehab program; however, patient is refusing at this time.

As a **palliative** measure, gave him 2 Tylox. Recheck first of the week and patient should call if he changes his mind regarding admission.

_____

_____

_____

24. 7-year-old with sore throat, difficulty swallowing, and headache for the past several days presents to the physician's office. Not improving regardless of aspirin, Tylenol, and gargling.

EXAM: Patient is **afebrile**. She has retro **TM** fluid on the left ear, which is **symptomatic**. The right side is normal. She has a considerable amount of **oropharyngeal** inflammation, with small, tender anterior cervical nodes. Lungs are clear to **auscultation**; heart, regular rate and rhythm without murmur.

IMPRESSION: Strep **tonsillitis**. Will treat with antibiotics, bed rest.

_____

_____

_____

_____

25. 9-year-old female with sore throat and cough that she has now had for about a week. Temperature in the office is 101.4; patient is **febrile**.

Skin is clear, eardrums are negative, pharynx is red. Cultures taken. Negative for Strep. Chest clear to auscultation. Heart tones regular without murmurs. Abdomen is soft, nontender.

IMPRESSION: **URI** with **pharyngitis**.

Amoxicillin, 250 mg tid for 10 days

_____

_____

_____

_____

26. 54-year-old female presents with stress at home. Issues regarding her current living situation with her boyfriend and her children have caused the patient to be unable to sleep or concentrate. Talked with patient at length regarding her stress level, approximately 15 minutes, and prescribed Trazodone 25 mg to take 1-2 hours before bed for the next few nights. We scheduled her to see a **psychologist** next week to begin resolving issues. Total visit time was 25 minutes.

Dx: Acute **anxiety, depressive disorder.**

_____

_____

_____

27. Patient presents for initial evaluation complaining of severe **pruritic** rash on her left and right **antecubital fossa** × 4 days. Reports rash began on her arms, erupted, and spread to her forearms and lower extremities. Also has multiple lesions across her chest area. Denies any new lotions, soaps, foods, pets, or clothes. No previous history of dermatitis. Denies fever, chills; other than rash, all other systems are unremarkable.

EXAM: **Diffuse** vesicular lesions across upper torso, forearms and thighs. Erythematous area of vesicular lesions in her right and left **popliteal fossa**. Vesicular lesions, etiology unknown.

Will prescribe **topical** hydrocortisone cream and use Benadryl for itching. If condition does not improve within 24-48 hours, patient should consider dermatology consult.

_____

_____

_____

28. Patient returns for evaluation of right **groin lesion**. He has been previously evaluated for this lesion, however, he feels it may have increased in size.

    Examination shows what appears to be a **lipoma** in the right groin area, appears **benign**. No sign of **hernia**, other masses, or **adenopathy.** Reassured patient and counseled him regarding the need to monitor size and contact us if he feels it is increasing further.

    _____

    _____

    _____

    _____

29. 82-year-old presents to the **ER** with episodes of shortness of breath when **supine** intermittently for the last few weeks. States feels OK until he lies down and tries to sleep. Denies chest pain, lower extremity swelling, but has had a dry cough for several days. Past history of **atrial fib** and **COPD**. Denies feeling of lightheadedness.

    EXAM: Vital signs, BP 142/78, temp 98.9

    Lungs: Clear to auscultation, no wheezes, **rales**, **rhonchi**

    Heart: Regular rate and rhythm, no murmurs

Abdomen: Soft, nontender, nondistended

Extremities: No **edema**, **cyanosis**

ECG: Normal sinus rhythm

CXR: Signs of COPD present; multiple cloudings on x-ray

DIAGNOSIS: **Exacerbation** of COPD

_____

_____

_____

_____

30. 22-year-old male caught foot on top step and fell at work, bruising the outer aspect of his right **tarsals**. X-rays are negative.

    IMPRESSION: **Contusion** of foot; patient to take **OTC** pain meds as needed.

    _____

    _____

    _____

    _____

2 Crucial Role of Physician Documentation

EXERCISES 1-5

Choose the best answer for the following questions.

1. Pertinent negatives are included in the _____ section of SOAP notes.
   a. history
   b. objective
   c. assessment
   d. plan

2. A review of systems is considered part of (the) _____.
   a. medical decision making
   b. family history
   c. social history
   d. examination

3. Title XVII of the Social Security Act of 1966 determined _____ was important to Medicare claims.
   a. qui tam action
   b. discharge summary
   c. medical necessity
   d. dictation

4. Which of the following statements is true?
   a. Dictated reports are easier to read than handwritten reports.
   b. Dictated reports are longer than handwritten reports.
   c. Dictated reports can be created more quickly than handwritten reports.
   d. Both a and c.

5. A _____ is considered an ancillary report.
   a. problem list
   b. medication record
   c. history and physical
   d. progress note

EXERCISES 6-10

Fill in the correct information for the following sentences.

6. A patient's complete history contains

   _____

   _____

7. Key components of all medical documentation include

   _____

   _____

8. Medical decision making requires

   _____

   _____

9. The cardinal rule of coding is

   _____

   _____

10. Guidelines for inpatient records are developed by

    _____

    _____

Determine the diagnostic statements in the following medical records that require assignment of ICD-9-CM codes.

EXERCISE 11

EMERGENCY ROOM RECORD

Name:		Age:	ER physician:
		DOB:	

Allergies/type of reaction:	Usual medications/dosages:
Penicillin and Naprosyn.	Lanoxin, 125 mg qd; isosorbide 30 mg half tablet qd; Lasix 20 mg one tablet bid; Lotensin 5 mg qd; aspirin one tablet qd; Plavix 75 mg po qd.

Triage/presenting complaint: 86-year-old was brought in for chest pain that was relieved with oxygen. Patient stated it was in the range of 5. By the time she got to the ER, the pain had completely resolved. During this time she was given some nitro that completely resolved the pain. Denies any nausea or vomiting at this time.
PAST MEDICAL HISTORY: CHF, angina, hypertension, and peripheral vascular disease.

Initial assessment:

Time	T	P	R	BP	Other:				

Medication orders:

Lab work: CBC shows WBC 7.8, hemoglobin 10.0, hematocrit 131.7, platelets 302. Metabolic panel showed glucose 120, BUN 20, creatinine 1.1, CPK 95. ALT is 117, AST 82, troponin 0, CPK 95.

X-ray: X-rays show cardiomegaly with no evidence of any infiltrate or pleural effusion.

Physician's report:

PHYSICAL EXAMINATION: Alert and oriented times three. At the time of examination, patient is chest-pain-free. T. 98.0, P. 89, R. 24, BP 128/69, saturating 99% on 3 liters.
HEENT: PERRLA, EOMI. Anicteric sclerae. Throat clear.
CHEST: Bilaterally clear with a few basilar crackles.
CARDIOVASCULAR: S1, S2 normal.
ABDOMEN: Soft, nontender.
EXTREMITIES: No edema, no cyanosis.
CNS: Grossly intact with no focal deficit.
PLAN: Increase isosorbide to 30 mg po qd and increase Lasix to 40 mg po qd. Follow up with primary care physician for the next couple of days. If the pain presents, return to the clinic to seek medical attention or come back to the emergency room.

Patient was discharged in stable condition.

Diagnosis:	Physician sign/date
ASSESSMENT: CHF, angina.	*Robert Rai MD*

Discharge	Transfer	Admit	Good	Satisfactory	Other:

GODFREY REGIONAL HOSPITAL
123 Main Street • Aldon, FL 77714 • (407) 555-1234

Answers

OFFICE NOTE

Date:	Vital signs:	T	R
Chief complaint:		P	BP

77-year-old comes in with pain in all the limbs, specifically the left elbow that has become swollen and tender. Patient has past history of gout in both ankles. States that the left elbow is swollen and has difficulty bending his arm. Unsure if he fell down. States that when he woke up this morning, his mattress was on the other side of the room and he was sleeping on the floor. Patient comes in with his nephew who confirms the above finding. Patient also has recently begun remembering events a little differently; however, is able to provide a history consistently without any problems.

MEDICATIONS: Cardura, Toprol, Softnen, nitro, Lanoxin, and Coumadin.

ALLERGIES: No known drug allergies.

Examination:

Alert and oriented times three; does not appear to be in any acute distress, does not appear to be dehydrated. T. 99.1, P. 49, R. 20, BP 137/88, saturating 97% on room air.

HEENT: PERRLA, EOML. Anicteric sclerae. Throat clear.

CHEST: Clear.

ABDOMEN: Soft, nontender.

EXTREMITIES: No edema, no cyanosis. Left elbow is swollen and tender.

LABS AND X-RAYS: CBC shows WBC 11.4, hemoglobin 16.1, hematocrit 46.5, platelets 149. X-rays of the left elbow do not show any specific fracture; however, questionable area of the left medial epicondyle. Either it has bony spur or is slightly moved away.

Impression:

ASSESSMENT: Most likely gouty arthritis.

Plan:

Will start on Celebrex 100 mg po bid. 15 tablets were given from the clinic. Also patient does not appear to take care of himself on a regular basis, and he does require some degree of assistance. Will get County Services involved for his health care. Patient advised to follow up with family physician in the next couple of days and was discharged from the clinic in stable condition.

William Obst MD

	Patient name:
	DOB:
	MR/Chart #:

GODFREY REGIONAL OUTPATIENT CLINIC
3122 Shannon Avenue • Aldon, FL 77712 • (407) 555-7654

Answers

OFFICE NOTE

Date:		Vital signs:	T		R	
Chief complaint:			P		BP	

S: Patient presents complaining of bilateral leg aches and left knee pain. He states that this has been bothering him off and on for a long period of time. He has had CVAs in the past. He has diabetes mellitus and alcoholic liver disease. He was sent up to Atlanta about 1–2 weeks ago with alcoholic encephalopathy. They treated him there for a few days and were able to send him home. He has mitral regurgitation and atrial fibrillation. He did have a heart cath about two years ago. He has had a couple CVAs in the past. Current medications are as listed on his ER sheet. He has no known allergies. He states that off and on for the last month his left knee has been painful for him, as have his legs through the upper legs and lower legs. It tends to be fairly nondescript.

Physical examination:

O: On examination, his left knee has a joint effusion and some mild decreased range of motion. Right knee is normal except for some arthritic changes but no effusion. His left knee is not warm to the touch. It is not erythematous. He has scattered areas of tenderness over his thighs and calves. It does not seem to be focused into any one region. There is a little bit of ankle edema but this is fairly typical for him. He has no evidence of respiratory distress at this time and has no other complaints in regards to his heart or lungs.

Assessment:

A: Arthritis, left knee with mild joint effusion; does not appear to be a septic knee. Scattered muscle aches and tenderness, probably related to deconditioning and his chronic health issues.

Plan:

P: Recommended exercise as much as he possibly can. Use Tylenol in limited amounts for his pain. Suggested using approximately half the usual dose of Tylenol, whatever strength he has. Discussed repeatedly and in detail how to split the recommended dose in half for each dose and for total daily requirements, and to try and get by on as little as he can. We discussed the metabolism of Tylenol to the liver and the fact that his liver doesn't "burn it up" as fast as it should. Discussed other procedures that can be done for the knee such as aspiration injection with cortisone, but did not recommend it at this time. We will have him reassess on a prn basis if any problems arise or if he seems to be worsening. Discussed his care at home. His wife does take care of him and they felt they could handle it at home. We offered hospitalization but the patient did not feel that this would be necessary.

Stony Knott, MD

	Patient name:
	DOB:
	MR/Chart #:

GODFREY REGIONAL OUTPATIENT CLINIC
3122 Shannon Avenue • Aldon, FL 77712 • (407) 555-7654

Answers

EXERCISE 14

OFFICE NOTE

Chief complaint: _____

Date: _____

Vital signs: BP_____ P_____ R_____

History:

S: 83-year-old female presents with difficulty swallowing since noon lunch. She states she had a few bites of some leftover ribs when she had difficulty swallowing. She states she has been unable to get anything down; even saliva comes back up. She has been gagging and vomiting all afternoon. She has had burning in her throat. She has been coughing up a lot of thick phlegm. She has had no prior history of ulcers or gastric problems. She currently takes Prinivil and Norvasc for hypertension, Glucotrol for diabetes, and is on three different eye drops for glaucoma. She is allergic to penicillin.

Exam:

O: On physical exam, her conjunctivae are injected and she is overdue for some drops, she states. Her pupils are equal, round, and reactive. TMs nondistended. Nasopharynx noncongested. Posterior pharynx is nonerythematous. Oropharynx without lesion. Lung sounds are clear. Heart is regular and without murmur. Abdomen is soft. There is no tenderness noted. Pressing in the epigastric area, however, increases the patient's symptoms in the mid chest where she feels this stuck food. Shortly, after pressing on her abdomen, she was given a glass of water, was able to swallow, and the water did go down and her symptoms resolved.

Diagnosis/assessment:

A: Dysphagia, suspect esophageal stricture.

P: Patient started on Protonix 40 mg, one po qd. She will fill that prescription tomorrow and call a specialist's office for evaluation for EGD, as most likely she has an esophageal stricture that will need to be dilated.

Felix Warden M.D.

Patient name: _____

Date of service: _____

GODFREY MEDICAL ASSOCIATES
1532 Third Avenue, Suite 120 • Aldon, FL 77713 • (407) 555-4000

Answers

OFFICE NOTE

Date:	Vital signs:	T	R
Chief complaint:		P	BP

S: Patient presents complaining of headache and dizziness. She woke in the middle of the night and had an episode of dizziness for about 15 minutes. She didn't sleep very well the rest of the night, and this morning she has had a headache on the left-hand side at the occiput and temporal region. She had a stroke in September where she lost half her vision and her right side became numb. This was very transient. She questions whether her left eye might be a little bit blurry but notices no other neurologic symptoms. The vertigo has completely resolved. She has a history of labyrinthitis and a hospitalization for this.

Physical examination:

O: On examination, neurologically, she appears to be intact. Romberg is very steady. Eyes: PERRLA. EOM normal. Ears appear clear. Normal strength upper and lower extremities.

Assessment:

A: Episode of vertigo, possibly labyrinthitis or possibly Ménière's disease, as she did describe a little bit of a pulsatile tinnitus at the time.

Plan:

P: Recommended observation for now. Discussed the headaches as likely being related to tension headaches and to use symptomatic treatment for this. We discussed having meclizine around to use for vertigo, and if she notices any worsening symptoms then she should be reevaluated.

Felix Wander MD

	Patient name:
	DOB:
	MR/Chart #:

GODFREY REGIONAL OUTPATIENT CLINIC
3122 Shannon Avenue • Aldon, FL 77712 • (407) 555-7654

Answers

OPERATIVE REPORT

Patient information:

Patient name:
DOB:
MR#:

Date:
Surgeon:
Anesthetist:

Preoperative diagnosis:

INDICATION:
The patient is a 7-year-old white male who reportedly fell off bleachers and suffered lacerations to his face along the inferior aspect of the lip on the right side, and also small lacerations over the lip itself and intraorally along the mucosa and just at the sulcus inferiorly near the mandible. The patient's family denies any loss of consciousness of the child, and he was brought immediately to the emergency room.

Postoperative diagnosis:

Procedure(s) performed:

Debridement irrigation, closure of facial and intraoral lacerations

Anesthesia:

Assistant surgeon:

Description of procedure:

In the operating room the patient underwent general anesthesia with endotracheal intubation. The face and mouth were then prepped and draped in the usual sterile fashion. The necrotic tissue from the edges of the wound were sharply debrided with a 15 blade scalpel and tenotomy scissors. Hemostasis was achieved with bipolar cautery. The intraoral lesions measured 1 cm along the mucosa near the commissure of the lip and 2.5 cm at the sulcus inferiorly. These lacerations were irrigated, bleeding was cauterized, necrotic tissue was debrided sharply, and it was closed with a running 4-0 Vicryl suture using locking stitches. The small laceration along the mucosa was closed with interrupted 4-0 Vicryl sutures.

The external lacerations measured 2.5 cm below the right side of the lower lip. This was debrided sharply and hemostasis was achieved with bipolar cautery. The laceration was closed in layers using 4-0 Vicryl for the deep layer to reapproximate the orbicularis oris muscle and 5-0 Vicryl for the subdermal layer; 5-0 plain gut was used to close the skin. A small portion of the laceration extended across the vermilion border and the majority of it was on the skin. A small 3-mm laceration oriented vertically on the lower lip was also closed with interrupted plain gut suture. And a small 3-mm laceration on his chin was closed also with interrupted plain gut.

The patient tolerated the procedure well. At the end of the procedure a plain x-ray of the face was taken to rule out any fractures. The patient was successfully extubated in the operating room and then taken to the PACU for recovery.

Maurice Doater, MD

GODFREY REGIONAL HOSPITAL
123 Main Street • Aldon, FL 77714 • (407) 555-1234

Answers

OPERATIVE REPORT

Patient information:	
Patient name: DOB: MR#:	Date: Surgeon: Anesthetist:

Preoperative diagnosis:

Posttraumatic arthritis, right wrist

Postoperative diagnosis:

Same

Procedure(s) performed:

Right wrist arthrodesis with application short-arm cast

Anesthesia:

Assistant surgeon:

Description of procedure:

The patient was placed supine on the operating room table and a satisfactory general anesthetic was given. Preoperative intravenous cephalosporin antibiotic was given. Pneumatic tourniquet was placed high on the left arm. The left hand, wrist, and forearm to proximal to the elbow were prepped sterilely with DuraPrep, and the left hand and wrist were draped in the usual sterile fashion. The dorsum of the wrist was shaved as needed prior to prepping and draping in the proposed incisional location. Tourniquet was inflated to 250 mm Hg.

Longitudinal skin incision was made on the dorsum of the hand and wrist from the area of the distal radius to the level of the mid shaft of the third metacarpal. The incision was carried through subcutaneous tissue. Hemostasis was achieved as necessary. Full-thickness skin flaps were raised. The extensor pollicis longus tendon was released from its sheath and was retracted during the procedure. The dorsal hump of the distal radius was then removed with rongeurs. Soft tissue was removed from the dorsal bones, including the lunate capitate and base of the third metacarpal. A burr was used to decorticate the posterior aspects of these bones as well as the joint surfaces between the radius and lunate, lunate and capitate, and capitate and third metacarpal. The wound was copiously irrigated with normal saline antibiotic solution. A nine-hole 3.5-mm dynamic compression plate was then bent in appropriate fashion to allow 10–20 degrees of extension at the wrist after arthrodesis. The prepared surfaces of the bone in between the radial lunate, lunocapitate, and capitate third metacarpal were filled with Collagraft. The plate was applied and attached to the radius and third metacarpal in compression type fashion. The overall alignment of the wrist was quite good. The plate was placed beneath the extensor pollicis longus tendon that was not damaged during the procedure.

The wound was copiously irrigated again with normal saline antibiotic solution. All fingers showed full range of motion passively after the procedure. The skin was closed full thickness with staples. Dry sterile dressings were applied, followed by sterile circumferential cast padding. Tourniquet was deflated. All drapes were removed including the tourniquet. Cast padding was applied to the elbow and a short-arm fiberglass cast was applied, not limiting flexion or extension to any joint of any finger. The patient tolerated the procedure well. There were no complications. She was awakened in the operating room and transported to the recovery room in stable condition.

Robert Chung MD

GODFREY REGIONAL HOSPITAL
123 Main Street • Aldon, FL 77714 • (407) 555-1234

Answers

EXERCISE 18

OPERATIVE REPORT

Patient information:	
Patient name: DOB: MR#:	CONSENT: Informed consent obtained from the patient after full disclosure of risks and indications to the patient.

Preoperative diagnosis:

Colonic polyps seen on air contrast barium enema in the sigmoid colon

Postoperative diagnosis:

ASSESSMENT:
1. Abnormal appearing fold/area in the cecum with surface appearing as a cauliflower sessile
2. Two sigmoid polyps, one pedunculated and one sessile, both snared and sent for histopathology
3. Moderate sized internal hemorrhoids

Procedure(s) performed:

Colonoscopy with hot biopsy and polypectomy with snare

Anesthesia:

Assistant surgeon:

Description of procedure:

After obtaining informed consent, the patient was brought to the OR and put in the left lateral position. IV line was maintained. IV sedation was given and vitals were monitored throughout the procedure that included pulse, pulse oximetry, blood pressure, respiratory rate, level of consciousness, and ECG monitoring. Digital rectal examination was done first, and then colonoscope Olympus GIF 140 was introduced and advanced all the way up to the cecum, identified by ileocecal valve and appendicular orifice. Of note of importance, she does have a lot of twist, almost a 360 twist in the area of transverse and descending colon, and also in the proximal ascending colon as well. Beyond the cecal valve was an area which appeared to be flat with cauliflower-looking appearance on top of which was an almost flat lesion, no pedicle, spread over approximately 0.8 mm in size in cross-section. No ulceration observed. It was a little bit friable, and I took a few biopsies, hot and cold, from that area. A minimum amount of blood oozing. The rest of the colon appeared normal. She had a few pockets of stools that were washed away. In the area of the sigmoid region, two polyps were identified, which were seen on air contrast barium enema. Both were in close approximation and were snared in toto and retrieved with suction. The rest of the colon was entirely normal. She does have moderate sized internal hemorrhoids.

PLAN:
Follow up with Pathology. Follow up in clinic in one to two weeks.

Patk Adam MD

GODFREY REGIONAL HOSPITAL
123 Main Street • Aldon, FL 77714 • (407) 555-1234

Answers

RADIOLOGY REPORT

MR#:
DOB:
Dr.

Clinical summary:

CT BRAIN WITHOUT CONTRAST

CLINICAL HISTORY:
Found on floor, passed out, left-side weakness, down unknown length of time, evaluate for bleed.

Abdomen:

Conclusion:

FINDINGS:
CT in sequential 4 and 8 mm axial images without IV contrast.

The study is remarkable for a large right temporoparietal lobe low-attenuating area somewhat geographically shaped extending to the calvaria; it completely effaces the right lateral ventricle in the mid and anterior region of the horn. The fourth ventricle is patent. There is no subfalcine herniation, no hemorrhage. Left side shows sharply demarcated, about 1-cm, low-attenuating change in the deep white matter of the left posterior parietal lobe; that's probably an old lacunar infarction. Suprasellar area shows the pituitary gland a little prominent.

There is a very large soft tissue scalp hematoma over the left parietal skull but there is no finding of fracture.

IMPRESSION:
Massive low-attenuating area in the right temporoparietal lobe. Differential includes a bland infarction; a malignancy can also have this appearance but the study was not done with contrast. Minimal subfalcine herniation. No downward transtentorial herniation. Effacement of the right lateral ventricle.

Ddt/mm

D:
T:

_____
Lisa Valhas, M.D.   Date

GODFREY REGIONAL HOSPITAL
123 Main Street • Aldon, FL 77714 • (407) 555-1234

Answers

RADIOLOGY REPORT

MR#:
DOB:
Dr.

Clinical summary:

CLINICAL INFORMATION:
Fell; right wrist pain

Abdomen:

Conclusion:

THREE VIEWS OF THE RIGHT WRIST:
There is a slightly comminuted distal radial articular surface fracture. This primarily involves the metaphysis with the accessory fracture line extending into the articular surface. There is no displacement or angulation. The ulna appears normal. There are degenerative changes at the first metacarpal carpal joint.

CONCLUSION:
Distal radial articular surface fracture

Ddt/mm

D:
T:

_____
Lisa Valhas, M.D.   Date

GODFREY REGIONAL HOSPITAL
123 Main Street • Aldon, FL 77714 • (407) 555-1234

Answers

EXERCISES 1-30

Complete steps 1 through 3 of the Diagnostic Worksheet for the following exercises. Step 4 will be completed after you have reviewed Chapters 4 and 5.

EXERCISE 1

EMERGENCY ROOM RECORD

Name:		Age: 6	ER physician:
Brandon Wilson		DOB: 11/08/19XX	Nancy Connelly

Allergies/type of reaction:	Usual medications/dosages:
None	

Triage/presenting complaint:

Patient presents with forehead laceration

Initial assessment:

Laceration appears clean, bleeding controlled

Time	T	P	R	BP	Other:				

Medication orders:

Lab work:

X-Ray:

Physician's report:

2-cm laceration. Forehead, after falling out of bed during the night
The wound was cleaned and irrigated all the way through the epidermis and dermis

After prep and Lidocaine block, the wound was approximated with interrupted 6-0 Ethilon
Suture removal in six days

Diagnosis:	Physician sign/date
Laceration forehead	*Nancy Connelly MD*

Discharge	Transfer	Admit	Good	Satisfactory	Other:

GODFREY REGIONAL HOSPITAL
123 Main Street • Aldon, FL 77714 • (407) 555-1234

Answers

PROGRESS NOTE

Chief complaint: Abdominal pain

Date: 01/04/XX

DOB: 05/11/XX

Vital signs: BP_____ P_____ R_____

MR/Chart #: 00368

History:

Patient with abdominal pain. Past history of Crohn's. Patient is tachycardic.

Exam:

Believe patient is going through drug withdrawal at this time. Recommended admission into a chemical drug rehab program. Patient refusing at this time.

Diagnosis/assessment:

As a palliative measure, I gave him 75/75 Demerol/Vistaril IM and five Tylox.
Recheck the first of the week.
If he wishes to reconsider admission, he will contact our office for arrangements.

Steny Kratt, MD

Patient name: Robert Sterne

Date of service: 01/04/XX

GODFREY REGIONAL OUTPATIENT CLINIC
3122 Shannon Avenue • Aldon, FL 77712 • (407) 555-7654

Answers

PROGRESS NOTE

Date: 02/05/XX	Vital signs:	T	R
Chief complaint: Sore throat, difficulty swallowing		P	BP

02/05/XX

This is a 7-year-old who has had a sore throat with some difficulty swallowing and a headache for the past two days. Not improving.

Examination:

She is afebrile. She has retro TM fluid on the left which is asymptomatic. The right side is normal. She has considerable amount of oropharyngeal inflammation, small tender anterior cervical node. Lungs are clear to auscultation. Heart, sinus without murmur.

Impression:

Strep tonsillitis

Plan:

She is placed on Amoxil 250 suspension tid for 10 days

Willen Obst MD

Patient name: Anne Novitz
DOB: 2/26/XX
MR/Chart #: 63223

GODFREY REGIONAL OUTPATIENT CLINIC
3122 Shannon Avenue • Aldon, FL 77712 • (407) 555-7654

Answers

PROGRESS NOTE

Date: 03/08/XX	Vital signs:	T		R	
Chief complaint: Sore throat/cough x 1 week		P		BP	

03/08/XX	9-year-old female with sore throat and cough which she has had now for about a week. Temperature in the office is 101.4

Examination:

Skin is clear. Ear drums negative, pharynx red. Culture taken.
Negative for strep. Chest clear to auscultation.
Heart tones regular w/o murmurs. Abdomen soft.

Impression:

URI with pharyngitis

Plan:

Amoxicillin 250 mg tid for 20 days

Willem Obst MD

Patient name: Anita White
DOB: 7/28/19XX
MR/Chart #: 67777

GODFREY REGIONAL OUTPATIENT CLINIC
3122 Shannon Avenue • Aldon, FL 77712 • (407) 555-7654

Answers

PROGRESS NOTE

Chief complaint: "Stressed"

Date: 04/06/XX

DOB: _____

Vital signs: BP_____ P_____ R_____   MR/Chart #: 52311 _____

History:

54-year-old female presented with stress, she just can't handle anymore.
Issues circle around behavior of adopted son age 17 and excessive sewing demands by a
daughter-in-law. Past history includes molestation and house robberies. Last several nights been
unable to sleep. Is having a nightmare about being robbed. She just can't take it anymore and
would like a sleeping pill.

Exam:

Diagnosis/assessment:

IMPRESSION:
Insomnia associated with nightmares/anxiety disorder
PLAN:
Issued Trazodone 25 mg to take 1–2 hours before bed for the next several nights. She is to
schedule visit with a psychologist to begin to resolve these issues on a more prolonged basis.

William Obst MD

Patient name: Sherry Prichet _____

Date of service: 04/06/XX

GODFREY REGIONAL OUTPATIENT CLINIC
3122 Shannon Avenue • Aldon, FL 77712 • (407) 555-7654

Answers

PROGRESS NOTE

Date:	Vital signs:	T		R	
Chief complaint:		P		BP	

Patient is here today complaining of several days of low abdominal discomfort
and severe pain that sounds like it might be bladder spasms.
She states when she gets the pain, she has trouble urinating.

Physical examination:

On exam, the abdomen is totally negative.
Pelvis and rectal are also entirely normal.

Laboratory findings:

Urinalysis is normal except 2+ glucose and blood sugar is 332. CBC normal.
Start her on glucophage 500 mg twice daily.
Start her on diabetic diet.
Prescribed Cystospaz for bladder spasms.
Obtain glucose meter. She already has one and she will monitor blood sugars.

Diagnosis:

Diabetes mellitus
Bladder spasms

Maurice Doater, MD

Patient name:
DOB:
MR/Chart #:

GODFREY REGIONAL OUTPATIENT CLINIC
3122 Shannon Avenue • Aldon, FL 77712 • (407) 555-7654

Answers

EXERCISE 7

PROGRESS NOTE

Date:	Vital signs:	T	R
Chief complaint:		P	BP

Patient is a 43-year-old female who comes in for evaluation of right buttock pain. Related for the past 6–8 weeks she has had persistent unrelenting right buttock pain which is non-positional. Has had several episodes of perianal paresthesia. Denies any difficulty with bladder or bowel habits.

Examination:

Impression:

Plan:

Discussed with patient at great length that a thorough orthopedic evaluation is warranted to rule out serious spinal abnormality or neurologic impairment. She is referred to Dr. Sprugg and I have asked her to let me know her progress.

Maurice Doater, MD

	Patient name:
	DOB:
	MR/Chart #:

GODFREY REGIONAL OUTPATIENT CLINIC
3122 Shannon Avenue • Aldon, FL 77712 • (407) 555-7654

Answers

PROGRESS NOTE

Date:	Vital signs:	T		R	
Chief complaint:		P		BP	

Patient comes in for follow-up. She has had a very hard month with severe and persistent fatigue as well as more problems with shortness of breath.
Patient has a long history of chronic obstructive pulmonary disease.

Review of systems:

Remarkable for fatigue, increased dyspnea
Slight increase in pedal edema

Examination:

BP 145/85, Pulse 90, Respirations 16
Chest shows decreased breath sounds
Cardiac exam unremarkable

Diagnosis:

COPD

Maurice Doater, MD

Patient name:
DOB:
MR/Chart #:

GODFREY REGIONAL OUTPATIENT CLINIC
3122 Shannon Avenue • Aldon, FL 77712 • (407) 555-7654

Answers

PROGRESS NOTE

Date:	Vital signs:	T		R	
Chief complaint:			P		BP

Patient presents for her initial evaluation complaining of severe pruritic rash on her left and right antecubital fossa X 4 days. She reports the rash began on her arms but has also erupted on her forearms and lower extremities. Also has multiple lesions across her chest. Denies any new lotions, soaps, detergents, clothes, pets. No different foods or exposure to poison ivy. Has no previous history of dermatitis.
Denies fevers, chills; other than rash all other systems are unremarkable.

Physical examination:

Diffuse vesicular lesions across the upper torso, forearms, and thighs.
She has erythematous area of vesicular lesions in her right and left popliteal fossa. Vesicular diffuse lesions, etiology unclear.

Assessment:

Plan:

Patient referred to dermatology for further evaluation and treatment.
Most likely this represents a viral exanthem. She was given topical hydrocortisone cream and advised to use Benadryl for itching.

Maurice Doater, MD

	Patient name:
	DOB:
	MR/Chart #:

GODFREY REGIONAL OUTPATIENT CLINIC
3122 Shannon Avenue • Aldon, FL 77712 • (407) 555-7654

Answers

PROGRESS NOTE

| Date: | Vital signs: | T | R |
| Chief complaint: | | P | BP |

Patient returns for evaluation of a right groin lesion. He has previously been evaluated for this lesion, however, feels there may have been a slight increase in size.

Physical examination:

Examination does show what appears to be a lipoma, or benign fatty lesion in the right groin area. No sign of hernia or other mass, no adenopathy.

Assessment:

Plan:

Reassured the patient and counseled him regarding the need to monitor the size and contact us if he continues to see an increase in size.

Maurice Doater, MD

Patient name:

DOB:

MR/Chart #:

GODFREY REGIONAL OUTPATIENT CLINIC
3122 Shannon Avenue • Aldon, FL 77712 • (407) 555-7654

Answers

PROGRESS NOTE

Date:	Vital signs:	T	R
Chief complaint:		P	BP 142/78

This 82-year-old male comes in today complaining of episodes of shortness of breath when supine intermittently for the last few weeks. He states he feels OK until he lies down or tries to go to sleep. Just as he falls asleep he will waken abruptly as if he can't catch his breath. Denies any chest pain and reports this only occurs when he is trying to lie down. Denies chest pain, lower extremity swelling, but has had a dry cough for the past few days. Has a past history of afib which has been well controlled. Denies any feeling of light-headedness.

Physical examination:

Lungs: Clear to auscultation, no wheezes, rales, rhonchi

Heart: Regular rate and rhythm, no murmurs, gallops, rubs

Abdomen: Soft, tender, non-distended, positive bowel sounds

Extremities: No edema, cyanosis, clubbing

ECG: Normal sinus rhythm

Diagnosis:

Orthopnea/rule out ventricular dysfunction

Maurice Doater, MD

Patient name:
DOB:
MR/Chart #:

GODFREY REGIONAL OUTPATIENT CLINIC
3122 Shannon Avenue • Aldon, FL 77712 • (407) 555-7654

Answers

PROGRESS NOTE

Date:	Vital signs:	T		R	
Chief complaint: Abdominal pain, vaginal bleeding		P		BP	

This 17-year-old female states her last menstrual period ended approximately 7–10 days ago. Presented today because she began heavy vaginal bleeding, with passage of clots, crampy lower abdominal pain and feeling weak.
She is on birth control pills but states she has only taken one tablet. Gravida 1 Para 1 female with history of normal vaginal delivery approximately one year ago.
No history of pelvic inflammatory disease.

Examination:

There is a minimal amount of blood in the vaginal vault. No tissue noted.
The cervix is normal in appearance and size. The os is closed. The fundus of the uterus was not well appreciated.

Laboratory findings:

Serum pregnancy was negative, WBC was 11,300 with normal hemoglobin and hematocrit.

Diagnosis/findings:

Vaginal bleeding
Possible PID

Maurice Doster, MD

Patient name:

DOB:

MR/Chart #:

GODFREY REGIONAL OUTPATIENT CLINIC
3122 Shannon Avenue • Aldon, FL 77712 • (407) 555-7654

Answers

PROGRESS NOTE

Chief complaint: _____

Date: _____

DOB: _____

Vital signs: BP_____   P_____   R_____   MR/Chart #: _____

History:

This 2-year-old male child presents with parent who states he had an ear infection two weeks ago, treated with Amoxicillin for 10 days. Patient's mother complains of cough, croupy sounding at times for several days and pulling on ears.

Exam:

Physical examination was unremarkable except for fiery-red tympanic membranes. Chest x-rays were negative.

Diagnosis/assessment:

Bilateral otitis media
Acute bronchitis

Maurice Doster, MD

Patient name: _____

Date of service: _____

GODFREY REGIONAL OUTPATIENT CLINIC
3122 Shannon Avenue • Aldon, FL 77712 • (407) 555-7654

Answers

PROGRESS NOTE

Date:	Vital signs:	T	R
Chief complaint:		P	BP

40-year-old female who presents history that she lifts heavy objects at work in the deli of a grocery store. She has developed right-sided flank pain and right back pain during the past few days. History of urinary tract infections. Denies dysuria, frequency or urgency at this time.

Physical examination:

Unremarkable except for back. Back is tender in the area of the right paravertebral muscles from approximately L1/2 to L4/L5. Patient is able to touch her toes, straight leg raises are negative.
Back x-rays reveal acute lower back sprain probably due to heavy lifting at place of employment.

Diagnosis:

Acute lower back sprain, probably due to employment
Urinary tract infection

Maurice Doater, MD

Patient name:
DOB:
MR/Chart #:

GODFREY REGIONAL OUTPATIENT CLINIC
3122 Shannon Avenue • Aldon, FL 77712 • (407) 555-7654

Answers

Chapter **3** **Determining Physician Diagnosis**

PROGRESS NOTE

Chief complaint: _____

Date: _____

DOB: _____

Vital signs: BP_____ P_____ R_____   MR/Chart #: _____

History:

This 28-year-old male states a 2-day history of swelling and mass to the left buttock area.
Denies any history of trauma or other history pertinent to this.

Exam:

Exam of the left buttock reveals an approximately 4 cm area of erthyma and induration to the
middle of the left buttock. There is increased warmth and/redness to this area, however, no
lymphangitis was noted.

Diagnosis/assessment:

IMPRESSION:
Abscess, left buttock
PLAN:
The abscess was incised and drained and the patient was instructed on proper follow-up care.

Stury Kratt, MD

Patient name: _____

Date of service: _____

GODFREY REGIONAL OUTPATIENT CLINIC
3122 Shannon Avenue • Aldon, FL 77712 • (407) 555-7654

Answers

PROGRESS NOTE

Chief complaint: <u>Fever/nasal drainage</u>

Date: <u>01/18/XX</u>

DOB: <u>4/16/20XX</u>

Vital signs:　　BP_____　P_____　R_____

MR/Chart #: <u>24481</u>

History:

This 9-month-old child with Down's syndrome brought in today by mother with onset of fever and thick greenish drainage from his nose. Also developed a cough again. No history of ear infections and has had a history of pneumonia.

Exam:

PE:　　General appearance of well-developed child in no acute distress

Head:　　Flat anterior fontanel

Ears:　　Canals small, cleared of cerumen

Neck:　　No adenopathy

Lungs:　　Clear, no wheezing but has noisy inspiratory respiration for which he had a recent bronchoscopy

Nose:　　He does have thick greenish drainage from his nose

Diagnosis/assessment:

ASSESSMENT:
Upper respiratory infection with symptoms of pulmonary infection
PLAN:
Continue with Ibuprofen and decongestants
Placed on Augmentin 200 mg twice daily

William Obst MD

Patient name: <u>Thomas Derringer</u>

Date of service: <u>01/18/XX</u>

GODFREY REGIONAL OUTPATIENT CLINIC
3122 Shannon Avenue • Aldon, FL 77712 • (407) 555-7654

Answers

Chapter **3**　**Determining Physician Diagnosis**

PROGRESS NOTE

Date: 04/22/XX	Vital signs:	T	R
Chief complaint: Injured wrist		P	BP

04/22/XX	14-year-old boy was doing "360s" on his pedal dirt bike when he fell off, landing on his left wrist. He notes tenderness and pain at the head of the radius.

Examination:

The x-ray indicates a minimal greenstick buckle from the dorsomedial aspect with perhaps a fine fracture line.

Impression:

Largely greenstick minimal fracture of the left radius.

Plan:

Placed in leatherette splint and instructed to wear for six weeks.
He is to follow up in four days.

Felix Wander M D

Patient name: Samuel Raimy
DOB: 12/12/19XX
MR/Chart #: 88615

GODFREY REGIONAL OUTPATIENT CLINIC
3122 Shannon Avenue • Aldon, FL 77712 • (407) 555-7654

Answers

PROGRESS NOTE

| Date: 04/24/XX | Vital signs: | T | | R | |
| Chief complaint: Swelling of thumb | | P | | BP | |

| 04/24/XX | 45-year-old male presents with swelling and redness of the volar aspect of the proximal phalangeal skin of his right thumb. He operates a body shop, works as a mechanic on a race car, and has been moving furniture at a garage sale over the past several days. It is presumptive for foreign body. The area is approximately 1.5 cm and the thumb is swollen and tender. |

Examination:

Soft tissue x-ray demonstrates no radiopaque foreign body.

Impression:

Probing would be of dubious wisdom.

Plan:

Plan is to give 1 gm Rocephin now and start Rx of Cephalexin 500 mg qid.
Instructed to soak thumb in hot water 20 minutes 4 times per day.
Follow-up in 3 days or earlier if needed.

Felix Warden MD

	Patient name: David Kopps
	DOB: 2/12/19XX
	MR/Chart #: 76337

GODFREY REGIONAL OUTPATIENT CLINIC
3122 Shannon Avenue • Aldon, FL 77712 • (407) 555-7654

Answers

PROGRESS NOTE

Date: 04/23/XX	**Vital signs:**	T	R
Chief complaint: Sore foot		P	BP

04/23/XX	22-year-old male at work caught foot between jack handle and steel tank bruising the outer aspect of his right foot.

Physical examination:

X-ray is negative.

Assessment:

Contusion of foot.

Plan:

Patient is to take over-the-counter salicylates or NSAIDs as needed for pain control. Follow-up in 2–4 days for additional check.

Felix Wander MD

Patient name: Jerold Farmington
DOB: 1/17/19XX
MR/Chart #: 99997

GODFREY REGIONAL OUTPATIENT CLINIC
3122 Shannon Avenue • Aldon, FL 77712 • (407) 555-7654

Answers

PROGRESS NOTE

| **Date:** 08/30/XX | **Vital signs:** | T | | R | |
| **Chief complaint:** Back pain | | P | | BP | |

| 08/30/XX | 36-year-old male comes in today with back pain that started yesterday after lifting. He has been unable to move since. He spent the night on the floor. He has been using ice which has helped some. He has a steady ache to the back. It is sharp when he tries to move. There is no pain, numbness, or tingling of the lower extremities. No bowel or bladder dysfunction. |

Examination:

On exam vital signs are normal. Straight leg raises are negative.
No motor or sensory deficits. Gait was not tested due to patient's pain.
LS spine x-rays were unremarkable.

Impression:

Low mechanical back pain

Plan:

He has some Lorcet he can use for pain. Will arrange PT follow-up.
Follow-up if no improvement from PT.

Felix Warden MD

Patient name: Michael Smith
DOB: 4/30/19XX
MR/Chart #: 43261

GODFREY REGIONAL OUTPATIENT CLINIC
3122 Shannon Avenue • Aldon, FL 77712 • (407) 555-7654

Answers

EXERCISE 21

OFFICE NOTE

Date:	Vital signs:	T	R
Chief complaint:		P	BP

SUBJECTIVE: Esther is an 83-year-old patient who was brought in after she had an episode of "tingling all over" and some dizziness "as if I were going to pass out." By the time she arrived here, the sensation had resolved. Upon review of the ambulance crew description of how they found her, they stated that she was oriented and cooperative, sitting in a chair. Skin was warm and dry, and she didn't have any difficulties with speech or weakness. She did have initial blood pressure of 200/100 and then, en route, she was lowered to 138/64. She was sating 100% on 1 liter. While here, Esther has had resolution of her symptoms as described above. She was not complaining of any pain. She felt better than she had at home. After interviewing her for a while, it was obvious that she has been feeling very weak for quite some time, and that this is an ongoing problem. She also has felt dyspnea with minimal exertion, which she had experienced after her surgery two years ago. She also states that yesterday she had an episode or two of vomiting clear material. She states she didn't have any accompanying diarrhea. This resolved later in the evening, and today she didn't have any and was able to eat well.

PAST MEDICAL HISTORY: CAD, SP CABG. Patient does not recall having had an acute myocardial infarction. Breast carcinoma SP lumpectomy. On tamoxifen, approximately a year ago. Hypothyroidism; on replacement. History of TIA some time ago that was worked up with carotid Dopplers. Unclear at this time what these rendered, but she was advised to take an aspirin a day.

MEDICATIONS: Tamoxifen, Synthroid, metoprolol, ASA, HCTZ, and potassium supplements.

ALLERGIES: None known.

Examination:

REVIEW OF SYSTEMS: It is equivocal whether she has had a low-grade fever at home or not, since she didn't take her temperature. She has had some chills and generalized weakness and malaise as above. Energy is very poor; appetite has been well maintained, and she usually sleeps very well. Vision: no blurred vision or diplopia.

HEENT: No facial pressures, sore throat, rhinorrhea, or earache.

RESPIRATORY: Denies cough, sputum production, or hemoptysis. No pleuritic chest pain.

CARDIOVASCULAR: As above.

GASTROINTESTINAL SYSTEM: No further episodes of nausea or vomiting; no hematemesis, no early satiety, no dysphagia. Denies any changes in bowel habits. No melena or hematochezia. No abdominal pain.

GENITOURINARY SYSTEM: No dysuria, frequency, or hematuria. The remainder is negative.

PHYSICAL EXAMINATION: Very pleasant elderly lady who appears frail. She is fully oriented and cooperative. Initial BP was 160/82; prior to discharge it was 148/74. She was sating 100% on 3 liters per nasal cannula. Temperature 98.1, pulse was in the 70s, regular; and monitor showed a normal sinus rhythm. Respiratory rate was normal. There were no difficulties with speech. HEENT: no facial asymmetries, no pallor, no jaundice. Hydration is fairly well maintained, although her lips are a little dry. PERRL, EOMI, no nystagmus. Oral examination is unremarkable. NECK: supple without lymphadenopathy or thyromegaly; no JVD noted, symmetric carotid upstrokes bilaterally. CHEST: lungs—respiration is quite shallow. EXTREMITIES: no edema. NEUROLOGICAL: is actually intact with mental status as above; no meningeal signs; CN 2-12 intact; motor strength is 4/4 in all four extremities, DTRs are 11 at bicipital and patellar levels; no sensory deficits elicited.

LABS & X-RAYS: Chest x-ray (portable) revealed heart of normal size, no infiltrates or effusions, and the surgical changes consistent with her CABG. I do not see over major differences with previous chest x-ray from over two years ago. EKG showed a normal sinus rhythm with a rate of 80 beats per minute. LAFB, incomplete RBBB, and diffuse IVCD. Labs showed glucose of 118, BUN 21, creatinine 0.7. All electrolytes were normal with potassium of 3.7; CK was 77, troponin 0, WBC count was 4.8 with normal differential, and hemoglobin and hematocrit were 12.8 and 35.6, respectively. Platelet count 251.

Impression:

Elderly lady presenting with resolved episode of diffuse tingling, unclear etiology. No focal findings on examination; no evidence of disease on x-rays or labs. Importantly, she has chronic dyspnea with minimal exertion.

Plan:

We discussed extensively with the patient and her son what the present situation brings up. I do not think that we are going to come up with the answer of why she is so short of breath for so long, and it certainly doesn't seem to be the main concern. The shortness of breath may be due to numerous factors, and these should be worked up on an outpatient basis. The patient was advised to take an extra potassium tablet daily for two days and to drink plenty of fluids. They were also advised to call tomorrow to make an appointment with her physician for follow-up. She may need further work-up, as her weakness and dyspnea have been persistent for so long. We reviewed all of these labs and chest x-rays with them. They agreed that the present problem has resolved and chronic problem needs to be worked up later. They feel comfortable trying it at home and will return if needed.

Felix Warden MD

	Patient name:
	DOB:
	MR/Chart #:

GODFREY REGIONAL OUTPATIENT CLINIC
3122 Shannon Avenue • Aldon, FL 77712 • (407) 555-7654

Answers

OFFICE NOTE

Date:		Vital signs:	T		R	
Chief complaint: Food reaction			P		BP	

S: This is a soon to be 66-year-old woman who says that since she was in her 30s, she would have some reaction when she ate certain foods, and this happened yesterday. It has been the same each time. She had eaten at some kind of church dinner but she says when she eats processed foods like Chicken McNuggets or something else, she will get a sensation that she has too much electrical activity in her head. The closest I can get as far as a description is some pressure, and then she feels her heart flip-flops and she feels funny. This happened yesterday so she came in early this morning to have things evaluated since she now has high blood pressure. Other than hypertension, she denies any other acute problems. She is on Diovan for her blood pressure once a day. She also has fibromyalgia. She has a codeine allergy. On review of systems, no HEENT complaints. Respiratory: negative. Cardiac: just this flip-flop sensation. No history of exertional or other kind of cardiac symptoms. GI: negative. GU: negative.

Examination:

O: On exam, this is an older woman who is in no distress. Her pressure was a little high to begin with, but it did come down and I think she was partly a little bit anxious. Her O_2 sats were fine. Pulse was stable. Eyes showed no papilledema. Neck had good carotid upstrokes without bruits. No nuchal rigidity. Lungs were clear. Heart is regular without any murmurs noted. Abdomen is negative. She moves all her extremities fine. Motor and sensory is intact. An EKG looks unremarkable.

Impression:

A: Vague symptoms. I can't exclude that she couldn't have some kind of weird reaction to MSG. It also may be just anxiety related with blood pressure elevation and palpitations.

Plan:

P: Discussion. She should continue on her Diovan. Her pressure at 174/93 actually isn't much higher than when she was in the clinic last. She was given an Rx for Lopressor 50 mg to take one a day when she has these episodes, #30 with a couple of refills. She will return if there are other problems. She was stable at discharge. She also had blood gases done that were normal.

Joe Palermo

Patient name:
DOB:
MR/Chart #:

GODFREY REGIONAL OUTPATIENT CLINIC
3122 Shannon Avenue • Aldon, FL 77712 • (407) 555-7654

Answers

EXERCISE 23

OPERATIVE REPORT

Patient information:	
Patient name:	Date:
DOB:	Surgeon:
MR#:	Anesthetist:

Preoperative diagnosis:

Right middle finger nail bed injury with subungual hematoma

Postoperative diagnosis:

Right middle finger nail bed injury with subungual hematoma with right middle nail bed laceration and necrotic nail bed with bone exposure

Procedure(s) performed:

PROCEDURE: Right middle finger nail plate removal, evacuation of subungual hematoma, debridement of necrotic nail bed, repair of nail bed laceration, suture removal

INDICATION FOR SURGERY: The patient is a 56-year-old white male who suffered a blunt trauma injury to his right middle finger approximately one week ago. He presented yesterday with this injury that had been repaired at an outside hospital emergency room. He now presents for evacuation of a subungual hematoma and repair of nail bed injuries.

Anesthesia:

Assistant surgeon:

Description of procedure:

The patient underwent a digital block of his right middle finger prior to coming into the operating room. There he underwent sedation, and his right hand and forearm were prepped and draped in the usual sterile fashion. A tourniquet was placed over his upper arm. At the beginning of the procedure, the hand was elevated and pressure was held for exsanguination. The tourniquet was inflated to 250 mm Hg pressure. Two sutures were removed from the nail plate and the skin using a blunt mosquito forceps. The nail plate was dissected off of the remaining nail bed and the nail plate was then removed. The underlying nail bed had a laceration across the mid portion and was necrotic at the distal portion along the radial side of the finger. The necrotic tissue was sharply debrided with a 15 blade scalpel. Upon completion of the nail bed debridement, there was exposed bone under the wound. The patient has a fracture of this distal phalanx, which was noted on preoperative x-ray. The wound was thoroughly irrigated with saline solution. The nail bed laceration in this open wound was then closed using 4-0 Vicryl suture. After repair of the nail bed and closure of this open wound, the nail bed and finger were assessed for bleeding by deflating the tourniquet. There was good hemostasis over the operative field. Preoperatively, it was noted that the patient's fingertip, which had been lacerated in the injury, was repaired but appeared dusky. A 25-gauge needle was poked into this flap of skin at the distal pulp of the finger and there was poor blood return. This suggests that there may be partial necrosis and loss of the skin in this part of the finger. The wound was then covered with antibiotic ointment, Xeroform gauze, clean gauze, and paper tape. It was then placed into a splint. The patient was then successfully taken to the PACU for recovery in stable condition.

GODFREY REGIONAL HOSPITAL *Patrick Chung MD*
123 Main Street • Aldon, FL 77714 • (407) 555-1234

Answers

OPERATIVE REPORT

Patient information:

Patient name:	Date:
DOB:	Surgeon:
MR#:	Anesthetist:

Preoperative diagnosis:

Morpheaform basal cell carcinoma of the nose

Postoperative diagnosis:

Morpheaform basal cell carcinoma of the nose

Procedure(s) performed:

Excision of basal cell carcinoma of the nose (2 cm × 1 1/4 cm). Full-thickness skin graft reconstruction of the nose from left preauricular donor site.

ESTIMATED BLOOD LOSS: Less than 10 cc

CLINICAL NOTE: The patient is a 60-year-old white female who has had recurrent basal cell carcinoma of the nose removed on two previous occasions. The last occasion was found to be consistent with morpheaform basal cell carcinoma with positive residual tumor present. She is being brought to the operating room for wide local excision with frozen sections and reconstruction using full-thickness skin graft.

Anesthesia:

IV sedation/attended local

Assistant surgeon:

Description of procedure:

OPERATIVE NOTE: The patient was brought to the operating room and placed on the operating room table in a supine position. IV sedation was administered, and using 1% lidocaine with 1:100,000 parts epinephrine. The nose and left preauricular regions were injected. The face was prepped and draped in sterile fashion. Using a marking pen, the area of visualized tumor with margins was marked along the dorsum and nasal tip region. Using 15-blade scalpel, an incision was made along the marked areas, measuring approximately 1 1/4 cm, and full-thickness skin graft was removed, labeled, and sent to Pathology for frozen and permanent sections. Frozen section showed residual tumor on the lateral 6 to 9 o'clock margins and additional section removed was clear on frozen section. Deep margins were clear. Meticulous hemostasis was obtained with bipolar and Bovie cautery. Left preauricular incision was made and an elliptical full-thickness skin tag taken from this region. It was cut to size and sutured in place with interrupted 6-0 nylon sutures to the nasal tip defect. The preauricular incision was undermined and then closed with running interlocking 5-0 nylon sutures. Bacitracin ointment was placed to both wounds, followed by Telfa dressing over the left preauricular area, and a Telfa pressure dressing over the left nasal tip skin graft site.

The patient was fully awakened from IV sedation and brought to the recovery room in stable condition, having tolerated the procedure well.

Adm Westy MD

GODFREY REGIONAL HOSPITAL
123 Main Street • Aldon, FL 77714 • (407) 555-1234

Answers

EXERCISE 25

OPERATIVE REPORT

Patient information:	
Patient name:	Date:
DOB:	Surgeon:
MR#:	Anesthetist:

Preoperative diagnosis:

1) Osteomyelitis, right 2nd distal phalanx.
2) Non-healing ulceration, right 2nd digit.

Postoperative diagnosis:

1) Osteomyelitis, right 2nd distal phalanx.
2) Non-healing ulceration, right 2nd digit.

Procedure(s) performed:

1) Amputation of the distal phalanx.
2) Removal of the nail plate and nail bed of the right distal phalanx.

Anesthesia:

Assistant surgeon:

Description of procedure:

The patient was brought back to the operating room, properly identified, and placed on the OR table in a supine position. Following IV sedation, the right 2nd digit was anesthetized with 3 cc of 50/50 mixture of 1% lidocaine plain and 0.5% Marcaine plain. The foot was then prepped and draped in the usual sterile, aseptic manner.

Attention then was directed to the distal aspect of the right 2nd digit where a fishmouth incision was placed at the distal top over the ulceration. The incision site was deepened down to the distal phalanx, which was noted to be open down through the cortical bone, and the bone was very soft. The soft tissue was freed from the distal phalanx plantarly, medially, and laterally. The dorsal attachment was noted to be void of coverage; the dorsal aspect of the phalanx was exposed and a void of soft tissue coverage under the nail plate. The nail plate was loose and the bone was exposed underneath the nail plate. The phalanx was removed from the surgical site in toto. The intermediate phalanx was inspected and noted to be healthy and had no breakdown. The nail plate was not attached except to the proximal nail fold. The nail plate was noted to be nonviable and void of nail bed secondary to the underlying bone exposure. The nail was then removed from the surgical site in toto. The area was then flushed with copious amounts of saline with Ancef in the solution. The redundant tissue was removed from the surgical site, closed with 4-0 Prolene. The foot was then dressed with adaptic 3x3 and Kling.

The patient tolerated the procedure well and left the OR with vital signs stable and vascular status intact to all digits.

Patrick Chung, MD

GODFREY REGIONAL HOSPITAL
123 Main Street • Aldon, FL 77714 • (407) 555-1234

Answers

OPERATIVE REPORT

Patient information:	
Patient name: DOB: MR#:	Date: Surgeon: Anesthetist:

Preoperative diagnosis:

1. Extremely comminuted, displaced, unstable, interarticular fracture of the distal radius, left wrist
2. Pre-existing longstanding navicular non-union with radioscaphoid and capitolunate degenerative arthritis, left wrist

Postoperative diagnosis:

1. Extremely comminuted, displaced, unstable, interarticular fracture of the distal radial left wrist
2. Pre-existing longstanding navicular non-union with radioscaphoid and capitolunate degenerative arthritis, left wrist

Procedure(s) performed:

Closed reduction and external fixation

Anesthesia:

Assistant surgeon:

Description of procedure:

The patient is under general anesthesia and LMA. He is positioned supine. The left upper extremity is placed on a hand table. A tourniquet is applied around the left arm. The patient received two grams of Ancef IV, 15 minutes prior to inflating the tourniquet. The fracture is examined under fluoroscopic imaging. With traction on the wrist, the fracture reduces very nicely on both views. The comminution of the articular surface is extremely severe. Placing the wrist in neutral dorsiflexion and volar flexion allows anatomic reduction of the articular surface of the distal radius on both views. The fracture is very unstable. There is an obvious non-union of a navicular fracture with radioscaphoid and capitolunate degenerative arthritis. The radial styloid is pointed in shape.

Prep and drape of the left upper extremity in the usual manner. The left upper extremity is exsanguinated with an Esmarch and the tourniquet inflated to 300 mm of mercury. Total tourniquet time was 60 minutes.

A 3-cm long skin incision is made on the dorsal radial aspect of the second metacarpal shaft. Deep dissection is done with scissors. The subcutaneous veins are identified and protected. A pre-drilling technique is used to insert a 3-mm self-tapping pin in the second metacarpal shaft. The first 3-mm pin is placed into the base of the second metacarpal. The second pin is placed perfectly parallel to the first pin using the appropriate guide. The soft tissues are irrigated with normal saline, removing all bone debris. The skin is partially closed around the pins, avoiding any tension of the skin around the pins. The closure of the skin is done using 4-0 nylon.

Another 3-cm long skin incision is made on the dorsal radial aspect of the forearm, in line with the dorsal radial incision on the hand. The incision is made 6–7 cm proximal to the radial styloid. Deep dissection is done with scissors. The superficial branch of the radial nerve is identified and protected. The radius shaft is exposed. A pre-drilling technique is used to insert perfectly parallel 3-mm self-tapping pins. The soft tissues are irrigated with normal saline, removing all bone debris, and the skin is partially closed using 4-0 nylon, avoiding any tension of the skin around the pins.

The external fixator clamps and rod are connected to the hat pins. The reduction is repeated using the same technique described previously. The wrist is placed in neutral position of dorsiflexion/volar flexion and in neutral deviation. After tightening the external fixator, the fracture is checked under fluoroscopic imaging. Alignment of the articular surface is excellent on both views. There is no shortening. Radial inclination and the tilt of the articular surface are restored. However, there is persistent instability of the fracture.

A bulky, non-adhesive dressing is applied around the hat pins. An ulnar gutter fiberglass splint is applied. Care is taken to carefully mold the splint over the wrist area. Alignment is re-examined after the cast has hardened, unchanged.

Surgery was well tolerated and the patient left the operating room for recovery in stable condition.

Patrick Chung, MD

GODFREY REGIONAL HOSPITAL
123 Main Street • Aldon, FL 77714 • (407) 555-1234

Answers

Chapter **3** Determining Physician Diagnosis

EXERCISE 27

OPERATIVE REPORT

Patient information:	
Patient name: DOB: MR#:	Date: Surgeon: Anesthetist:

Preoperative diagnosis:

Left knee internal derangement

Postoperative diagnosis:

1. Left knee radial and horizontal tear of the posterior horn and middle third of the lateral meniscus
2. Flap tear of the posterior horn of the medial meniscus
3. Grade II chondromalacia of the medial femoral condyle
4. Excessive lateral pressure syndrome

Procedure(s) performed:

1. Left knee arthroscopy
2. Partial lateral meniscectomy
3. Partial medial meniscectomy
4. Chondroplasty of the medial femoral condyle
5. Lateral retinacular release

Anesthesia:

Description of procedure:

The patient is under general anesthesia and endotracheal intubation. She received Ancef IV in holding. She is positioned supine. Knee laxity examination under general anesthesia is normal. The right lower extremity is placed in a well leg holder. A tourniquet is applied around the mid-thigh on the affected left lower extremity. A low-profile leg holder is applied around the tourniquet. The left lower extremity is exsanguinated with an Esmarch and the tourniquet is inflated to 300 mm Hg. Total tourniquet time was 60 minutes. Prep and drape of the left lower extremity in the usual manner.

Knee arthroscopy was done using two portals, anterolateral and anteromedial. The arthroscope was inserted anterolaterally. Instrumentation is through the anteromedial portal. Inflow is through the sheath of the arthroscope. The suprapatellar pouch looks normal. The medial and lateral gutters look normal. There is some fraying of the articular cartilage of the patella and trochlea. The patella is tilted laterally. Even beyond 60 degrees flexion, the patella remains tilted laterally. The cruciate ligaments are intact. In the lateral compartment there is a radial tear and a horizontal tear of the posterior horn and middle third of the lateral meniscus. The popliteus tendon looks normal. There is significant softening of the body of the meniscus. The articular cartilage of the lateral compartment is normal. A partial lateral meniscectomy is performed. The radial tear of the lateral meniscus is excised with baskets. The horizontal tear is sealed using an Oratec chondroplasty probe.

In the medial compartment there is a small sized flap tear of the posterior horn of the medial meniscus. The remaining meniscus is normal. The articular cartilage of the medial tibial plateau is normal. There is an area of grade II chondromalacia of the medial femoral condyle in its weight-bearing area at 45 degrees flexion. This area is 1.5 cm in size. A partial medial meniscectomy is performed with baskets, excising the small-sized flap tear of the posterior horn of the medial meniscus. The body of the meniscus is somewhat soft. A chondroplasty of the medial femoral condyle is performed, excising the unstable articular cartilage flaps with a 4.5 curved resector.

Finally, an arthroscopic lateral retinacular release is performed. The arthroscope is placed into the anteromedial portal. Patellar tracking is re-examined. The patella is tilted laterally even beyond 60 degrees flexion. A 4.5 resector is used to resect the fat pad anterolaterally. An Oratec chisel probe is next used to perform a limited lateral retinacular release. The release starts at the superior pole of the patella and extends towards the anterolateral portal. After the release is completed, the patella can be everted to 70 degrees. The patella tracks very nicely. Beyond 30 degrees flexion, the patella is well centered in the trochlear groove.

The knee is thoroughly irrigated, removing all soft tissue, cartilage, and meniscal debris. The arthroscopic cannulas are removed. The skin portals are closed with 4-0 nylon. 30 cc of Marcaine with epinephrine is injected inside the knee joint. Each portal is also injected with a few ccs of Marcaine without epinephrine. A bulky Jones dressing is applied. The tourniquet is released.

Surgery was well tolerated. The patient left the operating room to recovery in stable condition.

Patrick Chung, MD

GODFREY REGIONAL HOSPITAL
123 Main Street • Aldon, FL 77714 • (407) 555-1234

Answers

OPERATIVE REPORT

Patient information:

Patient name: Date:
DOB: Surgeon:
MR#:   Anesthetist:

Preoperative diagnosis:

1. Chronic maxillary sinusitis
2. Chronic ethmoid sinusitis
3. Deviated nasal septum
4. Nasal polyps

Postoperative diagnosis:

1. Chronic maxillary sinusitis
2. Chronic ethmoid sinusitis
3. Deviated nasal septum
4. Nasal polyps

Procedure(s) performed:

1. Bilateral endoscopic maxillary antrostomies with tissue removal
2. Bilateral endoscopic anterior ethmoidectomies
3. Septoplasty
4. Bilateral endoscopic nasal polypectomies

Anesthesia:

General

Assistant surgeon:

Description of procedure:

The patient was taken to the operating room and placed in the usual supine position. After induction of general anesthesia via endotracheal intubation, the patient was prepped and draped in the usual fashion for a clean uncontaminated procedure.

We first began by decongesting the nose with 4% cocaine on cottonoids. We then injected both sides of the nasal septum as well as the lateral nasal walls with 1% lidocaine with epinephrine.

We first performed the endoscopic sinus surgery on the left side because there were some very large polyps, in fact, some antral choanal polyps on the left side. The polyps were removed using the microdebrider. The uncinate process, the anterior ethmoid cells, and the natural ostium of the maxillary sinuses as well as a thick mucoid tissue within the sinus itself were all removed using the microdebrider. We then directed our attention to the septum where a left hemitransfixion incision was made. We performed a standard septoplasty with particular removal of the cartilage and bone that was compressing the right middle turbinate and obstructing the middle meatus on the right side. After this was done, we then resumed the sinus surgery, this time on the right side, and performed the exact same procedure with removal of the polyps, the anterior ethmoid cells, and the natural ostium of the maxillary sinus on the right-hand side.

After all this was done, the sinuses were thoroughly irrigated with normal saline solution. The left hemitransfixion incision on the septum was closed with a 5-0 plain gut suture. The mucoperichondrial flaps of the septum were closed with 4-0 plain gut in a basting suture fashion. The middle meatus on each side were packed with MeroGel packing. Doyle nasal splints were placed on each side of the septum, and 8-cm Merocel packs were placed on each side of the nose.

The patient tolerated the procedures well. There were no complications. The patient was subsequently moved directly to the recovery room in stable condition.

ESTIMATED BLOOD LOSS: 250 cc
COMPLICATIONS: None
COUNTS: Instrument count correct at the end of the procedure

Maurice Doater, MD

GODFREY REGIONAL HOSPITAL
123 Main Street • Aldon, FL 77714 • (407) 555-1234

Answers

EXERCISE 29

OPERATIVE REPORT

Patient information:

Patient name:
DOB:
MR#:

Preoperative diagnosis:

Left parotid tumor
CLINICAL NOTE:
The patient is a 73-year-old white male with an enlarging left parotid mass. Frozen section intraoperatively showed this to be a benign Warthin's tumor. The mass was approximately 2.5 cm in diameter and was closely adherent to the upper facial nerve branch divisions. The frontal branch of the facial nerve had to be peeled off the capsule of the tumor and was left intact.

Postoperative diagnosis:

Warthin's tumor, left parotid gland

Procedure(s) performed:

1. Left parotidectomy with facial nerve dissection
2. Left sternocleidomastoid muscle rotation flap

Anesthesia:

Description of procedure:

The patient was brought into the operating room and placed on the operating table in the supine position. General endotracheal anesthesia was performed. The left face was prepped and draped in sterile fashion and injected with saline with 1:100,000 parts epinephrine. A plane incision was injected subcutaneously with approximately 10 cc of the above. A modified Blair incision was made, extending along the preauricular crease around the earlobe and then on to the neck in curvilinear fashion. Incision was made with 15-blade scalpel and carried down through subcutaneous layer with Bovie cautery and meticulous dissection.

Using Metzenbaum scissors and meticulous dissection, with bipolar cautery, subcutaneous dissection just above the parotid fascia layer was performed and the facial flap was reflected anteriorly, exposing the parotid gland and tumor. The parotid tumor was in the preauricular area, just anterior to the tragal pointer of the ear cartilage, deep within the parotid gland.

Dissection was carried down along the preauricular region and tragal pointer tangentially to the anticipated course of the main trunk of the facial nerve. Hemostasis was obtained with bipolar cautery. Main trunk of the facial nerve was identified, and stylomastoid foramen was dissected out to the pes anserinus. Using cross-clamp technique, branches were followed that extended deep to the parotid tumor. Parotid tissue was cross-clamped and face observed for any facial movements, and then cut with 15-blade scalpel when clear. The parotid tumor was resected in a standard technique with the branches of the facial nerve visualized and preserved.

The mass was completely excised with several branches of the facial nerve, notably frontal and zygomatic branches dissected off the capsule of the tumor and preserved. Meticulous hemostasis was obtained with bipolar cautery and silk suture ties. Specimen was sent to Pathology for frozen and permanent section, and returned back showing Warthin's tumor.

The wound was irrigated copiously with normal saline and blotted dry. A superiorly based sternocleidomastoid muscle flap was made using the Bovie cautery and reflected up into the preauricular defect to cover the facial nerve to prevent scarring and Prey's syndrome. This was sutured with interrupted 3-0 chromic sutures to adjacent parotid fascia and preauricular soft tissue and fascia into position. A small diameter Jackson-Pratt drain was placed into the wound and brought out through a separate postauricular stab incision. It was sutured to the skin with 2-0 silk mattress sutures.

The wound was closed with inverted interrupted 3-0 chromic sutures for the deep subcutaneous layer and inverted interrupted 4-0 chromic sutures for the subcuticular layer. Skin was closed with running interlocking 5-0 nylon sutures with the exception of interrupted 5-0 nylon sutures around the earlobe. Bacitracin ointment was placed over the wound, followed by Telfa and light pressure dressing. The Jackson-Pratt was placed to self-suction.

The patient was awakened from general anesthesia, extubated, and brought to the recovery room in stable condition, having tolerated the procedure well.

Patk Adam MD

GODFREY REGIONAL HOSPITAL
123 Main Street • Aldon, FL 77714 • (407) 555-1234

Answers

OPERATIVE REPORT

Patient information:

Patient name:
DOB:
MR#:

Preoperative diagnosis:

Rectal bleeding

INDICATION FOR PROCEDURE:
This 42-year-old male has significant episodes of rectal bleeding and pain. By examination, he only has one external skin tag, no evidence of hemorrhoids. By history, this patient has a fissure.

Postoperative diagnosis:

Same, plus anal fissure

Procedure(s) performed:

Examination under anesthesia with left lateral internal sphincterotomy

Anesthesia:

Assistant surgeon:

Description of procedure:

After adequate preparation, 1% Xylocaine plain was used to infiltrate a peri-anal block. Examination of the anal canal does not show significant internal hemorrhoids. He does have a posterior anal fissure. The left lateral mucosa over the internal sphincter was incised and hemostasis achieved. Under direct vision, the sphincter was completely divided. The mucous membrane was then oversewn in a running locking fashion with 3-0 Vicryl.

The patient was taken to the recovery room in satisfactory condition.

Patrk Adam MD

GODFREY REGIONAL HOSPITAL
123 Main Street • Aldon, FL 77714 • (407) 555-1234

Answers

Using the ICD-9-CM Code Book

Complete step 4 of the Diagnostic Worksheet for Exercises 3-1 through 3-30 in Chapter 3.

5 V Codes and E Codes

Complete the following exercises by selecting the appropriate V codes and/or E codes as well as other necessary ICD-9-CM codes. Place the correct codes in the blanks provided. Note that the number of blank lines does not necessarily indicate the number of codes assigned.

V Code/E Code

1. Request expert medical advice _____

2. Well child _____

3. Postoperative visit for fractured distal radius _____

4. Contusions to the arms and legs due to accident at public facility _____

5. Laceration of the left fourth finger from powered lawn mower _____

6. Shortness of breath in a 7-year-old with history of asthma _____

7. Shortness of breath in a 27-year-old complaining of foot pain _____

8. Intrauterine pregnancy in a 35-year-old with history of previous miscarriage _____

9. 35-year-old presents with asthma exacerbation and states she has a history of miscarriage _____

10. Ankle pain as the result of tripping/falling during basketball game with diagnosis of sprained ankle _____

In Exercises 11 through 20, identify the proper sequencing of diagnostic codes. Determine whether it is appropriate to assign the V codes and/or E code as the primary diagnosis and whether it should be assigned a code. Place the correct ICD-9-CM codes in the blanks provided. The number of blank lines is not necessarily indicative of the number of correct ICD-9-CM codes.

11. Patient presents for screening colonoscopy. During the procedure, colon polyps are excised and the patient indicates that he has a strong family history of colon cancer.

    ICD-9-CM code(s):

    _____

    _____

    _____

12. Patient presents for annual recheck because of a previous diagnosis of breast cancer. She indicates she has been doing well; however, she has discovered a lump in her breast that she would like to have checked. After examination, the physician indicates it would be appropriate to obtain a mammogram and perhaps perform a breast biopsy. The breast biopsy specimen returns suspicious for malignancy.

    ICD-9-CM code(s):

    _____

    _____

    _____

13. Patient presents because of an accidental fall from a ladder at home. He complains of ankle swelling and a bruise on the leg above the knee. Examination and x-rays are negative.

    ICD-9-CM code(s):

    _____

    _____

    _____

14. A 3-year-old child is taken to the emergency department after a car accident in which she was a backseat passenger. Although the child remained secure in the child restraint seat, the mother insists on examination despite no obvious injuries or distress. A physical examination reveals no injuries, and the child is released.

    ICD-9-CM code(s):

    _____

    _____

    _____

15. Patient presents to the outpatient area for chemotherapy with a diagnosis of metastatic liver carcinoma, primary from the colon.

    ICD-9-CM code(s):

    _____

    _____

    _____

16. Patient presents to the emergency department after swallowing his mother's digoxin by accident. He complains of abdominal pain, nausea, and vomiting. A gastric lavage for ingested poisons is performed, the patient's symptoms are relieved, and he is released to his mother's care.

    ICD-9-CM code(s):

    _____

    _____

    _____

17. Patient presents for a recheck and possible cast change for her open distal radial fracture that occurred 2 weeks ago while roller skating.

    ICD-9-CM code(s):

    _____

    _____

    _____

18. Patient presents with complaint of shortness of breath. He gives a history of hypertension, COPD, and ingrown toenail. He receives a diagnosis of acute exacerbation of COPD, and steroids and medications are adjusted accordingly.

    ICD-9-CM code(s):

    _____

    _____

19. Patient presents for annual physical. During the course of the examination, the patient's hypertension and hypothyroid medications are checked and the patient is considered stable.

    ICD-9-CM code(s):

    _____

    _____

20. A 35-year-old female patient presents for a screening mammogram.

    ICD-9-CM code(s):

    _____

    _____

    _____

EXERCISES 21-40

Identify and assign the appropriate ICD-9-CM codes for the following medical records.

EXERCISE 21

OFFICE NOTE

Chief complaint: _____

Date: _____

Vital signs: BP_____ P_____ R_____

History:

SUBJECTIVE: This 74-year-old white female new patient with a history of polymyalgia presented after suddenly noticing and developing discomfort superficially at the right medial calf on the right lower extremity. She has noticed a knot and a swelling there and is concerned about a possible blood clot. She has a history of significant pulmonary conditions and has been the subject of multiple episodes of pneumonia. She states that she has not had any increased chest pain or shortness of breath.

Exam:

Pulse 81. Respiratory rate 18. Blood pressure 127/76. The patient is not out of breath. Her lungs are clear. Her heart is regular. Evaluation of the right calf shows a superficial clot right over a blood vessel on the medial surface of the calf approximately 1 3 of the way down from the tibial plateau. There is no leaking of fluid down the leg underneath the skin, and the calf muscle itself is flabby and not swollen.

Diagnosis/assessment:

IMPRESSION: Superficial blood vessel rupture, right lower extremity.

PLAN: We asked her to ice the area for the next couple of days and then apply heat to the area. We warned her of possible tracking of blood down the skin toward the ankle. We have given her antiembolic thigh-high stockings that she is to wear for the next 3–7 days, and she is to continue on her aspirin as before. She is to follow up with her primary care doctor on Thursday, to be monitored for potential complications to deep system. She is to return for any chest pain, shortness of breath, or evidence of infection in that area.

Maurice Doater, MD

Patient name: _____
Date of service: _____

GODFREY MEDICAL ASSOCIATES
1532 Third Avenue, Suite 120 • Aldon, FL 77713 • (407) 555-4000

Answers

OFFICE NOTE

Chief complaint: _____

Date: _____

Vital signs: BP_____ P_____ R_____

History:

This 50-year-old man developed epigastric pain radiating into his back 3 days ago after drinking about one six-pack of beer. That night he developed the hiccoughs and did a lot of belching. The next day he slept. Yesterday he felt improved and today he feels much improved. For the past 2 days, there has been no abdominal pain. His appetite has been poor. There has been no nausea or vomiting. His bowel function is regular. He has a history of alcohol abuse with abnormal liver function test. He also has psychiatric illness. He has had no surgery. His regular medications include Xanax and Zyprexa. He is allergic to sulfa.

Exam:

REVIEW OF SYSTEMS: He denies chest pain or palpitations. He has no cough or shortness of breath. There has been no dysuria or increased urinary frequency.

EXAMINATION: Reveals the patient to be alert. He is afebrile. Eyes are clear. Tympanic membranes appear normal. There is no nasal congestion. Mouth is moist. Throat reveals no redness or swelling. The neck is supple with no adenopathy. There is no heart murmur. Lungs are clear. The abdomen is soft and nontender. Bowel tones are active. Lab data include hemoglobin of 16.3; white count is 12,500. Chemistry panel includes calcium of 8.1, albumin is 3.4, bilirubin is 3.4, alkaline phosphatase is 202, AST 212, ALT 102, and sodium 126. Other values are within normal limits. Amylase is 75, CK is 117, and troponin is 0.3. Chest x-ray appears normal. EKG shows sinus rhythm with no acute change.

Diagnosis/assessment:

DIAGNOSIS:
1. Abdominal pain resolved
2. Abnormal liver function test probably secondary to alcoholism

DISPOSITION: Patient is to stay on a light diet. He admits to drinking about 1 six-pack of beer daily and was encouraged to stop drinking alcohol, which he has been able to do in the past. If he develops recurrent abdominal pain, vomiting, fever, or any other problem, he is to return to the office. Otherwise, he will follow up at the VA next week as scheduled. He was given copies of his lab reports.

Jay Corman MD

Patient name: _____

Date of service: _____

GODFREY MEDICAL ASSOCIATES
1532 Third Avenue, Suite 120 • Aldon, FL 77713 • (407) 555-4000

Answers

OFFICE NOTE

Date:	Vital signs:	T	R
Chief complaint:		P	BP

S: Arvin is here for assessment of a laceration. He is a 19-year-old who was involved in a motor vehicle accident approximately 2 hours prior to arrival. He says he was a passenger in the front seat of a car. He was not wearing a seatbelt and was sleeping when the car went into a ditch and hit an approach. He was then thrown forward and hit his head very forcefully on the dashboard. He is not certain if he lost consciousness or not. In any event, he sustained a gaping laceration just inferior to his left eyebrow. He is up to date on his tetanus immunization.

Physical examination:

O: Temperature 95. Pulse 70. Respirations 20. Blood pressure 110/64. In general, Arvin is alert, responsive, smells of alcohol, nontoxic appearing, and in no acute distress. Skin: There is a 3-centimeter total length laceration noted just inferior to the left eyebrow in the upper eye socket. It is quite gaping and fairly deep. It is an L-shaped configuration. No other injuries noted of the head.

HEENT: EOMI without nystagmus. PERRLA.

Assessment:

A: Laceration with layered repair.

Plan:

P: The wound was prepped with Betadine and anesthetized with 1% epinephrine. Four 4-0 Vicryl sutures were placed subcutaneously in the muscle layer to help bring together the edges of the wound. The wound edges were then approximated using eight 5-0 Ethilon sutures. The patient tolerated the procedure well. He was instructed in wound care and to return in a week for suture removal or prn before that if there are any other difficulties.

Maurice Doater, MD

	Patient name:
	DOB:
	MR/Chart #:

GODFREY REGIONAL OUTPATIENT CLINIC
3122 Shannon Avenue • Aldon, FL 77712 • (407) 555-7654

Answers

RADIOLOGY REPORT

MR#:
DOB:
Dr.

Clinical summary:

DIAGNOSIS:
Injured ribs

PART TO BE EXAMINED:
CXR and rt ribs

Abdomen:

Conclusion:

THREE VIEWS FOR RIGHT RIB DETAIL:
Recent fracture, anterior aspect of the right seventh rib and only slight displacement.

PA AND LATERAL CHEST:
Heart size and pulmonary vascularity normal. Lung fields are clear. No pleural fluid or pneumothorax. Harrington rods transfix the thoracolumbar spine. Previous coronary bypass procedure. No significant change since last CXR.

The recent fracture involving the anterior aspect of the right seventh rib, as noted on the right rib detail today, is not visualized clearly on the chest radiograph.

Ddt/mm

D:
T:

_____
Lisa Valhas, M.D.   Date

GODFREY REGIONAL HOSPITAL
123 Main Street • Aldon, FL 77714 • (407) 555-1234

Answers

RADIOLOGY REPORT

MR#:
DOB:
Dr.

Clinical summary:

EXAMINATION OF:
Chest (PA or AP and lateral)

CLINICAL SYMPTOMS:
Chest pain

Abdomen:

Conclusion:

PA AND LATERAL CHEST:
The bony structures are demineralized. There are surgical sutures in the sternum. There are small pleural effusions on each side. The heart is enlarged. The aorta is tortuous. The pulmonary vessels are congested. No area of confluent infiltrate is seen.

CONCLUSION:
Cardiomegaly with evidence of congestive heart failure.

Ddt/mm

D:
T:

_____
Lisa Valhas, M.D.   Date

GODFREY REGIONAL HOSPITAL
123 Main Street • Aldon, FL 77714 • (407) 555-1234

Answers

OFFICE NOTE

Date:	Vital signs:	T		R	
Chief complaint:		P		BP	

HISTORY: This 88-year-old new patient was lifting a pan, which fell on her right hand. She does have osteoporosis. Her medications are as listed. Her allergies are also as listed.

Physical examination:

Reveals an alert, pleasant elderly woman. There is ecchymosis and tenderness of the base of the proximal phalanx of the right middle finger. The skin is intact. Motion of the finger is limited. Sensation is intact. There is good capillary refill. X-rays of the right hand show no fracture.

Assessment:

DIAGNOSIS: Contusion, right hand.

Plan:

DISPOSITION: She is to elevate the hand with ice. She may take ibuprofen as needed. If she develops increased pain or any other problem she is to follow up with her usual physician.

Maurice Doater, MD

	Patient name:
	DOB:
	MR/Chart #:

GODFREY REGIONAL OUTPATIENT CLINIC
3122 Shannon Avenue • Aldon, FL 77712 • (407) 555-7654

Answers

EXERCISE 27

EMERGENCY ROOM RECORD

Name:		Age:	ER physician:
		DOB:	

Allergies/type of reaction:	Usual medications/dosages:

Triage/presenting complaint:	SUBJECTIVE: This is an 88-year-old female resident of a nursing home who was brought in by ambulance today after she was walking in the hallway and fell, striking the back of her head. There has been some question of possible heart arrhythmia. She has been very bradycardic ever since the ambulance service got to her. Currently, the patient is moaning and unable to provide any history.

Initial assessment:

Time	T	P	R	BP	Other:					

Medication orders:

Lab work:

X-ray:

Physician's report:

OBJECTIVE: This is a somewhat obtunded female who is moaning. Her BP is unable to be picked up. Pulse is unable to be picked up via monitors. With palpation of her femoral artery, pulse appeared to be about 20 beats per minute. She is hooked up on a cardiac monitor and this shows atrial activity, but only a rare ventricular capture. Pupils equal, round, and reactive to light. TMs are clear bilaterally. Oropharynx is clear. Neck is supple. No JVD. Heart is bradycardic. Lungs are clear to auscultation in all fields. Abdomen is soft, nontender, not distended. Extremities are free of any cyanosis, clubbing, or edema.

EMERGENCY ROOM COURSE: Patient did have an IV line established and was given IV atropine, 1 mg. This did not help her BP tremendously; therefore, with consultation with Dr. Obert, who is the internist on call and who had arrived in the ER to help resuscitate the patient, external pacing was done. She was set at a capture rate of 60 beats per minute and did well with this with a good pulse. Once she had her heart rhythm restored, she was alert. She was not complaining of any chest pain. No shortness of breath. She was unsure why she fell. EKG was done after the pacer was turned off because she was maintaining a sinus rhythm on her own. This revealed sinus bradycardia with first-degree AV block with a PR interval of 0.28 second. There was no ST-T wave elevation. There was some downward sloping of the ST segment in V5 and VS. There was evidence of a left bundle branch block. Chest x-ray was done, which was clear. Upon further examination of the patient, it did reveal a contusion to the back right side of her occiput with significant soft tissue ecchymosis, but no laceration that needed repair. This was cleansed. Neurological examination demonstrated movement in all four extremities. Toes were pointing downward bilaterally. Sensation was intact in distal extremities. A CT of her head was done, which revealed no bleed or acute findings per the radiologist's report. Troponin was 0.0. White count 13.2, hematocrit 39, Hgb 13.1, platelets 238.000. Glucose was elevated at 278, BUN 32, creatinine 1.7. This was up a little bit from her last readings. Albumin 3.1, alk phos 211, AST 46, ALT 85. This was up from normal levels of the previous tests. Sodium 135, potassium 3.7, chloride 99, bicarb 18. Patient remained stable and breathing on her own throughout her stay in the emergency room. Her heart remained in the sinus rhythm. It appeared to be a little bit tachycardic. EKG was repeated, which showed a sinus rhythm with a rate of 88 with continued first-degree AV block and left bundle branch block. Patient, who was diaphoretic and clammy when she came into the emergency room, then had normalizing of her body temperature with no further diaphoresis.

Diagnosis:	Physician sign/date
ASSESSMENT: This is an 88-year-old female with evidence of heart block now in sinus rhythm. No current evidence to suggest any acute ischemia. Neurological examination today demonstrates no focal findings. PLAN: Due to her heart block, patient was discussed with the cardiologist on call. He feels that the patient needs to be transferred down for further work-up and possible pacemaker placement; she will be transferred by ALS ambulance. She is in stable condition.	*Nancy Caully* MD

Discharge	Transfer	Admit	Good	Satisfactory	Other:

GODFREY REGIONAL HOSPITAL
123 Main Street • Aldon, FL 77714 • (407) 555-1234

Answers

EMERGENCY ROOM RECORD

Name:	Age:	ER physician:
	DOB:	

Allergies/type of reaction:	Usual medications/dosages:
none	none

Triage/presenting complaint:

S: The patient is a pleasant 47-year-old gentleman who was standing on a tire, cleaning the top of the cab of his truck. He lost his balance and landed on his right elbow. He had intense pain and was unable to flex or change position of his elbow. Given the severity of his injury and the acute pain, his wife notified the ambulance and he was brought into the ER. He had no LOC. No head injury. No shortness of breath, chest pain, GI/GU complaints. No previous trauma to the effected extremity.
FH: Noncontributory
ROS: See above.
PMH: He denies any previous hospitalizations or surgeries.
SH: He is married. He is an over-the-road truck driver. He does use tobacco.

Initial assessment:

Time	T	P	R	BP	Other:					

Medication orders:

Lab work:

X-ray: X-rays reveal a fracture dislocation of the distal humerus in the elbow joint and also a fracture of the distal radius, ulna, and scaphoid.

Physician's report:

O: The patient was in acute pain, alert, oriented, and able to converse. VS: T 98, O2 sat 100% on room air, P 90s, BP 170s/80s–90s. HEENT: AT/NC, PERRL, EOMI; conjunctivae and sclera are clear. Oropharynx clear. Neck supple. Lungs clear in all fields. Heart regular rate and rhythm; no murmurs or extra sounds. Abdomen soft and benign. Lower extremities within normal limits. Right upper extremity reveals an obvious dislocation with an open fracture. He is also tender across the distal radius and ulna. Sensation of the right and left upper extremities is equal and within normal limits.

EMERGENCY ROOM COURSE: The patient was seen and evaluated, an IV was placed, and he was treated with morphine for pain—a total of 18 mg over the course of the stay. He was also treated with 30 mg of IV Toradol. He was also treated with 1 g Ancef. He was given 75 mg Demerol and 50 mg Vistaril IM for transfer to another hospital.

Diagnosis:	Physician sign/date
A: Open fracture with fracture dislocation of the distal humerus, right elbow, and fracture of the distal radius, ulna, and scaphoid right arm. P: Transfer to the accepting hospital.	*Robert Rai MD*

Discharge	Transfer	Admit	Good	Satisfactory	Other:

GODFREY REGIONAL HOSPITAL
123 Main Street • Aldon, FL 77714 • (407) 555-1234

Answers

OFFICE NOTE

Date:		Vital signs:	T	R
Chief complaint:			P	BP

S: The patient is an 81-year-old new patient who, sometime two weeks prior to this visit, fell when deer hunting. He has fallen again and again, has recurrent right chest wall pain. He has had some dyspnea on exertion. He does, however, have chronic COPD and mild emphysema but he is restricting his breathing and has pain with each breath.

Physical examination:

O: He is afebrile. Pulse is 88. Respirations are 20 and splinted. Blood pressure is 142/76. HEENT: No signs of obvious trauma. Some memory deficit is noted. He denies any closed head injury with his initial injury. His fall last night was unexpected and caused by tripping. He had no syncopal episode, chest pain, or palpitations, and it did not appear by history to be a drop attack. Palpation of the neck revealed no crepitus but some arthritis. There was scant trapezius pain. Palpation along the right chest, however, revealed an area of exquisite tenderness without crepitus. The x-ray suggests that there is a fracture or at least a dislocation of the costochondral joint in this rib. There was no infiltrate and no effusion.

Assessment:

A: Right rib fracture, suspect 8th rib. Mild atelectasis.

Plan:

P: Treatment in the office is Toradol 30 mg IM. The patient is given a prescription for Toradol to use with meals and at bedtime routinely, but a limited prescription of five days is given. Heat and Aspercreme were discussed. The risk of atelectasis was explained in layman's terms. A forced deep inhalation was suggested.

Maurice Doates, MD

	Patient name:
	DOB:
	MR/Chart #:

GODFREY REGIONAL OUTPATIENT CLINIC
3122 Shannon Avenue • Aldon, FL 77712 • (407) 555-7654

Answers

OPERATIVE REPORT

Patient information:	
Patient name: DOB: MR#:	Date: Surgeon: Anesthetist:

Preoperative diagnosis:

Severe right heel abscess

INDICATIONS: The patient is a 54-year-old immune-suppressed rheumatoid who had presented with a severe abscess of his right heel. The patient returned today for the possibility of tobramycin bead removal and possibility for wound closure. Consent was obtained.

Postoperative diagnosis:

Severe right heel abscess

Procedure(s) performed:

1. Tobramycin bead removal
2. Irrigation and debridement
3. Wound closure

Anesthesia:

Assistant surgeon:

Description of procedure:

The patient was brought to the main operating room and positioned supine. After general anesthesia was adequately obtained, bandages were removed. The outside of the wound was noted to be healed up nicely. Therefore the right lower extremity was prepped and draped in the usual sterile fashion.

Sutures were cut, and serous fluid was identified within the wound; however, there was no evidence of purulence, no aroma. No evidence of necrosis either. Tobramycin beads were removed. The wound was again inspected, and again there was no evidence for infection. Therefore we ran 3000 cc of pulse-lavaged fluid throughout the wound. Small areas of devitalized tissue were sharply removed. Noted good granulation tissue throughout the bed. Again no evidence of osteomyelitis. After final irrigation was performed, we then reapproximated deep tissues with 3-0 Prolene, subcutaneous tissue with 3-0 Prolene, and closed the skin with 3-0 nylon. A sterile compression bandage was applied.

GODFREY REGIONAL HOSPITAL
123 Main Street • Aldon, FL 77714 • (407) 555-1234

Answers

OFFICE NOTE

Date:	Vital signs:	T	R
Chief complaint: Right hand injury		P	BP

HISTORY: This is a 44-year-old gentleman who was going to ride his horse. He had his hand in the bridle when the horse jerked up, and he injured his right middle and ring fingers with a deformity. He has a little blood coming around the nail too.

He is on Paxil. No other health problems. No allergies.

Physical examination:

O: On exam he has obvious deformities probably due to fractures of his right middle and ring finger. I am not sure if it is at the DIP joint or in the mid-phalanx at this point. He can feel to touch distally, but he isn't moving because of the pain. His little finger and ring finger are not really tender; color, movement, and sensation are intact in those. Color was good in the middle and ring finger too. X-rays show comminuted fractures with displacement impacting of his mid-phalanx of the ring and middle fingers.

Assessment:

A: Comminuted fractures of the mid-phalanx of the right middle and ring fingers.

Plan:

P: A hand surgeon was in the building, so I showed him the x-rays. He suggested just straightening the fingers out under some anesthesia and putting a volar splint on and then having him [the patient] see either himself or another hand surgeon after two days. That will allow the swelling to go down. I did do a digital block with just under 5 cc in each finger, of 2% lidocaine after a Betadine prep. After good anesthesia, each finger was grasped, pulled on the longitudinal aspect, and straightened out. With middle finger there was a fair amount of clunking but it did straighten out nicely. He was then put in a volar splint from the mid forearm with the wrist slightly in hyperextension and out past the fingers, the middle and ring fingers. Ace wrap was applied. He is to leave this on until he is rechecked. He can elevate the arm. He was given Tylenol #3 to use 1 to 2 q4h prn for pain, #30. He still had good color in the fingers. Sensation was not present because of anesthesia from the digital block. If he has any numbness that develops in his ring or little finger, he will loosen the bandages. He was stable at discharge, and he will need to bring his x-rays with him to see the hand surgeon or orthopedist.

Maurice Coates, MD

	Patient name:
	DOB:
	MR/Chart #:

GODFREY REGIONAL OUTPATIENT CLINIC
3122 Shannon Avenue • Aldon, FL 77712 • (407) 555-7654

Answers

EXERCISE 32

OFFICE NOTE

Date:		Vital signs:	T		R	
Chief complaint:			P		BP	

S: Patient presents to the office complaining of increasing shortness of breath. He was having gradually increasing shortness of breath over a long period of time. He had an angiogram a couple of years ago, and he states that his dyspnea has been present since that time. He also has had some episodes of mild chest tightness when he exerts himself, but as soon as he rests, it goes away fairly quickly. He has not been taking his furosemide. He has been taking his other medications as prescribed. He has not seen anybody for this for about two years. He usually follows with a cardiologist for his heart. He has a history of severe coronary artery disease, and the patient states that he has an ejection fraction of about 40 percent.

Examination:

O: On examination, patient appears mildly dyspneic as he arrives. His chest has a few bibasilar crackles. Heart regular rate and rhythm. No rubs, murmurs, or gallops are noted. Heart sounds are somewhat distant. He has a large chest. Abdomen is obese, soft, and nontender. Extremities 1 to 2+ edema at his ankles. We gave him Lasix 20 IV and obtained labs. His EKG showed no acute changes. His chest x-ray showed an enlarged heart but not a lot of fluid in his lung fields. Remainder of his labs were within acceptable limits.

Impression:

A: CHF.

Plan:

P: Patient has stated that the cardiologists have told him that there is not anything more that they can do for his coronary artery disease. We did discuss possibly starting him on a beta blocker for his CHF, but I would recommend follow-up with Cardiology before this is considered. The patient stated he would arrange a follow-up appointment with Cardiology to have this further assessed. We recommended strongly that he go ahead and start his Lasix, 40 mg daily, as prescribed previously. He hasn't been taking this for a very long period of time, with reason being that he doesn't like to void afterwards. We will discharge him to home, and we will have him reassessed on a prn basis if he has increasing dyspnea. Did recommend staying in a cool environment, maintaining adequate hydration, taking his furosemide regularly along with his other medications, and trying to rest as much as possible.

Jay Carson MD

	Patient name:
	DOB:
	MR/Chart #:

GODFREY REGIONAL OUTPATIENT CLINIC
3122 Shannon Avenue • Aldon, FL 77712 • (407) 555-7654

Answers

EXERCISE 33

EMERGENCY ROOM RECORD

Name:		Age:	ER physician:
		DOB:	

Allergies/type of reaction:	Usual medications/dosages:
Aspirin, codeine, and opiates.	Current medications—See list.

Triage/presenting complaint:

SUBJECTIVE: This 45-year-old woman presents by ambulance unresponsive. The patient reportedly sat down to eat dinner and ate a couple bits of potato. She then seemed to doze off and was snoring. People tried to wake her but they found her to be unresponsive. An ambulance was called, and upon their arrival, they noted her blood sugar to read low. The patient is a known diabetic and on Glucovance and Avandia. They were unable to arouse her and tried to give her a little Gluco paste in the mouth. They suctioned her and kept her on oxygen. The patient continued to be unresponsive and was brought to the emergency room.
Past medical history—mental retardation, depression, diabetes.

Initial assessment:

ASSESSMENT:
1. Low blood sugar.
2. Microcytic anemia.
3. Possible sleep apnea.

Time	T	P	R	BP	Other:					

Medication orders:

Lab work:

Labs show white blood count of 13,400 with hematocrit of 32.4 and MCV of 71.3. Normal electrolytes, BUN, creatinine, and a glucose of 109. Urine analysis is unremarkable.

X-ray:

Physician's report:

OBJECTIVE: Temperature 97, pulse 76, respiratory 24, blood pressure 18/74. Oxygen saturation is 92 percent on room air.

PHYSICAL EXAM: Shows patient to be unresponsive to even painful stimuli. She will not open her eyes and is snoring. She is breathing well on her own. HEENT shows pupils equal, round, and reactive to light and accommodation extraocular motion intact. Patient has normal nasal and oral mucosa. Neck is supple without adenopathy. Lungs are clear with good breath sounds in all four quadrants. Heart is regular rate and rhythm. Abdomen is soft, nontender with positive bowel sounds. Extremities show pre-tibular edema. Neurologically, the patient was initially unresponsive and snoring. After receiving 1 amp of D-50, she did awaken and returned to her normal state according to her friends.

PLAN: The patient is not usually on a strict diabetic diet, and her medications have been adjusted for that type of diet. However, the patient has come up to this area and is now on a fairly strict diet. She probably has not been receiving enough calories and so her blood sugar has become quite low.

She had an IV started and received 1 amp of D-50. She did awaken and became much more alert and responsive. Her friends here state that she is pretty much back to her normal status. Her blood count is mildly low and microcytic. This is probably a chronic condition. The patient also appears to be very sleepy at times and may be having some problems with sleep apnea, given her obesity and snoring respirations.

Diagnosis:	Physician sign/date
A physician from her area is present and will talk to her local doctor about readjusting her medications and doing further work-up for the anemia and sleep apnea problems. She was discharged home in stable condition.	*Robert Rai MD*

Discharge	Transfer	Admit	Good	Satisfactory	Other:

GODFREY REGIONAL HOSPITAL
123 Main Street • Aldon, FL 77714 • (407) 555-1234

Answers

OFFICE NOTE

Date:	Vital signs:	T		R	
Chief complaint:		P		BP	

SUBJECTIVE: This 85-year-old female new patient presents complaining of blood in her urine. The patient states that she started noticing the blood in her urine last night and it seemed to get quite dark. It has since cleared but she is concerned. She has not had any burning or pain with urination and denies any recent weight loss or illness.

Past medical history: High blood pressure, coronary artery bypass grafting six years ago, hysterectomy seven years ago for some type of tumor, which later required radiation therapy, and a pulmonary embolism.

Current medications: Lotensin, warfarin, Zocor, and a depression medication.

Allergies: Possibly Fragmin.

Physical examination:

OBJECTIVE: Temperature 97.6, pulse 78, respirations 18, and blood pressure 176/80.

PHYSICAL EXAM: Shows patient to be alert. She does not appear in any acute distress. HEENT shows pupils equal, round, and reactive to light and accommodation. Extraocular motion intact. The patient has normal oral and nasal mucosa. Neck is supple without adenopathy. The lungs are clear with good breath sounds in all four quadrants. Heart is regular rate and rhythm. Abdomen is soft, nontender, with positive bowel sounds. Back shows no spinal or CVA tenderness. Rectal exam shows heme-negative stool. No hemorrhoids are noted. A urinalysis shows 25 to 50 red blood cells with no white blood cells or bacteria. White blood count is 5.7 with hematocrit of 38.2. INR is 3.0.

Assessment:

Hematuria of unknown cause.

Plan:

The patient does have a history of hysterectomy for a cancer, and it is possible that she may have a bladder tumor. It seems to be clearing at this point, and we will contact her usual physician so that she can follow up with him on an outpatient basis. She is to return if she starts having any pain or worsening of her symptoms. She was to see her physician later this week.

Jay Corman MD

	Patient name:
	DOB:
	MR/Chart #:

GODFREY REGIONAL OUTPATIENT CLINIC
3122 Shannon Avenue • Aldon, FL 77712 • (407) 555-7654

Answers

Chapter **5** **V Codes and E Codes**

OFFICE NOTE

Date:	Vital signs:	T	R
Chief complaint:		P	BP

HISTORY: This 86-year-old woman slipped in the shower and fell, injuring her right wrist last evening. During the night she rolled out of the bed and seemed to re-injure the wrist. This morning she has increased pain and swelling. She has a history of heart disease with a pacemaker and hypertension. Her medications are as listed. There is no allergy to medicine.

Physical examination:

Reveals an alert, pleasant elderly woman. There is swelling and tenderness of the right wrist. The skin is intact. Function and sensation of the right hand are intact. X-rays of the right wrist show a non-displaced fracture of the distal radius. There is good capillary refill.

TREATMENT COURSE: A short-arm fiberglass splint was applied.

Assessment:

DIAGNOSIS: Non-displaced fracture to distal right radius

Plan:

DISPOSITION: She is to leave the splint in place. She will elevate the wrist with ice. She may take Tylenol as needed. She was given Darvocet that she may take for more severe pain. If she develops increased pain, weakness, or numbness of the hand or any other problems, she is to go to the emergency room; otherwise, in about 10 days she will follow up with her usual physician.

	Patient name:
	DOB:
	MR/Chart #:

GODFREY REGIONAL OUTPATIENT CLINIC
3122 Shannon Avenue ¥ Aldon, FL 77712 ¥ (407) 555-7654

Answers

OFFICE NOTE

Chief complaint: _____

Date: _____

Vital signs: BP_____ P_____ R_____

History:

S: This 67-year-old female new patient presents with a complaint of neck discomfort, right knee discomfort, left ankle discomfort, and an abrasion on her nose after she fell out of bed this evening. She was asleep after going to bed at approximately 11:00 p.m. and was evidently having a nightmare. Her husband noted that she was screaming. She fell to the floor as she was attempting to get out of bed. She immediately woke up and was alerted to the situation and was able to stand to her feet and come to the clinic. She is mainly concerned about her neck pain.

Exam:

O: On physical exam, she is afebrile. Pulse is 90. Respirations 22. Blood pressure 169/104. Her pulse is 90. She is in no obvious distress, other than some abrasions and some bruises noted. She has a mildly stiff neck. Pupils are equal, round, and reactive to light and accommodating. Extraocular muscles are intact. Funduscopic exam is grossly normal. She has a small abrasion over her nose. There is no nasal crepitus. There is no zygomatic crepitus noted. There is no obvious tooth damage. She has no bite marks on her tongue or inside her mouth. There are no lesions in the throat. Neck is supple with no lymphadenopathy. No palpable thyroid abnormalities. She has stiffness over the posterior aspect. No specific exquisite tender points. She exhibits fairly normal range of motion in flexion, extension, side bending, and rotation. Sensation in the arms is normal. Deep tendon reflexes normal throughout. No obvious wrist, elbow, or shoulder injury. She has a large bruise on her right wrist from an IV today. She did have a colonoscopy today and was given midazolam and meperidine for sedation earlier today. Chest reveals normal lung sounds and normal heart sounds. No thoracic or lumbar tenderness to palpation. She exhibits normal thoracic and lumbar range of motion. Her gait is unaffected and normal. Hips are without crepitus and specific pain. She has had some chronic right hip pain but nothing new since her fall tonight. Lower extremities reveal a bruise over the medial aspect of the right knee. She exhibits normal range of motion with normal weightbearing, however. She has a skin abrasion and contusion of the left lower extremity just superior to the ankle. She exhibits normal range of motion of the ankle and normal weightbearing as well.

Diagnosis/assessment:

A: 1. Questionable night terror—evidently husband states she has had several episodes of this in the past. Initially, it was thought that maybe some of her symptoms were due to her sedation for her colonoscopy; however, her husband states that this has happened frequently over the last couple of years. 2. Contusion, right medial knee. 3. Skin abrasion and contusion, left lower extremity superior to the ankle. 4. Abrasion of the nose.

P: Ice to affected areas. Rest. Follow-up with her usual physician. A sleep study may need to be considered if this has been a chronic issue for her. Any further symptoms, headaches, or worsening neck pain should result in another visit to the physician.

William Obst MD

Patient name: _____

Date of service: _____

GODFREY MEDICAL ASSOCIATES
1532 Third Avenue, Suite 120 • Aldon, FL 77713 • (407) 555-4000

Answers

EXERCISE 37

OPERATIVE REPORT

Patient information:

Patient name:	Date:
DOB:	Surgeon:
MR#:	Anesthetist:

Preoperative diagnosis:

1. Comminuted, markedly displaced fracture of the distal mid 1/3 junction of the left tibia and fibula with associated bacterial infection, and delayed union
2. Status post multiple debridement and insertion of antibiotic impregnated methyl methacrylate beads

Postoperative diagnosis:

Same

Procedure(s) performed:

Operative, multicultures of fracture site, removal of methyl methacrylate and antibiotic beads from distal lower leg fracture site, wound irrigation, local debridement, and lysis of adhesions

Anesthesia:

Assistant surgeon:

Description of procedure:

The patient was brought to the operating room and placed under spinal anesthesia without episode. Tourniquet was applied high on the proximal aspect of the left thigh. The extremity was then prepped and draped in the usual sterile fashion from the tourniquet level distally. The extremity was elevated for exsanguination of venous blood and tourniquet inflated to 300 mm of mercury pressure. Following this, approach was made to the distal anterior aspect of the lower leg, utilizing previous old surgical scar in a slightly curvilinear fashion; the most posterior aspect of the distal incision was extended anteriorly to the most medial portion of the old scar in an extensile fashion. This allowed access to both the anteromedial methyl methacrylate antibiotic beads and the direct anterior methyl methacrylate impregnated antibiotic bead.

Sharp dissection was taken down through the skin and subcutaneous tissue. Care was taken to protect neurovascular and tendinous structures. The previous open wound area, measuring approximately 1 1/2 cm in widest diameter, directly over one of the methyl methacrylate beads, was quite easily discernible. Utilizing meticulous sharp and blunt dissection, the entire anteromedial antibiotic impregnated methacrylate bead construct was removed. There did not appear to be any gross drainage/infection at the site of bead placement or at the site of the fracture. Multiple cultures were obtained, including Gram stain of the area, and cultures for aerobic and anaerobic organisms.

Following this, dissection was continued directly medial, that is anteriorly, where the second antibiotic impregnated methyl methacrylate bead construct was easily discernible, and it likewise was removed. The latter was directly anteriorly placed over the periosteum at the distal fracture site. Again, this area did not disclose any gross evidence of pus. The area was further developed to allow release of adhesions between the ankle dorsiflexor tendons and the overlying skin. Following mobilization of this fibrous tissue, passive mobilization of the ankle could be facilitated; inversion/eversion motion was also facilitated without the persistence of cutaneous periosteal adhesions.

Following extensive irrigation of the area utilizing copious amounts of sterile saline mixed with vancomycin and tobramycin solution, the wound was subsequently closed in layers using widely spaced interrupted simple sutures of 4-0 nylon. A Penrose drain was left percutaneously exposed through the site of the previous small open wound to allow for egress of any seroma or drainage from the operative field. Tourniquet was released prior to skin closure with excellent and immediate return of distal circulation, excellent capillary refill, and pink toes. Following application of sterile Adaptic gauze and multiple layers of sterile 4 × 4s and sterile soft roll cast padding, the extremity was subsequently immobilized in a knee-high fiberglass splint overwrapped with an Ace bandage.

The patient tolerated the procedure quite well, was taken to postoperative recovery, and subsequently returned to the medical-surgical unit in good condition. No intraoperative or immediate postoperative difficulties were noted.

Patrick Chung, MD

GODFREY REGIONAL HOSPITAL
123 Main Street • Aldon, FL 77714 • (407) 555-1234

Answers

OPERATIVE REPORT

Patient information:

Patient name:	Date:
DOB:	Surgeon:
MR#:	Anesthetist:

Preoperative diagnosis:

Avulsive crush injury, right long and ring fingers

INDICATIONS: Patient is a 33-year-old right-hand–dominant white male who caught his right hand in a brake press at work. The wounds were examined. Consent was obtained for shortening of the fingers and partial wound closure.

Postoperative diagnosis:

Same

Procedure(s) performed:

Irrigation, debridement, bone shortening, and partial closure, left long and ring fingers

Anesthesia:

Local

Assistant surgeon:

Description of procedure:

EBL: Minimal

TOURNIQUET TIME: 0

COMPLICATIONS: None apparent

The patient was brought to the main operating room and positioned supine. After anesthesia placed a digital block under sterile conditions, the left upper extremity was prepped and draped in the usual sterile fashion. Ragged ends of bone that were protruding through the wound were trimmed back with a rongeur, and on the right finger, it was taken back to the level of the DIPJ as it was marked comminuted. Devitalized tissue was excised with a #15 blade and tenotomy scissors as appropriate.

I then reapproximated the flexor and extensor tendons over the tip of the bone with 2-0 Ethibond sutures. I then utilized 4-0 nylon to loosely approximate the edges, leaving the central portion open to further granulate into place. Bacitracin was applied as well as a sterile light compression bandage.

The patient was returned to PAR in stable condition without apparent complication.

IMMUNIZATION: The patient was given tetanus prophylaxis as well as 3.1 gm Timentin IV.

DISCHARGE INSTRUCTIONS: The patient will be discharged to home. He is to keep the wound clean and dry. He is also given outpatient antibiotics and pain medications. He should follow up with myself in 48 hours for a wound check.

Robert Chong MD

GODFREY REGIONAL HOSPITAL
123 Main Street • Aldon, FL 77714 • (407) 555-1234

Answers

EXERCISE 39

OPERATIVE REPORT

Patient information:	
Patient name: DOB: MR#:	Date: Surgeon: Anesthetist:

Preoperative diagnosis:

Left distal radius fracture

Postoperative diagnosis:

Same

Procedure(s) performed:

Open reduction, internal fixation of left distal radius fracture; long-arm splinting; fluoroscopy

Anesthesia:

Assistant surgeon:

Description of procedure:

The patient was taken to the operating room, and after general anesthesia was administered, her left upper extremity was examined under fluoroscopy. It was noted that the fracture was unstable and would slide back into the volarly displaced position after reduction. The decision was made to do an open reduction internal fixation at that point. The arm was prepped and draped in a sterile fashion. A well padded pneumatic tourniquet had been applied around the upper arm, and after exsanguination of the extremity with an Esmarch, it was inflated to 200 mm Hg.

Standard volar approach to the distal forearm was made. The brachioradialis was palpated and a longitudinal incision was made. The radial artery was identified and protected. It was taken laterally. Dissection down to the pronator was done and it was divided off its insertion on the radius. The fracture site was identified. The fracture was reduced, and a small T plate off of the small fragment set was used to hold the fracture on the volar surface using buttressing type effect. One screw was placed in the sliding hole and fluoroscopy was used to assess the fracture position as well as hardware placement. Each of these was felt to be acceptable, and therefore additional cortical screws were placed proximally. A single cancellous screw was placed distally. Care was taken to remain out of the growth plate. The hardware being in place, the fracture site was identified under fluoroscopy using AP and lateral views. It was felt that hardware position as well as fracture reduction were acceptable. The wound was irrigated out copiously. The pronate was closed back down with 2-0 Vicryl. The subcutaneous tissue was closed with 2-0 Vicryl. The skin was closed with 4-0 Biosyn and Steri-strips. A sterile dressing and long arm sugar tong type splint were applied.

The patient was taken to the recovery room in stable condition. Of note, the tourniquet was deflated prior to wound closure and the wound had minimal bleeding. The radial artery was pulsating and had good flow.

Patrick Chung, MD

GODFREY REGIONAL HOSPITAL
123 Main Street • Aldon, FL 77714 • (407) 555-1234

Answers

OPERATIVE REPORT

Patient information:	
Patient name:	Date:
DOB:	Surgeon:
MR#:	Anesthetist:

Preoperative diagnosis:

CC: Elbow injury
Patient suffered extremity injury as a result of a fall on arm. Patient sustained additional injuries stating she feel off back of 1-ft step, hitting the back of her head on the concrete. She is complaining of altered vision in the left eye, but denies headache, nausea, or vomiting.

Symptoms are contained to the left elbow and are described by the patient as severe.

Allergies: Aspirin, Codeine

Postoperative diagnosis:

TREATMENT:
OCL splint applied. Device is fit appropriately and neurovascular exam remains intact.

Laceration is repaired with 3 sutures through the subcutaenous with 3-0 Nylon. Wound was covered with sterile dressing. Antibiotic ointment was applied over suture line.

Procedure(s) performed:

Partial first ray amputation, left lower extremity

Anesthesia:

Assistant surgeon:

Description of procedure:

REVIEW OF SYSTEMS:
Neuro: Negative headache, dizziness, confusion, numbness, tingling, weakness
MS: Positive joint pain, negative back pain, neck pain
GI: Negative nausea, vomiting, chills
Eyes: Positive visual changes, negative pain
EXAM:
General, well-nourished 47-year-old in no acute distress. Vital signs are reviewed.
HEENT: PERRLA. EOMI
Chest: No visibile signs of trauma.
CV: Regular rate and rhythm.
GI: Abdoment, no signs of trauma
MS: 1-cm laceration, left elbow. No active bleeding, no foreign bodies noted.
   Range of motion decreased secondary to pain. Moderate amount of tissue.
   Swelling. Severe tenderness to palpation.
Skin: Intact throughout without significant abrasion.
Neuro: Alert and oriented ×3
X-Ray: Left elbow, positive proximal olecranon fracture

Robert Rai MD

GODFREY REGIONAL HOSPITAL
123 Main Street • Aldon, FL 77714 • (407) 555-1234

Answers

EXERCISES 1-30

For the following exercises, complete steps 1 through 4 of the Diagnostic Worksheet. You will complete the E & M Worksheet for these exercises after finishing Chapter 11.

EXERCISE 1

PROGRESS NOTE

Date: 04/15/XX	Vital signs:	T	R
Chief complaint: Runny nose, cough, congestion		P	BP

SUBJECTIVE:
27-year-old with cold for two weeks, runny nose, cough, sinus congestion.
Also has had some diarrhea and vomited several times.

Examination:

OBJECTIVE:
Vitals are stable HEENT: Throat - some congestion, no exudate.
Sinuses are non-tender. NECK: No lymphadenopathy. CHEST: Clear.
ABDOMEN:
Soft, non-tender. Equal bowel sounds.

Impression:

Viral syndrome

Plan:

Reassurance
Sudafed for sinus congestion
Motrin for pain
Immodium for diarrhea

Jay Corm mo

Patient name: Shana Kurtz
DOB: 1/10/19XX
MR/Chart #: 73684

GODFREY REGIONAL OUTPATIENT CLINIC
3122 Shannon Avenue • Aldon, FL 77712 • (407) 555-7654

Answers

PROGRESS NOTE

Date: 02/12/XX

Chief complaint: Cough for 2 weeks

Vital signs:	T		R
	P		BP

4-month-old is brought in with complaint he has been having a cough for over 2 weeks. Now he has a fever and coughs a lot. Also fussy. He is eating fair.

Examination:

Temperature 101, pulse 140, respirations 36. No use of accessory muscles.
Throat: some congestion. Ears: bilaterally does reveal red eardrum on the left with absent-like reflex. Normal vesicular breathing. No rhonchi or crackles.
Chest x-ray, PA & lateral is negative
CBC normal

Impression:

Bilateral otitis media. Probably pneumonia.

Plan:

Augmentin 125 mg per 5 ml.
1 tsp tid x 10 days

Jay Corrum mo

Patient name: Erik Schmitt

DOB: 10/08/20XX

MR/Chart #: 10084

GODFREY REGIONAL OUTPATIENT CLINIC
3122 Shannon Avenue • Aldon, FL 77712 • (407) 555-7654

Answers

EXERCISE 3

<table>
<tr><td colspan="2">PROGRESS NOTE</td></tr>
<tr>
<td>Date: 03/12/XX</td>
<td>Vital signs: T   R</td>
</tr>
<tr>
<td>Chief complaint: Productive cough x 2–3 days</td>
<td>P   BP</td>
</tr>
</table>

03/12/XX   Patient complains of 2–3 day history of non-productive cough. Coughing, all nocturnal. Nyquil has not helped. Patient also reports fever during the past 24 hours.

Physical examination:

Alert, non-ill appearing white female. Vital signs are stable.
HEENT: Clear. Pharyngeal congestion. Lungs clear, abdomen soft with active bowel sounds.

Rapid strep is negative. CBC and chest x-ray negative.

Assessment:

Acute bronchitis

Plan:

Jay Corman MD

Patient name: Rachel Lynne
DOB: 11/07/19XX
MR/Chart #: 90681

GODFREY REGIONAL OUTPATIENT CLINIC
3122 Shannon Avenue • Aldon, FL 77712 • (407) 555-7654

Answers

PROGRESS NOTE

| Date: 01/12/XX | Vital signs: | T | | R | |
| Chief complaint: Abdominal pain | | P | | BP | |

| 01/12/XX | 32-year-old presents with pain in the upper right quadrant for over 1 week. This comes and goes. This is not associated with food. It hurts to walk. No chest pain. No shortness of breath. No nausea or vomiting. No diarrhea or constipation. He had a cholescystectomy over 10 years ago. He has a history of diabetes and takes medication, although doesn't remember the name. As this is a new patient to our facility, we do not have records regarding this medication. |

Physical examination:

Alert, oriented, active, vitals stable. Temperature 98.3, BP 120/80, pulse 110. Abdomen: Reveals right upper quadrant scar. On palpation he is tender in right upper quadrant area. Liver is felt just below the right costal margin. Otherwise, good bowel sounds. Chest is clear. His CBC, liver panel and BUN and creatinine are unremarkable. Abdomen x-ray was negative.

Assessment:

IMPRESSION:
Epigastric and RUQ pain, probably gastritis

Jay Corm MD

Plan:

	Patient name: Bradley Hinter
	DOB: 1/04/19XX
	MR/Chart #: 14434

GODFREY REGIONAL OUTPATIENT CLINIC
3122 Shannon Avenue • Aldon, FL 77712 • (407) 555-7654

Answers

PROGRESS NOTE

Chief complaint: _____

Date: 03/18/XX _____   DOB: 02/13/20XX _____

Vital signs: BP_____ P_____ R_____   MR/Chart #: 08006 _____

History:

1-year-old new patient who was seen approximately one week ago for immunizations, MMR and HIB vaccine. Today presents with mild cough that has progressed where she is now running a fever, more irritable and fussy, cough has increased having a bit of a sore throat type symptomatology and some troubles with swallowing and such.

Exam:

The one tympanic membrane does look red and inflamed at this point. Throat is a little red also. Neck is supple, lungs are clear. Heart, regular rate and rhythm. Abdomen seems benign.

Diagnosis/assessment:

Otitis and pharyngitis
Cefzil 125 per 5 tsp bid for ten days. Tylenol as needed.

Jay Coram MD

Patient name: Brandy Kemper _____

Date of service: 03/18/XX _____

GODFREY REGIONAL OUTPATIENT CLINIC
3122 Shannon Avenue • Aldon, FL 77712 • (407) 555-7654

Answers

PROGRESS NOTE

Date: 05/10/XX	Vital signs:	T	R
Chief complaint: Back pain		P	BP

Here today with complaints of back pain. Tells me that earlier today he lifted the garbage and immediately got some discomfort in the right upper part of his back. Tells me it didn't cause any numbness or tingling. It is not restricting his ability to move, but with pressure applied he complains of pain.

Examination:

Alert, responsive, frail in his stature, but does not appear in distress.
Musculoskeletal: Back is erect without abrasion or deformity. Complains of pain with palpation along the wing of the scapula on the right side. Range of motion is appropriate.

Impression:

Upper back pain

Plan:

Use arthritis medicine previously prescribed as has a history of rheumatoid arthritis. Avoid excessive strain or activity.

Felix Wander MD

Patient name: Charles Diets
DOB: 10/21/19XX
MR/Chart #: 07331

GODFREY REGIONAL OUTPATIENT CLINIC
3122 Shannon Avenue • Aldon, FL 77712 • (407) 555-7654

Answers

PROGRESS NOTE

Date: 03/18/XX	Vital signs:	T	R
Chief complaint: Twisted ankle/basketball		P	BP

03/18/XX — 20-year-old male was playing basketball yesterday and twisted right ankle. It is quite swollen. 2 view x-ray of ankle is negative.

Examination:

Impression:

Lateral ankle sprain

Plan:

Ace wrap and crutches. Non-weight bearing 1 week.
May take Tylenol 1000 mg qid or equivalent OTC non-steroidal.
If no improvement in the next 3–5 days, should return for additional follow-up.

Jay Corm MD

Patient name: Devin McMurphy
DOB: 11/01/19XX
MR/Chart #: 11400

GODFREY REGIONAL OUTPATIENT CLINIC
3122 Shannon Avenue • Aldon, FL 77712 • (407) 555-7654

Answers

EMERGENCY ROOM RECORD

Name:		Age: 20	ER physician:
Lisa Bird		DOB: 8/4/19XX	Nancy Connelly

Allergies/type of reaction: | **Usual medications/dosages:**

Triage/presenting complaint:

Rash on the side of abdomen

Initial assessment:

Fine red rash scattered over back and abdomen
No allergies/skin problems

Time	T	P	R	BP	Other:					

Medication orders:

Benadryl 50 mg IM

Lab work:

X-Ray:

Physician's report:

20-year-old woman presents with onset pyritic rash on left side of abdomen. Came on just this evening as driving home in the last hour. She has not had any history of skin problems in the past. Not taking any medications. Denies any recent upper respiratory infection. Her health has been good.

PHYSICAL: General appearance is that of well-developed female in no acute distress. Examination of her back and abdomen revealed randomly scattered hives.

ASSESSMENT: Urticaria

PLAN: Benadryl 50 mg IM and then 50 mg PO TID prn. Cautioned her about sedation.

Diagnosis:	Physician sign/date
Urticaria	*Nancy Connelly* MD

Discharge	Transfer	Admit	Good	Satisfactory	Other:

GODFREY REGIONAL HOSPITAL
123 Main Street • Aldon, FL 77714 • (407) 555-1234

Answers

EXERCISE 9

Date:	Vital signs:	T	R
Chief complaint:		P	BP

This 68-year-old established patient presents because she is having cataract surgery and is here for her preoperative evaluation. She has already seen the cardiologist and reports he has taken an ECG and evaluated her for her history of atrial fibrillation and cleared her for surgery. We will review and evaluate her history of hypertension to determine her stability at this time. She is on her usual medications.

Examination:

Lungs—clear. Heart—regular rhythm with a rate of 72. Abdomen—negative. No peripheral edema. She does state she has been having some leg pain and she will return following her surgery for evaluation of her leg pain.

Impression:

Labs pending although I expect them to return as normal.
We will forward a copy to the outpatient surgery center prior to her surgery.

Plan:

Cleared for cataract surgery scheduled for next Wednesday, September 21, 20XX.

Maurice Doater, MD

	Patient name:
	DOB:
	MR/Chart #:

GODFREY REGIONAL OUTPATIENT CLINIC
3122 Shannon Avenue • Aldon, FL 77712 • (407) 555-7654

Answers

PROGRESS NOTE

Date:	Vital signs:	T	R
Chief complaint:		P	BP

Patient presents with leg pain especially in her right calf. She stated she can only walk about 15–20 yards before her leg hurts. She currently walks about 2 miles. However, states she must stop intermittently due to pain. She stops, the pain subsides or completely resolves.

Physical examination:

Upon exam, she has femoral, posterior tibial, dorsalis pedis and popliteal pulses present on the left. Dorsalis pedis and posterior pulses however are somewhat faint. Color, temperature are good on the right and left. I cannot appreciate the popliteal on the right, and the dorsalis pedis and posterior tibial are quite faint on the right as well.

Assessment:

Certainly given the symptoms, I would suspect she has an obstruction between the femoral and popliteal area on the right leg. I will refer her to a vascular surgeon for further evaluation and treatment.

Maurice Doater, MD

Plan:

Patient name:

DOB:

MR/Chart #:

GODFREY REGIONAL OUTPATIENT CLINIC
3122 Shannon Avenue • Aldon, FL 77712 • (407) 555-7654

Answers

EXERCISE 11

PROGRESS NOTE

Chief complaint: _____

Date: _____   DOB: _____

Vital signs: BP_____   P_____   R_____   MR/Chart #: _____

History:

Established patient arrives complaining of stress incontinence and some lower abdominal pain and she feels her abdomen may have some slight swelling.

Exam:

On pelvic examination, she does have a slight cystocele. Rectal is normal. Her abdomen may be a little distended, although I am not sure. I will schedule her for a barium enema and we may need to do a CT scan. I suggested she develop a schedule for the bathroom on a regular basis to see if this controls her stress incontinence. If not, we will recommend urological evaluation.
Urinalysis shows no signs of infection and no other symptoms apparent for her stress incontinence.

Diagnosis/assessment:

IMPRESSION:
Stress incontinence
Abdominal pain, possibly due to previous history of GI reflux

Maurice Doater, MD

Patient name: _____
Date of service: _____

GODFREY REGIONAL OUTPATIENT CLINIC
3122 Shannon Avenue • Aldon, FL 77712 • (407) 555-7654

Answers

PROGRESS NOTE

| Date: | Vital signs: | T | R |
| Chief complaint: | | P | BP |

This 34-year-old female patient presents following a fall over the weekend. She presents with a slight bruise and contusion over the left knee as well as an abrasion to the knee. She complains mainly of pain to the left hand and wrist. There is some swelling over the distal ulna, however, no tenderness and complete range of motion. X-ray reveals no fracture. She experiences tenderness in the area of the navicular bone. We will therefore treat her with a splint for her wrist sprain

Examination:

X-ray reveals no fracture. She experiences tenderness in the area of the navicular bone.

Impression:

Plan:

We will therefore treat her with a splint for her wrist sprain and recheck in 10-14 days.

Maurice Doater, MD

| Patient name: |
| DOB: |
| MR/Chart #: |

GODFREY REGIONAL OUTPATIENT CLINIC
3122 Shannon Avenue • Aldon, FL 77712 • (407) 555-7654

Answers

PROGRESS NOTE

Date:		Vital signs:	T		R
Chief complaint:			P		BP

Patient comes in as a result of an accident last Wednesday where a company truck ran over her left foot. The truck stayed over the foot for a number of seconds before the driver put the truck in reverse. She was initially taken to the hospital ER. X-rays were performed that did not reveal a fracture. She has moderately severe pain in the dorsum of the right foot. She was instructed to wrap the ankle with an elastic bandage and remain non-weight bearing with the use of crutches for the next 7–10 days.

Examination:

The patient remains with some swelling over the dorsum of the foot, and it is exquisitely tender in the dorsal area. She has adequate range of motion over the ankle and toes and seems neurovascularly intact.

Impression:

Plan:

ASSESSMENT: Contusion of the left foot with minimal swelling, pain. Patient will ice the injury and she was given a prescription for pain. If not resolved within the next 3–5 days, she will call for reevaluation.

Maurice Doates, MD

Patient name:
DOB:
MR/Chart #:

GODFREY REGIONAL OUTPATIENT CLINIC
3122 Shannon Avenue • Aldon, FL 77712 • (407) 555-7654

Answers

PROGRESS NOTE

Date:	Vital signs:	T	R
Chief complaint:		P	BP

Patient presents for a recheck of his laceration of the left middle finger. This has healed excellently. Laceration repair was approximately 3 weeks ago, with suture removal one week ago. Patient denies pain, discharge, redness, swelling or any signs of infection. He has not been working with this injury.

Physical examination:

Exam reveals left middle finger healing well. Wound edges well approximated. No discharge, no swelling, no erythema, no increased warmth or heat over the area. No evidence of infection. Nail bed looks fine as does the nail.

Assessment:

Resolving/healing laceration, left middle finger.

Plan:

Patient may return to work full duty without restrictions. As the wound is well approximated, it is not required to be covered any more. At this time, no repeat visit will be necessary. Patient is to report any problems for reevaluation.

Maurice Doater, MD

	Patient name:
	DOB:
	MR/Chart #:

GODFREY REGIONAL OUTPATIENT CLINIC
3122 Shannon Avenue • Aldon, FL 77712 • (407) 555-7654

Answers

EXERCISE 15

PROGRESS NOTE

Chief complaint: _____

Date: _____

Vital signs:　BP_____　P_____　R_____

History:

Patient presents with complaints as follows: (1) Occasional problem where food seems to get stuck in his esophagus. It does not seem related to activity, and usually he does not have much pain, although if it gets stuck long enough it does cause him some discomfort. (2) He reports a cough, for approximately the last 5&6 weeks which has been non-productive. He does not smoke, and has been around no chemicals or pesticides to his knowledge. He does have a history of allergies, and has been in good health otherwise.

Exam:

Patient appears well
HEENT: Negative
Neck: Negative
Lungs: Clear
Heart: Regular rate, sinus rhythm
Abdomen: Negative
　　　　No lymphadenopathy

Diagnosis/assessment:

Send for chest x-ray for his cough and to rule out bronchitis or other pulmonary involvement. I will recommend referral to a gastroenterologist for his difficult

Maurice Doster, MD

Patient name: _____

Date of service: _____

GODFREY REGIONAL OUTPATIENT CLINIC
3122 Shannon Avenue ¥ Aldon, FL 77712 ¥ (407) 555-7654

Answers

PROGRESS NOTE

Date:	Vital signs:	T		R	
Chief complaint:		P		BP	

Patient presents today with sore throat and nasal congestion she reports for the past 48–72 hours. Nasal congestion is yellow in color. She is presently breastfeeding a three-month-old baby. No allergies to medications and currently on no meds.

Examination:

Sclera clear. Conjunctivae pale. Ears with bulging translucent tympanic membranes. Nasal mucosa edematous. Moist posterior pharynx is hyperemic. No anterior cervical adenopathy. Lungs clear to auscultation, no rales, wheezes, rhonchi. Heart regular rate and rhythm. Extremities without cyanosis or edema.

Impression:

ASSESSMENT: Pharyngitis
                 Sinusitis
                 Probable upper respiratory infection

Plan:

Will place her on Amoxicillin 500 mg TID X 10 days. She may want to check with her pediatrician to see if it would be safe to take an antihistamine and decongestant such as Dimetapp.

Stony Kraut, MD

Patient name:

DOB:

MR/Chart #:

GODFREY REGIONAL OUTPATIENT CLINIC
3122 Shannon Avenue • Aldon, FL 77712 • (407) 555-7654

Answers

PROGRESS NOTE

Date:	Vital signs:	T	R
Chief complaint:		P	BP

Patient presents with history of dark red blood mixed with bowel movements over the past 2–3 days. He has had blood mixed in his stool in the past attributed to hemorrhoids. He has had several flexible sigmoidoscopies over the years due to a history of diverticulosis. He denies any fever, abdominal pain, diarrhea. He has seen no blood for the last 2 days.

Examination:

On examination, external exam reveals some redundant perianal flesh.
Digital exam reveals enlarged, smooth prostate. No masses felt. Hemoccult was negative. Anascopic exam reveals several internal hemorrhoids. No active bleeding at this time.

Impression:

Plan:

Should symptoms return, he is to call us for further evaluation and discussion regarding other treatment options, including surgery for his hemorrhoids.

Maurice Doater, MD

Patient name:

DOB:

MR/Chart #:

GODFREY REGIONAL OUTPATIENT CLINIC
3122 Shannon Avenue • Aldon, FL 77712 • (407) 555-7654

Answers

PROGRESS NOTE

Date:	Vital signs:	T	R
Chief complaint:		P	BP

This 19-year-old female states her last menstrual period ended approximately two weeks ago. Today she began heavy vaginal bleeding with passage of clots, crampy lower abdominal pain, and she felt weak. She is on birth control oral contraceptives.

Physical examination:

Gravida I para I, history of normal vaginal delivery approximately one year ago. History of pelvic inflammatory disease prior to pregnancy.
There is a minimal amount of blood in the vaginal vault. No tissue noted. Cervix is normal in appearance. The os is closed. The fundus of the uterus is not well appreciated. Serum pregnancy test was negative. WBC was 11,300 with normal HgB and HcT.

Assessment:

Vaginal bleeding, possibly involving past pelvic inflammatory disease.

Plan:

Felix Wander MD

	Patient name:
	DOB:
	MR/Chart #:

GODFREY REGIONAL OUTPATIENT CLINIC
3122 Shannon Avenue • Aldon, FL 77712 • (407) 555-7654

Answers

EXERCISE 19

PROGRESS NOTE

Date: 02/28/XX		Vital signs:	T	R
Chief complaint:	Bitten by cat several days ago, swollen hand		P	BP

02/28/XX	HISTORY: 52-year-old female presents as a new patient with complaint that her housecat bit her several days ago while she was trying to coax it out of a corner. History of hypertension, hyperlipidemia. The cat bit her on the hand, second through fourth fingers on the left hand, and a small bite on the right hand as well. Fingers are swollen. Cat ran away and has not been caught. It has not had rabies series but has never been outdoors. MEDS: Atenolol, Norvasc, Relafen, Zantac, Premarin ALLERGIES: None known TETANUS: Unknown date of last tetanus

Examination:

Vitals are stable at 98.5 temp, 110 pulse and BP controlled at 120/85. In general she is a pleasant, alert female in no distress. Hands—has swelling over the index and long fingers of the left hand with numerous tiny puncture marks over the dorsum of the fingers and palm. She has full range of motion. Some bruising and discoloration.

Impression:

ASSESSMENT: Cat bites to hands

Plan:

Augmentin 875 mg bid
Tetanus booster given

Jay Corm MD

	Patient name: Debborah Walton
	DOB: 1/8/19XX
	MR/Chart #: 03663

GODFREY REGIONAL OUTPATIENT CLINIC
3122 Shannon Avenue • Aldon, FL 77712 • (407) 555-7654

Answers

PROGRESS NOTE

Date: 03/01/XX	Vital signs:	T	R
Chief complaint: Severe back pain		P	BP

03/01/XX

30-year-old female presents to the office for the first time in approximately four years as she has been enlisted in the Navy and stationed overseas during that time. Presents with very severe back pain that may have begun three months ago while spending a whole day rubbing floors. She has been bothered off and on for some time and has seen a chiropractor and a physical therapist.

Most recently, she bent down to pick up some garbage in a trash bag and immediately observed extreme low back pain. She went numb from the waist down but this recovered in about one minute. She has been limping around since then in a typical back pain posture.

Physical examination:

Because of the severity of her complaints, an x-ray of the lumbar spine reveals narrowing of the L5-S1 disc space. The possibility of discogenic back pain does exist.
Clinically, there is no loss of sensation below the waist, the left leg is somewhat hypoesthetic compared to the right. Straight leg raising is virtually impossible due to excruciating pain.

Assessment:

Lumbosacral pain

Plan:

Flexeril 10 mg qid for 1–2 weeks, Darvocet N100 four times a day for 1–2 weeks.
Because of significant history of constipation and finding of same on x-ray, suggested a Dulcolax tablet and ounce of milk of magnesia until her constipation clears.

Jay Corm MD

	Patient name: Heather Maddan
	DOB: 2/28/19XX
	MR/Chart #: 55885

GODFREY REGIONAL OUTPATIENT CLINIC
3122 Shannon Avenue • Aldon, FL 77712 • (407) 555-7654

Answers

EXERCISE 21

OFFICE NOTE

Chief complaint: _____

Date: _____

Vital signs: BP_____ P_____ R_____

History:

SUBJECTIVE: This 69-year-old white female presents after developing left back pain. She feels as if it has come forward somewhat but is indistinct in the anterior part of the chest. The patient states that it is worse after movement and today it began after sleep. She felt it may or may not go into the left arm. It is not associated with diaphoresis, nausea, vomiting, cough, or pleuritic chest pain. She states that the pain is actually in the back. The patient is a smoker and has hypertension. She says she has had her cholesterol checked in the past and it was felt to be normal. There is a positive family history of MI in her brother and there is no diabetes.

Exam:

Temperature 98.8, pulse 76, respiratory 20, blood pressure 175/101. Patient is not in any acute distress. The ears are clear. The throat is clear. The neck is supple. The lungs are clear. The heart is regular. The abdomen is soft, and having the patient sit up, there is perivertebral knot that I can actually push on and elicit the pain on the left side, parallel to the scapula off the vertebral column. She states that this is the discomfort that she is having and this reproduces the pain acutely. Lab work includes white count 10.7, hemoglobin 13.2, hematocrit 39, platelet count 3.6, CK 36; troponin is less then 0.3, sodium 141, potassium 3.3, BUN 15, creatinine 0.7, glucose 88; LFTs are within normal limits. Her chest x-ray shows COPD but no acute pulmonary disease. Her EKG is read as normal sinus rhythm. I do not see any unusual T waves.

Diagnosis/assessment:

IMPRESSION: Muscle strain upper left back

PLAN: She is to take 2 Advil 3 times a day for the next 7 days as needed. We have discussed the application of heat to the area with a heating pad or a heat patch to be used as directed. We have given her some Vicodin for relief of the discomfort, 1 2 to 1 pill po q4h prn for severe pain. We have asked her to follow up with her usual physician in 48 hours as needed. She is to return for any worsening symptoms.

Steny Knott MD

Patient name: _____

Date of service: _____

GODFREY MEDICAL ASSOCIATES
1532 Third Avenue, Suite 120 • Aldon, FL 77713 • (407) 555-4000

Answers

OFFICE NOTE

Chief complaint: _____

Date: _____

Vital signs: BP_____ P_____ R_____

History:

This 69-year-old woman was shopping this afternoon when she developed some lower abdominal cramping. She had a bowel movement and appeared to pass some red blood that she estimates at 2–3 teaspoons. She has no abdominal pain at this time. There has been no nausea or vomiting. Four days ago, she was started on iron for upcoming knee surgery. She has a history of acid peptic disease with prior upper GI bleeds. She also has hypertension. Her medications are as listed. She states that she occasionally takes an ibuprofen. She is allergic to penicillin.

Exam:

REVIEW OF SYSTEMS: She denies chest pain or palpitations. There has been no cough or shortness of breath. She has no dysuria or increased urinary frequency. She is a nonsmoker. She does not drink alcohol.

EXAMINATION: Reveals an alert, pleasant woman. Eyes are clear. Tympanic membranes appear normal. There is no nasal congestion. Mouth is moist. Throat reveals no redness or swelling. The neck is supple with no adenopathy. There is no heart murmur. Lungs are clear. The abdomen is soft and nontender. There is no mass. Bowel tones are active. There is a small amount of red blood on the perianal skin. Digital exam reveals good sphincter tone. There is no rectal mass or fissure palpable. Anoscopy shows a small amount of red blood in the anal canal, but no active bleeding or a bleeding site was seen. She is noted to have formed stool that does not appear black or grossly bloody. Lab data includes hemoglobin of 12.7. White count is 9,100.

Diagnosis/assessment:

DIAGNOSIS: Rectal bleeding probably secondary to anal irritation from iron-induced constipation.

DISPOSITION: She is to stop the iron for the next several days and take Surfak bid. She is also to increase her intake of fluids and fiber. If she develops continued rectal bleeding, abdominal pain, vomiting, or any other problem, she is to return to the office. Otherwise, in 2 days she will make telephone contact with her usual physician who was called and agreed with the above plan.

Maurice Doater, MD

Patient name: _____

Date of service: _____

GODFREY MEDICAL ASSOCIATES
1532 Third Avenue, Suite 120 • Aldon, FL 77713 • (407) 555-4000

Answers

EXERCISE 23

OFFICE NOTE

Date:	Vital signs:	T		R	
Chief complaint:			P		BP

SUBJECTIVE: This 86-year-old white male with a history of significant COPD presents with chest discomfort and coughing. This began 2 days ago and has become increasingly worse. He states that he has a severe pain with coughing and he can't get the phlegm out; when he does cough, the pain in his chest is worse, and when he is resting, he has no discomfort. He had not been having any fevers, and he does state that he has a tenacious sputum. He is allergic to penicillin and sulfa. He has steroid-dependent COPD.

Physical examination:

Patient does not appear in any acute distress. Temperature is 97.5, pulse 86, respiratory 24, blood pressure 149/84. Oxygen saturation is 94 percent on 2 liters per minute. The ears have wax on the left; right ear is clear. The throat is pink and dry. The patient is not in respiratory distress with breathing. His lungs have diminished breath sounds bilaterally. Rare crackles in the bases. His white count is 8.6, hemoglobin 12.1, platelet 187. Chest x-ray shows no acute pulmonary disease when compared to films from December.

Assessment:

IMPRESSION: Bronchitis with pleurisy.

Plan:

Since the patient is on a steroid at present, it will be inappropriate to treat him with a non-steroidal. Because of his discomfort with his cough, we will go ahead and start him on Tylenol #3,1 po q6h prn severe cough only. We have given him 5 and gave him another prescription for 8. He has Tessalon pearls at home, and I have asked him to use as directed by his physician. If he is having trouble with the cough, then he is to use the Tylenol with codeine, but he is not to use it every 6 hours, only as needed. We have started him on Levaquin at 500 mg p.o. QD, and we have given him a 7-day course. We have asked him to follow up with his primary care doctor in 3 days. He is to return for any worsening symptoms.

Willem Obet MD

Patient name:
DOB:
MR/Chart #:

GODFREY REGIONAL OUTPATIENT CLINIC
3122 Shannon Avenue • Aldon, FL 77712 • (407) 555-7654

Answers

OFFICE NOTE

Date:	**Vital signs:** T	R
Chief complaint: Swollen, painful right leg	P	BP

S: This new patient is a 63-year-old gentleman who, about a week ago, had problems with pain in his right elbow. He developed swelling in his right elbow, as well as swelling in the right knee and calf with some discomfort. He saw his usual physician who felt he had tendinitis. He presented because he has had increased pain and swelling in his calf, and it hurts to bear weight. He has also noticed a little bit of bruising down below his ankle. There is no history of injury. He is on Celebrex, 200 mg daily, as of Wednesday. His health problems are significant for cervical dystonia for which he gets Botox periodically, and he also takes Clonopin and Flexeril. He has no allergies. He has no history of high blood pressure, diabetes, heart disease, GI disease, or urinary problems. He hasn't had any fever, chills, or other symptoms.

Physical examination:

O: He is afebrile. On exam of his elbow, he has just slight loss of full extension, but otherwise good stipulation, pronation. Elbow is nontender, and there is no warmth or redness. Exam of the right knee reveals a little swelling around the knee; it is not hot or red. The popliteal spaces feel symmetrical. He also has pain with squeezing of the calf with some edema in the lower extremity, but not much in the foot. Squeezing the calf is tender and Homans' sign is tender also. Concern was DVT versus Baker's cyst. He was sent for Doppler study, and it showed no DVT, but did confirm a Baker's cyst.

Assessment:

A: Right Baker's cyst

Plan:

P: Discussion. He should use ice, continue with the Celebrex, and follow up with his usual physician to discuss what he would like to do further about the symptomatic problem.

Stony Kratt, MD

Patient name:
DOB:
MR/Chart #:

GODFREY REGIONAL OUTPATIENT CLINIC
3122 Shannon Avenue • Aldon, FL 77712 • (407) 555-7654

Answers

EXERCISE 25

OFFICE NOTE

Date:	Vital signs:	T	R
Chief complaint:		P	BP

HISTORY: This 56-year-old man, who lives in a CBRF, this morning was noted to have swelling of his legs. There has been no injury. Patient has Down syndrome, Alzheimer's disease, and a seizure disorder. His medications are as listed. There is no allergy to medicine. He is nonverbal and unable to give any history.

Physical examination:

Eyes are clear. TMs appear normal. There is no nasal congestion. Mouth is moist. Throat reveals no redness or swelling. The neck is supple. There is no adenopathy. Heart rhythm is regular. There is no murmur. Lungs are clear. The abdomen is obese but soft with no apparent tenderness. There is edema of both lower legs, worse on the left. There is no apparent calf tenderness or palpable cord. Lab data include hemoglobin of 14.6; white count is 5000. Chemistry panel includes alkaline phosphatase of 169; other values are within normal limits. EKG shows sinus rhythm with no acute change. Chest x-ray shows no active pulmonary disease. Venous Doppler of the left leg appears normal.

Assessment:

DIAGNOSIS: Leg swelling

Plan:

DISPOSITION: Staff will restrict the patient's salt intake and recommend he elevate his legs when sitting. If they note increased swelling, discoloration, fever, or any other problem, he is to be sent to the emergency room or follow up with his usual physician.

Stany Kractt, MD

	Patient name:
	DOB:
	MR/Chart #:

GODFREY REGIONAL OUTPATIENT CLINIC
3122 Shannon Avenue • Aldon, FL 77712 • (407) 555-7654

Answers

EMERGENCY ROOM RECORD

Name:		Age:	ER physician:
		DOB:	

Allergies/type of reaction:	Usual medications/dosages:

Triage/presenting complaint:

CHIEF COMPLAINT: Collapse

SUBJECTIVE: This gentleman has a long history of bad disease. He has been known to have ischemic coronary disease, dysrhythmia, COPD, and diabetes. He has been on oxygen and multiple medications. There is a standing health care power of attorney, and advanced directives are written in his chart where he clearly states he would not want any heroic treatments, just comfort care only. Today he was out feeding chickens without his oxygen on and collapsed. There was apparently some response initially, and a couple of nitroglycerin were given before 911 was called. There were attempts to try to direct CPR over the phone. First responder came somewhere between 8 and 15 minutes afterwards and started CPR. The ambulance arrived 15 or 20 minutes afterwards, and he was transported 30 minutes en route. En route the automatic defibrillator deployed a shock three times and CPR was accomplished; a Combivent tube was placed.

Initial assessment:

Time	T	P	R	BP	Other:					

Medication orders:

Lab work:

X-ray:

Physician's report:

On arrival to the emergency room, he had no palpable pulse or blood pressure. His rhythm complex showed a slow neuro complex QRS. Without a pulse, he was judged to be in pulseless CIA. He was given atropine and then epinephrine and his pulse did speed up and was palpable. He then went back into V fib and was re-shocked. He then went back into V tachycardia and was shocked. Approximately 50 minutes after the arrest with recurrent V tachycardia, V fibrillation, and with no response to treatment, efforts were called. He had dilated fixed pupils. He was judged expired at approximately 0945.

Diagnosis:	Physician sign/date
ASSESSMENT: Expired. Cause of death likely myocardial infarction and contributing factors of longstanding coronary disease, intermittent dysrhythmias, COPD, and diabetes. PLAN: Appropriate notifications.	*Nancy Cauley* MD

Discharge	Transfer	Admit	Good	Satisfactory	Other:

GODFREY REGIONAL HOSPITAL
123 Main Street • Aldon, FL 77714 • (407) 555-1234

Answers

OFFICE NOTE

Chief complaint: _____

Date: _____

Vital signs: BP_____ P_____ R_____

History:

SUBJECTIVE: This 78-year-old female claims she woke up feeling short of breath and a little chest pain. She was here about 24 hours ago with dizziness, weakness, and emesis and was diagnosed with benign positional vertigo. She was prescribed Antivert that she says she is using, but it isn't helping. The patient agreed to be seen by me when she realized ambulance costs to another city wouldn't be covered.

PAST MEDICAL HISTORY: Seems to be positive for a number of emergency visits for similar complaints. She does have an artificial porcine valve and apparently has had bypass surgery.

MEDICATIONS: Vioxx, Tagament, Slow Iron, Norvasc, and the Antivert mentioned.

ALLERGIES: Apparently to Tylenol, ASA, ibuprofen, and, I believe, sulfa.

Exam:

She is afebrile. Vital signs are stable. She seems to be sleepy but is also anxious. Color is normal. She is not diaphoretic. NECK: supple. JVP is flat. Carotids are normal. CHEST: clear with good air entry bilaterally. Heart sounds are normal. She has aortic stenosis type murmur. ABDOMEN: soft and nontender, perhaps a little mild tenderness in the left upper quadrant. Pulses are normal.

LAB AND X-RAYS: ECG did not reveal any acute changes.

TREATMENT: She was originally given sublingual nitro, which she said helped. By the time the lab results came back, she had talked to the nurse and came to the conclusion that she had overreacted when she woke up, was likely just anxious, but now was feeling fine. She wants to go home.

Diagnosis/assessment:

1. Questionable anxiety

PLAN: She will go home on the usual medications.

William Olx MD

Patient name: _____

Date of service: _____

GODFREY MEDICAL ASSOCIATES
1532 Third Avenue, Suite 120 • Aldon, FL 77713 • (407) 555-4000

Answers

RADIOLOGY REPORT

MR#:
DOB:
Dr.

Clinical summary:

CLINICAL INFORMATION:
Fell down stairs

Abdomen:

Conclusion:

AP UPRIGHT STANDING BOTH KNEES AND A LATERAL VIEW OF EACH KNEE:
The radiographs demonstrate no evidence of joint effusion on the right or on the left. There are early degenerative changes for a patient of this age group. Subchondral sclerosis is seen in the tibial plateaus and there are osteophytes arising from the tibial spines, the posterior aspect of each patella, and at the insertion of each quadriceps tendon.

CONCLUSION:
1. No acute fracture is identified
2. There is minimal degenerative change for a patient of this age group

Ddt/mm

D:
T:

_____
Lisa Valhas, M.D.   Date

GODFREY REGIONAL HOSPITAL
123 Main Street • Aldon, FL 77714 • (407) 555-1234

Answers

EXERCISE 29

OPERATIVE REPORT

Patient information:	
Patient name:	Date:
DOB:	Surgeon:
MR#:	Anesthetist:

Preoperative diagnosis:

Skin lesion over right flank and back, possible melanoma in situ

Postoperative diagnosis:

Skin lesion over right flank and back, possible melanoma in situ

Procedure(s) performed:

Excision of right flank and back skin lesions with complex closure

INDICATION FOR SURGERY:
The patient is a 47-year-old white female with shave biopsies of lesions over her right flank and back. The specimens were not clearly labeled and it is unclear which of these areas was truly a melanoma in situ. The other lesion is consistent with some atypia. Because of the uncertainty of the diagnosis for melanoma in the location, both lesions are being excised with the presumptive diagnosis of melanoma in situ.

Anesthesia:

Assistant surgeon:

Description of procedure:

The patient was placed in a left decubitus position. The areas were prepped and draped in the usual sterile fashion. The skin and subcutaneous tissue around these lesions were anesthetized with 1% lidocaine with epinephrine. A total of 22 cc of local anesthetic was used. Fusiform incisions were made around these lesions, allowing for a 0.5 cm border. The border was marked around the biopsy scar. The scar over the right flank measured 1.5 cm and the scar over the back measured 0.8 cm. After the fusiform incisions were made, further dissection was carried out with the scalpel. Separate instruments were used for both locations. When the specimen was removed, it was sent to Pathology for permanent sections.

Using skin hooks, the wound edges were retracted, and electrocautery was used to extensively undermine the wound edges to allow for tension-free closure. Once the wound edges were thoroughly mobilized in the subcutaneous plane, bleeding was controlled with electrocautery. The wound was then thoroughly irrigated with saline solution. The right flank wound was then closed with 3-0 Vicryl for the deep layer and running 3-0 nylon for the skin. The lesion over the back was also extensively mobilized by retracting the wound edges with skin hooks and using electrocautery to undermine the skin flaps. The bleeding was controlled with electrocautery, and the deep layer was closed with 3-0 Vicryl suture and the skin was closed with running 2-0 nylon suture.

The patient tolerated the operation well, and the wounds were cleaned and covered with antibiotic ointment and pressure dressings. The patient was then taken to the postanesthesia care unit for recovery in stable condition.

Maurice Doater, MD

GODFREY REGIONAL HOSPITAL
123 Main Street • Aldon, FL 77714 • (407) 555-1234

Answers

OPERATIVE REPORT

Patient information:	
Patient name: DOB: MR#:	Date: Surgeon: Anesthetist:

Preoperative diagnosis:

Recurrent squamous cell carcinoma of the oral cavity

Postoperative diagnosis:

Recurrent squamous cell carcinoma of the oral cavity

Procedure(s) performed:

Laser ablation of recurrent squamous cell carcinoma of the left anterior floor of mouth/mandibular alveolar mucosa/and left anterior tongue

ESTIMATED BLOOD LOSS: Less than 5 cc

CLINICAL NOTE: The patient is an 82-year-old white female who several years ago underwent wide local resection of left anterior and lateral tongue and floor of mouth, squamous cell carcinoma. She had full-course radiation therapy postoperatively. She has been doing well, when on routine follow-up visit was found to have recurrent squamous cell carcinoma that was biopsied in the office and confirmed the above. She is being brought to the operating room for resection/ablation.

Anesthesia:

General

Assistant surgeon:

Description of procedure:

OPERATIVE NOTE: The patient was brought in the operating room and placed on the operating room table in a supine position. General anesthesia was administered endotracheally with a special laser tube. The left anterior tongue/floor of mouth and alveolar area of tumor were seen and examined circumferentially. With margins this was marked with Bovie cautery prior to injecting with 1% lidocaine with 1:100,000 epinephrine. Using a hand-held laser set at 15 watts, super pulse power was applied around the circumference of the lesion, and dysplasia was circumscribed with the laser. The central tumor and dysplastic tissue were then ablated and vaporized with the laser. Specimens were sent from the left anterior tongue/anterior and posterior alveolar mucosal margins and left floor of mouth deep margins from the patient after ablation of the tumor. All these returned back negative for residual squamous cell carcinoma except the posterior alveolar margin that showed one small foci of carcinoma. This area was further ablated with the laser to destroy any residual tumor. There was adequate hemostasis obtained. There was meticulous hemostasis throughout the procedure. The patient was then awakened from general anesthesia, extubated, and brought to the recovery room in stable condition, having tolerated the procedure well.

Maurice Doater, MD

GODFREY REGIONAL HOSPITAL
123 Main Street • Aldon, FL 77714 • (407) 555-1234

Answers

7 Coding Special Complexities

EXERCISES 1-10

Provide codes for the following cases.

1. 54-year-old female with long-term history of vaginitis and candidiasis. Also has carbuncle of her vagina. Sees the OB/GYN because of vaginal pain. Irrigation of the vagina is performed for the vaginal carbuncle and medications are prescribed for this condition as well as the vaginitis that is found.

   ICD-9-CM code(s): _____

   _____

2. Patient presents to the cardiologist as a referral from his primary care physician. Patient has reported elevated blood pressure for the past 2 to 3 weeks with diagnosis of hypertension. Referred for further evaluation and treatment because the PCP has been unable to control the hypertension with medications at this point.

   Patient undergoes both ECG and echocardiogram. Patient is diagnosed with malignant hypertension, and medications are prescribed accordingly.

   ICD-9-CM code(s): _____

   _____

3. Patient presents to the emergency department with complaints of abdominal pain. On questioning by the ED physician, the patient relates a 1-week history of abdominal pain. Her father passed away at that time, and she has been under a great deal of stress.

   Examination is unremarkable. Patient is weepy, depressed, and affect appears flat.

   Treatment for situational depression with abdominal pain.

   ICD-9-CM code(s): _____

   _____

4. Patient presents with a nondisplaced closed fracture of the radius and ulna of the forearm. Patient also has a puncture wound of the upper thigh that occurred at the time of this incident as well as multiple bruises to the forearm, leg, and foot.

   ICD-9-CM code(s): _____

   _____

5. Patient has superficial and partial-thickness burns of the right hand as the result of a kitchen fire.

   ICD-9-CM code(s): _____

   _____

6. Patient presents for assessment of high-risk pregnancy. She is approximately 24 weeks and has had significant spotting during her first trimester. Today she has no complaints and comes in for her regularly scheduled OB appointment. Vitals are stable; she has had no problems since her last visit and will return in 2 weeks for her next follow-up appointment.

   ICD-9-CM code(s): _____

   _____

7. OB patient who is 24 weeks' pregnant presents for 3-hour glucose tolerance test to rule out gestational diabetes.

   ICD-9-CM code(s): _____

   _____

8. Patient presents for independent medical evaluation ordered by the employer's workers' compensation carrier. The patient has been disabled from work and the carrier has requested additional input regarding the extent of the disability.

   ICD-9-CM code(s): _____

   _____

9. Patient presents with BP of 220/140. Last month the patient was seen with a BP of 120/80.

   ICD-9-CM code(s):

   _____

10. Patient is referred to cardiology for evaluation of possible malignant hypertension. Patient has already been diagnosed with hypertension; however, further evaluation is made.

    ICD-9-CM code(s): _____

    _____

Identify errors in the code assignments in the following coding scenarios. These could include such errors as the following:

- Signs and symptoms that do not need codes
- Incorrect ICD-9-CM codes
- Wrong order assigned to ICD-9-CM codes

11. Patient with history of breast cancer presents for lump in breast.

    Code(s) assigned: V10.3

                          611.72

    Coding error(s) identified:

    _____

    _____

    Correct code(s) assignment:

    _____

    _____

12. Patient with LUQ and RUQ abdominal pain gives a history of hypertension and DM.

    Code(s) assigned: 789.00

                          401.9

                          250.0

    Coding error(s) identified:

    _____

    _____

    Correct code(s) assignment:

    _____

    _____

13. Patient presents with complaints of back pain that may have begun 3 months ago while lifting a heavy object.

    Code(s) assigned: 724.5

                          E927

    Coding error(s) identified:

    _____

    _____

    Correct code(s) assignment:

    _____

    _____

14. Red, mattery eye that is diagnosed as conjunctivitis may be lacrimal duct obstruction.

    Code(s) assigned: 379.99

                          372.30

                          375.54

    Coding error(s) identified:

    _____

    _____

    Correct code(s) assignment:

    _____

    _____

15. Patient presents with complaints of headache, probably migraine in nature. She also stated she has a history of hypertension and hypothyroidism.

    Code(s) assigned: 346.9

                          401.9

                          244.9

    Coding error(s) identified:

    _____

    _____

    Correct code(s) assignment:

    _____

    _____

16. Patient presents with complaints of heart racing and beating fast. He is diagnosed with tachycardia and indicates he has a history of tachycardia as well.

    Code(s) assigned: 785.0

                          V12.50

    Coding error(s) identified:

    _____

    _____

    Correct code(s) assignment:

    _____

    _____

17. Patient presents for tonsillectomy due to chronic adult tonsillitis. He also reports medical conditions of hypertension and acne.

Code(s) assigned: 463

401.9

706.1

Coding error(s) identified:

_____

_____

Correct code(s) assignment:

_____

_____

18. Patient presents with abdominal pain, and laboratory tests indicated elevated liver enzymes and possible pancreatitis.

Code(s) assigned: 577.0

Coding error(s) identified:

_____

_____

Correct code(s) assignment:

_____

_____

19. Patient presents with abdominal pain. Laboratory results and x-rays indicate the presence of kidney calculi as well as cholecystitis. Surgery will be planned as soon as possible.

Code(s) assigned: 575.10

574.2

Coding error(s) identified:

_____

_____

Correct code(s) assignment:

_____

_____

20. Patient presents for shoulder x-ray with clinical diagnosis of shoulder pain that resulted from a fall several months ago. X-ray suggests the possibility of rotator cuff tear. Additional studies and perhaps a shoulder arthroscopy will be performed for a more definitive diagnosis.

Code(s) assigned: 719.41

E888.9

Coding error(s) identified:

_____

_____

Correct code(s) assignment:

_____

_____

In addition to identifying the coding errors, discuss how you, as the coder for these physicians, could recommend improvements to their documentation to correct these errors or clarify the medical conditions.

Assign the appropriate ICD-9-CM diagnostic codes for the following patient records. The Diagnostic Worksheet may be used, or code them directly after the steps discussed in the worksheet method.

EXERCISE 21

EMERGENCY ROOM RECORD

Name:	Age:	ER physician:
	DOB:	

Allergies/type of reaction:	Usual medications/dosages:

Triage/presenting complaint:	Patient is in with complaints of her usual headache. She is age 54. She has recurrent headache complaints. It is almost monthly. At this point, she has been seeing a neurologist for this problem.

Initial assessment:

Recurrent headaches

Time	T	P	R	BP	Other:				

Medication orders:

Lab work:

X-Ray:

Physician's report:

Her headache began at 5:30 PM with some nausea and vomiting. Has had Demerol and Vistaril pretty consistently in the past for this. She has tried Toradol in the past as well as Compazine and other things without relief.

She is scheduled for surgery for a carotid endarterectomy on the left. There has been no preop done as far as she is able to tell me. There is an unclear history of exactly what is going on there. She seems to feel that this is going to resolve her headaches.

PHYSICAL EXAM: She appears uncomfortable. She appears quite a bit older than her stated age. Vitals are stable.

HEENT: Relatively unremarkable. She has a tough time opening her eyes because of her photophobia. Tympanic membranes look OK. Throat is OK. Neck is supple. Don't appreciate any carotid bruits. Lungs clear. Heart, regular rate and rhythm. Gait is normal.

Diagnosis:	Physician sign/date
PLAN: I guess we will go with usual 75 mg of Demerol and 75 mg of Vistaril IM for her at this point. She should go home, go to bed, and get some fluids and then follow-up if ongoing troubles. She should keep her scheduled surgery appointment.	*Robert Rai MD*
Discharge Transfer Admit Good Satisfactory Other:	

GODFREY REGIONAL HOSPITAL
123 Main Street • Aldon, FL 77714 • (407) 555-1234

Answers

PROGRESS NOTE

Date:	Vital signs:	T	R
Chief complaint: Mattery left eye		P	BP

Examination:

SUBJECTIVE:
3-week-old female infant delivered vaginally at 34 weeks gestation. Stayed in the NICU for 10 days. Did not require ventilator. She had newborn jaundice and was treated and improved. She is breast-fed and nursing well. Baby has had green, mattery left eye for approximately 3 days. Mother has been providing eye care to the area cleaning from the inner canthus to the outer canthus and avoiding crossing over to the other eye. No fever, no feeding difficulties, she continues to nurse very well. No other concerns.

Examination:

OBJECTIVE:
Tiny neonate with good color, actively moving extremities. No acute distress. Temperature 97.4 axillary, pulse 140, respirations 130. Head normocephalic and atraumatic. Anterior fontanelle is soft and flat. Right eye is unremarkable. Left eye shows mild erythema of the upper lid. Lot of green matter along the lashes. Pupils equal and reactive to light. Red reflex is unremarkable. Throat is nonerythematous. Uvula is midline. Neck is supple without adenopathy. No thyromegaly. Chest, clear to auscultation bilaterally. Heart S1 and S2 without murmur. Genitourinary normal external female genitalia. Extremities, hips abduct evenly and without clicks. Abdomen soft. No edema or rash. Neuro: Motor grossly intact.

Impression:

ASSESSMENT:
Conjunctivitis, left eye. This may also be lacrimal duct obstruction, bacterial, viral or chemical.

Plan:

Treat with Erythromycin ointment 0.5% to left eye bid. Continue eye care and washing from inner canthus to outer. Follow-up if not improved or worsening symptoms.

William Obrt MD

Patient name:

DOB:

MR/Chart #:

GODFREY REGIONAL OUTPATIENT CLINIC
3122 Shannon Avenue • Aldon, FL 77712 • (407) 555-7654

Answers

PROGRESS NOTE

Chief complaint: _____

Date: _____

Vital signs: BP_____   P_____   R_____

History:

76-year-old comes in with complaints of heart pounding. She had an episode last night lasting about 25 minutes and another episode this morning. Her Norvasc has been increased to 10 mg already. No chest pain, shortness of breath, paroxysmal nocturnal dyspnea or orthopnea.

Exam:

On exam, vital signs are stable. Blood pressure is 150/81, HEENT is unremarkable. Lungs clear. Heart, regular S1 S2. Urinalysis showed small leukocytes. Abdomen is soft, extremities no edema.

An ECG shows normal sinus rhythm with no acute STT changes. Urinalysis showed small leukocytes. BMP was normal.

Diagnosis/assessment:

IMPRESSION:
History of tachycardia

PLAN:
Consider Holter monitor, follow-up with cardiologist.

Steny Kratt, MD

Patient name: _____

Date of service: _____

GODFREY REGIONAL OUTPATIENT CLINIC
3122 Shannon Avenue • Aldon, FL 77712 • (407) 555-7654

Answers

EMERGENCY ROOM RECORD

Name:		Age:	ER physician:
		DOB:	

Allergies/type of reaction:	Usual medications/dosages:
Allergies to codeine	Coumadin 4.5 mg po qd

Triage/presenting complaint:

REASON FOR VISIT: Difficulty with speech
This 72-year-old female with past history of CVA presents for symptoms that started on Friday. Apparently she had an episode which lasted approximately 15 minutes not being able to express her words. She says her thoughts were clear but she was unable to say the words she wanted to say. In conjunction with that, she had some pain along the left temporal and parietal region. No visual symptoms. No obvious facial drooping according to witnesses. No weakness or paresthesias in her arms or legs. Since then has felt excessively tired and

Initial assessment:

Expressive aphasia most likely due to TIA or small stroke. Symptoms have resolved at this time.
Remains fatigued but no neurologic symptoms.

Time	T	P	R	BP	Other:					

Medication orders:

Lab work:

X-Ray:

Physician's report:

PAST MEDICAL HISTORY:
Significant for CVA involving her right hand. She was involved in PT for approximately one month. Back to about 90 to 95% function. Workup at that time included an echocardiogram and carotid Dopplers which she says are normal. No symptoms since that time.

REVIEW OF SYSTEMS:
Otherwise unremarkable. No upper respiratory problems. Did have an eye infection and was treated with antibiotics a couple weeks ago. No chest pain, palpitations, shortness of breath. No abdominal complaints. No dysuria or joint pain.

On exam, patient is alert and oriented. Memory is intact to conversation. HEENT exam reveals pupils equal, round and reactive to light. Extraocular eye movements are intact. No obvious facial asymmetry is noted. Oral pharynx is pink and moist. Uvula and tongue midline. Neck supple, no carotid bruits appreciated. Carotid upstrokes are of good quality and equal bilaterally. Lungs are clear to auscultation bilaterally. Heart sounds are regular, no murmurs, rubs, or gallops.

Neurological exam: cranial nerves II through XII grossly intact. Motor exam reveals good strength in both upper and lower extremities. NO gross sensory deficits. Deep tendon reflexes are of good quality and equal bilaterally. Romberg is negative. Patient able to do tandem finger to nose as well as moving her heel up and down without difficulty. Rapid alternating movements were not tested. Able to ambulate without difficulty. No ataxia or limp.

INR today is 2.6

Diagnosis:	Physician sign/date
PLAN: Already off Coumadin, discussed adding a baby aspirin. She would like to discuss these options with her private doctor. Feel this is reasonable as she is stable at this time. She does have a residual headache, however, if neurologic symptoms reemerge or worsen she should have a CT scan done emergently. Continue Coumadin 4.5 mg po q day.	*Robert Rai MD*

Discharge	Transfer	Admit	Good	Satisfactory	Other:

GODFREY REGIONAL HOSPITAL
123 Main Street • Aldon, FL 77714 • (407) 555-1234

Answers

EMERGENCY ROOM RECORD

Name:		Age:	ER physician:
		DOB:	

Allergies/type of reaction:	Usual medications/dosages:
	Depakote 250 mg tid Zoloft 50 mg po qd Depo-Provera 1 injection q3m

Triage/presenting complaint:	REASON FOR VISIT: Seizure

19-year-old female with known history of seizure disorder since age 13. Apparently had a tonic/clonic seizure at home today lasting approximately 10 minutes. Did not have any urinary or bowel incontinence. Sounds like she fell over the edge of a coffee table landing on her stomach bumping her head against the wall. Did not lose consciousness and did not seem to hit her head hard. Takes Depakote 250 mg po tid. Denies any history of recent alcohol use. Mom recently brought her home from a Developmental Center last week following a lot of stress going on at home as well as the week of a move from their house to an apartment home.

Has also been complaining of chronic intermittent pain in the lower abdomen. Urinary pregnancy test and UA have been negative. Exam in the ER approximately 1 week ago was unremarkable. Now today she continues to complain of persistent pain and in the exam room is crying with spasms of pain and clutching her

Initial assessment:	1. Seizure in 19-year-old with known history. Stable at this time. 2. Persistent lower abdominal pain. Has history of ovarian cyst which is a possibility 3. Mild mental retardation 4. Depression with dysfunctional social situation

Time	T	P	R	BP	Other:				

Medication orders:	

Lab work:	

X-Ray:	

X-rays of abdomen were unremarkable. No significant stool in colon.

Physician's report:

PAST MEDICAL HISTORY: Seizure disorder, history of ovarian cyst, depression, mild mental retardation

FAMILY HISTORY: Noncontributory

SOCIAL HISTORY: Somewhat dysfunctional over the past year. Was under custody of dad for past year until he admitted her to Developmental Center. Was resident there until approximately 1 week ago when mom brought her home with her. Custody is through Catholic Health Services. No known history of smoking or alcohol use, but has been sexually active at least for past month.

REVIEW OF SYSTEMS: No upper respiratory complaints. No headaches or visual problems. No sore throat, no chest pain, no shortness of breath, no hemoptysis. Abdominal complaints recurrent over last few weeks. Intermittent sharp to crampy pain in lower abdomen. Denies having any change in bowel habits. No blood in stools. No constipation or diarrhea. No dysuria. Did throw up once in ER.

PHYSICAL EXAM: Patient sleepy and appears postictal. Vital signs are stable, temp 99.2, pulse 88, respirations 20, BP 113/88. HEENT reveals head atraumatic. Visual inspection and palpation at base of skull reveals no abrasions, bruises, or lacerations. Pupils equal, round and reactive to light. Small conjunctival hemorrhage noted lateral aspect of eye. Extraocular eye movements intact. Clear oropharynx, pink and moist. Uvula is midline. Tongue is midline. Neck is supple, lungs clear to auscultation. Heart sounds are regular without murmurs or gallops. Abdomen is soft, bowel sounds are present. Patient exhibits no tenderness over abdomen with stethoscope. Percussion over the lower abdomen reveals some winching and voluntary guarding but no rebound is appreciated. GU and rectal exam not performed.

Patient seems quite sleepy. Exam was unremarkable. Quite irritable, and did have 2–3 episodes of significant discomfort related to lower abdomen where she was crying and screaming quite loudly.

Diagnosis:	Physician sign/date
PLAN: Tylenol #3 for discomfort. Increased Depakote to 500 mg in AM, 250 mg mid-day and 250 PM. Needs additional evaluation in the next 24–48 hours for her abdominal pain.	*Nancy Caulley MD*

Discharge	Transfer	Admit	Good	Satisfactory	Other:

GODFREY REGIONAL HOSPITAL
123 Main Street • Aldon, FL 77714 • (407) 555-1234

Answers

EXERCISE 26

PROGRESS NOTE

Date:		Vital signs:	T		R	
Chief complaint:				P		BP

This 86-year-old is status post total hip arthroplasty performed approximately 1 week ago for an infected hip prosthesis. Culture of the infected prosthesis indicated strep and the patient was initially treated in the hospital with IV antibiotics. At discharge, the patient was put on oral antibiotics and was told to return for follow-up.

Examination:

Patient presents today with no complaints. The arthroplasty site appears intact with no redness or swelling present. The incision site is clean and dry. No apparent infection at this time.

Impression:

Plan:

Continue antibiotics for the next 5 days and return for staple removal in approximately 5 days.

Maurice Doaters, MD

	Patient name:
	DOB:
	MR/Chart #:

GODFREY REGIONAL OUTPATIENT CLINIC
3122 Shannon Avenue • Aldon, FL 77712 • (407) 555-7654

Answers

PROGRESS NOTE

Date:	Vital signs:	T	R
Chief complaint:		P	BP

This 65-year-old male has a history of angina and called the office requesting work-in due to chest tightness over the past several days. Patient relates a one week history of chest pain and pain radiating through the shoulder and down the back. Past medical history is significant for myocardial infarction in the distant past.

Physical examination:

Exam of head, heart, lungs and abdomen are unremarkable. ECG as well as pulsed wave Doppler echocardiography are performed. Initial assessment is unstable angina with impending MI. Other medical conditions include hypertension, coronary artery disease and hypothyroidism.

Assessment:

Arrangements are made to transport the patient for admission. During that time, the patient suffered a massive myocardial infarct of the anterior wall. Patient is defibrillated twice and cardiopulmonary resuscitation is performed by the physician for over 45 minutes until the rescue squad arrival.

Plan:

	Patient name:
	DOB:
	MR/Chart #:

GODFREY REGIONAL OUTPATIENT CLINIC
3122 Shannon Avenue • Aldon, FL 77712 • (407) 555-7654

Answers

EXERCISE 28

PROGRESS NOTE

Date:	Vital signs:	T	R
Chief complaint:		P	BP

14-year-old female patient presents following treatment for strep throat. The patient was seen approximately 4 days ago with positive strep test and treated with Erythromycin. Today she presents with complaints of nausea and vomiting over the past 24–48 hours. Abdominal cramping and pain are quite severe and the patient indicates she has not been able to keep anything down for the past 2 days as a result.

Physical examination:

Assessment:

Gastritis as a result of Erythromycin

Plan:

Patient is advised to discontinue the use of Erythromycin and prescribed an alternative antibiotic.

Maurice Doater, MD

	Patient name:
	DOB:
	MR/Chart #:

GODFREY REGIONAL OUTPATIENT CLINIC
3122 Shannon Avenue • Aldon, FL 77712 • (407) 555-7654

Answers

PROGRESS NOTE

Date:	Vital signs:	T		R	
Chief complaint:		P		BP	

Patient's mother phoned our office approximately one hour ago and indicated she believed her 3-year-old had swallowed some of her prescription medications. She was instructed to gather all her prescription medication bottles and proceed immediately to the emergency room where she presents at this time.

Physical examination:

The child appears to be in no distress, playing and running about the emergency room. Lab tox screens were run for the medications presented by the mother which were all negative.

Assessment:

Plan:

Mother is instructed to watch the child for any signs of distress, decreased level of activity, etc. and return immediately if any of these signs are present.

Robert Rai MD

Patient name:

DOB:

MR/Chart #:

GODFREY REGIONAL OUTPATIENT CLINIC
3122 Shannon Avenue • Aldon, FL 77712 • (407) 555-7654

Answers

EMERGENCY ROOM RECORD

Name:		Age:	ER physician:
		DOB:	

Allergies/type of reaction:	Usual medications/dosages:

Triage/presenting complaint:	Patient is a 46-year-old who had hysterectomy performed approximately one week ago. She called our office this morning complaining of fever, nausea, and vomiting over the past 24 hours.

Initial assessment:

Time	T	P	R	BP	Other:					

Medication orders:

Lab work:

X-Ray:

Physician's report:

Upon arrival, the patient relates a 24-hour history of nausea, vomiting, and abdominal tenderness. Of note, the patient has an indwelling catheter which was inserted postoperatively due to her inability to void. She was to return to the office postoperatively on the 3rd postop day for possible removal of the catheter.

Urine sample taken from the catheter is positive for red and white blood cells. Urine culture is performed and the patient is given antibiotics.

Diagnosis:	Physician sign/date
Bladder infection due to indwelling catheter	*Maurice Doater, MD*

Discharge	Transfer	Admit	Good	Satisfactory	Other:

GODFREY REGIONAL HOSPITAL
123 Main Street • Aldon, FL 77714 • (407) 555-1234

Answers

PROGRESS NOTE

Chief complaint: _____

Date: _____

Vital signs: BP_____ P_____ R_____

History:

This 43-year-old female was seen as a result of having right ear pain for the last 3–4 days. She states the pain radiates to the side of her face and neck. Also complains of sore throat and increased pain to touch underneath her ear. No head pain, neck pain, no cough, cold, flu, no rhinorrhea, no congestion.

Allergies: Codeine
Medications: Calan SR 240 mg for HTN
FH/SH: Non-contributory

Exam:

Vital Signs: Temp 99.6, pulse 64, respirations 18, BP 128/74
HEENT: Ears show bilaterally clear tympanic membranes. Nose slightly congested. Throat clear. Only slight redness and injection of the peritonsillar region. Submental nodes are markedly tender on right side.
Neck: Supple, full ROM without any limitation

Diagnosis/assessment:

Right neck lymphadenopathy, early pharyngitis. Patient will be started on Amoxil 500 mg tid.

Maurice Doater, MD

Patient name: _____
Date of service: _____

GODFREY REGIONAL OUTPATIENT CLINIC
3122 Shannon Avenue • Aldon, FL 77712 • (407) 555-7654

Answers

EMERGENCY ROOM RECORD

Name:		Age:	ER physician:
		DOB:	

Allergies/type of reaction:	Usual medications/dosages:
Penicillin	None

Triage/presenting complaint: Patient presents to the emergency room complaining of fever off and on since seven days ago. States he has also had some chills and urinary urgency. Denies sore throat, nausea, vomiting, diarrhea, and cough. Also states has been having some low back pain and headache occasionally with the fever.

Initial assessment:

Time	T	P	R	BP	Other:				

Medication orders:

Lab work:

X-Ray:

Physician's report:

PMH: HTN
SH: Non-smoker, married
PHYSICAL EXAM:
Vitals: Temp 103.6, pulse 96, respirations 20, BP 168/88
Lungs: Clear to auscultation, no wheezes or crackles
Heart: Regular rate and rhythm
Abdomen: Nondistended, positive bowel sounds, non-tender
LABORATORY FINDINGS:
Chest x-ray shows left lower lobe atelectasis, urinalysis shows findings compatible with urinary tract infection.

Diagnosis:	Physician sign/date
Left lower lobe atelectasis Patient will be treated with Cipro for his left lower lobe atelectasis and urinary tract infection symptoms.	*Nancy Caully MD*

Discharge	Transfer	Admit	Good	Satisfactory	Other:

GODFREY REGIONAL HOSPITAL
123 Main Street • Aldon, FL 77714 • (407) 555-1234

Answers

EMERGENCY ROOM RECORD

Name:	Age:	ER physician:
	DOB:	

Allergies/type of reaction:	Usual medications/dosages:
	Unknown

Triage/presenting complaint: This 53-year-old male patient comes to the emergency room after being found unresponsive. Patient has a known history of lung carcinoma and has been told to expect this outcome at some time in the near future.

Initial assessment:

Time	T	P	R	BP	Other:					

Medication orders:

Lab work:

X-Ray:

Physician's report:

Patient was found by paramedics in sinus bradycardia with a pressure. IV started and patient was intubated on the scene. Atropine and epinephrine were administered on several occasions without development of a pressure. Patient placed on pacemaker but no pressure or pulse developed.

Past medical history: Lung carcinoma

Social history/FM: Unknown

Review of systems: Unable to elicit from patient

PHYSICAL EXAM:

On arrival, no pulse, no respirations, no blood pressure, undergoing cardiopulmonary resuscitation. Pupils fixed and dilated, corneal reflexes absent. Heart sounds not heard, no spontaneous respiratory effort. No peripheral pulses, femoral pulses felt. Patient has been unresponsive without blood pressure or pulse for approximately 45–50 minutes and pronounced dead.

Diagnosis:	Physician sign/date
Cardiorespiratory arrest History of lung carcinoma	*Robert Rai MD*

Discharge	Transfer	Admit	Good	Satisfactory	Other:

GODFREY REGIONAL HOSPITAL
123 Main Street • Aldon, FL 77714 • (407) 555-1234

Answers

PROGRESS NOTE

Date:	Vital signs:	T		R	
Chief complaint:		P		BP	

HISTORY OF ILLNESS:
This 54-year-old female known to this practice presents due to abdominal pain, primary mid-abdominal and epigastric area. Pain has lasted approximately two weeks. Accompanied by nausea, vomiting, and diarrhea. Some vomitus has had blood streaks in it and she has had some slight red rectal bleeding. Has already had a gallbladder workup which was negative. Has no history of ulcer disease, pancreatitis. No chest pain.

PAST MEDICAL HISTORY:
Arthritis, hypertension, hypothyroidism. Status post hysterectomy, bilateral salpingo-oophorectomy.

Physical examination:

Vital signs: BP 184/94, pulse 104, temp 96.7

Chest: Clear

Heart: Unremarkable

Abdomen: Soft, some tenderness in epigastric area

LABORATORY FINDINGS: CBC showed hematocrit of 43, WBC of 7100, platelet count of 327,000 and amylase returned at 502. Abdominal series was negative.

Assessment:

DIAGNOSIS:
Acute pancreatitis

Plan:

I spoke with the patient at length regarding the need for hospitalization to stabilize her condition. She consented and arrangements were made for her direct admission. I will see her later this afternoon at the hospital.

Maurice Doater, MD

	Patient name:
	DOB:
	MR/Chart #:

GODFREY REGIONAL OUTPATIENT CLINIC
3122 Shannon Avenue • Aldon, FL 77712 • (407) 555-7654

Answers

PROGRESS NOTE

Date:		Vital signs:	T		R	
Chief complaint:			P		BP	

Patient is status post coronary bypass grafting approximately one year ago. Today, she developed a rapid pulse of approximately 145, no chest pain, no SOB, but indicates she felt weak as a result.
PAST MEDICAL HISTORY: As above
MEDICATIONS: Verapamil, dogixon, coumadin, iron

Physical examination:

Vital signs: BP 150/66, pulse 136, and irregular, temp 97.2
Chest: Clear
Heart: Rhythm is irregular
Abdomen: Soft and non-tender
LABORATORY FINDINGS:
ECG showed atrial flutter 125–145. Chest x-ray showed cardiomegaly.
Patient given 5 mg Verapamil and converted to sinus rhythm at a rate of 85 almost immediately.

Assessment:

DIAGNOSIS:
Atrial flutter, converted
Cardiomegaly

Plan:

Patient will be admitted to Cardiology Services at the hospital.

Maurice Doater, MD

Patient name:
DOB:
MR/Chart #:

GODFREY REGIONAL OUTPATIENT CLINIC
3122 Shannon Avenue • Aldon, FL 77712 • (407) 555-7654

Answers

EXERCISE 36

PROGRESS NOTE

Date:	Vital signs:	T	R
Chief complaint:		P	BP

This 19-year-old female was seen in the emergency room approximately four days ago with complaint of headache and underwent a CAT scan and lumbar puncture at that time. She was discharged from the ER on unknown medications and presents today with complaint of continuing headache, worse when she stands up and better when she lies down. Experiences vomiting when upright, no hematemesis, had diarrhea, but none presented. No abdominal pain, no rashes, no diplopia, blurred vision, numbness, tingling of extremities, no back pain.

FAMILY HISTORY: Diabetes

MEDICATIONS: Other than those prescribed in ER, unknown

ALLERGIES: None

Physical examination:

Vital signs: Temp 98.4, pulse 84, BP 110/68

Neck: Supple, no cervical adenopathy, oral mucosa pink, moist

Heart: Regular rate and rhythm without murmur

Abdomen: Non-tender and soft, no guarding, rigidity, no masses

Assessment:

DIFFERENTIAL DIAGNOSIS:
Probably post LP headache. Possible syndrome gastroenteritis.

Plan:

TREATMENT:
Patient will be admitted to observation status for 23-hour stay and evaluation.

Maurice Doater, MD

	Patient name:
	DOB:
	MR/Chart #:

GODFREY REGIONAL OUTPATIENT CLINIC
3122 Shannon Avenue • Aldon, FL 77712 • (407) 555-7654

Answers

HISTORY AND PHYSICAL EXAMINATION

Admitted:

Medical record number:

This 59-year-old patient presents for admission with a prior history of "small vessel disease" in her heart per the patient and chest pain that developed today. She was seen in my office at approximately 1:00 PM today where she developed chest pain, dull aching pain in her chest which radiated into the left chest, across over to the right, down her left arm. She experiences shortness of breath and nausea and was administered Nitroglycerin. She was sent for admission and further evaluation and treatment.

Past medical history:

Some of her old records are not available. However, patient has no history of myocardial infarction, and a negative heart cath in 1997 at which time her previous cardiologist reported she had small vessel disease. She also has hypertension and diabetes.

Family and social history:

Heart disease in grandmother and brother
Previous smoker

Review of systems:

Physical exam:

Vital signs: Stable

Heart: Regular

Abdomen: Soft, non-tender

Extremities: No peripheral edema, calf tenderness. EKG shows sinus rhythm. Chest x-ray normal, cardiac enzymes were normal.

Laboratory/radiology:

X-ray

Assessment:

DIAGNOSIS: Chest pain, Hypertension, Diabetes

Plan:

She is being admitted for further evaluation and treatment at this time.

GODFREY REGIONAL HOSPITAL
123 Main Street • Aldon, FL 77714 • (407) 555-1234

Answers

EXERCISE 38

EMERGENCY ROOM RECORD

Name:		Age:	ER physician:
		DOB:	

Allergies/type of reaction: | **Usual medications/dosages:**

None

Triage/presenting complaint: Patient is a 24-year-old female who states she slipped and fell today and landed directly on her left side. Right after she fell, she began having lower abdominal pain and vaginal bleeding. She states her menstrual cycle completed approximately 7–10 days ago. She denies vaginal discharge.

Initial assessment:

Time	T	P	R	BP	Other:					

Medication orders:

Lab work:

X-Ray:

Physician's report:

REVIEW OF SYSTEMS: Denies neck or head trauma or pain, chest pain, shortness of breath.
Denies vomiting, fever, chills, diarrhea, dysuria, pelvic pain.
SH/FH: Non-contributory
PMH/SURGICAL HISTORY: None
PHYSICAL EXAMINATION:
Vital signs: Temp 98.8, pulse 114, BP 96/69
HEENT: Pupils, equal round and reactive to light
Neck: Supple, non-tender
Chest: Clear to auscultation
Heart: Regular rate and rhythm no murmurs, gallops, rubs
Abdomen: Showed tenderness to deep palpation mid lower abdomen as well as right lower quadrant and left lower quadrant.
Pelvic: Shows blood at the introitus. Speculum exam showed blood in the vaginal vault cleared with approximately six large swabs equal to approximately 1/2 cup. Exam showed no lacerations or tears.

Diagnosis: | **Physician sign/date**

Acute abdominal pain, status post fall
Vaginal bleeding
Rule out possible ruptured ovarian cyst
Possible hematoma intra-abdominal injury

Robert Rai MD

Discharge   **Transfer**   **Admit**   **Good**   **Satisfactory**   **Other:**

GODFREY REGIONAL HOSPITAL
123 Main Street • Aldon, FL 77714 • (407) 555-1234

Answers

PROGRESS NOTE

Chief complaint: _____

Date: _____

Vital signs: BP_____ P_____ R_____

History:

Established patient returns complaining of pain behind her left knee for about one week. She works as a maid and does some strenuous work but does not recall any specific injury.

Exam:

On examination, she has marked tenderness over the popliteal area on the left, none of the right. Negative Homan's sign. Calf on the left measures 1/4 inch greater than right. She has no chest pain, no shortness of breath. Note she indicates she has had similar pains in the past, which were treated with anti-inflammatories and muscle relaxants with good results.

Diagnosis/assessment:

Leg pain, cannot rule out DVT
Prescribe Naprosyn, use elevation and heat. Schedule her for Doppler study ASAP.

Maurice Doater, MD

Patient name: _____
Date of service: _____

GODFREY REGIONAL OUTPATIENT CLINIC
3122 Shannon Avenue • Aldon, FL 77712 • (407) 555-7654

Answers

PROGRESS NOTE

Date:	Vital signs:	T		R	
Chief complaint:		P		BP	

Patient walked in today saying she had a cold, sore throat and chest from coughing. Her symptoms started approximately one week ago. She has nasal congestion, yellow in color.

Examination:

Temperature is 100.5. Cerumen is noted in right ear canal. Unable to visualize tympanic membrane. Left ear canal is bulging and translucent. No pre or postauricular nodes. Nasal mucosa edematous and erythematous. Does have some anterior cervical adenopathy. Posterior pharynx is pink. Lungs are clear after cough, cough is upper airway.

Impression:

DIAGNOSIS:
Sinusitis
Allergic rhinitis
Upper respiratory infection

Plan:

Maurice Doater, MD

Patient name:

DOB:

MR/Chart #:

GODFREY REGIONAL OUTPATIENT CLINIC
3122 Shannon Avenue • Aldon, FL 77712 • (407) 555-7654

Answers

RADIOLOGY REPORT

MR#:
DOB:
Dr.

Clinical summary:

DIAGNOSIS:
Size and dates

PART TO BE EXAMINED:
OB US

Abdomen:

Conclusion:

OB ULTRASOUND:
There is a single viable intrauterine pregnancy in a breech presentation. Average ultrasound age is 18 weeks 0 days. Normal amount of amniotic fluid. Placenta is posterior and to the right with no placenta previa abruptio. No fetal abnormality evident.

Ddt/mm

D:
T:

_____
Lisa Valhas, M.D.   Date

GODFREY REGIONAL HOSPITAL
123 Main Street • Aldon, FL 77714 • (407) 555-1234

Answers

RADIOLOGY REPORT

MR#:
DOB:
Dr.

Clinical summary:

DIAGNOSIS:
Postpartum bleeding × 3 months

PART TO BE EXAMINED:
Pelvic US

Abdomen:

Conclusion:

PELVIC ULTRASOUND:
Patient is 3 months post partum and presents with vaginal bleeding. Anteverted uterus top normal in size. There is relative thickening and irregularity to the endometrium over a length of 2.9 centimeters and with a width of 1.2 centimeters; this is a nonspeci c nding, but in view of the patient's history, abnormality such as some residual placenta or other products of gestation cannot be excluded. Both ovaries appear normal. No mass or abnormal uid collection in the pelvis.

Ddt/mm

D:
T:

_____
Lisa Valhas, M.D.   Date

GODFREY REGIONAL HOSPITAL
123 Main Street • Aldon, FL 77714 • (407) 555-1234

Answers

RADIOLOGY REPORT

MR#:
DOB:
Dr.

Clinical summary:

DIAGNOSIS:
Size, dates, and position

PART TO BE EXAMINED:
OB ultrasound

Abdomen:

Conclusion:

OB ULTRASOUND EXAM:
The technologist performed the exam and hard-copy images are reviewed.

Single intrauterine pregnancy with fetus in the breech position. Placenta is located posteriorly and to the left in the uterus and does not appear low-lying. Normal volume of amniotic fluid. Fetal cardiac motion observed by the technologist. Fetal anatomy appears within normal limits on the images provided. Average ultrasound age estimated to be 27 weeks 2 days. Refer to the OB worksheet for other measurements.

Ddt/mm

D:
T:

_____
Lisa Valhas, M.D.   Date

GODFREY REGIONAL HOSPITAL
123 Main Street • Aldon, FL 77714 • (407) 555-1234

Answers

EXERCISE 44

OPERATIVE REPORT

Patient information:	
Patient name: DOB: MR#:	Date: Surgeon: Anesthetist:

Preoperative diagnosis:

Saw injury to right small finger

Postoperative diagnosis:

1. Open proximal phalanx fracture
2. Traumatic arthrotomy of the proximal interphalangeal joint
3. Ulnar-sided digital neurovascular laceration
4. Complex laceration of the entire fifth digit

Procedure(s) performed:

1. Debridement and irrigation of open proximal phalanx fracture
2. Debridement and irrigation of open proximal interphalangeal joint
3. Debridement, irrigation, and primary repair of complex laceration (approximately 5 cm)
4. Digital nerve repair
5. Pinning of proximal phalanx fracture
6. Short-arm splint application
7. Fluoroscopy

Anesthesia:

Assistant surgeon:

Description of procedure:

The patient was taken to the operating room where, after general anesthesia was administered, the right upper extremity was prepped and draped in a sterile fashion. The skin edges were debrided as needed. The joint was debrided of any foreign bodies. Minimal foreign material was actually seen. The fracture was curetted and irrigated out copiously as well. Copious amounts of antibiotic irrigation were used for lavage. Once this was completed, the wound was extended for about 1 cm proximally and distally to help identify the neurovascular bundle. This was identified. The digital artery had a segmental loss and it was coagulated. The digital nerve was injured over about a 2-cm segment. However, the nerve was felt to be repairable. The fracture site was somewhat unstable and, therefore, a single pin was placed from the radial aspect distally to proximally under fluoroscopic guidance. The fracture was stable after this, and excellent alignment was obtained as visualized on multiple planes with fluoroscopy. The digital nerve was repaired with 4 epineural sutures using 8-0 nylon. The PIP joint had to be flexed to about 15 degrees to allow for repair without significant tension. Once this was completed, the wound was once again irrigated out copiously with antibiotic irrigation solution. The complex laceration was closed with multiple simple and vertical mattress nylon sutures.

Xeroform and bulky hand dressing and a short-arm dorsal blocking splint were applied. Of note, the tourniquet was deflated prior to the end of the procedure, and the finger had good capillary refill and good color. Hemostasis was obtained as needed during the procedure with

Patrick Chsay MD

GODFREY REGIONAL HOSPITAL
123 Main Street • Aldon, FL 77714 • (407) 555-1234

Answers

OPERATIVE REPORT

Patient information:

Patient name:
DOB:
MR#:

Date:
Surgeon:
Anesthetist:

Preoperative diagnosis:

Comminuted fracture, left distal radius, closed

Postoperative diagnosis:

Comminuted fracture, left distal radius, closed

Procedure(s) performed:

Closed reduction with external fixation, fracture, left distal radius utilizing fluoroscopy

Anesthesia:

Assistant surgeon:

Description of procedure:

The patient was placed supine on the operating room table and a satisfactory general anesthetic was given. Preoperative intravenous cephalosporin antibiotic was given. Pneumatic tourniquet was placed high about the left arm but did not require inflation during this procedure. The left hand, wrist, and forearm to proximal to the elbow were prepped sterilely with DuraPrep, and the left wrist and hand were draped in the usual sterile fashion. Pins were placed in the usual fashion via full-thickness skin incisions and spreading of the subcutaneous tissue down to bone. Drilling was performed within a soft tissue protector that was placed all the way down to bone. Pins were then placed. Two pin sites needed to be revised because of the soft bone in these areas. Two pins were proximal to the fracture and two pins were distal. Each pin was placed on the radial aspect of either the radius or second metacarpal. External fixator was applied and a closed reduction of the fracture was performed and the bolts of the fixator were tightened down. The fracture was lengthened as needed. Fluoroscopy was used to view the fracture site in AP and lateral views, and it was extremely close to anatomic position with good restoration of the articular joint surface, as well as the alignment of the distal radius on the AP and lateral views.

The pin sites were copiously irrigated with normal saline antibiotic solution and closed over the pins as needed with 3-0 nylon. Neosporin ointment and dry sterile dressings were applied.

The patient tolerated the procedure well. There were no complications. She was awakened in the operating room and transported to the recovery room in stable condition.

Patrick Chung, MD

GODFREY REGIONAL HOSPITAL
123 Main Street • Aldon, FL 77714 • (407) 555-1234

Answers

OPERATIVE REPORT

Patient information:	
Patient name:	Date:
DOB:	Surgeon:
MR#:	Anesthetist:

Preoperative diagnosis:

Stiffness post-total knee arthroplasty, right knee

Postoperative diagnosis:

Same

Procedure(s) performed:

Right knee manipulation under anesthesia and injection

Anesthesia:

Assistant surgeon:

Description of procedure:

After suitable general anesthesia had been achieved, a gentle manipulation was performed on the right knee. Pressure was applied on the proximal tibia and the knee gradually flexed. Prior to the manipulation, knee flexion was 65 and after manipulation went to 115. Scar tissue bands were noted to pop while this manipulation was performed.

Using sterile technique, the patient's right knee was then injected with 18 cc of Marcaine and 80 mg of Kenalog.

The patient tolerated the procedure well and returned to the recovery room in stable condition.

[signature]

GODFREY REGIONAL HOSPITAL
123 Main Street • Aldon, FL 77714 • (407) 555-1234

Answers

OPERATIVE REPORT

Patient information:

Patient name: Date:
DOB: Surgeon:
MR#:   Anesthetist:

Preoperative diagnosis:

Displaced fracture, left distal radius, extra-articular, closed

Postoperative diagnosis:

Displaced fracture, left distal radius, extra-articular, closed

Procedure(s) performed:

Closed reduction of fracture, left distal radius with percutaneous pinning, utilization of fluoroscopy, application short-arm cast

Anesthesia:

Assistant surgeon:

Description of procedure:

The patient was placed supine on the operating room table and a satisfactory general anesthetic was given. Preoperative intravenous cephalosporin antibiotic was given. No pneumatic tourniquet was used. The left hand, wrist, and forearm to proximal to the elbow were prepped sterilely with DuraPrep, and the left wrist area was draped in the usual sterile fashion. A closed reduction of the left distal radius was performed and visualized fluoroscopically. It was in essentially anatomic reduction on AP and lateral views and showed minimal instability. The decision, therefore, was made to perform percutaneous pinning rather than external fixation. Two smooth K-wires were drilled from the radial styloid across the fracture site to engage the proximal fracture fragment cortex. There was excellent stability at the fracture. It was viewed fluoroscopically with stress and was noted to be quite stable. Neosporin ointment was applied to the pin sites, followed by Jergen balls with the pins cut at appropriate lengths. Dry, sterile dressings were applied, followed by sterile circumferential cast padding. All drapes were removed. Cast padding was applied for short-arm cast application and a short-arm fiberglass cast was applied.

The patient tolerated the procedure well. There were no complications. He was awakened in the operating room and transported to the recovery room in stable condition.

GODFREY REGIONAL HOSPITAL
123 Main Street • Aldon, FL 77714 • (407) 555-1234

Answers

OPERATIVE REPORT

Patient information:	
Patient name: DOB: MR#:	Date: Surgeon: Anesthetist:

Preoperative diagnosis:

Nonhealing diabetic ulcer, plantar surface of the right 5th MP

Postoperative diagnosis:

Same

Procedure(s) performed:

Resection of distal right 5th metatarsal head and debridement of plantar ulcer

Anesthesia:

Assistant surgeon:

Description of procedure:

After sterile preparation of the right foot, infiltration of 1% plain Xylocaine was carried out, digital block was made, and incision was made laterally over the right MP joint and up on to the 5th metatarsal, carried down to the metatarsal. A periosteal elevator was used to isolate this area. Then using a rongeur, the entire metatarsal head was removed. Sizable bleeders that could be noted were cauterized, and attention was directed to the plantar surface where this was debrided. Following this, the wound was closed with interrupted 4-0 nylon, and a bulky dressing was placed.

The patient was given routine postoperative instructions. Darvocet-N 100, 1-2 q4h prn pain. She will be seen in the clinic for dressing change on Monday.

Patrick Chug MD

GODFREY REGIONAL HOSPITAL
123 Main Street • Aldon, FL 77714 • (407) 555-1234

Answers

OFFICE NOTE

Date:	Vital signs:	T		R	
Chief complaint:		P		BP	

HISTORY: This 90-year-old man who is a resident of a nursing home presents with a 2-day history of intermittent left lateral chest pain, which varies with respiration. He has an occasional nonproductive cough but denies increased shortness of breath. There has been no injury to the chest. He has a history of coronary artery disease with congestive heart failure and COPD. His medications are as listed. He is allergic to Vancenase.

Physical examination:

REVIEW OF SYSTEMS: He denies anterior chest pain or palpitations. His appetite has been good. He has no abdominal pain. His bowel function is regular. He had a large bowel movement today. There has been no dysuria or increased urinary frequency.

EXAMINATION: Reveals the patient to be afebrile. He is alert. Eyes are clear. Tympanic membranes appear normal. There is no nasal congestion. Mouth is moist. Throat reveals no redness or swelling. The neck is supple with no adenopathy. There is no heart murmur. Lungs are clear. The abdomen is soft and nontender. There is no chest wall tenderness. There is 1+ pitting edema of both lower legs. There is no calf tenderness. Lab data include hemoglobin of 12.5; white count is 6300. Chemistry panel includes a BUN of 29 and other values are within normal limits. D–dimer is positive. ECG shows what appears to be atrial fibrillation with a ventricular rate on right of 56. There are no acute changes. Chest x-ray shows COPD but no active pulmonary disease.

Assessment:

DIAGNOSIS: Pleuritic left chest pain

Plan:

DISPOSITION: He is to continue his regular medications. He may take Tylenol as needed. If he develops increased pain, shortness of breath, fever, or any other problem, he is to go to the emergency room; otherwise, he will follow up with his usual physician next week regarding further evaluation. The above was discussed with patient and his son.

Jay Corm md

	Patient name:
	DOB:
	MR/Chart #:

GODFREY REGIONAL OUTPATIENT CLINIC
3122 Shannon Avenue • Aldon, FL 77712 • (407) 555-7654

Answers

EXERCISE 50

EMERGENCY ROOM RECORD

Name:	Age:	ER physician:
	DOB:	

Allergies/type of reaction:	Usual medications/dosages:
States it was like "penmycin," which maybe was a penicillin or erythromycin.	Prevacid

Triage/presenting complaint:

HISTORY OF PRESENT ILLNESS: Michael presents to the ER with complaints of pain now for the past few days. He has had flu-like symptoms for some days, with achy joints and feeling feverish, has had sweats, some chills. About two weeks ago, he had cough and cold symptoms, which seemed to be getting a little bit better now. He started with fatigue and symptoms mentioned above. He vomited a few times but hasn't had any vomiting the last few days. He has been passing gas, and he has had diarrhea earlier this week. He has had no firm stool yesterday and today, but he is passing gas as mentioned. He has had no urinary symptoms, no frequency, urgency, dysuria, or hematuria. He has had no noted changes in his stools as far as blood. He has some back discomfort, which is rather generalized underneath the ribs and goes around to the abdomen. He appears not SOB, and he has not had chest pain. The cough seems to be a little bit better at this time.

PAST MEDICAL HISTORY: He has had previous fracture of the left extremity and status-post fracture. After taking anti-inflammatories, developed some GI problems and he has been on Prevacid since then.

Initial assessment:

Time	T	P	R	BP	Other:				

Medication orders:

Lab work: CBC shows a normal white count, and his liver enzymes are markedly elevated. We'll get an amylase on him; it is pending at this time.

X-ray: Chest x-ray is unremarkable.

Physician's report:

REVIEW OF SYSTEMS: As noted in the HPI

PHYSICAL EXAMINATION:

VITALS: He is afebrile. BP is stable

HEENT: TMs normal; oral mucosa is pink and moist; throat is pink and moist, no exudate.

NECK: supple, no adenopathy. Negative carotid bruits.

LUNGS: clear

CARDIAC: Rate and rhythm is regular. No murmurs, clicks, or rubs.

ABDOMEN: Has good bowel sounds in all four quadrants. He has had no tenderness, no rebound, or guarding. No organomegaly or masses.

BACK: He has no spinal or CVA tenderness.

EXTREMITIES: intact. He has a trace of edema on the left lower extremity.

Diagnosis:	Physician sign/date
ASSESSMENT: Elevated liver enzymes with upper abdominal pain; probable cholelithiasis. PLAN: We'll go ahead and admit him to the hospital and get an ultrasound in the morning.	*Robert Rai MD*

Discharge	Transfer	Admit	Good	Satisfactory	Other:

GODFREY REGIONAL HOSPITAL
123 Main Street • Aldon, FL 77714 • (407) 555-1234

Answers

8 | ICD-10-CM

EXERCISES 1-10

Indicate the appropriate ICD-10-CM category for each of the following terms. Choose from Service Category (**SC**), Body System (**BS**), or Objective (**O**).

SC/BS/O

1. Occlusion _____

2. Destruction _____

3. Imaging _____

4. Ear, nose, and sinus _____

5. Transplantation _____

6. Subcutaneous tissue _____

7. Tendons _____

8. Placement _____

9. Radiation oncology _____

10. Mental health services _____

EXERCISES 11-15

Choose or fill in the best answer in the following exercises.

11. Name the three chapters (or volumes) of the ICD-10-CM. _____
_____
_____

12. List three body systems in the ICD-10-CM.
_____
_____
_____
_____

13. In ICD-10-CM, the _____ character indicates the affected body system.

    a. first
    b. second
    c. third
    d. fourth

14. ICD-10-CM codes have _____ alphanumeric digits.

    a. ten
    b. five
    c. three
    d. six

15. Which qualifier denotes a diagnostic procedure?

    a. Z
    b. Y
    c. X
    d. D

9 Determining Codeable Services

EXERCISES 1-3

Choose the best answer for each of the following questions.

1. On the claim form, CPT codes should be listed in what order?
   a. least significant service first
   b. the order in which services appear on the record
   c. most significant service first
   d. none of the above

2. The same guidelines and rules apply to CPT codes and ICD-9-CM codes.
   a. true
   b. false

3. _____ is NOT a chapter of CPT.
   a. Psychiatry
   b. Pathology
   c. Medicine
   d. Evaluation and Management

EXERCISES 4-10

Place the following steps in the proper order.

4. Provide information that supports or clarifies. _____

5. Identify key words and phrases necessary to assign codes for services. _____

6. Determine additional specific information regarding the services. _____

7. Assign the correct CPT code(s) from the CPT book. _____

8. Determine the appropriate chapter from which services will be assigned. _____

9. Identify specifics about procedures or services being performed. _____

10. Determine the correct order for billing services and procedures. _____

Identify and assign the appropriate ICD-9-CM codes for the following medical records, and identify services that will need to have the appropriate CPT codes assigned.

EXERCISE 11

OFFICE NOTE

Date:	Vital signs:	T		R	
Chief complaint:		P		BP	

SUBJECTIVE: This 38-year-old man presents with drainage from his right little finger. The patient suffered an injury to the back of his right fingers in an accident 7 days ago. He had the skin partially peeled off, and it has been healing slowly. The other fingers seem to have healed well, but he still has some drainage right at the PIP joint of the little finger. It is sort of orange and reddish, and he is a little concerned about it. He has not noticed a lot of redness or swelling in the area.

Past medical history—Smoker

Current medications—Vicodin

Allergies—None

Last tetanus shot was two years ago.

Examination:

OBJECTIVE: Temperature 97.8, pulse 64, respiratory 16, BP 102/60.

Shows patient to be alert. The right hand shows good pulses, sensation, and capillary refill. The patient has full range of motion of each finger, including the little finger. At the PIP joint of the back of the little finger, there is an open area with some serosanguineous discharge. No pus is noted. No swelling is noted. No red streaks are noted.

Impression:

Right little finger serosanguineous discharge.

Plan:

Patient was told that this is fairly normal and that it will take time for the joint to heal. He was to rest it and to use soap and water on it. He was to follow up with his physician in 7–10 days if it had not healed. He was to return or see his physician sooner if he developed any redness, swelling, or pus and was discharged home in stable condition.

Maurice Doates, MD

Patient name:
DOB:
MR/Chart #:

GODFREY REGIONAL OUTPATIENT CLINIC
3122 Shannon Avenue • Aldon, FL 77712 • (407) 555-7654

Answers

EXERCISE 12

EMERGENCY ROOM RECORD

Name:	Age:	ER physician:
	DOB:	

Allergies/type of reaction:	Usual medications/dosages:
None.	Allegra, prednisone, potassium, Prilosec, stool softener, Niferex, Lotensin, Carafate, dapsone, Pamelor, and insulin.

Triage/presenting complaint:

SUBJECTIVE: This 67-year-old woman presents by ambulance after 2 occurrences of unresponsive episodes. The patient is usually in a nursing home but is visiting a relative. The patient usually goes to bed around 9:00 p.m., but they have been keeping her up tonight and they were getting her to the bathroom at 1:00 this morning. While sitting on the toilet, the patient suddenly became unresponsive and started having a little bit of twitching of her right arm. They were unable to hold her up on the toilet, and after a couple of minutes, she seemed to come around and was completely alert again. They called the ambulance, and upon its arrival, the ambulance personnel noted that she had an unresponsive episode with a very fine tremor of her right arm, which lasted only about a minute. She again became completely responsive afterwards. Her blood sugar was checked and noted to be normal at the scene. She does not appear to have any postictal state, and her blood pressure in the ambulance was initially around a systolic of 80. The patient denies any pain and feels completely back to normal in the emergency room. She is acting normally according to her relatives.

Past medical history: Stroke in August 4 years ago, causing left-sided weakness; myocardial infarction 2 years ago; and diabetic

Initial assessment:

Time	T	P	R	BP	Other:					

Medication orders:

Lab work:

Laboratories show a normal urinalysis with a white blood count of 14,700 with only 4 bands. Hematocrit is 4.6 with essentially normal electrolytes, BUN, and creatinine. Glucose was 150. CPK was less than 20 and troponin was less than 0.3.

X-ray:

A chest x-ray shows some mild increased heart size and some possible vasculature changes but is pretty much unremarkable.

Physician's report:

OBJECTIVE: Temperature 95.3, pulse 103, respirations 16, and blood pressure 116/66. Oxygen saturation 91% on room air.

PHYSICAL EXAM: Shows patient to be alert. She does not appear in any distress. HEENT shows pupils equal, round, and reactive to light and accommodation. Extraocular motion intact. The patient has normal oral and nasal mucosa. Neck is supple. The lungs are clear with some slight upper airway wheezes. Heart is regular rate and rhythm. Abdomen is soft, nontender with positive bowel sounds. Extremities all show red patches on her legs, which seem to be fading. She does have 11 pretibial edema. EKG shows a sinus tachycardia with no ischemic changes.

PLAN: The patient usually goes to bed around 9:00 p.m. and takes several medications at night. This includes the Pamelor that makes her very sleepy. I do not feel that the patient had a seizure episode, since she did not have any postictal state. I feel it most likely they got her up onto the toilet and that she had a vaso vagal reaction with a short syncopal episode. The patient was mildly hypotensive according to the ambulance personnel, but her blood pressure had come up well in the emergency room. She has been alert and was kept in the emergency room for over 2 hours. She did not have any more episodes and felt well. She was given an albuterol nebulizer treatment because of the slight wheezes in her lungs, and her oxygen saturation came up to 94% on room air. I feel her elevated white blood count is secondary to the prednisone that she has recently started on because of the rash on her legs. She remained stable in the emergency room, and the family will take her home and have her rest. They were to follow her usual schedule more closely. She was to return if she had any further problems. The patient was discharged home in stable condition.

Diagnosis:	Physician sign/date
ASSESSMENT: Syncopal episodes	*Nancy Caulfy MD*
Discharge Transfer Admit Good Satisfactory Other:	

GODFREY REGIONAL HOSPITAL
123 Main Street • Aldon, FL 77714 • (407) 555-1234

Answers

OFFICE NOTE

Chief complaint: _____

Date: _____

Vital signs: BP_____ P_____ R_____

History:

SUBJECTIVE: This 77-year-old white female presents to the office for the first time with actually two complaints. She has been having some pubic pressure and increased urinary frequency, which she has noted for the last day without fever. She has a long-standing history of bladder problems and recurrent UTIs and has been treated successfully both with sulfa drugs and fluoroquinolones in the past. She is allergic to Macrodantin. She has not been vomiting or having any unusual fevers. Today, however, she had noticed a large amount of blood after going to the bathroom to urinate. She states that she does have a history of external hemorrhoids and has had a colonoscopy in the past, which was said to be normal 3 years ago. She has not been losing any weight. She is being presently evaluated for angina and is on Coumadin for having a past CVA. She will be having a treadmill test on Wednesday.

Exam:

Patient is not in acute distress. Temperature 97.9, pulse 86, respiratory 18, blood pressure 160/88. The conjunctivae are not pale, and the patient has good facial color. Lungs are clear. The heart is regular. The abdomen is overweight. Bowel sounds are present; unable to palpate any masses. Rectally, the patient has thrombosed external hemorrhoid that looks like it had recently bled. There is no blood in this area at the present time, and there is no active bleeding noted. Anoscopy is performed, and some stool noted at the end of the anoscope; a cotton swab is placed and stool sample is taken. This is found to be heme-negative. Lab work showed white count 10.9, hemoglobin of 13.3, platelet count of 286, INR of 3.0, and urine consistent with a urinary tract infection.

Diagnosis/assessment:

IMPRESSION:
1. External hemorrhoidal bleeding has stopped on its own.
2. UTI

PLAN: Patient is given instructions in hemorrhoidal care and is started on Anusol-HC of 1 prn bid 5–7 days as needed; 14 are given without a refill. We have asked her also to use Tucks as needed. We have in addition started her on Bactrim DS, 1 po bid for 7 days, and have asked her to follow up with her usual physician in 7–10 days. We have explained to her that she may need repeat colonoscopy and that she should discuss this with her physician. She should return for any worsening bleeding.

Maurice Doates, MD

Patient name: _____

Date of service: _____

GODFREY MEDICAL ASSOCIATES
1532 Third Avenue, Suite 120 • Aldon, FL 77713 • (407) 555-4000

Answers

EMERGENCY ROOM RECORD

Name:			Age:	ER physician:
			DOB:	

Allergies/type of reaction:	Usual medications/dosages:

Triage/presenting complaint:	Knife wound, left thigh

S: This is a 22-year-old male who was at a party, and someone got upset and stabbed him with a pocket knife. He has a scratch along his abdomen and a wound to his left thigh. His tetanus is up to date. He has no other injuries. He may be allergic to erythromycin. No routine medications.

Initial assessment:

Time	T	P	R	BP	Other:				

Medication orders:

Lab work:

X-ray:

Physician's report:

O: He has about a 6-cm scratch midline of his abdomen that does not require any care. He has a 3.5-cm vertical laceration to the lateral aspect of his left thigh that goes through the subcutaneous fat down to the vascular layer of the thigh muscle. This is nicked, but there does not seem to be any muscle injury, and there is no active bleeding, so that does not need any repair. CMS was intact distally.

P: Betadine. Local 1% plain Xylocaine for anesthesia. He had suture repair with 4 vertical mattress and 6 simple of 4-0 Ethilon and dressing applied. Wound sheet given. Suture removal in eight days. Return for signs of infection. He was advised he would have an achy thigh muscle for a while because of the nick to the muscle fascia. He can use ibuprofen for pain. He was stable at discharge.

Diagnosis:	Physician sign/date
A: Laceration, left lateral thigh	Nancy Cauley MD
Discharge Transfer Admit Good Satisfactory Other:	

GODFREY REGIONAL HOSPITAL
123 Main Street • Aldon, FL 77714 • (407) 555-1234

Answers

OFFICE NOTE

Chief complaint: _____

Date: _____

Vital signs: BP_____ P_____ R_____

History:

S: The patient is a 65-year-old gentleman who presents today with some trouble swallowing since this morning. Associated with this he has a sensation that he has a hard time taking a deep breath. He had oatmeal and some toast this morning. He didn't think anything got caught, but he is having trouble swallowing and he spits things up. He has had occasional problems with dysphagia in the past, but just a few months ago he had an EGD and there was no evidence of esophageal strictures. He did have a hiatal hernia in addition to some ulcers. I just recently saw him because of edema and leg pain and had made some medication changes. The pain pills helped and his pain is less. The fluid in his legs is down with the metolazone, but he stopped the pain pills because he thought they could be contributing to his symptoms. He has insulin-dependent diabetes, hypertension, atrial fibrillation, mitral regurgitation, alcoholism with cirrhosis, COPD, previous TIA, chronic renal failure, and CHF. His medications are as [noted] previously except for he is not on Bumex, as I had stopped that a couple of days ago and put him on metolazone 5 mg daily. He has no allergies. He has had no trouble with swelling of his tongue or lips. He hasn't had a rash.

Exam:

O: On exam, he is afebrile. Vital signs look stable. His lips and tongue are not swollen. His posterior pharynx looks unremarkable. Neck feels unremarkable. Lungs are clear. Heart is unchanged. Edema is less in his legs and his legs are less tense. We did a chest x-ray and that looks unremarkable.

Diagnosis/assessment:

A: Dysphagia. I suspect he has some kind of esophageal motility problem. He was able to drink some fluid and he felt it went down.

P: Discussion. We did try a Maxi mist treatment with albuterol and also SQ epi and that really didn't affect his symptoms, so I don't think it is an allergic problem. He is to be set up for a swallowing study and stay on just a liquid diet for now. He was stable at discharge.

William Olsen MD

Patient name: _____

Date of service: _____

GODFREY MEDICAL ASSOCIATES
1532 Third Avenue, Suite 120 • Aldon, FL 77713 • (407) 555-4000

Answers

Chapter **9** **Determining Codeable Services**

EXERCISE 16

EMERGENCY ROOM RECORD

Name:		Age:	ER physician:
		DOB:	

Triage/presenting complaint:

S: This 94-year-old female was brought in by her granddaughter because of severe substernal chest discomfort that awoke her at approximately 12:15 a.m. She immediately came here because of severe chest and upper mid-back discomfort. Nursing was transferring her from the wheelchair to the ER cot when she went unresponsive and was found to be without respirations and pulseless. They immediately were able to get her on the cot, lifted her up, and initiated ACLS protocol. They immediately put a cardiac monitor on and found her to be in ventricular fibrillation and immediately shocked her at 200 joules. A rhythm did appear on the monitor that was apparently sinus. She had a bradycardic rate and was still pulseless and spontaneously reverted back into ventricular fibrillation. She was then shocked at 300 joules, again converting into a sinus rhythm. A pulse was then palpated. Chest compressions were started with immediate intubation by paramedics on the scene here in the hospital. CPR was continued in between shocks when she was found to be pulseless until she was shocked again. After the second shock, as noted, she was in a sinus bradycardia with a palpable pulse.

Lab work:

Her laboratory results showed a CBC revealing a white count of 11,500 with 36 percent neutrophils, 54 percent lymphocytes, hemoglobin 13, and platelets 266. Her initial troponin was 0.9. Her urinalysis was unremarkable other than 2 to 4 white blood cells. Basic metabolic profile revealed a glucose of 130, BUN of 38, creatinine 1.3, sodium 142; and potassium was mildly low at 3.3. Chloride was 106, CO_2 27, calcium 8.9, magnesium 2.9; AST and ALT were normal. LDH: 667, CK: 110.

Physician's report:

O: Approximately 5 minutes later, I arrived on the scene in the ER and found the patient to be in a sinus rhythm at a rate of 120 to 140 with a blood pressure of 200/100. Her pupils were approximately 3 millimeters and equal and sluggish. She did start to wake up and was rather restless and agitated. Any time her blood pressure would be taken, she would flex. There was questionable posturing noted at times. Her lung sounds were heard in both lungs after she was intubated. She was placed on the ventilator with a tidal volume of initially 900 by the medics. This was decreased to 800. She was initially hyperventilated, and her ABGs returned, showing O2 sats over 400 and a CO2 that was low at 26. The respiratory rate was decreased from 20 down to 16, and her tidal volume, as noted, was decreased down to 800. Repeat ABGs thereafter showed a PO2 of 477, PCO2 of 28, and a pH of 7.47. After she converted with the second shock, she was started on lidocaine. After a 50 cc bolus, she was started on a 30 cc drip. Life Flight was called immediately by nursing and paramedics. At approximately 1:00 a.m. she started to have more frequent PVCs. Her blood pressure was rather high, in the 220s/130. Her lidocaine drip was increased to 50 cc. 12-lead EKG was taken at that time as well, showing acute MI in the inferior, anterior, and lateral leads. She was starting to get even more restless. She was given an mg of Versed. Chest x-ray was taken and showed adequate tube placement. No obvious pulmonary edema. Lung fields actually looked rather clear. Approximately 7 minutes later, she was still rather agitated. She was given a second mg of Versed. Two IVs were started initially: one for the lidocaine drip, and a second extra IV was also started. Her temperature was noted to be 94. A Baer hugger was placed. She was then given 5 mg of Lopressor IV. Her blood pressure came down to the 150 to 140 systolic/80 diastolic. She was given 4 mg of morphine also at that same time. A Foley catheter was then also placed. NG tube was inserted. At approximately 1:40 a.m., another mg of Versed was given for a total of 3 mg up until this point. Her temperature had increased to 97.2 rectally. She continued to be rather agitated. Another 4 mg of Versed was given.

At approximately 1:50 a.m. Life Flight arrived. A repeat temperature showed tympanic temp of 94.2. Another 2 mg of Versed was given, and the paramedics from Life Flight also gave Zemuron to paralyze her. Just prior to this she actually looked rather alert. Her eyes were focusing on me, and she was still rather agitated. Care was then transferred to the ER physician at the receiving hospital to be taken over by the Life Flight crew. She was transferred via Life Flight to the receiving hospital for further evaluation and treatment. Further considerations and treatment had included a nitro drip, which we decided not to start after her blood pressure dropped in the 150s to 140 systolic after the Lopressor. Also, possibility of thrombolytic was considered. I consulted the receiving physicians at this time. Because of her age, it is felt that the risks outweigh the benefits for her. I also discussed with the patient's daughter and granddaughter the risks of thrombolytic therapy, and their decision at this time was to withhold thrombolytics.

Diagnosis:	Physician sign/date
IMPRESSION: 1. Cardiorespiratory arrest with a witnessed code. 2. Ventricular fibrillation converted with 300 joules. 3. Acute anterolateral and anteroseptal and inferior myocardial infarction. 4. Mild hypokalemia. PLAN: As noted above, the patient was transferred in critical condition to a receiving hospital under the care of the ER physician.	*Nancy Caulby* MD

Discharge   Transfer   Admit   Good   Satisfactory   Other:

GODFREY REGIONAL HOSPITAL
123 Main Street • Aldon, FL 77714 • (407) 555-1234

Answers

EXERCISE 17

EMERGENCY ROOM RECORD

Name:		Age:	ER physician:
		DOB:	

Allergies/type of reaction:	Usual medications/dosages:

Triage/presenting complaint: SUBJECTIVE: Patient is a 1-year-old brought in by his mom with concerns of burns to the fingertips of his middle and ring fingers on his right hand. Mom states that she was baking cookies when he reached onto the counter and touched the hot cookie pan. He started crying right away. Mom took his fingers and ran them under cool and cold water. Then after that, she brought him up to the emergency department.

Initial assessment:

Time	T	P	R	BP	Other:				

Medication orders:

Lab work:

X-ray:

Physician's report:

PHYSICAL EXAMINATION: Reveals on the tips of the middle and ring fingers of the right hand there is an area of whiteness. He does pull back a little bit when these are palpated very lightly; these don't appear to be vesicular but may soon become vesicles. He has surrounding erythema around this, basically just involving minimally proximal to the DIP fold on the palmar aspect of these fingers. He also has some erythema on the small finger pad, but there doesn't appear to be any vesicle here.

PLAN: We did apply Silvadene ointment and a bandage. Recommend that she continue keeping these covered. Continue with an antibiotic ointment cream. Watch for any signs of infection and return to the clinic should he have any signs of infection.

Diagnosis:	Physician sign/date
ASSESSMENT: 2nd degree burns to the fingertips of the middle and ring fingers of the right hand with 1st degree burns to the small fingertip of the right hand.	*Nancy Cauley MD*

Discharge	Transfer	Admit	Good	Satisfactory	Other:

GODFREY REGIONAL HOSPITAL
123 Main Street • Aldon, FL 77714 • (407) 555-1234

Answers

OFFICE NOTE

Chief complaint: _____

Date: _____

Vital signs: BP_____ P_____ R_____

History:

S: This is a 65-year-old gentleman complaining of epistaxis. He has had it intermittently for a week and a half. It is on the right side today. He was actually just in hospital in another city, and was here last month. He has diabetes, hypertension, atrial fibrillation, mitral regurgitation, cirrhosis related to alcoholism, coronary artery disease with previous MI, previous CVA, congestive heart failure, and renal insufficiency. He isn't on any blood thinners other than aspirin. He is on numerous medications that are listed.

Exam:

O: On exam his pressure is not bad. He has a little dried scab of blood in the left nostril so I didn't touch that. On the right side he had just some oozing from the septum that looked raw. I did put a little epinephrine on a cotton swab in there, left it on for awhile, and removed it, and I used a little silver nitrate to cauterize that side of the septum. He is to use a little Vaseline in the left side. He has been on an Atrovent nasal spray for a drippy nose with eating. I told him that this could be causing his problem as it does cause drying and is a known side effect, so he should stop that. He can continue to use his saline nasal spray. He was stable at discharge.

Diagnosis/assessment:

Willen Obst MD

Patient name: _____

Date of service: _____

GODFREY MEDICAL ASSOCIATES
1532 Third Avenue, Suite 120 • Aldon, FL 77713 • (407) 555-4000

Answers

EMERGENCY ROOM RECORD

Name:		Age:	ER physician:
		DOB:	

Allergies/type of reaction:	Usual medications/dosages:
None	None

Triage/presenting complaint:

S: This is a 46-year-old gentleman who was brought in by ambulance for assessment of increasing and worsening shortness of breath. He has a long history of COPD for unknown reasons. It is a debate as to whether it is from his smoking or a welding problem, but in any event, he is totally disabled because of his lungs. He is monitored by a pulmonologist and takes all the medications listed. He started having difficulty a week ago and has been getting progressively worse to the point where tonight he just was extremely winded. He was quite diaphoretic with this but didn't really have any substernal chest pain. He complained of a diffuse chest pain that he thought was from his lungs. A lot of trouble with deep breaths, however. He does have home O2, which he used, but it didn't help, so an ambulance was called. No nausea or vomiting. He does not have a history of MI. He has never had any operations. No temperature.

PMH: He denies any previous hospitalizations or surgeries.

SH: He is married. He is an over-the-road truck driver. He does use tobacco.

FH: Noncontributory

ROS: See above.

Initial assessment:	

Time	T	P	R	BP	Other:				

Medication orders:

Lab work:

Blood gases show a pH of 7.29 with a PCO2 of 73, PO2 of 52, with O2 sats of 87% on 10 liters.

X-ray:

Physician's report:

O: Pulse 135. General: alert, responsive, oriented, quite tachypneic, has a rebreathing mask on, and appears to be in some moderate distress. Chest: Very poor air movement, and I could hear some rhonchi with rales bilaterally, but he is not wheezing. Cardiovascular: normal S1, S2 with a very rapid rate but regular rhythm.

P: Discussed the situation with his pulmonologist. In light of the fact that he could be heading towards some mechanical assistance for breathing, we will send him to the pulmonologist's hospital for further evaluation and treatment.

Diagnosis:	Physician sign/date
A: COPD with acute exacerbation and impending ARDS	*Robert Rai MD*

Discharge	Transfer	Admit	Good	Satisfactory	Other:	

GODFREY REGIONAL HOSPITAL
123 Main Street • Aldon, FL 77714 • (407) 555-1234

Answers

EXERCISE 20

EMERGENCY ROOM RECORD

Name:	Age:	ER physician:
	DOB:	

Allergies/type of reaction:	Usual medications/dosages:
Penicillin	Zoloft 50 mg qd and decongestant spray.

Triage/presenting complaint:

SUBJECTIVE: Patient is a 41-year-old gentleman who presents by ambulance today complaining of shortness of breath. He reports he was sitting watching TV when he started to feel short of breath, get tingly in his hands and feet, and just generally not feel well. He was a little bit nauseous with it. He wasn't having any chest pain or pressure with it. He did have a Cardiolite in September that was negative. Also had some pulmonary function tests indicative of some chronic obstructive pulmonary disease. He has had some intermittent spells of shortness of breath. He also reports he was started on Zoloft last week for some anxiety. He had been on 25 mg a day and just bumped up to 50 mg a day. He also gives a history of bipolar disorder. He is not sure when his last manic episode was, but certainly feels it has been in the last few years. Those records are in another city where he lived previously. He has not seen anyone in Mental Health here.

PAST MEDICAL HISTORY: Otherwise negative per his report.

SOCIAL HISTORY: The patient denies any alcohol use. He smokes about a pack a day, although he says this is quite a bit cut down from his past. He is not currently working.

Initial assessment:

Time	T	P	R	BP	Other:				

Medication orders:

Lab work:

CBC is within normal limits. Chemistry panel within normal limits. CK is 56, troponin 0. EKG shows a normal sinus rhythm with no acute changes.

X-ray:

Physician's report:

OBJECTIVE: Thin gentleman, fairly anxious appearing. Color is good. P 86, R 12, BP 109/85, O2 sat 98% on 3 liters when he arrived from the ambulance. CHEST: lungs bilaterally clear to auscultation. HEART: regular rate and rhythm without murmurs. ABDOMEN: positive bowel sounds. Soft, nontender. Nondistended. EXTREMITIES: normal strength and sensation. No cyanosis or edema.

PLAN:
1. Given that he had a normal Cardiolite fairly recently and symptoms are not terribly suggestive of heart disease, as well as all the normal labs and EKG, I think we are fairly safe in saying that this is probably not cardiac related.
2. I discussed with the patient that I am concerned that the Zoloft may be worsening some of his anxiety symptoms and may actually be causing some more manic symptoms. I have asked him to stop the Zoloft. I did give him some Xanax, 0.5 mg po q6h prn. 20 tabs given. It was discussed with him that this is not a long-term solution, but more short-term to help with the immediate anxiety symptoms.
3. I have set up for the patient to be seen at the mental health center tomorrow.

Diagnosis:	Physician sign/date
ASSESSMENT: An episode of shortness of breath; suspect some anxiety. I would also be concerned that he may be going into a more manic episode, especially given the recent starting of Zoloft. No evidence on exam or laboratory and EKG testing of heart disease.	*Nancy Caully* MD

Discharge	Transfer	Admit	Good	Satisfactory	Other:

GODFREY REGIONAL HOSPITAL
123 Main Street • Aldon, FL 77714 • (407) 555-1234

Answers

OFFICE NOTE

Date:	Vital signs:	T		R	
Chief complaint:		P		BP	

SUBJECTIVE: Esther is an 83-year-old patient who was brought in after she had an episode of "tingling all over" and some dizziness "as if I were going to pass out." By the time she arrived here, the sensation had resolved. Upon review of the ambulance crew description of how they found her, they stated that she was oriented and cooperative, sitting in a chair. Skin was warm and dry, and she didn't have any difficulties with speech or weakness. She did have initial blood pressure of 200/100 and then, en route, she was lowered to 138/64. She was sating 100% on 1 liter. While here, Esther has had resolution of her symptoms as described above. She was not complaining of any pain. She felt better than she had at home. After interviewing her for a while, it was obvious that she has been feeling very weak for quite some time, and that this is an ongoing problem. She also has felt dyspnea with minimal exertion, which she had experienced after her surgery two years ago. She also states that yesterday she had an episode or two of vomiting clear material. She states she didn't have any accompanying diarrhea. This resolved later in the evening, and today she didn't have any and was able to eat well.
PAST MEDICAL HISTORY: CAD, SP CABG. Patient does not recall having had an acute myocardial infarction. Breast carcinoma SP lumpectomy, approximately a year ago. On tamoxifen. Hypothyroidism; on replacement. History of TIA some time ago that was worked up with carotid Dopplers. Unclear at this time what these rendered, but she was advised to take an aspirin a day.
MEDICATIONS: Tamoxifen, Synthroid, metoprolol, ASA, HCTZ, and potassium supplements.
ALLERGIES: None known.

Examination:

REVIEW OF SYSTEMS: It is equivocal whether she has had a low-grade fever at home or not, since she didn't take her temperature. She has had some chills and generalized weakness and malaise as above. Energy is very poor; appetite has been well maintained, and she usually sleeps very well. Vision: no blurred vision or diplopia.
HEENT: No facial pressures, sore throat, rhinorrhea, or earache.
RESPIRATORY: Denies cough, sputum production, or hemoptysis. No pleuritic chest pain.
CARDIOVASCULAR: As above.
GASTROINTESTINAL SYSTEM: No further episodes of nausea or vomiting; no hematemesis, no early satiety, no dysphagia. Denies any changes in bowel habits. No melena or hematochezia. No abdominal pain.
GENITOURINARY SYSTEM: No dysuria, frequency, or hematuria. The remainder is negative.
PHYSICAL EXAMINATION: Very pleasant elderly lady who appears frail. She is fully oriented and cooperative. Initial BP was 160/82; prior to discharge it was 148/74. She was sating 100% on 3 liters per nasal cannula. Temperature 98.1, pulse was in the 70s, regular; and monitor showed a normal sinus rhythm. Respiratory rate was normal. There were no difficulties with speech. HEENT: no facial asymmetries, no pallor, no jaundice. Hydration is fairly well maintained, although her lips are a little dry. PERRL, EOMI, no nystagmus. Oral examination is unremarkable. NECK: supple without lymphadenopathy or thyromegaly; no JVD noted, symmetric carotid upstrokes bilaterally. CHEST: lungs—respiration is quite shallow. EXTREMITIES: no edema. NEUROLOGICAL: is actually intact with mental status as above; no meningeal signs; CN 2-12 intact; motor strength is 4/4 in all four extremities, DTRs are 11 at bicipital and patellar levels; no sensory deficits elicited.
LABS & X-RAYS: Chest x-ray (portable) revealed heart of normal size, no infiltrates or effusions, and the surgical changes consistent with her CABG. I do not see other major differences with previous chest x-ray from over two years ago. EKG showed a normal sinus rhythm with a rate of 80 beats per minute. LAFB, incomplete RBBB, and diffuse IVCD. Labs showed glucose of 118, BUN 21, creatinine 0.7. All electrolytes were normal with potassium of 3.7; CK was 77, troponin 0, WBC count was 4.8 with normal differential, and hemoglobin and hematocrit were 12.8 and 35.6, respectively. Platelet count 251.

Impression:

Elderly lady presenting with resolved episode of diffuse tingling, unclear etiology. No focal findings on examination; no evidence of disease on x-rays or labs. Importantly, she has chronic dyspnea with minimal exertion.

Plan:

We discussed extensively with the patient and her son what the present situation brings up. I do not think that we are going to come up with the answer of why she is so short of breath for so long, and it certainly doesn't seem to be the main concern. The shortness of breath may be due to numerous factors, and these should be worked up on an outpatient basis. The patient was advised to take an extra potassium tablet daily for two days and to drink plenty of fluids. They were also advised to call tomorrow to make an appointment with her physician for follow-up. She may need further work-up, as her weakness and dyspnea have been persistent for so long. We reviewed all of these labs and chest x-rays with them. They agreed that the present problem has resolved and chronic problem needs to be worked up later. They feel comfortable trying it at home and will return if needed.

Felix Wander MD

	Patient name:
	DOB:
	MR/Chart #:

GODFREY REGIONAL OUTPATIENT CLINIC
3122 Shannon Avenue • Aldon, FL 77712 • (407) 555-7654

Answers

EXERCISE 22

OFFICE NOTE

Date:	Vital signs:	T		R	
Chief complaint: Food reaction		P		BP	

S: This is a soon to be 66-year-old woman who says that since she was in her 30s, she would have some reaction when she ate certain foods, and this happened yesterday. It has been the same each time. She had eaten at some kind of church dinner but she says when she eats processed foods like Chicken McNuggets or something else, she will get a sensation that she has too much electrical activity in her head. The closest I can get as far as a description is some pressure, and then she feels her heart flip-flops and she feels funny. This happened yesterday so she came in early this morning to have things evaluated since she now has high blood pressure. Other than hypertension, she denies any other acute problems. She is on Diovan for her blood pressure once a day. She also has fibromyalgia. She has a codeine allergy. On review of systems, no HEENT complaints. Respiratory: negative. Cardiac: just this flip-flop sensation. No history of exertional or other kind of cardiac symptoms. GI: negative. GU: negative.

Examination:

O: On exam, this is an older woman who is in no distress. Her pressure was a little high to begin with, but it did come down and I think she was partly a little bit anxious. Her O_2 sats were fine. Pulse was stable. Eyes showed no papilledema. Neck had good carotid upstrokes without bruits. No nuchal rigidity. Lungs were clear. Heart is regular without any murmurs noted. Abdomen is negative. She moves all her extremities fine. Motor and sensory is intact. An EKG looks unremarkable.

Impression:

A: Vague symptoms. I can't exclude that she couldn't have some kind of weird reaction to MSG. It also may be just anxiety related with blood pressure elevation and palpitations.

Plan:

P: Discussion. She should continue on her Diovan. Her pressure at 174/93 actually isn't much higher than when she was in the clinic last. She was given an Rx for Lopressor 50 mg to take one a day when she has these episodes, #30 with a couple of refills. She will return if there are other problems. She was stable at discharge. She also had blood gases done that were normal.

John Palermo MD

	Patient name:
	DOB:
	MR/Chart #:

GODFREY REGIONAL OUTPATIENT CLINIC
3122 Shannon Avenue • Aldon, FL 77712 • (407) 555-7654

Answers

OPERATIVE REPORT

Patient information:	
Patient name: DOB: MR#:	Date: Surgeon: Anesthetist:

Preoperative diagnosis:

Right middle finger nail bed injury with subungual hematoma

Postoperative diagnosis:

Right middle finger nail bed injury with subungual hematoma with right middle nail bed laceration and necrotic nail bed with bone exposure

Procedure(s) performed:

PROCEDURE: Right middle finger nail plate removal, evacuation of subungual hematoma, debridement of necrotic nail bed, repair of nail bed laceration, suture removal

INDICATION FOR SURGERY: The patient is a 56-year-old white male who suffered a blunt trauma injury to his right middle finger approximately one week ago. He presented yesterday with this injury that had been repaired at an outside hospital emergency room. He now presents for evacuation of a subungual hematoma and repair of nail bed injuries.

Anesthesia:

Assistant surgeon:

Description of procedure:

The patient underwent a digital block of his right middle finger prior to coming into the operating room. There he underwent sedation, and his right hand and forearm were prepped and draped in the usual sterile fashion. A tourniquet was placed over his upper arm. At the beginning of the procedure, the hand was elevated and pressure was held for exsanguination. The tourniquet was inflated to 250 mm Hg pressure. Two sutures were removed from the nail plate and the skin using a blunt mosquito forceps. The nail plate was dissected off of the remaining nail bed and the nail plate was then removed. The underlying nail bed had a laceration across the mid portion and was necrotic at the distal portion along the radial side of the finger. The necrotic tissue was sharply debrided with a 15 blade scalpel. Upon completion of the nail bed debridement, there was exposed bone under the wound. The patient has a fracture of this distal phalanx, which was noted on preoperative x-ray. The wound was thoroughly irrigated with saline solution. The nail bed laceration in this open wound was then closed using 4-0 Vicryl suture. After repair of the nail bed and closure of this open wound, the nail bed and finger were assessed for bleeding by deflating the tourniquet. There was good hemostasis over the operative field. Preoperatively, it was noted that the patient's fingertip, which had been lacerated in the injury, was repaired but appeared dusky. A 25-gauge needle was poked into this flap of skin at the distal pulp of the finger and there was poor blood return. This suggests that there may be partial necrosis and loss of the skin in this part of the finger. The wound was then covered with antibiotic ointment, Xeroform gauze, clean gauze, and paper tape. It was then placed into a splint. The patient was then successfully taken to the PACU for recovery in stable condition.

GODFREY REGIONAL HOSPITAL
123 Main Street • Aldon, FL 77714 • (407) 555-1234

Answers

OPERATIVE REPORT

Patient information:	
Patient name: DOB: MR#:	Date: Surgeon: Anesthetist:

Preoperative diagnosis:

Morpheaform basal cell carcinoma of the nose

Postoperative diagnosis:

Morpheaform basal cell carcinoma of the nose

Procedure(s) performed:

Excision of basal cell carcinoma of the nose (2 cm × 1 1⁄4 cm). Full-thickness skin graft reconstruction of the nose from left preauricular donor site.

ESTIMATED BLOOD LOSS: Less than 10 cc

CLINICAL NOTE: The patient is a 60-year-old white female who has had recurrent basal cell carcinoma of the nose removed on two previous occasions. The last occasion was found to be consistent with morpheaform basal cell carcinoma with positive residual tumor present. She is being brought to the operating room for wide local excision with frozen sections and reconstruction using full-thickness skin graft.

Anesthesia:

IV sedation/attended local

Assistant surgeon:

Description of procedure:

OPERATIVE NOTE: The patient was brought to the operating room and placed on the operating room table in a supine position. IV sedation was administered, and using 1% lidocaine with 1:100,000 parts epinephrine. The nose and left preauricular regions were injected. The face was prepped and draped in sterile fashion. Using a marking pen, the area of visualized tumor with margins was marked along the dorsum and nasal tip region. Using 15-blade scalpel, an incision was made along the marked areas, measuring approximately 1¼ cm, and full-thickness skin graft was removed, labeled, and sent to Pathology for frozen and permanent sections. Frozen section showed residual tumor on the lateral 6 to 9 o'clock margins and additional section removed was clear on frozen section. Deep margins were clear. Meticulous hemostasis was obtained with bipolar and Bovie cautery. Left preauricular incision was made and an elliptical full-thickness skin tag taken from this region. It was cut to size and sutured in place with interrupted 6-0 nylon sutures to the nasal tip defect. The preauricular incision was undermined and then closed with running interlocking 5-0 nylon sutures. Bacitracin ointment was placed to both wounds, followed by Telfa dressing over the left preauricular area, and a Telfa pressure dressing over the left nasal tip skin graft site.

The patient was fully awakened from IV sedation and brought to the recovery room in stable condition, having tolerated the procedure well.

Adam Westy MD

GODFREY REGIONAL HOSPITAL
123 Main Street • Aldon, FL 77714 • (407) 555-1234

Answers

OPERATIVE REPORT

Patient information:	
Patient name: DOB: MR#:	Date: Surgeon: Anesthetist:

Preoperative diagnosis:

1) Osteomyelitis, right 2nd distal phalanx.
2) Non-healing ulceration, right 2nd digit.

Postoperative diagnosis:

1) Osteomyelitis, right 2nd distal phalanx.
2) Non-healing ulceration, right 2nd digit.

Procedure(s) performed:

1) Amputation of the distal phalanx.
2) Removal of the nail plate and nail bed of the right distal phalanx.

Anesthesia:

Assistant surgeon:

Description of procedure:

The patient was brought back to the operating room, properly identified, and placed on the OR table in a supine position. Following IV sedation, the right 2nd digit was anesthetized with 3 cc of 50/50 mixture of 1% lidocaine plain and 0.5% Marcaine plain. The foot was then prepped and draped in the usual sterile, aseptic manner.

Attention then was directed to the distal aspect of the right 2nd digit where a fishmouth incision was placed at the distal top over the ulceration. The incision site was deepened down to the distal phalanx, which was noted to be open down through the cortical bone, and the bone was very soft. The soft tissue was freed from the distal phalanx plantarly, medially, and laterally. The dorsal attachment was noted to be void of coverage; the dorsal aspect of the phalanx was exposed and a void of soft tissue coverage under the nail plate. The nail plate was loose and the bone was exposed underneath the nail plate. The phalanx was removed from the surgical site in toto. The intermediate phalanx was inspected and noted to be healthy and had no breakdown. The nail plate was not attached except to the proximal nail fold. The nail plate was noted to be nonviable and void of nail bed secondary to the underlying bone exposure. The nail was then removed from the surgical site in toto. The area was then flushed with copious amounts of saline with Ancef in the solution. The redundant tissue was removed from the surgical site, closed with 4-0 Prolene. The foot was then dressed with adaptic 3x3 and Kling.

The patient tolerated the procedure well and left the OR with vital signs stable and vascular status intact to all digits.

Patrick Chung MD

GODFREY REGIONAL HOSPITAL
123 Main Street • Aldon, FL 77714 • (407) 555-1234

Answers

EXERCISE 26

OPERATIVE REPORT

Patient information:	
Patient name: DOB: MR#:	Date: Surgeon: Anesthetist:

Preoperative diagnosis:

1. Extremely comminuted, displaced, unstable, interarticular fracture of the distal radius, left wrist
2. Pre-existing longstanding navicular non-union with radioscaphoid and capitolunate degenerative arthritis, left wrist

Postoperative diagnosis:

1. Extremely comminuted, displaced, unstable, interarticular fracture of the distal radial left wrist
2. Pre-existing longstanding navicular non-union with radioscaphoid and capitolunate degenerative arthritis, left wrist

Procedure(s) performed:

Closed reduction and external fixation

Anesthesia:

Assistant surgeon:

Description of procedure:

The patient is under general anesthesia and LMA. He is positioned supine. The left upper extremity is placed on a hand table. A tourniquet is applied around the left arm. The patient received two grams of Ancef IV, 15 minutes prior to inflating the tourniquet. The fracture is examined under fluoroscopic imaging. With traction on the wrist, the fracture reduces very nicely on both views. The comminution of the articular surface is extremely severe. Placing the wrist in neutral dorsiflexion and volar flexion allows anatomic reduction of the articular surface of the distal radius on both views. The fracture is very unstable. There is an obvious non-union of a navicular fracture with radioscaphoid and capitolunate degenerative arthritis. The radial styloid is pointed in shape.

Prep and drape of the left upper extremity in the usual manner. The left upper extremity is exsanguinated with an Esmarch and the tourniquet inflated to 300 mm of mercury. Total tourniquet time was 60 minutes.

A 3-cm long skin incision is made on the dorsal radial aspect of the second metacarpal shaft. Deep dissection is done with scissors. The subcutaneous veins are identified and protected. A pre-drilling technique is used to insert a 3-mm self-tapping pin in the second metacarpal shaft. The first 3-mm pin is placed into the base of the second metacarpal. The second pin is placed perfectly parallel to the first pin using the appropriate guide. The soft tissues are irrigated with normal saline, removing all bone debris. The skin is partially closed around the pins, avoiding any tension of the skin around the pins. The closure of the skin is done using 4-0 nylon.

Another 3-cm long skin incision is made on the dorsal radial aspect of the forearm, in line with the dorsal radial incision on the hand. The incision is made 6–7 cm proximal to the radial styloid. Deep dissection is done with scissors. The superficial branch of the radial nerve is identified and protected. The radius shaft is exposed. A pre-drilling technique is used to insert perfectly parallel 3-mm self-tapping pins. The soft tissues are irrigated with normal saline, removing all bone debris, and the skin is partially closed using 4-0 nylon, avoiding any tension of the skin around the pins.

The external fixator clamps and rod are connected to the hat pins. The reduction is repeated using the same technique described previously. The wrist is placed in neutral position of dorsiflexion/volar flexion and in neutral deviation. After tightening the external fixator, the fracture is checked under fluoroscopic imaging. Alignment of the articular surface is excellent on both views. There is no shortening. Radial inclination and the tilt of the articular surface are restored. However, there is persistent instability of the fracture.

A bulky, non-adhesive dressing is applied around the hat pins. An ulnar gutter fiberglass splint is applied. Care is taken to carefully mold the splint over the wrist area. Alignment is re-examined after the cast has hardened, unchanged.

Surgery was well tolerated and the patient left the operating room for recovery in stable condition.

Patrick Chung MD

GODFREY REGIONAL HOSPITAL
123 Main Street • Aldon, FL 77714 • (407) 555-1234

Answers

OPERATIVE REPORT

Patient information:

Patient name:
DOB:
MR#:

Date:
Surgeon:
Anesthetist:

Preoperative diagnosis:

Left knee internal derangement

Postoperative diagnosis:

1. Left knee radial and horizontal tear of the posterior horn and middle third of the lateral meniscus
2. Flap tear of the posterior horn of the medial meniscus
3. Grade II chondromalacia of the medial femoral condyle
4. Excessive lateral pressure syndrome

Procedure(s) performed:

1. Left knee arthroscopy
2. Partial lateral meniscectomy
3. Partial medial meniscectomy
4. Chondroplasty of the medial femoral condyle
5. Lateral retinacular release

Anesthesia:

Description of procedure:

The patient is under general anesthesia and endotracheal intubation. She received Ancef IV in holding. She is positioned supine. Knee laxity examination under general anesthesia is normal. The right lower extremity is placed in a well leg holder. A tourniquet is applied around the mid-thigh on the affected left lower extremity. A low-profile leg holder is applied around the tourniquet. The left lower extremity is exsanguinated with an Esmarch and the tourniquet is inflated to 300 mm Hg. Total tourniquet time was 60 minutes. Prep and drape of the left lower extremity in the usual manner.

Knee arthroscopy was done using two portals, anterolateral and anteromedial. The arthroscope was inserted anterolaterally. Instrumentation is through the anteromedial portal. Inflow is through the sheath of the arthroscope. The suprapatellar pouch looks normal. The medial and lateral gutters look normal. There is some fraying of the articular cartilage of the patella and trochlea. The patella is tilted laterally. Even beyond 60 degrees flexion, the patella remains tilted laterally. The cruciate ligaments are intact. In the lateral compartment there is a radial tear and a horizontal tear of the posterior horn and middle third of the lateral meniscus. The popliteus tendon looks normal. There is significant softening of the body of the meniscus. The articular cartilage of the lateral compartment is normal. A partial lateral meniscectomy is performed. The radial tear of the lateral meniscus is excised with baskets. The horizontal tear is sealed using an Oratec chondroplasty probe.

In the medial compartment there is a small sized flap tear of the posterior horn of the medial meniscus. The remaining meniscus is normal. The articular cartilage of the medial tibial plateau is normal. There is an area of grade II chondromalacia of the medial femoral condyle in its weight-bearing area at 45 degrees flexion. This area is 1.5 cm in size. A partial medial meniscectomy is performed with baskets, excising the small-sized flap tear of the posterior horn of the medial meniscus. The body of the meniscus is somewhat soft. A chondroplasty of the medial femoral condyle is performed, excising the unstable articular cartilage flaps with a 4.5 curved resector.

Finally, an arthroscopic lateral retinacular release is performed. The arthroscope is placed into the anteromedial portal. Patellar tracking is re-examined. The patella is tilted laterally even beyond 60 degrees flexion. A 4.5 resector is used to resect the fat pad anterolaterally. An Oratec chisel probe is next used to perform a limited lateral retinacular release. The release starts at the superior pole of the patella and extends towards the anterolateral portal. After the release is completed, the patella can be everted to 70 degrees. The patella tracks very nicely. Beyond 30 degrees flexion, the patella is well centered in the trochlear groove.

The knee is thoroughly irrigated, removing all soft tissue, cartilage, and meniscal debris. The arthroscopic cannulas are removed. The skin portals are closed with 4-0 nylon. 30 cc of Marcaine with epinephrine is injected inside the knee joint. Each portal is also injected with a few ccs of Marcaine without epinephrine. A bulky Jones dressing is applied. The tourniquet is released.

Surgery was well tolerated. The patient left the operating room to recovery in stable condition.

Patrick Chung md

GODFREY REGIONAL HOSPITAL
123 Main Street • Aldon, FL 77714 • (407) 555-1234

Answers

OPERATIVE REPORT

Patient information:

Patient name:
DOB:
MR#:

Date:
Surgeon:
Anesthetist:

Preoperative diagnosis:

1. Chronic maxillary sinusitis
2. Chronic ethmoid sinusitis
3. Deviated nasal septum
4. Nasal polyps

Postoperative diagnosis:

1. Chronic maxillary sinusitis
2. Chronic ethmoid sinusitis
3. Deviated nasal septum
4. Nasal polyps

Procedure(s) performed:

1. Bilateral endoscopic maxillary antrostomies with tissue removal
2. Bilateral endoscopic anterior ethmoidectomies
3. Septoplasty
4. Bilateral endoscopic nasal polypectomies

Anesthesia:

General

Assistant surgeon:

Description of procedure:

The patient was taken to the operating room and placed in the usual supine position. After induction of general anesthesia via endotracheal intubation, the patient was prepped and draped in the usual fashion for a clean uncontaminated procedure.

We first began by decongesting the nose with 4% cocaine on cottonoids. We then injected both sides of the nasal septum as well as the lateral nasal walls with 1% lidocaine with epinephrine.

We first performed the endoscopic sinus surgery on the left side because there were some very large polyps, in fact, some antral choanal polyps on the left side. The polyps were removed using the microdebrider. The uncinate process, the anterior ethmoid cells, and the natural ostium of the maxillary sinuses as well as a thick mucoid tissue within the sinus itself were all removed using the microdebrider. We then directed our attention to the septum where a left hemitransfixion incision was made. We performed a standard septoplasty with particular removal of the cartilage and bone that was compressing the right middle turbinate and obstructing the middle meatus on the right side. After this was done, we then resumed the sinus surgery, this time on the right side, and performed the exact same procedure with removal of the polyps, the anterior ethmoid cells, and the natural ostium of the maxillary sinus on the right-hand side.

After all this was done, the sinuses were thoroughly irrigated with normal saline solution. The left hemitransfixion incision on the septum was closed with a 5-0 plain gut suture. The mucoperichondrial flaps of the septum were closed with 4-0 plain gut in a basting suture fashion. The middle meatus on each side were packed with MeroGel packing. Doyle nasal splints were placed on each side of the septum, and 8-cm Merocel packs were placed on each side of the nose.

The patient tolerated the procedures well. There were no complications. The patient was subsequently moved directly to the recovery room in stable condition.

ESTIMATED BLOOD LOSS: 250 cc
COMPLICATIONS: None
COUNTS: Instrument count correct at the end of the procedure

Maurice Doater, MD

GODFREY REGIONAL HOSPITAL
123 Main Street • Aldon, FL 77714 • (407) 555-1234

Answers

OPERATIVE REPORT

Patient information:

Patient name:
DOB:
MR#:

Preoperative diagnosis:

Left parotid tumor
CLINICAL NOTE:
The patient is a 73-year-old white male with an enlarging left parotid mass. Frozen section intraoperatively showed this to be a benign Warthin's tumor. The mass was approximately 2.5 cm in diameter and was closely adherent to the upper facial nerve branch divisions. The frontal branch of the facial nerve had to be peeled off the capsule of the tumor and was left intact.

Postoperative diagnosis:

Warthin's tumor, left parotid gland

Procedure(s) performed:

1. Left parotidectomy with facial nerve dissection
2. Left sternocleidomastoid muscle rotation flap

Anesthesia:

Description of procedure:

The patient was brought into the operating room and placed on the operating table in the supine position. General endotracheal anesthesia was performed. The left face was prepped and draped in sterile fashion and injected with saline with 1:100,000 parts epinephrine. A plane incision was injected subcutaneously with approximately 10 cc of the above. A modified Blair incision was made, extending along the preauricular crease around the earlobe and then on to the neck in curvilinear fashion. Incision was made with 15-blade scalpel and carried down through subcutaneous layer with Bovie cautery and meticulous dissection.

Using Metzenbaum scissors and meticulous dissection, with bipolar cautery, subcutaneous dissection just above the parotid fascia layer was performed and the facial flap was reflected anteriorly, exposing the parotid gland and tumor. The parotid tumor was in the preauricular area, just anterior to the tragal pointer of the ear cartilage, deep within the parotid gland.

Dissection was carried down along the preauricular region and tragal pointer tangentially to the anticipated course of the main trunk of the facial nerve. Hemostasis was obtained with bipolar cautery. Main trunk of the facial nerve was identified, and stylomastoid foramen was dissected out to the pes anserinus. Using cross-clamp technique, branches were followed that extended deep to the parotid tumor. Parotid tissue was cross-clamped and face observed for any facial movements, and then cut with 15-blade scalpel when clear. The parotid tumor was resected in a standard technique with the branches of the facial nerve visualized and preserved.

The mass was completely excised with several branches of the facial nerve, notably frontal and zygomatic branches dissected off the capsule of the tumor and preserved. Meticulous hemostasis was obtained with bipolar cautery and silk suture ties. Specimen was sent to Pathology for frozen and permanent section, and returned back showing Warthin's tumor.

The wound was irrigated copiously with normal saline and blotted dry. A superiorly based sternocleidomastoid muscle flap was made using the Bovie cautery and reflected up into the preauricular defect to cover the facial nerve to prevent scarring and Prey's syndrome. This was sutured with interrupted 3-0 chromic sutures to adjacent parotid fascia and preauricular soft tissue and fascia into position. A small diameter Jackson-Pratt drain was placed into the wound and brought out through a separate postauricular stab incision. It was sutured to the skin with 2-0 silk mattress sutures.

The wound was closed with inverted interrupted 3-0 chromic sutures for the deep subcutaneous layer and inverted interrupted 4-0 chromic sutures for the subcuticular layer. Skin was closed with running interlocking 5-0 nylon sutures with the exception of interrupted 5-0 nylon sutures around the earlobe. Bacitracin ointment was placed over the wound, followed by Telfa and light pressure dressing. The Jackson-Pratt was placed to self-suction.

The patient was awakened from general anesthesia, extubated, and brought to the recovery room in stable condition, having tolerated the procedure well.

Patk Adam MD

GODFREY REGIONAL HOSPITAL
123 Main Street • Aldon, FL 77714 • (407) 555-1234

Answers

EXERCISE 30

OPERATIVE REPORT

Patient information:

Patient name:
DOB:
MR#:

Preoperative diagnosis:

Rectal bleeding

INDICATION FOR PROCEDURE:
This 42-year-old male has significant episodes of rectal bleeding and pain. By examination, he only has one external skin tag, no evidence of hemorrhoids. By history, this patient has a fissure.

Postoperative diagnosis:

Same, plus anal fissure

Procedure(s) performed:

Examination under anesthesia with left lateral internal sphincterotomy

Anesthesia:

Assistant surgeon:

Description of procedure:

After adequate preparation, 1% Xylocaine plain was used to infiltrate a peri-anal block. Examination of the anal canal does not show significant internal hemorrhoids. He does have a posterior anal fissure. The left lateral mucosa over the internal sphincter was incised and hemostasis achieved. Under direct vision, the sphincter was completely divided. The mucous membrane was then oversewn in a running locking fashion with 3-0 Vicryl.

The patient was taken to the recovery room in satisfactory condition.

Patrick Adam MD

GODFREY REGIONAL HOSPITAL
123 Main Street • Aldon, FL 77714 • (407) 555-1234

Answers

10 Using CPT

EXERCISES 1-5

1. Name the four categories of radiology services.

   _____

   _____

   _____

   _____

2. A _____ indicates a new code in the CPT-4.

   a. period
   b. number 1
   c. question mark
   d. vertical line

3. Similar to ICD-9-CM, CPT contains indented entries.

   a. true
   b. false

4. _____ procedures have no specific procedural code assigned.

   a. add-on
   b. revised
   c. global
   d. unlisted

5. Modifiers have _____ digits.

   a. one
   b. two
   c. three
   d. four

EXERCISES 6-15

Identify where the following services are located.

	Chapter	Subsection
6. Cholecystectomy	_____	_____
7. Nasal endoscopy	_____	_____
8. Acute hepatitis panel	_____	_____
9. Digital neuroplasty	_____	_____
10. Hospital observation	_____	_____
11. Elbow arthrectomy	_____	_____
12. Right heart catheterization	_____	_____
13. Home visit for hemodialysis	_____	_____
14. Lacrimal gland biopsy	_____	_____
15. Kidney transplantation	_____	_____

EXERCISES 16-25

Identify the Chapter of CPT and further breakdown associated with identifying the proper assignment for the following services. Also identify what information, if any, is missing to most correctly assign the correct CPT codes.

16. Destruction benign lesion, arm

    Step 1: CPT chapter: _____

    Step 2: _____

    Step 3: _____

    Step 4: _____

    Step 5: _____

    Step 6: _____

    Step 7: _____

    Step 8: _____

    Additional information/clarification needed (if any):

    _____

17. Diagnostic knee arthroscopy

   Step 1: CPT chapter: _____

   Step 2: _____

   Step 3: _____

   Step 4: _____

   Step 5: _____

   Step 6: _____

   Step 7: _____

   Step 8: _____

   Additional information/clarification needed (if any):

   _____

18. Open reduction, radial fracture

   Step 1: CPT chapter: _____

   Step 2: _____

   Step 3: _____

   Step 4: _____

   Step 5: _____

   Step 6: _____

   Step 7: _____

   Step 8: _____

   Additional information/clarification needed (if any):

   _____

19. Excision, benign lesion, arm, 2.0 cm

   Step 1: CPT chapter: _____

   Step 2: _____

   Step 3: _____

   Step 4: _____

   Step 5: _____

   Step 6: _____

   Step 7: _____

   Step 8: _____

   Additional information/clarification needed (if any):

   _____

20. Closure, simple, leg

   Step 1: CPT chapter: _____

   Step 2: _____

   Step 3: _____

   Step 4: _____

   Step 5: _____

   Step 6: _____

   Step 7: _____

   Step 8: _____

   Additional information/clarification needed (if any):

   _____

21. Office visit, problem-focused history/exam, low medical decision making

   Step 1: CPT chapter: _____

   Step 2: _____

   Step 3: _____

   Step 4: _____

   Step 5: _____

   Step 6: _____

   Step 7: _____

   Step 8: _____

   Additional information/clarification needed (if any):

   _____

22. Office visit, established patient, detailed history/ exam, moderate medical decision making

Step 1: CPT chapter: _____

Step 2: _____

Step 3: _____

Step 4: _____

Step 5: _____

Step 6: _____

Step 7: _____

Step 8: _____

Additional information/clarification needed (if any):

_____

23. Bronchoscopy with bronchial alveolar lavage

Step 1: CPT chapter: _____

Step 2: _____

Step 3: _____

Step 4: _____

Step 5: _____

Step 6: _____

Step 7: _____

Step 8: _____

Additional information/clarification needed (if any):

_____

24. Insertion of central venous catheter, age 65, with port

Step 1: CPT chapter: _____

Step 2: _____

Step 3: _____

Step 4: _____

Step 5: _____

Step 6: _____

Step 7: _____

Step 8: _____

Additional information/clarification needed (if any):

_____

25. Colonoscopy with polypectomy by snare technique

Step 1: CPT chapter: _____

Step 2: _____

Step 3: _____

Step 4: _____

Step 5: _____

Step 6: _____

Step 7: _____

Step 8: _____

Additional information/clarification needed (if any):

_____

Identify and assign the appropriate CPT codes for the following reports.

EXERCISE 26

OFFICE NOTE

Date:		Vital signs:	T		R	
Chief complaint:			P		BP	

HISTORY: This 90-year-old man who is a resident of a nursing home presents with a 2-day history of intermittent left lateral chest pain, which varies with respiration. He has an occasional nonproductive cough but denies increased shortness of breath. There has been no injury to the chest. He has a history of coronary artery disease with congestive heart failure and COPD. His medications are as listed. He is allergic to Vancenase.

Physical examination:

REVIEW OF SYSTEMS: He denies anterior chest pain or palpitations. His appetite has been good. He has no abdominal pain. His bowel function is regular. He had a large bowel movement today. There has been no dysuria or increased urinary frequency.

EXAMINATION: Reveals the patient to be afebrile. He is alert. Eyes are clear. Tympanic membranes appear normal. There is no nasal congestion. Mouth is moist. Throat reveals no redness or swelling. The neck is supple with no adenopathy. There is no heart murmur. Lungs are clear. The abdomen is soft and nontender. There is no chest wall tenderness. There is 1+ pitting edema of both lower legs. There is no calf tenderness. Lab data include hemoglobin of 12.5; white count is 6300. Chemistry panel includes a BUN of 29 and other values are within normal limits. D–dimer is positive. ECG shows what appears to be atrial fibrillation with a ventricular rate on right of 56. There are no acute changes. Chest x-ray shows COPD but no active pulmonary disease.

Assessment:

DIAGNOSIS: Pleuritic left chest pain

Plan:

DISPOSITION: He is to continue his regular medications. He may take Tylenol as needed. If he develops increased pain, shortness of breath, fever, or any other problem, he is to go to the emergency room; otherwise, he will follow up with his usual physician next week regarding further evaluation. The above was discussed with patient and his son.

Jay Corm mo

	Patient name:
	DOB:
	MR/Chart #:

GODFREY REGIONAL OUTPATIENT CLINIC
3122 Shannon Avenue • Aldon, FL 77712 • (407) 555-7654

Answers

EXERCISE 27

OFFICE NOTE

Chief complaint: _____

Date: _____

Vital signs: BP_____ P_____ R_____

History:

SUBJECTIVE: This 92-year-old man presents complaining of a rash. The patient was sent over from a nursing home because he started having a rash on his face and on both thighs. He started with this rash 2 to 3 days ago, but it seems to be getting a little worse on the face today. The patient states that he is not having any pain or itching in the areas and has not had any fevers. Denies any difficulty breathing or shortness of breath.

Past medical history: Dementia, anemia, TURP, and hard of hearing.

Current medications: Paxil, Metamucil, and vitamin B12.

Allergies: none.

Exam:

OBJECTIVE: Temperature 97.1, pulse 70, respirations 18, and blood pressure 190/84.

PHYSICAL EXAM: Shows patient to be alert. He seems to be answering questions fairly well. HEENT shows pupils equal, round, and reactive to light and accommodation. Extraocular motion intact. The patient has normal oral and nasal mucosa. There is a pink ring around the eyes and on the sides of the cheeks and down onto just below the mouth. It is slightly swollen. Neck is supple without adenopathy. The lungs are clear. Heart is regular rate and rhythm. Abdomen is soft, nontender with positive bowel sounds. Extremities all show good range of motion and pulses. The skin only shows the rash on the face and also a deep red rash that is flat on both anterior thighs. These are large rashes with a large red patch. They do not have any areas of tenderness. Laboratories show white blood count of 5.5 with hematocrit of 32.8.

Diagnosis/assessment:

ASSESSMENT: Rash of unknown etiology

PLAN: The patient does not appear to be itching at the area, and I do not feel it is an allergic type of reaction. It appears to be more of an edema on the face but not on the legs. They seem to be 2 different types of rashes. There does not appear to be any type of infection, and at this point the patient will be tried on prednisone on a declining dose over the next 7 days. He does not appear to be in any respiratory distress, and they were to watch closely for any difficulty breathing. He was to follow up with his physician in 2 days to evaluate whether or not he will require a dermatologic consult or if his physician can determine what is going on with his rash. The patient was discharged home in stable condition.

Jay Corm MD

Patient name: _____

Date of service: _____

GODFREY MEDICAL ASSOCIATES
1532 Third Avenue, Suite 120 • Aldon, FL 77713 • (407) 555-4000

Answers

EMERGENCY ROOM RECORD

Name:	Age:	ER physician:
	DOB:	

Allergies/type of reaction:	Usual medications/dosages:

Triage/presenting complaint:	HISTORY: 77-year-old man, at about 8:30 tonight, was eating a piece of steak that hung up in his lower esophagus. Since then, he has been unable to drink water without regurgitating. He

has a long history of similar esophageal obstruction that usually resolves spontaneously. He had one prior EGD about 6 years ago. He has a past history of repair of an abdominal aortic aneurysm complicated by a BK amputation on the right because of an embolus. His medications include Persantine and Coumadin. There is no allergy to medicine.

Initial assessment:

Time	T	P	R	BP	Other:				
Medication orders:									

Lab work:	Lab data include a hemoglobin of 15.2; white count is 10,800. Chemistry panel includes a glucose of 164. Other values are within normal limits. INR is 3.4.

X-ray:	Chest x-ray shows no active pulmonary disease.

PhysicianÕs report:

REVIEW OF SYSTEMS: He denies chest pain or palpitations. He has no cough or shortness of breath. He denies abdominal pain. His bowel function is regular. He has no dysuria.

EXAMINATION: Reveals an alert, pleasant, elderly gentleman. Eyes are clear. TMs appear normal. There is no nasal congestion. Mouth is moist. Throat reveals no redness or swelling. The neck is supple with no adenopathy. Heart rhythm is regular. There is no murmur. Lungs are clear. The abdomen is soft and nontender. EKG shows sinus rhythm and appears normal.

EMERGENCY ROOM COURSE: A saline lock was inserted. He was given 1 mg of glucagon intravenously. He was observed for approximately one hour and was still unable to swallow water without regurgitating.

Diagnosis:	Physician sign/date
Esophageal obstruction. DISPOSITION: Endoscopist called to perform EGD and foreign body removal.	*Robert Rai MD*
Discharge Transfer Admit Good Satisfactory Other:	

GODFREY REGIONAL HOSPITAL
123 Main Street • Aldon, FL 77714 • (407) 555-1234

Answers

EXERCISE 29

RADIOLOGY REPORT

MR#:
DOB:
Dr.

Clinical summary:

CLINICAL INFORMATION:
Right lobectomy 2 years ago, lung CA

Abdomen:

Conclusion:

CT OF THE CHEST:
Axial scans were obtained at 7-mm intervals through the lung fields. The patient was then given 150 ccs Isovue intravenously and axial scans were obtained at 7-mm intervals through the entire chest. Comparison is made with the prior exam.

There are changes from previous pulmonary resection on the right. The upper lobe bronchus is not present, so presumably the entire upper lobe was resected.

There is no pulmonary nodule. The major bronchi are otherwise normal. There is no adenopathy. There is no enhancing lesion.

Scans into the upper abdomen show no focal abnormality in the liver. The right adrenal is enlarged, as on the previous study. It measures about 3 cm in greatest dimension, unchanged.

CONCLUSION:
1. Stable appearance of CT of the chest when compared with the previous study
2. The enlarged right adrenal is stable as well

Ddt/mm

D:
T:

_____
Lisa Valhas, M.D.   Date

GODFREY REGIONAL HOSPITAL
123 Main Street • Aldon, FL 77714 • (407) 555-1234

Answers

RADIOLOGY REPORT

MR#:
DOB:
Dr.

Clinical summary:

CLINICAL INFORMATION:
Fell and injured right hand and rib area

Abdomen:

Conclusion:

THREE VIEWS OF THE RIGHT HAND:
There is a faint transverse lucency through the base of the 5th metacarpal. This may represent a small undisplaced and incomplete fracture, but could also simply be artifact. If the patient has symptoms in this area, one could obtain follow-up radiographs to further assess in several weeks' time. Elsewhere there is no focal bony abnormality. Degenerative changes are seen at the radiocarpal joint as well as the interphalangeal joints.

CONCLUSION:
Possible incomplete, undisplaced fracture base of the 54th metacarpal (see discussion above)

CHEST PA AND LATERAL:
The heart size and the vasculature are normal. There is neither in ltrate nor effusion. Degenerative changes are seen.

CONCLUSION:
No active disease in the chest

Ddt/mm

D:
T:

_____
Lisa Valhas, M.D.   Date

GODFREY MEDICAL ASSOCIATES
1532 Third Avenue, Suite 120 • Aldon, FL 77713 • (407) 555-4000

Answers

RADIOLOGY REPORT

MR#:
DOB:
Dr.

Clinical summary:

DIAGNOSIS:
Follow-up abnormal chest

PART TO BE EXAMINED:
Chest

Abdomen:

Conclusion:

SINGLE PA VIEW OF THE CHEST:
The nodular opacity seen in the left lung base previously is not as well demonstrated on this exam. Although it may lie just beneath the nipple marker, I believe that this finding is still indeterminate. Would recommend CT of the chest to exclude a pulmonary nodule. Scattered interstitial infiltrate in the right mid lung and both costophrenic angles has not changed significantly. Tortuous aorta. Prominent fat pad at the cardiac apex. Focal eventration, right hemidiaphragm. Chest otherwise negative.

LIMITED CHEST FLUOROSCOPY:
This was performed to evaluate the indeterminate nodular opacity in left lung base seen on prior chest x-ray. Under fluoroscopy, I was unable to identify the vague nodular opacity seen on the previously described chest x-ray. Although this could represent a nipple shadow or a density in the chest wall soft tissues or bones, I still believe a pulmonary nodule cannot be excluded, and would recommend CT of the chest in further evaluation.

Ddt/mm

D:
T:

_____
Lisa Valhas, M.D.   Date

GODFREY REGIONAL HOSPITAL
123 Main Street • Aldon, FL 77714 • (407) 555-1234

Answers

OPERATIVE REPORT

Patient information:

Patient name: Date:
DOB: Surgeon:
MR#:   Anesthetist:

Preoperative diagnosis:

Traumatic scalp wound with bone exposure

Postoperative diagnosis:

Traumatic scalp wound with bone exposure

Procedure(s) performed:

Debridement and irrigation of traumatic scalp wound with flap coverage

INDICATION FOR SURGERY: The patient is a 76-year-old white male who initially fell from a seawall. He suffered a traumatic injury to his scalp with bone exposure, excessive bleeding, and had a foreign body within the scalp tissue. He did not seek medical attention initially and approximately three days later presented to the emergency room with an infected wound. There he underwent initial debridement and irrigation of his wound along with antibiotic therapy. He now presents for elective closure of his scalp following debridement and irrigation.

Anesthesia:

Assistant surgeon:

Description of procedure:

The patient was brought to the operating room and placed in supine position on the operating room table. After adequate general anesthesia and endotracheal intubation, the patient was prepped and draped in the usual sterile fashion. Using 1% lidocaine with epinephrine 1:100,000, a total of 20 cc of local anesthesia was used to infiltrate the scalp tissue around the wound. The wound measured approximately 12 cm × 6 cm in greatest dimensions. There was approximately 3.5 cm of exposed bone at the center of the wound. Currently, there is no purulence, crepitus or fluctuance or erythema associated with this wound, and there is no foreign body within it. However, there is still some necrotic material in the scalp wound. After adequate infiltration and anesthesia of area, skin hooks were used to retract the wound edges, and debridement was performed to tissue and fascia. Fibrinous material and other necrotic tissue was debrided with a curet. After the skin edges, subcutaneous tissue, muscle, and fascia were all thoroughly debrided and cleaned, the scalp was extensively undermined circumferentially. The wound was pulled together; however, it was not able to cover the area of bone exposure, thus a flap was constructed by incising the scalp over the left temporal area to allow for a rotation of the scalp flap into the central portion of the wound to cover the exposed bone. After the flap had been incised, it was mobilized with blunt and sharp dissection. Hemostasis was achieved with electrocautery. After the flap had been adequately immobilized, the wound was thoroughly irrigated with three liters of normal saline solution mixed in with 50,000 units of Bacitracin.

After the wound and the flap had been thoroughly cleansed with irrigation, hemostasis was rechecked with electrocautery. After adequate hemostasis was achieved, the wound edges were reapproximated with interrupted 0 Vicryl sutures. In addition, 2-0 Vicryl was used to close the remaining areas. After closure of the deep layer, the rotation flap covered all of the exposed bone and the wound edges were not under tension. The skin was then closed with interrupted 2-0 nylon using simple stitches. The posterior and lateral aspects of the incisions were closed with running 3-0 nylon sutures.

The patient tolerated the procedure well. The wound was cleaned and covered with Bacitracin ointment, 4 × 4s, fluffs, and Kerlix rolls. The patient in the operating room was successfully extubated and taken to PACU for recovery. He went to PACU in stable condition.

Adm Westg MD

GODFREY REGIONAL HOSPITAL
123 Main Street • Aldon, FL 77714 • (407) 555-1234

Answers

EXERCISE 33

EMERGENCY ROOM RECORD

Name:	Age:	ER physician:
	DOB:	

Allergies/type of reaction:	Usual medications/dosages:
Codein	

Triage/presenting complaint:	CC: Fall/injury, pain Patient fell and hit head on coffee table PAST MEDICAL HISTORY: DJD, HTN
Initial assessment:	ROS: Negative nausea, vomited, headache Tripped, no loss of consciousness, no headache Integumentary: Negative for rashes Constitutional: Negative for fever All other systems have been reviewed and are negative

Time	T	P	R	BP	Other:					

Medication orders:

Fosamax 70 mg once a week, Norvasc 2.5 mg daily

Lab work:

X-ray:

PhysicianŌs report:

EXAM:
General: White 71-year-old male, well nourished and in acute distress
HEENT: 1-cm laceration to occipital scalp. Eyes, pupils equal, round and reactive to light, extraocular motion intact
Respiratory: Respirations unlabored with symmetric chest expansion. Lungs sound equal and clear bilaterally.
CV: Regular rate and rhythm
Abdomen: Soft, non-tender to palpation without guarding
Skin: Normal, except for 1-cm laceration on the occipital scalp
PROCEDURE:
The area was prepped and draped and the wound was clensed thoroughtly with betadine. Wound was irrigated with copious amounts of NS. Skin closure was accomplished with 2 staples.

Diagnosis:	Physician sign/date
IMPRESSION: 1-cm scalp laceration Patient received discharge instructions and was related from the ED.	*Robert Rai MD*

Discharge	Transfer	Admit	Good	Satisfactory	Other:

GODFREY REGIONAL HOSPITAL
123 Main Street • Aldon, FL 77714 • (407) 555-1234

Answers

OPERATIVE REPORT

Patient information:

Patient name:
DOB:
MR#:

Date:
Surgeon:
Anesthetist:

Preoperative diagnosis:

1. Intraoral tumor
2. Right nasal ala skin lesion

Postoperative diagnosis:

1. Intraoral tumor
2. Right nasal ala basal cell carcinoma measuring 0.9 cm

Procedure(s) performed:

OPERATIVE PROCEDURE:
Excision of intraoral tumor, excision of right nasal ala basal cell carcinoma with bilobed flap reconstruction
INDICATIONS FOR SURGERY:
The patient is a 70-year-old white female who presents with an intraoral lesion that has been slowly growing for the past several months, as well as a lesion on her nose over the right alar dome. She now presents for elective excision and treatment of these lesions.

Anesthesia:

Assistant surgeon:

Description of procedure:

The patient was brought to the operating room and placed supine on the operating room table. After adequate general anesthesia and endotracheal intubation, the patient was prepped and draped in the usual sterile fashion. Using 1% lidocaine with epinephrine, the skin and subcutaneous tissue around the lesion of the right alar dome were anesthetized. After adequate local anesthesia and epinephrine effect, a shave biopsy was performed of this basal cell carcinoma that measured 0.9 cm in size. The specimen was sent to Pathology and came back positive for basal cell carcinoma, all margins involved. The patient then had a 3-mm margin excised and sent to Pathology with sutures orienting the pathologist. Frozen section of this excision was negative for any tumor at the margins. A bilobed flap was outlined along the right nasal sidewall. Using skin hooks, the bilobed flap was undermined widely in the submuscular plane. Once this myocutaneous flap was adequately mobilized, the remaining wound edges were also mobilized to allow for closure without tension. The flap was then in-set using 5-0 Vicryl sutures for the deep layer and a combination of 5-0 and 6-0 nylon sutures for the skin. Please note that during flap transfer, the skin, subcutaneous tissue, and nasal muscle were transferred together with the flap.

Using separate instruments, separate syringe and needles, the intraoral lesion was anesthetized with 1% lidocaine with epinephrine for the epinephrine effect. After adequate time had elapsed, the lesion was excised with a #15 blade scalpel. The cheek was retracted with a small intraoral retractor, and the specimen was sent to Pathology for permanent sections. Hemostasis was achieved with electrocautery. The mucosa was then closed with running and locking 2-0 chromic sutures. At the end of the procedure, the patient was successfully extubated in the operating room. Her face had been cleaned and the suture line was covered with Bacitracin ointment.

At the end of the procedure, the patient was taken to PACU for recovery in stable condition.

Maurice Doaters, MD

GODFREY REGIONAL HOSPITAL
123 Main Street • Aldon, FL 77714 • (407) 555-1234

Answers

EXERCISE 35

OPERATIVE REPORT

Patient information:	
Patient name: DOB: MR#:	Date: Surgeon: Anesthetist:

Preoperative diagnosis:

Left knee ACL tear, probable meniscal tear

Postoperative diagnosis:

1. Left knee ACL tear
2. Complex tear of the posterior horn of the medial meniscus
3. Flap tear and degenerative fraying of the free edge of the lateral meniscus
4. Large area of grade IV chondromalacia of the weight area of the medial femoral condyle

Procedure(s) performed:

1. Left knee arthroscopy
2. Partial medial meniscectomy
3. Partial lateral meniscectomy
4. Medial femoral condyle chondroplasty

Anesthesia:

Assistant surgeon:

Description of procedure:

The patient is under general anesthesia and LMA. He is supine. He received Ancef IV in holding. Lachman test is positive 21. Pivot shift test is positive. Medial and lateral laxities are within normal limits. The right lower extremity is placed in a well leg holder. A tourniquet is applied around the mid thigh on the affected left lower extremity. A low-profile leg holder is applied around the tourniquet. The left lower extremity is exsanguinated with an Esmarch. The tourniquet is inflated to 300 mm Hg. Total tourniquet time was 57 minutes. Prep and drape of the left lower extremity in the usual manner.

Knee arthroscopy was done using two portals, anterolateral and anteromedial. The arthroscope was inserted anterolaterally. Instrumentation is through the anteromedial portal. Inflow is through the sheath of the arthroscope. There is a very small amount of normal appearing synovial fluid inside the knee joint.

There is a mild amount of cartilage debris inside the joint. The suprapatellar pouch looks normal. The patellofemoral joint has normal tracking. There are very mild degenerative changes in the patellofemoral joint with fraying of the articular cartilage. In the medial gutter there is a plica extending towards the fat pad, making visualization of the medial compartment somewhat difficult. The 4.5 resector is inserted through the anterior medial portal and the medial plica is excised. A partial debridement of the fat pad is performed to improve visualization. The anterior cruciate ligament is completely torn mid substance. The posterior cruciate ligament looks normal. The tibial stump of the anterior cruciate ligament is excised. In the lateral compartment the articular cartilage looks normal. There is a flat horn of the lateral meniscus. There is also some degenerative fraying of the tree edge of the lateral meniscus. The popliteus tendon looks normal. A basket is used to excise the flap tear and the degenerative fraying of the free edge of the lateral meniscus. Next the edge of the meniscus is smoothed using an Oratec chondroplasty probe. In the medial compartment there is a very complex tear of the posterior horn of the medial meniscus. There is significant thinning of the articular cartilage of the medial tibial plateau. There is a large area of grade IV chondromalacia involving the weight-bearing area of the medial femoral condyle. This area is weight bearing at 45 degrees flexion. The complex tear of the posterior horn of the medial meniscus is excised using baskets. The free edge of the meniscus is smoothed using the Oratec chondroplasty probe. The large area of grade IV chondromalacia is treated next. The unstable articular cartilage flaps are completely debrided. The area is almost 4 cm in diameter. A microfracture technique is used to treat the area of grade IV chondromalacia.

The knee is thoroughly irrigated, removing all soft tissue and cartilage debris. The cannulas are removed. The skin portals are closed with 4-0 nylon. 30 cc of Marcaine with epinephrine are injected inside the knee joint. Each portal is also injected with a few ccs of Marcaine without epinephrine.

Patrick Chrup, MD

The patient was transferred to the recovery room and is in good condition.

GODFREY REGIONAL HOSPITAL
123 Main Street • Aldon, FL 77714 • (407) 555-1234

Answers

OPERATIVE REPORT

Patient information:	
Patient name: DOB: MR#:	Date: Surgeon: Anesthetist:

Preoperative diagnosis:

Left leg squamous cell carcinoma

Postoperative diagnosis:

Left leg squamous cell carcinoma

Procedure(s) performed:

Excision of left leg CA with full-thickness skin graft and complex repair of the left thigh.

Anesthesia:

Assistant surgeon:

Description of procedure:

Under local anesthesia with Xylocaine 1% (used about 20 cc) and IV sedation by anesthesiologist, the left leg was prepped with Betadine, sterile towel draped, and incised. The lesion was in the distal leg at the anterior side and it is about 2 cm. I infiltrated the skin at this area and I did circular incision around the lesion, staying about 8 mm from the edge of it. Cut through the skin and subcutaneous tissue and sent the specimen to the pathologist. They told me the margin was free of tumor. Hemostasis was done with cautery.

We were then supposed to do a split-thickness skin graft from the left thigh, but the dermatome was not available, so I had to do it full-thickness skin graft. I cut the skin in the left upper thigh area anteriorly with Xylocaine 1% and used about 12 cc. Then I did an elliptical incision about 3 inches × 1 inch, cut the skin and subcutaneous tissue, took the lesion off, and then mobilized the skin flap on both sides of the thigh, superiorly and inferiorly. Hemostasis was done with cautery. Closed the edges together with chromic.

3-0 without tension, and the subcutaneous tissue and the skin was approximated with nylon 3-0 and a mattress suture. I applied sterile dressing, then cleaned the skin graft from the subcutaneous fat, and applied it over the left leg and sutured it in interrupted layers with nylon 4-0. I applied Vaseline gauze and a cotton ball on the top of it. I tied the suture on top of it and applied sterile dressing. I put an Ace bandage over the dressing of the graft. The patient tolerated the procedure well.

GODFREY REGIONAL HOSPITAL
123 Main Street • Aldon, FL 77714 • (407) 555-1234

Rachel Perez MD

Answers

EXERCISE 37

OPERATIVE REPORT

Patient information:	
Patient name:	Date:
DOB:	Surgeon:
MR#:	Anesthetist:

Preoperative diagnosis:

Osteochondral flap, right patella

INDICATIONS: 14-year-old white male who has had persistent mechanical symptoms as well as effusion in the right knee. MRI was consistent with osteochondral flap of the patella. Alternatives, risks, and possible complications were carefully discussed with him and his family. Operative intervention was desired. Consent was obtained.

Postoperative diagnosis:

Osteochondral flap, right patella

Procedure(s) performed:

Diagnostic arthroscopy, right; debridement osteochondral flap, right knee; drilling, right patella

Anesthesia:

General

Assistant surgeon:

Description of procedure:

EBL: Minimal

TOURNIQUET TIME: 25 minutes at 300 mm Hg

COMPLICATIONS: None apparent

DESCRIPTION OF OPERATION:
The patient was brought to the main operating room and positioned supine. After general anesthesia was adequately obtained, a tourniquet was placed around the right proximal thigh. 1 gm Ancef was given IV. The right lower extremity was prepped and draped in the usual sterile fashion. The limb was elevated and the tourniquet inflated.

The arthroscope was placed through the standard inferolateral portal, with outflow through the superolateral portal, and instrumentation from the inferomedial portal. No effusion was noted upon entering the joint. The patella revealed an osteochondral flap roughly in the central portion of the patella, lining up with the trochlea. It was very unstable, barely being attached in one corner only. It was felt to be irreparable as it was nearly displaced. There was also some fraying of the cartilage surrounding this region. There was also relatively thickened plica (though it did not feel pathologic) noted in the superomedial corner. Gutters otherwise clear; no loose bodies were identified. Medial and lateral compartments were pristine as well as ACL and PCL.

A shaver was placed within the joint and margins were debrided back and again noted to be a very unstable OCD-type lesion. Therefore a grabber was used to remove the two fragments basically falling out of the crater. I then beveled the crater back with the shaver. Through a small stab incision over the dorsum of the patella, I placed multiple .045 drill holes directly into the lesion, visualizing it through the arthroscope. After this, I placed the shaver back in the joint and cleaned out debris and completed the beveling. Then I irrigated out the knee and removed the arthroscopic equipment. I instilled 0.25% Marcaine as we removed the arthroscope. A sterile compression bandage was applied, and the tourniquet was deflated.

The patient was awakened and returned to PAR in stable condition without apparent complication.

Patrick Chung md

GODFREY REGIONAL HOSPITAL
123 Main Street • Aldon, FL 77714 • (407) 555-1234

Answers

OPERATIVE REPORT

Patient information:

Patient name:	Date:
DOB:	Surgeon:
MR#:	Anesthetist:

Preoperative diagnosis:

Left small finger proximal phalanx fracture

INDICATIONS FOR PROCEDURE: The patient is a 29-year-old white male who reports suffering a crush injury to his left non-dominant hand in a press at work. This resulted in small wounds over the hand that have now healed, as well as a fracture of the proximal aspect of the proximal phalanx of the left small finger. He now presents for elective repair of his fracture.

Postoperative diagnosis:

Same

Procedure(s) performed:

Open reduction and K-wire fixation of left small finger proximal phalanx fracture

Anesthesia:

Assistant surgeon:

Description of procedure:

The patient underwent an axillary block and was then brought to the operating room and placed supine on the operating room table. After adequate sedation, the patient's left arm was prepped and draped in the usual sterile fashion. A tourniquet had been placed over the upper arm. The left hand and forearm were exsanguinated with an Esmarch bandage and the tourniquet was deflated to 250 mm Hg pressure. Please note that the tourniquet time for the operation was 25 minutes.

Next, using a zigzag pattern over the proximal aspect of the left small finger, a 15-blade scalpel was used to make a skin incision. Blunt dissection was carried out with tenotomy scissors. Small crossing veins were cauterized with a bipolar cautery. Further dissection identified the extensor tendon over the proximal phalanx. This was incised longitudinally with a fresh 15-blade scalpel. Then with the use of a periosteal elevator, the underlying fracture site was defined.

Using dissection with the periosteal elevator, the fibrous tissue hematoma within the fracture site and a small piece of bone were removed. After this was removed, the area was irrigated with saline solution mixed in with Bacitracin. Next, the fracture site was reduced by rotating the fracture and pulling on the finger. Once there was good reduction of the fracture fragment, K-wires were passed to keep the fracture reduced. Then 0.035 K-wires were used, crossing each other from the ulnar and radial aspects of the finger. The K-wire positions were confirmed using fluoroscopy. After good reduction was achieved, the K-wires were cut. The tourniquet was deflated and hemostasis was achieved with bipolar cautery. The extensor tendon was repaired with running 4-0 Vicryl sutures. Next, the skin was closed with interrupted 4-0 nylon sutures. The wound was then cleaned. Caps were placed on the K-wires. Xeroform and Bacitracin were placed over the K-wires and incision, and 4 × 4 fluffs were placed in between the fingers and around the K-wire pins for padding. The hand was wrapped in cast padding and two 10-plys of 4-inch plaster were applied along the volar and ulnar aspects of the hand to maintain the fingers and hand in reduction. This was then wrapped with 3-inch and 4-inch Ace wraps.

The patient tolerated the procedure well. He was then taken to the PACU for recovery in stable condition.

Patrick Chug MD

GODFREY REGIONAL HOSPITAL
123 Main Street • Aldon, FL 77714 • (407) 555-1234

Answers

EXERCISE 39

OPERATIVE REPORT

Patient information:

Patient name:
DOB:
MR#:

Preoperative diagnosis:

Right hydrocele, possible hernia

Postoperative diagnosis:

Same

Procedure(s) performed:

Right high ligation of hernia sac and hydrocelectomy

Anesthesia:

Assistant surgeon:

Description of procedure:

The patient was brought to the operating room, placed under general anesthesia. After prepping and draping was completed, incision was made in the lower abdominal skin-fold, through the skin with a scalpel, through the subcutaneous tissues with a Bovie exposing the external inguinal ring. The cord was dissected up along with the hernia sac. Circumferential dissection was carried out, and the hernia sac was then carefully dissected away from the cord structures and they were preserved. The sac was divided, rotated upon itself several revolutions, and suture-ligated with 3-0 silk. The hydrocele was then opened and imbricated back with two silk sutures. Hydrocele fluid was expressed. I then closed the subcutaneous tissues with Vicryl, the skin with undyed Vicryl, followed by Mastisol, Steri-Strips, and an OpSite dressing.

The patient tolerated the procedure without any obvious abnormalities.

Patk Adam MD

GODFREY REGIONAL HOSPITAL
123 Main Street • Aldon, FL 77714 • (407) 555-1234

Answers

RADIOLOGY REPORT

MR#:
DOB:
Dr.

Clinical summary:

DIAGNOSIS:
Follow-up, both-bone forearm fracture

PART TO BE EXAMINED:
Right forearm

Abdomen:

Conclusion:

TWO VIEWS OF THE RIGHT FOREARM:
Comparison is made with previous views of the right forearm dated 7-3-xx. On today's exam an overlying cast obscures bony detail. The previously described fractures of the distal right radial and ulnar shafts are again demonstrated. The fracture involving the distal right radial shaft has been reduced, and the previously described signi cant palmar angulation is no longer present. Alignment of the radial fracture fragment is satisfactory. As previously described, the distal right ulnar shaft fracture is an incomplete fracture. Once again, I can only con rm normal alignment of the radial head with the capitellum on one view, and thus if radial head dislocation is a clinical consideration, I would recommend AP and lateral views of the right elbow in further evaluation.

Ddt/mm

D:
T:

_____
Lisa Valhas, M.D.   Date

GODFREY REGIONAL HOSPITAL
123 Main Street • Aldon, FL 77714 • (407) 555-1234

Answers

RADIOLOGY REPORT

MR#:
DOB:
Dr.

Clinical summary:

Abdomen:

Conclusion:

MRA EXAMINATION OF THE CAROTID ARTERIES:
Time-of-flight and phase-contrast technique used. There is mild to moderate motion artifact, which compromises the images. The common external and internal carotid arteries bilaterally do contain signal and no gross abnormality is noted. The vertebral arteries bilaterally also contain flow.

MRI EXAMINATION OF THE CIRCLE OF WILLIS:
Right and left carotid arteries, proximal anterior, middle, and posterior cerebral arteries, and distal basilar artery are imaged and these vessels contain flow. No definite evidence of a focal aneurysm by this method of imaging.

The internal carotid arteries near the base of the skull on either side not well imaged on the MRA examination.

Ddt/mm

D:
T:

_____
Lisa Valhas, M.D.   Date

GODFREY REGIONAL HOSPITAL
123 Main Street • Aldon, FL 77714 • (407) 555-1234

Answers

RADIOLOGY REPORT

MR#:
DOB:
Dr.

Clinical summary:

CLINICAL INFORMATION:
Chest nodule

Abdomen:

Conclusion:

CT OF THE CHEST:
There is a prior chest radiograph obtained four years ago. The patient's recent chest radiograph, obtained at a Godfrey Regional Hospital, has not been delivered for review.

Axial scans were obtained through the chest at 10-mm intervals. Subsequently, 2-mm scans were obtained though a 10-mm nodule in the left upper lobe. Subsequently, the patient was given 150 ccs of Isovue intravenously, and axial scans were obtained through the chest at 7-mm intervals. Following this, 2-mm scans were obtained through the nodular density in the left upper lobe.

The slightly ovoid lobule in the left upper lobe measures 10 mm in diameter. It has a Hounsfield density of 27 on the pre-enhanced images and approximately 28 on the post-enhanced images. This indicates that it is not enhancing.

Since the nodule was apparently identifiable on a chest radiograph, it must contain sufficient calcification to be identifiable at this small size. Hounsfield measurements are probably artifactually low due to partial volume affect. For this reason, the finding is most consistent with small granuloma. Review of an old chest radiograph obtained here two years ago shows a marginal density overlying the left 7th rib in about this location, so it has probably been present since that time.

When the old chest radiograph arrives, we will compare it with the current study.

No additional pulmonary abnormality is identified. The major bronchi are normal. The hilar mediastinal structures are normal.

Scans into the upper abdomen show numerous calculi in the gallbladder. The adrenals are normal.

1. Small non-enhancing nodule left upper lobe (see discussion above)
2. The old radiographs will be reviewed when they arrive.
3. Cholelithiasis

Ddt/mm

D:
T:

_____
Lisa Valhas, M.D.   Date

GODFREY REGIONAL HOSPITAL
123 Main Street • Aldon, FL 77714 • (407) 555-1234

Answers

EXERCISE 43

OPERATIVE REPORT

Patient information:	
Patient name:	Date:
DOB:	Surgeon:
MR#:	Anesthetist:

Preoperative diagnosis:

1. Endometrial hyperplasia treated with Provera; this is a re-evaluation
2. Stenotic cervix

Postoperative diagnosis:

FINDINGS:
1. Uterus six weeks size, severe retroversion
2. Severe scarring of the cervical os, impenetrable with Pratt dilator and lacrimal duct. Ultrasound guidance was used to aid in the dilatation but was unable to be done secondary to scarring.
3. Ultrasound findings as above

Procedure(s) performed:

Attempted cervical dilatation and curettage that could not be done; scar tissue was far too thick; lacrimal ducts were used; surgeon unable to safely develop a canal into the endocervical canal; ultrasound guidance was used, endometrium was found to be 1.2 mm thick, retroverted uterus, simple cyst on the right ovary, 2 × 1 cm, no change times one year. Attempt to dilate with guidance still failed secondary to severe scarring and distortion of the endocervical canal. The procedure was not able to be adequately done at this time.

Anesthesia:

Light mask anesthesia

Assistant surgeon:

Description of procedure:

After obtaining informed consent, the patient was taken to the operating room and placed in the dorsal supine position, and placed under light mask anesthesia. The patient was prepped and draped in the usual sterile fashion. She was placed in the lithotomy position with Allen stirrups. Weighted speculum was placed in her introitus after being prepped and draped. Single-tooth tenaculum was placed in the 12 o'clock position of the cervix. She was attempted to be dilated with Pratt dilators but an adequate cervical opening could not be found. Lacrimal ducts were used from the smallest size to the medium size; unable to penetrate the external os through various attempts at cervical opening. Ultrasound was called in for ultrasound guidance. The uterus was found to be retroverted, and a 1.2-mm simple cyst was noted on the right ovary, unchanged from previous evaluation. Again, attempts were made to dilate under ultrasound guidance, and again, no tract could be made from the external os at all through several attempts secondary to the thin endometrial lining. As the result of the difficulty and inability to properly dilate, the procedure was deemed completed at this time.

The patient was taken to the recovery room in stable condition. Instrument counts and sponge counts were correct times two.

COMPLICATIONS: Severe scarring

ESTIMATED BLOOD LOSS: Zero

IV FLUIDS: 400 cc

URINE OUTPUT: Not available

Rachel Perez MD

GODFREY REGIONAL HOSPITAL
123 Main Street • Aldon, FL 77714 • (407) 555-1234

Answers

OPERATIVE REPORT

Patient information:

Patient name:
DOB:
MR#:

CONSENT:
Informed consent was obtained from the patient after full
disclosure of risks and indications to the patient.

Preoperative diagnosis:

Elevated liver enzymes

Postoperative diagnosis:

Same

Procedure(s) performed:

Subcutaneous liver biopsy

Anesthesia:

Assistant surgeon:

Description of procedure:

After obtaining informed consent, the patient was brought in the room and put in a left lateral position. IV line was maintained,
IV sedation was given with 2 mg Ativan prior to the procedure. Then the area of the liver span was mapped out by percussion,
confirmed with ultrasound during expiratory and inspiratory phases. The area of biopsy site was chosen and then the area was
cleaned. The patient was in the supine position. Patient was infiltrated with 2% Xylocaine in the skin and the deeper tissue all
the way up to the liver capsule. A small nick was made on the skin with a scalpel, 1 cm to 1/2 inch deep, and then the ASAP
gun was introduced and advanced all the way into the liver capsule. The patient was asked to hold her breath and then we
inserted the ASAP gun into the liver. We obtained core biopsy, which was immediately taken out and sent for histopathology.

Follow up with routine post-biopsy instructions.

Patk Adam MD

GODFREY REGIONAL HOSPITAL
123 Main Street • Aldon, FL 77714 • (407) 555-1234

Answers

OPERATIVE REPORT

Patient information:

Patient name:
DOB:
MR#:

Date:
Surgeon:
Anesthetist:

Preoperative diagnosis:

1) Recurrent, and chronic ethmoid and maxillary sinusitis; 2) Bilateral inferior turbinate hypertrophy; 3) Septal deformity; 4) Nasal obstruction

INDICATION:
51-year-old female with history of recurrent and chronic sinusitis, confirmed on exam and CT scan. She also has a nasal obstruction secondary to bilateral inferior turbinate hypertrophy and a traumatic septal deformity.

Postoperative diagnosis:

Same

Procedure(s) performed:

1. Bilateral endoscopic anterior ethmoidectomy
2. Bilateral endoscopic maxillary antrostomy
3. Bilateral inferior turbinate reduction with radiofrequency

Anesthesia:

Assistant surgeon:

Description of procedure:

After consent was obtained, the patient was taken to the operating room and placed on the operative table in a supine position. After an adequate level of IV sedation was obtained, the patient was draped in an appropriate manner for a nasal and sinus surgery. The patient's nose was packed with cotton pledgets soaked with 4% cocaine. After several minutes, intranasal injection of 1% Xylocaine with 1:100,000 units epinephrine was made. Nasal hairs were trimmed. Attention first focused on the right side. Utilizing the sinuscope, the middle turbinate was medialized. Local solution was then infiltrated into the uncinate process. A similar procedure was then performed on the left side. Attention then refocused on the right, where utilizing a sickle knife and microdebrider, the uncinate process was removed. The anterior ethmoids were then cleared of hypertrophic mucosa. The maxillary sinus ostia were then cleared of the hypertrophic mucosa and the ostia were widened in the posterior and inferior directions. Retained secretions were suctioned. The area was then packed with cotton pledgets soaked with 1:50,000 units epinephrine. A similar procedure then performed on the left uncinate process, anterior ethmoids, and maxillary sinus ostia. That area was also packed with cotton pledgets soaked with the epinephrine solution. Subsequently, the inferior turbinates were addressed. The anterior mucosa was treated with the radiofrequency to 400 joules on each side. With completion of this, there was an adequate nasal airway. As such, the septoplasty portion was not performed. She had some mild right anterior septal deformity, septal deflection, and also a left superior mid septal deflection, which at this time did not appear to be obstructing the airway. As such, no further work was done. The ethmoid cavities were then packed lightly with Surgicel and Bacitracin ointment. Nasal dressing was then applied. Patient tolerated the procedure well, and there was no break in technique. Patient was awakened and taken to the recovery room in good condition.

Fluids administered: 800 cc of RL

Estimated blood loss: Less than 25 cc

Preoperative medications: 12 mg of Decadron IV

Maurice Doater, MD

GODFREY REGIONAL HOSPITAL
123 Main Street • Aldon, FL 77714 • (407) 555-1234

Answers

11 Evaluation and Management Services

EXERCISES 1-20

Use the patient charts found in Chapter 3, Exercises 1 through 20, to complete an E & M Worksheet for each exercise.

EXERCISES 21-55

Assign E & M codes for Exercises 21 through 55 as appropriate. The steps reviewed in the diagnostic documentation and E & M worksheets for determining the correct diagnostic and E & M codes may be used for assistance.

CRITICAL THINKING EXERCISES

Also in the following exercises, identify missing elements that would permit items in the chart to be coded at a higher level. Describe how to educate the physician to include this information in the future.

PROGRESS NOTE

Date:		Vital signs:	T	R
Chief complaint:	43-year-old female with right ear pain and sore throat.		P	BP

43-year-old female was seen as a result of having right ear pain for the last 3–4 days. She states the pain radiates to the side of her face and neck. Also complains of sore throat and increased pain to touch underneath her ear. No head pain, neck pain, no cough, cold, flu, no rhinorrhea, no congestion.

ALLERGIES: Codeine

MEDICATIONS: Calan SR 240 mg for HTN

FH/SH: Non-contributory

Physical examination:

Vital Signs: Temp 99.6, pulse 64, respirations 18, BP 128/74

HEENT: Ears show bilaterally clear tympanic membranes. Nose slightly congested. Throat clear. Only slight redness and injection of the peritonsillar region. Submental nodes are markedly tender on right side.

Neck: Supple, full ROM without any limitation

Assessment:

DIAGNOSIS:
Right neck lymphadenopathy, early pharyngitis

Plan:

Patient will be started on Amoxil 500 mg tid

Maurice Doater, MD

Patient name:
DOB:
MR/Chart #:

GODFREY REGIONAL OUTPATIENT CLINIC
3122 Shannon Avenue • Aldon, FL 77712 • (407) 555-7654

Answers

EXERCISE 22

<table>
<tr><td colspan="2">PROGRESS NOTE</td></tr>
<tr><td colspan="2">Date:</td><td>Vital signs:</td><td>T</td><td>R</td></tr>
<tr><td colspan="2">Chief complaint: 44-year-old with fever</td><td></td><td>P</td><td>BP</td></tr>
</table>

Patient presents to the emergency room complaining of fever off and on since seven days ago. States he has also had some chills and urinary urgency. Denies sore throat, nausea, vomiting, diarrhea and cough. Also states has been having some low back pain and headache occasionally with the fever.

PMH: HTN   ALLERGIES: Penicillin

MEDICATION: None   SH: Non-smoker, married

Examination:

VITALS: Temp 103.6, pulse 96, respirations 20, BP 168/88
LUNGS: Clear to ausculation, no wheezes or crackles
HEART: Regular rate and rhythm
ABDOMEN: Non-distended, positive bowel sounds, non-tender
LABORATORY FINDINGS:
Chest x-ray shows left lower lobe atelectasis, Urinalysis shows findings compatible with urinary tract infection

Impression:

DIAGNOSIS: Left lower lobe atelectasis

Plan:

Patient will be treated with Cipro for his left lower lobe atelectasis and urinary tract infection symptoms.

Maurice Doater, MD

Patient name:
DOB:
MR/Chart #:

GODFREY REGIONAL OUTPATIENT CLINIC
3122 Shannon Avenue • Aldon, FL 77712 • (407) 555-7654

Answers

EMERGENCY ROOM RECORD

Name:		Age:	ER physician:
		DOB:	

Allergies/type of reaction:	Usual medications/dosages:
None	

Triage/presenting complaint:

53-year-old unresponsive

Initial assessment: This 53-year-old male patient comes to the emergency room after being found unresponsive. Patient has a known history of lung carcinoma and has been told to expect this outcome at some time in the near future. Patient was found by paramedics in sinus bradycardia with a pressure. IV started and patient was intubated on the scene. Atropine and epinephrine were administered on several occasions without development of a pressure. Patient placed on pacemaker but no pressure or pulse developed.

Time	T	P	R	BP	Other:					

Medication orders:

Lab work:

X-Ray:

PhysicianÕs report:

PAST MEDICAL HISTORY: Lung carcinoma
MEDICATIONS: Unknown
SOCIAL HISTORY/FM: Unknown
REVIEW OF SYSTEMS: Unable to elicit from patient
PHYSICAL EXAM:
On arrival, no pulse, no respirations, no blood pressure, undergoing cardiopulmonary resuscitation. Pupils fixed and dilated, corneal reflexes absent. Heart sounds not heard, no spontaneous respiratory effort. No peripheral pulses, femoral pulses felt. Patient has been unresponsive without blood pressure or pulse for approximately 45–50 minutes and pronounced dead.

Diagnosis:	Physician sign/date
Cardiorespiratory arrest History of lung carcinoma	*Maurice Doater, MD*

Discharge	Transfer	Admit	Good	Satisfactory	Other:

GODFREY REGIONAL HOSPITAL
123 Main Street • Aldon, FL 77714 • (407) 555-1234

Answers

EXERCISE 24

PROGRESS NOTE

Date:		Vital signs:	T		R	
Chief complaint:	54-year-old female 2 week history of abdominal pain		P		BP	

HISTORY OF PRESENT ILLNESS:
This 54-year-old female known to this practice presents due to abdominal pain, primary mid-abdominal and epigastric area. Pain has lasted approximately two weeks. Accompanied by nausea, and vomiting and diarrhea. Some vomitus has had blood streaks in it and she has had some slight red rectal bleeding. Has already had a gallbladder workup which was negative. Has no history of ulcer disease, pancreatitis. No chest pain.
PAST MEDICAL HISTORY:
Arthritis, hypertension, hypothyroidism. Status post hysterectomy, bilateral salpingoophorectomy.

Examination:

VITAL SIGNS: BP 184/94, pulse 104, temp 96.7
CHEST: Clear
HEART: Unremarkable
ABDOMEN: Soft, some tenderness in epigastric area
LABORATORY FINDINGS:
CBC showed hematocrit of 43, WBC of 7100, platelet count of 327,000 and amylase returned at 502. Abdominal series was negative.

Impression:

DIAGNOSIS: Acute pancreatitis

Plan:

I spoke with the patient at length regarding the need for hospitalization to stabilize her condition. She consented and arrangements were made for her direct admission. I will see her later this afternoon at the hospital.

Maurice Doates, MD

Patient name:
DOB:
MR/Chart #:

GODFREY REGIONAL OUTPATIENT CLINIC
3122 Shannon Avenue • Aldon, FL 77712 • (407) 555-7654

Answers

PROGRESS NOTE

Date:	Vital signs:	T	R
Chief complaint: 74-year-old female with rapid heartbeat		P	BP

Patient is status post coronary bypass grafting approximately one year ago. Today, she developed a rapid pulse of approximately 145, no chest pain, no SOB, but indicates she felt weak as a result.

PAST MEDICAL HISTORY: As above

MEDICATIONS: Verapamil, dogixon, Coumadin, Iron

Physical examination:

VITAL SIGNS: BP 150/66, pulse 136, and irregular, temp 97.2
CHEST: Clear
HEART: Rhythm is irregular
ABDOMEN: Soft and non-tender
LABORATORY FINDINGS:
ECG showed atrial flutter 125–245. Chest x-ray showed cardiomegaly.
Patient given 5 mg Verapamil and converted to sinus rhythm at a rate of 85 almost immediately. Patient will be admitted to Cardiology Services at the hospital.

Assessment:

DIAGNOSIS:
Atrial flutter, converted
Cardiomegaly

Plan:

Felix Warden M

Patient name:
DOB:
MR/Chart #:

GODFREY REGIONAL OUTPATIENT CLINIC
3122 Shannon Avenue • Aldon, FL 77712 • (407) 555-7654

Answers

EXERCISE 26

Date:	Vital signs:	T	R
Chief complaint: 19-year-old female with headache		P	BP

This 19-year-old female was seen in the emergency room approximately four days ago with complaint of headache and underwent a CAT scan and lumbar puncture at that time. She was discharged from the ER on unknown medications and presents today with complaint of continuing headache, worse when she stands up and better when she lies down. Experiences vomiting when upright, no hematemesis, had diarrhea, but none presented. No abdominal pain, no rashes, no diplopia, blurred vision, numbness, tingling of extremities, no back pain.

FAMILY HISTORY: Diabetes

MEDICATIONS: Other than those prescribed in ER, none

ALLERGIES: None

Examination:

VITAL SIGNS: Temp 98.4, pulse 84, BP 110/68

NECK: Supple, no cervical adenopathy, oral mucosa pink, moist

HEART: Regular rate and rhythm without murmur

ABDOMEN: Non-tender and soft, no guarding, rigidity, no masses

Impression:

DIFFERENTIAL DIAGNOSIS:
Probably post LP headache. Possible syndrome gastroenteritis.

Plan:

TREATMENT:
Patient will be admitted to observation status for 23 hour stay and evaluation.

Felix Wander MD

Patient name:
DOB:
MR/Chart #:

GODFREY REGIONAL OUTPATIENT CLINIC
3122 Shannon Avenue • Aldon, FL 77712 • (407) 555-7654

Answers

HISTORY AND PHYSICAL EXAMINATION

Admitted:

Medical record number:

CHIEF COMPLAINT: 59-year-old with chest pain

This 59-year-old patient presents for admission with a prior history of "small vessel disease" in her heart per the patient and chest pain that developed today. She was seen in my office at approximately 1:00 P.M. today where she developed chest pain, dull aching pain in her chest which radiated into the left chest, across over to the right, down her left arm. She was experiencing shortness of breath and nausea and was administered Nitroglycerin and sent her for admission and further evaluation and treatment.

Past medical history:

Some of her old records are not available. However, patient has no history of myocardial infarction, and a negative heart cath in 19XX at which time her previous cardiologist reported she had small vessel disease. She also has hypertension and diabetes.

Family and social history:

Heart disease in grandmother and brother
Previous smoker

Review of systems:

Physical exam:

VITAL SIGNS: Stable

HEART: Regular

ABDOMEN: Soft, non-tender

EXTREMITIES: No peripheral edema, calf tenderness

EKG shows sinus rhythm. Chest x-ray normal, cardiac enzymes were normal. She is being admitted for further evaluation and treatment at this time.

Laboratory/radiology:

X-ray

Assessment:

DIAGNOSIS: Chest pain, Hypertension, Diabetes

Plan:

Maurice Doates, MD

GODFREY REGIONAL HOSPITAL
123 Main Street • Aldon, FL 77714 • (407) 555-1234

Answers

EXERCISE 28

EMERGENCY ROOM RECORD

Name:		Age:	ER physician:
		DOB:	

Allergies/type of reaction:	Usual medications/dosages:
	None

Triage/presenting complaint:

24-year-old vaginal bleeding with fall

Initial assessment:

Patient is a 24-year-old female who states she slipped and fell today and landed directly on her left side. Right after she fell, she began having lower abdominal pain and vaginal bleeding. She states her menstrual cycle completed approximately 7–10 days ago. She denies vaginal discharge.

Time	T	P	R	BP	Other:				

Medication orders:

Lab work:

X-Ray:

PhysicianŌs report:

REVIEW OF SYSTEMS:
Denies neck or head trauma or pain, chest pain, shortness of breath. Denies vomiting, fever, chills, diarrhea, dysuria, pelvic pain.
SH/FH: Non-contributory
MEDICATIONS: None
PMH/SURGICAL HISTORY: None
PHYSICAL EXAMINATION:
VITAL SIGNS: Temp 98.8, pulse 114, BP 96/69
HEENT: Pupils, equal round and reactive to light
NECK: Supple, non-tender
CHEST: Clear to auscultation
HEART: Regular rate and rhythm no murmurs, gallops, rubs
ABDOMEN: Showed tenderness to deep palpation mid lower abdomen as well as right lower quadrant and left lower quadrant
PELVIC: Shows blood at the introitus. Speculum exam showed blood in the vaginal vault cleared with approximately six large swabs equal to approximately 1/2 cup. Exam showed no lacerations or tears.

Diagnosis:	Physician sign/date
Acute abdominal pain, status post fall Vaginal bleeding Rule out possible ruptured ovarian cyst Possible hematoma intra-abdominal injury	*Nancy Caudly MD*

Discharge	Transfer	Admit	Good	Satisfactory	Other:

GODFREY REGIONAL HOSPITAL
123 Main Street • Aldon, FL 77714 • (407) 555-1234

Answers

PROGRESS NOTE

Chief complaint: *Maid with knee pain*

Date: _____

Vital signs: BP_____   P_____   R_____

History:

Established patient returns complaining of pain behind her left knee for about one week. She works as a maid and does some strenuous work but doesn't recall any specific injury. On examination, she has marked tenderness over the popliteal area on the left, none on the right. Negative Homans̄ sign. Calf on the left measures 1/4 inch greater than right. She has no chest pain, no shortness of breath. Note she indicates she has had similar pains in the past, which were treated with anti-inflammatories and muscle relaxants with good results.

Exam:

Diagnosis/assessment:

Leg pain, cannot rule out DVT

Prescribe Naprosyn, use elevation and heat. Schedule her for Doppler study ASAP.

Maurice Doater, MD

Patient name: _____

Date of service: _____

GODFREY REGIONAL OUTPATIENT CLINIC
3122 Shannon Avenue • Aldon, FL 77712 • (407) 555-7654

Answers

OUTPATIENT CLINIC NOTE

| Date: | Vital signs: | T | | R | |
| Chief complaint: Walk in with cold, sore throat and chest | | P | | BP | |

Patient walked in today saying she had a cold, sore throat and chest from coughing. Her symptoms started approximately one week ago. She has nasal congestion, yellow in color.

Physical examination:

Temperature is 100.5. Cerumen is noted in right ear canal. Unable to visualize tympanic membrane. Left ear canal is bulging and translucent. No pre or postauricular nodes. Nasal mucosa edematous and erythematous. Does have some anterior cervical adenopathy. Posterior pharynx is pink. Lungs are clear after cough, cough is in upper airway.

Assessment:

DIAGNOSIS:
Sinusitis
Allergic rhinitis
Upper respiratory infection

Plan:

Felix Wanda MD

| Patient name: |
| DOB: |
| MR/Chart #: |

GODFREY REGIONAL OUTPATIENT CLINIC
3122 Shannon Avenue • Aldon, FL 77712 • (407) 555-7654

Answers

PROGRESS NOTE

Date: 09/01/XX	Vital signs:	T		R	
Chief complaint: Temperature		P		BP	

09/01/XX	This 3-year-old male comes in with a temperature of 100.5 degrees. Denies any pain, but mother has noted him to be lethargic. Patient has had frequent ear infections in the past. He also has history of strep throat.

Physical examination:

Alert male, lethargic, but responsive
Not in acute respiratory distress
TEMPERATURE: 101, Pulse 120, BP 120/80
NECK: No lymphadenopathy or stiffness. Full ROM
LUNGS: Clear with upper respiratory sound, but no wheezing
CARDIAC: Regular rate and rhythm
HEENT: Reveals dull red right TM. Oropharyngeal exam normal.

Assessment:

Right otitis media

Plan:

Treat with Zithromaz 200 per 5.
Given Auralgan suspension, 3 drops to right ear.

Felix Wander M

Patient name: John Roberts
DOB: 4/1/XX
MR/Chart #: 65487

GODFREY REGIONAL HOSPITAL
123 Main Street • Aldon, FL 77714 • (407) 555-1234

Answers

EXERCISE 32

EMERGENCY ROOM RECORD

Name: Stacy Moor	Age: 3	ER physician: Nancy Connelly
	DOB: 5/4/XX	

Allergies/type of reaction:	Usual medications/dosages:
None	

Triage/presenting complaint:

Hurt shoulder

Initial assessment:

3-year-old complains of shoulder pain

Time	T	P	R	BP	Other:					

Medication orders:

Lab work:

X-Ray:

PhysicianŌs report:

3-year-old seen with history of trauma to right shoulder. Mom was lifting him up.
On exam, he has both internal and external flexion and extension, abduction and adduction.
Bursitis
Parents reassured; if symptoms persist will x-ray

Diagnosis:	Physician sign/date
Bursitis	*Nancy Connelly* MD

Discharge	Transfer	Admit	Good	Satisfactory	Other:

GODFREY REGIONAL HOSPITAL
123 Main Street • Aldon, FL 77714 • (407) 555-1234

Answers

PROGRESS NOTE

Date: 06/14/XX	Vital signs:	T	R
Chief complaint: Finger pain		P	BP

06/14/XX	Patient brought in by mom and dad with complaint of smashing 2 middle fingers in a cart. The child is crying because of pain. Mother states that patient has been regular on immunizations.

Examination:

It looks like he has bluish discoloration with possible crushed injury on tip of his middle finger, both hands. X-rays show questionable hairline fracture of the distal phalanx tip of the left middle finger.

Impression:

Plan:

Plan to keep icing the area and use Capital with Codeine 1 tsp q 8 hr for the next 2 days. Follow up in office next Monday and use finger protectors.

Maurice Doater, MD

Patient name: Darryl Hanson
DOB: 3/19/XX
MR/Chart #: 65465

GODFREY REGIONAL OUTPATIENT CLINIC
3122 Shannon Avenue • Aldon, FL 77712 • (407) 555-7654

Answers

OUTPATIENT RECORD

Date: 06/11/XX	Vital signs:	T	R
Chief complaint:		P	BP

SUBJECTIVE:
Patient brought in by father with complaint that he fell from a tree about 5 feet yesterday afternoon. Injured his right arm and right knee. No significant swelling or bruising noted. He started having more pain today. On twisting his arm, they decided to come in and get it evaluated.

Physical examination:

OBJECTIVE:
On exam, he has good power and strength in his left upper and right upper extremity. He is able to pronate and supinate with good ROM. Able to flex and extend his arm against resistance. Mild tenderness on dorsal aspect of left forearm. Otherwise unremarkable exam. Right knee exam within normal limits. Good ROM. Lachman's and drawer signs are negative. Mild bruising over anterior aspect of knee just below the patella. X-rays of left forearm and elbow are done, x-ray of right knee also. No obvious fracture of injuries seen.

Assessment:

Soft tissue injuries of left forearm and right knee.

Plan:

Will start on Ibuprofen 400 mg po q 8 h pn for 5 days.
Use ice packs every 6–8 hours.

Felix Warden MD

	Patient name:
	DOB:
	MR/Chart #:

GODFREY REGIONAL HOSPITAL
123 Main Street • Aldon, FL 77714 • (407) 555-1234

Answers

EMERGENCY ROOM RECORD

| Name: | Age: 12 | ER physician: |
| Timothy Rodriguez | DOB: 8/3/19XX | Nancy Connelly |

Allergies/type of reaction:

Usual medications/dosages:

Triage/presenting complaint:

Wasp sting

Initial assessment:

Wasp sting in child with history of asthma

| Time | T | P | R | BP | Other: | | | | |

Medication orders:

Benadryl 25 mg po

Lab work:

X-Ray:

PhysicianŌs report:

Patient brought with complaint that a wasp stung the boy in back of his left ear. Been putting ice on the area. Boy has past medical history for asthma. Stating he feels dizzy and feels SOB. Peak flow done averaging 240.
LUNGS: Clear bilaterally
ABDOMEN: Soft non-tender
HEENT: Unremarkable
CARDIAC: Stable
EXTREMITIES: Good skin turgor

Diagnosis:

Insect bite from wasp

Physician sign/date

Nancy Connelly MD

| Discharge | Transfer | Admit | Good | Satisfactory | Other: |

GODFREY REGIONAL HOSPITAL
123 Main Street • Aldon, FL 77714 • (407) 555-1234

Answers

EXERCISE 36

PROGRESS NOTE

Date: 09/20/XX	Vital signs:	T	R
Chief complaint: Ear pain		P	BP

09/20/XX	7-year-old with history of recurrent otitis media externa. S/P 3 PE tube placements. Comes in with yellowish drainage from ear with pain on right side. No upper respiratory symptoms such as cough, cold, fevers, chills.

Examination:

Alert, oriented, not in acute distress.
Ear: Reveals yellowish drainage with significant swelling external auditory canal. Rest of HEENT is unremarkable.
Neck: Reveals no lymphadenopathy or stiffness
Lung: Clear to auscultation and percussion

Impression:

Plan:

Right otitis media and externa, S/P tube bilat
Will treat with Corticosporin susp 3 drops rt ear
Zithromax 200 per 5.
Return for recheck in 7–10 days.

William Obst MD

Patient name: Brianna Morten
DOB: 6/6/XX
MR/Chart #: 98788

GODFREY REGIONAL HOSPITAL
123 Main Street • Aldon, FL 77714 • (407) 555-1234

Answers

OUTPATIENT RECORD

Date: 07/07/XX	Vital signs:	T		R	
Chief complaint:		P		BP	

SUBJECTIVE:
Comes in with twisted left ankle. It happened last night around 8 PM. She hit a hole in the driveway while walking which resulted in this incident.
ALLERGIES: None
CURRENT MEDS: Prozac and Synthroid

Physical examination:

OBJECTIVE:
Alert, oriented female. BP 102/68, respirations 18, pulse 72. Temp 98 degrees. O2 sat 98% on room air.
Left ankle minimally swollen, tender over the lateral malleolar area. Good range of motion. Good pulses.
X-ray reveals no fracture.

Assessment:

Left ankle sprain.

Plan:

Elevate the leg, ice, immobilize with Swede-O splint. Give Tylox 5 tablets,
1–2 tablets 3 times a day for pain.

Maurice Doates, MD

	Patient name:
	DOB:
	MR/Chart #:

GODFREY REGIONAL HOSPITAL
123 Main Street • Aldon, FL 77714 • (407) 555-1234

Answers

PROGRESS NOTE

Date: 03/17/XX	Vital signs:	T		R	
Chief complaint:			P		BP

SUBJECTIVE:
5-year-old comes in with his father complaining of stiffness over the right side of the neck. About an hour earlier, his shirt was caught in a machine that pulled him towards it but he was able to extricate himself. Then started complaining of pain and stiffness. Prior to this, no upper respiratory symptoms, ear pain, sore throat, cough or phlegm. No fever, no chills.

Examination:

OBJECTIVE:
Alert male, no acute distress. Weight 59 pounds. Pulse 100, Temperature 98.4 degrees. Examination of the right neck reveals a tense trapezius muscle. There is no lymphadenopathy. The muscle is more tense when he is upright than when he is lying down.
LUNGS: Clear
HEENT: Unremarkable

Impression:

ASSESSMENT:
Torticollis, right trapezius muscle

Plan:

Apply ice. Ibuprofen 200 mg tid for 3 days. Rest.

Felix Warden MD

Patient name:
DOB:
MR/Chart #:

GODFREY REGIONAL HOSPITAL
123 Main Street • Aldon, FL 77714 • (407) 555-1234

Answers

PROGRESS NOTE

Date: 06/13/XX	Vital signs:	T	R
Chief complaint: Insomnia		P	BP

06/13/XX

This 45-year-old has a 6 month history of insomnia. She also has had hypercholesterolemia for the past 4 years, most recently her serum cholesterol was 292. She has been given Niacin in doses of 2000 mg daily; however, it only dropped to 262. She also gets "weepy" pre-menstrual.

Allergies: Codeine

Review of systems:
Some bloating after meals. Has urinary frequency and has extremely cold extremities where she wears gloves in the house in the winter.

Family history:
Mother had valvular heart disease, colitis, and gallstones. Father had heart attack. Brother has stomach problems.
Habits: Drinks coffee and rare alcohol.

Examination:

Impression:

ASSESSMENT:
Borderline hypercholesterolemia
Reactive hypoglycemia
Insomnia
Pre-menstrual syndrome
Cold extremities and dry skin

Plan:

Will refer to psychologist as her insominia seems to be triggered by several social stressors in her life at this time.

Maurice Doater, MD

Patient name: Alberta Rhode
DOB: 4/2/XX
MR/Chart #: 32121

GODFREY REGIONAL HOSPITAL
123 Main Street • Aldon, FL 77714 • (407) 555-1234

Answers

Chapter **11 Evaluation and Management Services**

EMERGENCY ROOM RECORD

Name:	Age: 19	ER physician:
Jessica Carol	DOB: 4/20/XX	Nancy Connelly

Allergies/type of reaction:	Usual medications/dosages:

Triage/presenting complaint:

Seizures

Initial assessment:

Time	T	P	R	BP	Other:				

Medication orders:

Lab work:

X-Ray:

Physician's report:

19-year-old comes in today brought by ambulance with grand mal seizure times four. She has been seizing every 1-2 minutes for 30 seconds. Had upper extremity jerking. Gave her some Valium IV to start an IV and switched to IV Ativan. Seizures do not appear normal. Jerks to the upper extremities in an odd-like fashion with forward flexion and extension of her arms. Talked to her mom out in the hall and questioned whether the seizures were real. Does have some psychological issues. Psych just took her off antidepressants due to drug interactions. Vital signs are stable. Cranial nerves II through XII intact. TMs clear. Pharynx is clear.

IMPRESSION: Pseudoseizures

Diagnosis:	Physician sign/date
Pseudoseizures	*Nancy Connelly* MD
Discharge Transfer Admit Good Satisfactory	Other:

GODFREY REGIONAL HOSPITAL
123 Main Street • Aldon, FL 77714 • (407) 555-1234

Answers

OFFICE NOTE

Date:	Vital signs:	T		R	
Chief complaint:		P		BP	

77-year-old comes in with pain in all the limbs, specifically the left elbow that has become swollen and tender. Patient has past history of gout in both ankles. States that the left elbow is swollen and has difficulty bending his arm. Unsure if he fell down. States that when he woke up this morning, his mattress was on the other side of the room and he was sleeping on the floor. Patient comes in with his nephew who confirms the above finding. Patient also has recently begun remembering events a little differently; however, is able to provide a history consistently without any problems.

MEDICATIONS: Cardura, Toprol, Softnen, nitro, Lanoxin, and Coumadin.

ALLERGIES: No known drug allergies.

Examination:

Alert and oriented times three; does not appear to be in any acute distress, does not appear to be dehydrated. T. 99.1, P. 49, R. 20, BP 137/88, saturating 97% on room air.

HEENT: PERRLA, EOML. Anicteric sclerae. Throat clear.

CHEST: Clear.

ABDOMEN: Soft, nontender.

EXTREMITIES: No edema, no cyanosis. Left elbow is swollen and tender.

LABS AND X-RAYS: CBC shows WBC 11.4, hemoglobin 16.1, hematocrit 46.5, platelets 149. X-rays of the left elbow do not show any specific fracture; however, questionable area of the left medial epicondyle. Either it has bony spur or is slightly moved away.

Impression:

ASSESSMENT: Most likely gouty arthritis.

Plan:

Will start on Celebrex 100 mg po bid. 15 tablets were given from the clinic. Also patient does not appear to take care of himself on a regular basis, and he does require some degree of assistance. Will get County Services involved for his health care. Patient advised to follow up with family physician in the next couple of days and was discharged from the clinic in stable condition.

Willen Obt MD

	Patient name:
	DOB:
	MR/Chart #:

GODFREY REGIONAL OUTPATIENT CLINIC
3122 Shannon Avenue • Aldon, FL 77712 • (407) 555-7654

Answers

EMERGENCY ROOM RECORD

Name:		Age:	ER physician:
		DOB:	

Allergies/type of reaction:	Usual medications/dosages:
Penicillin and Naprosyn.	Lanoxin, 125 mg qd; isosorbide 30 mg half tablet qd; Lasix 20 mg one tablet bid; Lotensin 5 mg qd; aspirin one tablet qd; Plavix 75 mg po qd.

Triage/presenting complaint: 86-year-old was brought in for chest pain that was relieved with oxygen. Patient stated it was in the range of 5. By the time she got to the ER, the pain had completely resolved. During this time she was given some nitro that completely resolved the pain. Denies any nausea or vomiting at this time. PAST MEDICAL HISTORY: CHF, angina, hypertension, and peripheral vascular disease.

Initial assessment:

Time	T	P	R	BP	Other:					

Medication orders:

Lab work: CBC shows WBC 7.8, hemoglobin 10.0, hematocrit 131.7, platelets 302. Metabolic panel showed glucose 120, BUN 20, creatinine 1.1, CPK 95. ALT is 117, AST 82, troponin 0, CPK 95.

X-ray: X-rays show cardiomegaly with no evidence of any infiltrate or pleural effusion.

PhysicianÕs report:

PHYSICAL EXAMINATION: Alert and oriented times three. At the time of examination, patient is chest-pain-free. T. 98.0, P. 89, R. 24, BP 128/69, saturating 99% on 3 liters.

HEENT: PERRLA, EOMI. Anicteric sclerae. Throat clear.

CHEST: Bilaterally clear with a few basilar crackles.

CARDIOVASCULAR: S1, S2 normal.

ABDOMEN: Soft, nontender.

EXTREMITIES: No edema, no cyanosis.

CNS: Grossly intact with no focal deficit.

PLAN: Increase isosorbide to 30 mg po qd and increase Lasix to 40 mg po qd. Follow up with primary care physician for the next couple of days. If the pain presents, return to the clinic to seek medical attention or come back to the emergency room.

Patient was discharged in stable condition.

Diagnosis:	Physician sign/date
ASSESSMENT: CHF, angina.	*Robert Rai MD*

Discharge	Transfer	Admit	Good	Satisfactory	Other:

GODFREY REGIONAL HOSPITAL
123 Main Street • Aldon, FL 77714 • (407) 555-1234

Answers

OFFICE NOTE

Chief complaint: _____

Date: _____

Vital signs: BP_____ P_____ R_____

History:

SUBJECTIVE: This 74-year-old white female new patient with a history of polymyalgia presented after suddenly noticing and developing discomfort superficially at the right medial calf on the right lower extremity. She has noticed a knot and a swelling there and is concerned about a possible blood clot. She has a history of significant pulmonary conditions and has been the subject of multiple episodes of pneumonia. She states that she has not had any increased chest pain or shortness of breath.

Exam:

Pulse 81. Respiratory rate 18. Blood pressure 127/76. The patient is not out of breath. Her lungs are clear. Her heart is regular. Evaluation of the right calf shows a superficial clot right over a blood vessel on the medial surface of the calf approximately 1 3 of the way down from the tibial plateau. There is no leaking of fluid down the leg underneath the skin, and the calf muscle itself is flabby and not swollen.

Diagnosis/assessment:

IMPRESSION: Superficial blood vessel rupture, right lower extremity.

PLAN: We asked her to ice the area for the next couple of days and then apply heat to the area. We warned her of possible tracking of blood down the skin toward the ankle. We have given her antiembolic thigh-high stockings that she is to wear for the next 3–7 days, and she is to continue on her aspirin as before. She is to follow up with her primary care doctor on Thursday, to be monitored for potential complications to deep system. She is to return for any chest pain, shortness of breath, or evidence of infection in that area.

Maurice Doater, MD

Patient name: _____

Date of service: _____

GODFREY MEDICAL ASSOCIATES
1532 Third Avenue, Suite 120 • Aldon, FL 77713 • (407) 555-4000

Answers

EMERGENCY ROOM RECORD

Name:	Age:	ER physician:
	DOB:	

Allergies/type of reaction:	Usual medications/dosages:
No known drug allergies.	Aspirin, metoprolol, Lopressor, Lanoxin, Prevacid, Coumadin, isosorbide, K-Dur, lisinopril, Lasix, hydrocodone prn for leg pain, Metamucil.

Triage/presenting complaint:

Initial assessment:

SUBJECTIVE: 73-year-old brought in by family. He comes in with episodes of coughing up blood in the morning—a few red clots. Patient has a history of nasopharyngeal carcinoma. Was given radiation therapy followed by chemotherapy according to patient. Patient states that he had similar episode a long time ago when he was diagnosed with pulmonary congestion. Was put in the hospital at that time. Recently had an extensive evaluation earlier this year for his chest, including CT scanning, etc., which was negative for any mass. Patient states this morning he coughed and saw a couple clots that he spitted out. Denies any fever or chills. No respiratory problem otherwise, no shortness of breath. Patient does feel tired. He has an appointment to see his primary care doctor in the next couple of days for repeat upper endoscopy. No fever, no chills. No urinary symptoms, no joint swelling. No hematemesis, no melena. Appetite has been fairly good; eating OK.

Time	T	P	R	BP	Other:				

Medication orders:

Lab work:

Labs show PT 20, INR 2.78 (therapeutic). CBC shows WBC 5.9, hemoglobin 11.8, hematocrit 33.2, platelet 162. Comprehensive metabolic panel showed glucose of 135, BUN 34, creatinine 1.4. Amylase is 147, CPK 39. Liver function within normal limits, troponin 0.

X-ray:

Chest x-ray shows some degree of cardiomegaly, no pleural effusion. No pulmonary congestion. No mass or infiltrates seen.

Physician's report:

PHYSICAL EXAMINATION: Alert and oriented times three. Does not appear to be in any acute distress. T. 97.4, P. 75, R. 16, BP in the range of 89/53 asymptomatic, saturating 94% on room air.

HEENT: PERRLA, EOMI. Anicteric sclerae. Throat clear.

CHEST: Clear. A few basal crackles.

ABDOMEN: Soft, nontender.

EXTREMITIES: No edema, no cyanosis.

I advised patient to return to the clinic immediately if any further episodes or if he develops any dizziness or increased tiredness or notices any black, tarry stool or hematemesis. Discussed with Dr. Doate regarding patient condition. Will schedule for a CT scan of chest abdomen to look for any reason for elevated amylase. Patient to follow up with Dr. Seers in the next couple of days after the above tests are done. Will also give pain medication, Percocet 1 mg, PO tid to qid for his back pain. Patient was discharged from the ER in stable condition.

Diagnosis:	Physician sign/date
ASSESSMENT: Hemoptysis, apparently no evidence of current bleeding at this time. His blood pressure I have checked in the previous reports and as per patient also; it usually runs low. He otherwise is totally asymptomatic, no evidence of hematemesis or melena. The episodes of hemoptysis were in the morning; hasn't repeated again yet.	*Nancy Cauley* MD

Discharge	Transfer	Admit	Good	Satisfactory	Other:

GODFREY REGIONAL HOSPITAL
123 Main Street • Aldon, FL 77714 • (407) 555-1234

Answers

OFFICE NOTE

Date:		Vital signs:	T	R
Chief complaint:			P	BP

73-year-old fell down at home today while carrying a box. She complains of pain on the mid lateral thigh and in the left hip area. Was brought in by ambulance secondary to difficulty ambulating. This accident happened a couple of hours before she got here. Denies any nausea or vomiting. No numbness or tingling sensation. No loss of consciousness either before the fall or afterwards.

MEDICATIONS: Actos 30 mg a day, Aciphex 20 mg a day, verapamil, doxepin, Zocor, sucralfate.

ALLERGIES: Morphine sulfate, Novocain, and Demerol.

PAST MEDICAL HISTORY: Diabetes, peptic ulcer disease, hypertension, and hypercholesterolemia.

Physical examination:

REVIEW OF SYSTEMS: Patient has a persistent cough, productive for the past several weeks. Has been treated with antibiotics but has not had relief of symptoms—is still putting out greenish sputum. Some degree of chills at home.

Alert and oriented times three, does not appear to be in acute distress. T 98.0, P 70, R 20, BP 122/67, saturating 89%. When she arrived, 97% with 2 liters oxygen. However, when oxygen was taken off later, it was 92% on room air. HEENT: PERRLA, EOMI. Anicteric sclerae. Throat clear. Ears clear. CHEST: coarse rhonchi, no wheezing, no crackles. CARDIOVASCULAR: S1, S2 normal. ABDOMEN: soft. Tenderness in the left hip joint. Straight leg raising test positive. Pain on lateral rotation of the hip; however, can elevate both legs on her own. Muscle power 5/5 all over; reflexes 21.

LAB AND X-RAY: Chest x-ray negative for any infiltrate, pleural effusion, or cardiomegaly. X-ray done of the left hip and pelvis—both negative for fracture or dislocation.

Assessment:

Upper respiratory infection/bronchitis. Negative for any fracture of the hip, most likely contusion or pulled muscle.

Plan:

Advised patient to take it easy. Was put on Percocet one tablet po qid as needed for pain control. Will also start on Zithromax Z-Pak as well for bronchitis and Robitussin-AC 1 tsp, po tid for ten days. Follow up with primary care physician in the next couple of days. Seek medical attention if she develops any severe pain or difficulty walking.

Felix Warden MD

Patient name:
DOB:
MR/Chart #:

GODFREY REGIONAL OUTPATIENT CLINIC
3122 Shannon Avenue • Aldon, FL 77712 • (407) 555-7654

Answers

EXERCISE 46

OFFICE NOTE

Date:	Vital signs:	T	R
Chief complaint:		P	BP

Patient is 4 years old, and her parents bring her in because she sustained trauma to her back and the back of her head. She was sledding down a hill, did not wait as she was asked to, and the sled went down and started to spin around. Finally she hit a tree with her back. She also apparently hit the back of her head. She never had loss of consciousness, cried right away, and has been complaining of back pain since.

The patient is otherwise healthy. Her vaccinations are up to date.

Examination:

PHYSICAL EXAMINATION: Well nourished and developed, no acute distress. Interactive and cooperative. Vital signs are stable. She was actually quite playful also by the end of the interview. HEENT: normocephalic, atraumatic. No pallor or jaundice. Hydration is normal. Both TMs are intact without discharges. Neck supple without lymphadenopathy. Lungs: clear to auscultation. Heart: regular rate and rhythm. No murmurs or tachycardia. Back: no asymmetries, no evidence of trauma. She is a little sore on palpation of the lumbar area without any specific tenderness. Neurological exam is intact. Abdominal exam is negative. Her gait is normal.

Impression:

Status post trauma to the back without loss of consciousness. Concerned for kidney trauma.

Plan:

Will obtain a UA. If this is negative, I think that she should be treated symptomatically with acetaminophen for pain relief. If indeed her UA is negative, as expected, then she will be discharged and asked to come back if she has worsening symptoms.

Jay Corson MD

	Patient name:
	DOB:
	MR/Chart #:

GODFREY REGIONAL OUTPATIENT CLINIC
3122 Shannon Avenue • Aldon, FL 77712 • (407) 555-7654

Answers

EMERGENCY ROOM RECORD

Name:	Age:	ER physician:
	DOB:	

Allergies/type of reaction:	Usual medications/dosages:
Penicillin	Zoloft 50 mg qd and decongestant spray.

Triage/presenting complaint:

CHIEF COMPLAINT: Collapse
An ambulance was summoned to the house after the patient was found collapsed on the floor. No CPR was done when they arrived. ECG initially showed some ventricular fibrillation. A shock was unsuccessful. Intubation was unsuccessful. He then had a Combi-tube placed. CPR was performed throughout, and he was transported to the hospital.

Initial assessment:

Time	T	P	R	BP	Other:					

Medication orders:

Lab work:

X-ray:

Physician's report:

When he arrived, CPR was being done adequately. There was fair to good ventilation of the lungs with a Combi-tube. No IV had been successfully placed. Anesthesia was present and exchanged the Combi-tube for a T-tube. There was good ventilation bilaterally, but his color remained somewhat dusky. He had rhonchi in both lungs. He was in asystole. IVs were started—initially 2 mg of epinephrine through the ET tube, and then additional epinephrine through the IV. He had 2 mg of atropine IV. Attempted external pacing with 120 milliamps output created some muscle movement of pectoralis, but there was no capture of the hearts. He remained asystolic when there was no CPR or pacing and essentially died a cardiac death.

Of note, time down with no CPR before the ambulance arrived was at least 5 minutes, probably closer to 8.

Additional history from family: He had fallen around noon today, and afterwards the family noticed he had a little bit of slurred speech. He has a history of intermittent atrial fibrillation. He is on Coumadin. His son has had coronary stents, and there is a question if he has stents. He has a history of COPD, and near the time he was being evaluated for his cardiovascular unresponsiveness, the family indicated that he had not wanted CPR.

Diagnosis:	Physician sign/date
CAUSE OF DEATH: Probable stroke. Cannot rule out myocardial infarction. Clearly sudden death. Patient with multiple risk factors.	
Usual physician is Dr. Smith. Message has been left for him to call back. No signs of foul play. His daughter and son who live with him were here. Several neighbors were here. Other family members have been contacted. Representative from cathedral has been here. Grandson is here, as well as former daughter-in-law.	*Robert Rai MD*
We are contacting the organ donation group, but because of his age, he is an unlikely organ donor, and no autopsy was requested by us.	

Discharge	Transfer	Admit	Good	Satisfactory	Other:

GODFREY REGIONAL HOSPITAL
123 Main Street • Aldon, FL 77714 • (407) 555-1234

Answers

EXERCISE 48

OFFICE NOTE

Chief complaint: _____

Date: _____

Vital signs: BP_____ P_____ R_____

History:

S: This is a 26-year-old white female who is brought in by friends after she was riding as a passenger on a snowmobile and she fell off the back end. The patient states that she was going about 80 miles an hour. Bystanders say she was only going about 40 miles per hour. They evidently hit a bump, and she went airborne and fell onto her shoulders on a smooth trail. It didn't sound like she hit anything other than the ground. She has pain from the base of her neck down to her tailbone. It seems to be worse in her low back. She does have a history of previous low back injuries. The accident occurred at approximately 2300 hours. She denies any numbness or tingling. She does not have loss of consciousness. She was wearing a helmet.

Exam:

O: On examination, the patient is awake, alert, and appropriate. She is moving all extremities well. She complains of pain mostly in the low back. We palpated in this region with the patient laying flat, and she has tenderness more in the paraspinal muscles than over the spinous processes. She has spasm and tenderness up the paraspinal muscles involving most of her lower thoracic and lumbar spine. Also a little bit in the paraspinal muscles of her cervical spine. Her head was blocked by the nurse as soon as she got here. Lateral C-spine appeared normal down through C7. Therefore, completion of cervical, lumbosacral, and thoracic spine was obtained. She did not appear to have any acute fractures. There is a question of a very slight old compression fracture in her lower thoracic spine, but this was subtle and did not appear to be acute.

Diagnosis/assessment:

A: Contusion, back after falling off a snowmobile. History of low back pain.

P: Cyclobenzaprine 10 mg qhs, Ibuprofen OTC three tablets four times a day. Tylenol in addition to this prn for pain. Recommended being up and walking at least once every hour for about five minutes and to try to avoid any heavy lifting. She is to try and maintain physical activity as much as possible. If she seems to worsen or doesn't improve over the next couple of weeks, then consider follow-up to consider physical therapy. In the meantime, she should use her pain as her guide for her activities.

Felix Wander MD

Patient name: _____

Date of service: _____

GODFREY MEDICAL ASSOCIATES
1532 Third Avenue, Suite 120 • Aldon, FL 77713 • (407) 555-4000

Answers

EMERGENCY ROOM RECORD

Name:	Age:	ER physician:
	DOB:	

Allergies/type of reaction:	Usual medications/dosages:

Triage/presenting complaint:

S: The patient is a 12-year-old child visiting this community for the first time. She was staying with her aunt. She and her aunt had been taking a nap. The aunt woke up, was puttering around the house, and then looked in on the patient when she awakened with a c/o severe headache, c/o numbness on the left side of the face, hand, and leg. The aunt became alarmed and brought her to the ER. When seen in the ER, the child was crying continuously complaining that "it hurts, it hurts." She was nauseated and vomited twice. The location of the pain was not clear, but from time to time, she would describe pain in her head; other times, in her extremities, and would be inconsistent about the complaints. Dimming the lights in the room decreased her complaints. She demonstrated a waxing and waning course with lapsing into rest and calmness for several minutes, followed by an accelerating c/o pain that was nonspecific, followed by vomiting. She exhibited at least two and possibly three of these cycles during the ER period. Attempts to draw blood, insert an IV, and accomplish a CT scan were all met with hysterical objection and strenuous resistance.

Initial assessment:

Time	T	P	R	BP	Other:					

Medication orders:

Lab work:

X-ray:

Physician's report:

O: On physical exam, optic fundi could initially be visualized when she was more cooperative. The optic fundi showed sharp disks and normal vascular pattern. PERRLA. EOMI with no nystagmus or weakness. There was no facial asymmetry. TMs were normal. Oropharynx showed a symmetric palate and tongue motion. There were no palpable masses in the neck. She showed symmetric ROM of upper and lower extremities. DTRs were brisk and symmetric. Romberg normal. Tandem walk normal. Finger pursuit, finger midline, heel shin were normal.

Following the initial examination, her symptoms seemed to deteriorate, and as attempts at diagnostic procedures were made, her level of objection and c/o discomfort accelerated. Over the next hour and a half, an attempt was made to locate an on-call pediatric neurologist to discuss the case. The child's vital signs remained stable throughout that time, although she continued to cry out almost continuously during that waiting period. An adult neurologist was contacted at another hospital who felt that she could not be helpful because she was not a pediatric neurologist.

Finally, a pediatric neurologist was located at another hospital. He agreed that she needed urgent transfer and evaluation under sedation if necessary. Arrangements were made with the ambulance service and she was transferred.

Total patient contact time: 1½ hours

Diagnosis:	Physician sign/date
	Nancy Conoly MD

Discharge	Transfer	Admit	Good	Satisfactory	Other:

GODFREY REGIONAL HOSPITAL
123 Main Street • Aldon, FL 77714 • (407) 555-1234

Answers

EXERCISE 50

OFFICE NOTE

Chief complaint: _____

Date: _____

Vital signs: BP_____ P_____ R_____

History:

This 82-year-old woman, who is a nursing home resident, noted throat irritation after swallowing her pills this morning. For months she has noted shortness of breath in the morning. Her breathing improves over the course of the day. She has no cough or sputum production. She takes nebulized albuterol twice daily. She also has a longstanding history of bladder pressure and feeling that her bladder is not emptying. She also has arthritic pain. She had taken a brief course of Celebrex with significant relief but has now run out. There is a history of cerebral palsy with spasticity. She is known to have an abdominal aneurysm and has chronic anxiety. Her medications are as listed. There is no allergy to medicine.

Exam:

Reveals an alert, pleasant elderly woman. Eyes are clear. Mouth is moist. Throat reveals no redness or swelling. The neck is supple with no adenopathy. There is no heart murmur. Lungs are clear. The abdomen is soft and nontender. There is no bladder distension. There is no calf tenderness or ankle edema. Lab data include a hemoglobin of 12.5; white count is 6600. Urinalysis is negative. Chest x-ray shows COPD but no infiltrate or congestive heart failure.

TREATMENT COURSE: The patient was initially seen by another physician who prescribed Mylanta with Xylocaine that seemed to soothe her throat. She had no difficulty swallowing water. After voiding, a Foley catheter was inserted, and no significant residual urine was found.

Diagnosis/assessment:

1. Throat irritations
2. COPD
3. Neurogenic bladder
4. Degenerative arthritis

DISPOSITION: She is to continue her medications. Her Celebrex, 100 mg bid, was refilled. She and her daughter were told that if she continues to have difficulty swallowing, she will need a barium swallowing study. If she has increased difficulty swallowing, she is to follow up with her personal physician.

Stong Knott MD

Patient name: _____

Date of service: _____

GODFREY MEDICAL ASSOCIATES
1532 Third Avenue, Suite 120 • Aldon, FL 77713 • (407) 555-4000

Answers

OFFICE NOTE

Date:	Vital signs:	T		R	
Chief complaint:		P		BP	

S: Patient presents complaining of bilateral leg aches and left knee pain. He states that this has been bothering him off and on for a long period of time. He has had CVAs in the past. He has diabetes mellitus and alcoholic liver disease. He was sent up to Atlanta about 1–2 weeks ago with alcoholic encephalopathy. They treated him there for a few days and were able to send him home. He has mitral regurgitation and atrial fibrillation. He did have a heart cath about two years ago. He has had a couple CVAs in the past. Current medications are as listed on his ER sheet. He has no known allergies. He states that off and on for the last month his left knee has been painful for him, as have his legs through the upper legs and lower legs. It tends to be fairly nondescript.

Physical examination:

O: On examination, his left knee has a joint effusion and some mild decreased range of motion. Right knee is normal except for some arthritic changes but no effusion. His left knee is not warm to the touch. It is not erythematous. He has scattered areas of tenderness over his thighs and calves. It does not seem to be focused into any one region. There is a little bit of ankle edema but this is fairly typical for him. He has no evidence of respiratory distress at this time and has no other complaints in regards to his heart or lungs.

Assessment:

A: Arthritis, left knee with mild joint effusion; does not appear to be a septic knee. Scattered muscle aches and tenderness, probably related to deconditioning and his chronic health issues.

Plan:

P: Recommended exercise as much as he possibly can. Use Tylenol in limited amounts for his pain. Suggested using approximately half the usual dose of Tylenol, whatever strength he has. Discussed repeatedly and in detail how to split the recommended dose in half for each dose and for total daily requirements, and to try and get by on as little as he can. We discussed the metabolism of Tylenol to the liver and the fact that his liver doesn't "burn it up" as fast as it should. Discussed other procedures that can be done for the knee such as aspiration injection with cortisone, but did not recommend it at this time. We will have him reassess on a prn basis if any problems arise or if he seems to be worsening. Discussed his care at home. His wife does take care of him and they felt they could handle it at home. We offered hospitalization but the patient did not feel that this would be necessary.

Stony Knott, MD

	Patient name:
	DOB:
	MR/Chart #:

GODFREY REGIONAL OUTPATIENT CLINIC
3122 Shannon Avenue • Aldon, FL 77712 • (407) 555-7654

Answers

OFFICE NOTE

Date:	Vital signs:	T		R	
Chief complaint:		P		BP	

Examination:

S: This 62-year-old female with longstanding asthma/COPD was seen last week by her usual physician and diagnosed with bronchitis/pneumonia and started on Levaquin. She took it two days and stated it made her sick to her stomach, so she stopped it. She has now been off of antibiotics for five days. She complains of increased wheezing and cough productive of green sputum. She has been more short of breath and she presents for evaluation.

Examination:

O: On exam, she is afebrile. Temp is 97. Pulse is 92. Respirations are 20. Blood pressure 119/88. O2 sats are 95% on room air. She is alert and oriented 3 3. She is in no obvious distress and only mildly dyspneic at rest. Pupils equal, round, and reactive. Conjunctivae noninjected. TMs nondistended and nonerythematous. Right TM is a little injected. Ear canals are without lesion. Nasopharynx is noncongested with septum midline. Posterior pharynx is mildly erythematous. Neck reveals no lymphadenopathy. Lung sounds revealed diffuse, coarse, expiratory wheezes throughout both lungs. Heart sounds are distant and regular without murmur. Abdomen is obese, soft, and nontender. Extremities are without cyanosis. There is no edema. She was given albuterol with Atrovent nebulization. Her dyspnea improved but she continues to have coarse wheezes. She was given Solu-Medrol 125 mg IM. Chest x-ray shows a questionable early right lower lobe infiltrate. She has a white count of 10,200 with normal differential. Hemoglobin is 14.1. Platelets are 281.

Impression:

A: 1. Early acute right lower lobe pneumonia. 2. Exacerbation of COPD/asthma.

Plan:

P: She is given Zithromax Z-Pak as directed, since she did not tolerate the Levaquin. She will use her albuterol neb. at home as needed. She is also given a Medrol dose pack, which she will start later this afternoon. She will follow up in the clinic if she is not improving over the next 3–4 days.

Jay Carman MD

Patient name:

DOB:

MR/Chart #:

GODFREY REGIONAL OUTPATIENT CLINIC
3122 Shannon Avenue • Aldon, FL 77712 • (407) 555-7654

Answers

OFFICE NOTE

Date:		Vital signs:	T		R	
Chief complaint:			P		BP	

S: 28-year-old gentleman presents with a severe sore throat; is unable to even swallow Tylenol at this time because his throat is so sore. He has had fever and chills today.

Physical examination:

O: On exam, his temp is 98.2. Pulse is 95. Respirations are 20. Blood pressure is 144/23. He is lying on the cot in the exam room with his coat over his shoulders and a blanket over that. He is in moderate distress from his sore throat and he has a muffled sounding voice. His TMs are nondistended and nonerythematous. Conjunctivae are noninjected. Pupils are equal, round, and reactive. Nasopharynx: noncongested with septum midline. Posterior pharynx is very erythematous with large tonsillar hypertrophy and white and yellow exudate seen in the tonsillar crypts. Neck reveals lymphadenopathy along the cervical chain. Lung sounds are clear. Heart is regular rate and rhythm without murmur.

Assessment:

A: Acute tonsillitis/pharyngitis.

Plan:

P: Patient is given Bicillin CR 1.2 milliunits IM. He will rest and take Tylenol as needed for fever, drink plenty of fluids, and follow up if worsening occurs over the course of the next 24 hours or if not improving in the next two days.

Willen Olst MD

	Patient name:
	DOB:
	MR/Chart #:

GODFREY REGIONAL OUTPATIENT CLINIC
3122 Shannon Avenue • Aldon, FL 77712 • (407) 555-7654

Answers

EMERGENCY ROOM RECORD

Name:	Age:	ER physician:
	DOB:	

Allergies/type of reaction:	Usual medications/dosages:

Triage/presenting complaint:

S: This is an 84-year-old white female who became suddenly unresponsive. She was witnessed to go down. The attendant at her nursing home immediately called 911. Upon arrival, the ambulance personnel stated that she appeared to be in a fine fibrillation. She was shocked and went into an asystole, was run through the asystole protocol, and was able to be revived to a PEA but with full-dose atropine and epinephrine 34 and pacing. The best rhythm that could be obtained was a pulseless electrical activity.

Initial assessment:

O: Upon arrival, she was noted to have excellent pulses with CPR in progress. Rhythm appeared to be initially PEA. This degenerated into asystole. CPR was commenced. We gave one more milligram of epinephrine and this again developed some electrical activity of a very wide complex, but no pulse was generated with this. Because of the extremely poor prognosis with this situation, we opted to cease CPR, having gone through the protocol and generating only PEA.

Time	T	P	R	BP	Other:					

Medication orders:

Lab work:

X-ray:

Physician's report:

P: The patient does have cancer and therefore is not a candidate for organ donation. We inquired about autopsy. I stated that I felt there was no reason that this would need to be done, and the family and the attendant at her nursing home concurred. She has no first-degree relatives, only nieces and nephews. Many of them were present at this time. All lines and tubes were discontinued.

Diagnosis:	Physician sign/date
A: Probable cause of death: acute MI.	*Robert Rai MD*

Discharge	Transfer	Admit	Good	Satisfactory	Other:

GODFREY REGIONAL HOSPITAL
123 Main Street • Aldon, FL 77714 • (407) 555-1234

Answers

OFFICE NOTE

Date:	Vital signs:	T	R
Chief complaint:		P	BP

S: Patient presents complaining of headache and dizziness. She woke in the middle of the night and had an episode of dizziness for about 15 minutes. She didn't sleep very well the rest of the night, and this morning she has had a headache on the left-hand side at the occiput and temporal region. She had a stroke in September where she lost half her vision and her right side became numb. This was very transient. She questions whether her left eye might be a little bit blurry but notices no other neurologic symptoms. The vertigo has completely resolved. She has a history of labyrinthitis and a hospitalization for this.

Physical examination:

O: On examination, neurologically, she appears to be intact. Romberg is very steady. Eyes: PERRLA. EOM normal. Ears appear clear. Normal strength upper and lower extremities.

Assessment:

A: Episode of vertigo, possibly labyrinthitis or possibly Ménière's disease, as she did describe a little bit of a pulsatile tinnitus at the time.

Plan:

P: Recommended observation for now. Discussed the headaches as likely being related to tension headaches and to use symptomatic treatment for this. We discussed having meclizine around to use for vertigo, and if she notices any worsening symptoms then she should be reevaluated.

Felix Wander MD

	Patient name:
	DOB:
	MR/Chart #:

GODFREY REGIONAL OUTPATIENT CLINIC
3122 Shannon Avenue • Aldon, FL 77712 • (407) 555-7654

Answers

12 Anesthesia Services

Identify the appropriate anesthesia CPT procedure code(s) and any physical status or qualifying circumstances. If time is listed, calculate the time units in 10-minute increments.

1. Blepharoplasty repair on an 86-year-old male with severe CAD and uncontrolled hypertension. Administration of anesthesia began at 10:15 AM and ended at 11:10 AM.

   CPT code(s): _____

   Physical status modifier(s): _____

   Qualifying circumstance(s): _____

   Time units: _____

2. Needle biopsy of the thyroid performed on an otherwise healthy 35-year-old female.

   CPT code(s): _____

   Physical status modifier(s): _____

   Qualifying circumstance(s): _____

   Time units: _____

3. Anesthesia for a cesarean section in an otherwise healthy 45-year-old female who is undergoing a repeat c-section. Anesthesiologist entered OR at 10:00 AM, began administration at 10:30 AM, ended administration of anesthesia at 11:15 AM.

   CPT code(s): _____

   Physical status modifier(s): _____

   Qualifying circumstance(s): _____

   Time units: _____

4. Knee arthroscopy; anesthesia time 1 hour 10 minutes.

   CPT code(s): _____

   Physical status modifier(s): _____

   Qualifying circumstance(s): _____

   Time units: _____

5. Modified radical mastectomy on a 67-year-old female with CAD, hypertension, carcinoma of the breast with metastatic spread to spine.

   CPT code(s): _____

   Physical status modifier(s): _____

   Qualifying circumstance(s): _____

   Time units: _____

6. Heart transplant. Anesthesia began 8:00 AM, ended at 3:00 PM, on an 86-year-old male. Patient with severe heart disease/failure who has been hospitalized until transplant becomes available. Patient not expected to survive without heart transplant.

   CPT code(s): _____

   Physical status modifier(s): _____

   Qualifying circumstance(s): _____

   Time units: _____

7. Emergency cesarean section on 35-year-old healthy female. Anesthesia time: 1 hour only.

   CPT code(s): _____

   Physical status modifier(s): _____

   Qualifying circumstance(s): _____

   Time units: _____

8. Lithotripsy procedure for gallstones in 47-year-old male with mild systemic disease; surgery time 25 minutes.

   CPT code(s): _____

   Physical status modifier(s): _____

   Qualifying circumstance(s): _____

   Time units: _____

9. Repair of open ankle fracture, 15-year-old male, anesthesia time 1 hour, 18 minutes.

CPT code(s): _____

Physical status modifier(s): _____

Qualifying circumstance(s): _____

Time units: _____

10. Anesthesia for open ankle fracture, performed by surgeon; anesthesia time 1 hour, 18 minutes.

CPT code(s): _____

Physical status modifier(s): _____

Qualifying circumstance(s): _____

Time units: _____

Identify the appropriate anesthesia codes for the following medical records.

EXERCISE 11

OPERATIVE REPORT

Patient information:
Patient name: DOB: MR#:

Preoperative diagnosis:
Abnormal calcifications left breast

Postoperative diagnosis:
Same History of breast cancer

Procedure(s) performed:
Left needle localization and breast biopsy

Anesthesia:
Local with sedation

Assistant surgeon:

Description of procedure:
Procedure start time: 0900 AM   Procedure stop time: 0925 AM Anesthesia start time: 0910 AM   Anesthesia stop time: 0925 AM

The patient was placed in the supine position. The left breast was prepped and draped in the usual fashion. An incision was made along the superior aspect of the areola and dissection was carried down to the tip of the wire incorporating 1 inch of breast tissue in each direction so as to incorporate all calcifications. A second specimen had to be obtained in order to obtain the most proximal one. The specimens were send to radiology for confirmation that all calcifications had been removed. Once confirmation was obtained, the area was irrigated, hemostasis was obtained. The wound was approximated with a running 3-9 Monocryl. Benzoin, Steri-strips and Tegaderm were applied and the patient was taken to the recovery room in satisfactory condition.

Adm Westy MD

GODFREY REGIONAL HOSPITAL
123 Main Street • Aldon, FL 77714 • (407) 555-1234

Answers

OPERATIVE REPORT

Patient information:

Patient name:
DOB:
MR#:

Preoperative diagnosis:

Question of basal cell carcinoma of left nare
Uncontrolled hypertension
Severe COPD

Postoperative diagnosis:

Basal cell carcinoma of left nare

Procedure(s) performed:

1 Wide excision basal cell carcinoma of left nare with frozen section
2 Harvesting of split-thickness skin graft from the left neck and application of graft to site of excision of left nare

Patient admitted for surgery today. She had seen me because of the lesion on the left nare. Because of the size, and the fact this could not be closed by primary repair, I advised wide excision and skin graft. She was admitted this morning for the same. On admission we took her to the x-ray department. We are going to do the procedure under IV sedation with monitored anesthesia.

Anesthesia:

Assistant surgeon:

Description of procedure:

| Procedure start time: | 1000 AM | Procedure stop time: | 1100 AM |
| Anesthesia start time: | 1010 AM | Anesthesia stop time: | 1045 AM |

In surgery the patient was properly positioned. The left name was cleaned with Hibiclens and draped. The donor site for the left neck was cleaned with Hibiclens and draped. The operation was started. First the graft was harvested. An appropriate skin segment was harvested from the left neck. This was a full-thickness skin segment. Following this the donor site was repaired primarily with interrupted sutures of 3-0 nylon. Next the tumor site was marked out with a marking pen and infiltrated with 2% Xylocaine as was the donor site and then excised adequately with margins. It was then submitted for frozen section exam, which showed it was basal cell carcinoma but all margins were free. Then the full-thickness skin was prepared for split-thickness skin graft portion, then sutured in place and held in place with sutures. Operation was terminated and the patient was then taken from surgery to the Recovery Room in satisfactory condition.

Rachel Perez MD

GODFREY REGIONAL HOSPITAL
123 Main Street • Aldon, FL 77714 • (407) 555-1234

Answers

EXERCISE 13

OPERATIVE REPORT

Patient information:

Patient name:
DOB:
MR#:

Preoperative diagnosis:

Deflated right reconstructive breast implant

Postoperative diagnosis:

Deflated right reconstructive breast implant

Procedure(s) performed:

Replacement of implant
This 69-year-old female had undergone a right breast reconstruction post mastectomy using a tissue expander and implant technique. Shortly after tattooing her nipple areolar complex, she noted that her implant was increasingly soft and smaller. On examination, it was apparent that her implant was deflating.

Anesthesia:

Assistant surgeon:

Description of procedure:

A pinpoint hole on the posterior aspect of the implant was found. The only explanation for this is that it seems reasonable the implant may have flipped over at the time of the tattooing when local anesthetic was infiltrated beneath the areola. The new implant set in the existing pocket nicely and no further modifications to the pocket were necessary.

Procedure start time: 0800 AM   Procedure stop time: 0850 AM
Anesthesia start time: 0810 AM   Anesthesia stop time: 0855 AM

The patient was brought to the Operating room where uncomplicated general anesthesia was induced. The surgical site was prepped and Duraprep and routine sterile drapes applied. The existing inframammary incision was reopened sharply and extended to the implant capsule and the implant extracted. The only defect in the implant appeared to be a pinpoint hole on the posterior aspect of the implant. The wound was irrigated with dilute Betadine solution and a new breast implant was selected. This was a McGhann Style 363LF saline filled textured breast implant, Serial #5364xx, Lot #583740xx. The implant was inspected and prepared and inserted using a no touch technique and inflated with normal saline to 450 ccs. The implant sat nicely in the existing pocket and the size seemed to be appropriate. Accordingly, the wound was closed with running 3-0 Vicryl for the implant capsule and mascular fascia. Buried interrupted 4-9 Biosyn for the buried dermal closure and running 5-0 plain gut for the skin. Steri-strips were used to cover the wound followed by sterile dressing. The patient was moved to the Recovery Room in excellent condition.

Adam Westy MD

GODFREY REGIONAL HOSPITAL
123 Main Street • Aldon, FL 77714 • (407) 555-1234

Answers

EXERCISE 14

OPERATIVE REPORT

Patient information:

Patient name:
DOB:
MR#:

Preoperative diagnosis:

Lesion right forehead

Postoperative diagnosis:

Same

Procedure(s) performed:

Excision lesion right forehead

Anesthesia:

Assistant surgeon:

Description of procedure:

Procedure start time: 1100 AM   Procedure stop time: 1135 AM
Anesthesia start time: 1106 AM   Anesthesia stop time: 1130 AM

The patient was admitted for excision of this lesion, which appeared suddenly over the past 2-3 weeks. We had planned to do this last week but the patient developed a temperature, which was aborted until today. The procedure was to be done under general anesthesia because it was clear we could not do this with local as the patient was very excitable.

The patient was brought to surgery, general anesthesia was administered. The right temple lesion was clearly evident, measuring 1 × 1 cm, pigmented, mole-type lesion. The reason we are excising it was because of the sudden history and sudden appearance. The area was cleaned with saline, infiltrated with 2% Xylocaine then excised completely and submitted for pathology. Hemostasis was achieved using hand-held cautery device. Wound was closed with sutures of 5-9 Prolene. Antibiotic ointment was applied. Patient was discharged back to parents for follow-up.

Rachel Perez MD

GODFREY REGIONAL HOSPITAL
123 Main Street • Aldon, FL 77714 • (407) 555-1234

Answers

EXERCISE 15

Answers

13 Surgery Services

EXERCISES 1-45

Using the Surgery Coding Worksheet, determine the necessary elements to identify the correct codes for surgeries in the following medical charts.

EXERCISE 1

OPERATIVE REPORT

Patient information:

Patient name:
DOB:
MR#:

Preoperative diagnosis:

Left breast mass
Rule out breast carcinoma

Postoperative diagnosis:

Same

Procedure(s) performed:

Anesthesia:

Assistant surgeon:

Description of procedure:

55-year-old female presented with a left breast mass, which was recommended for left breast biopsy. The options, risks, alternative treatments, and exact nature of the procedure were described in detail to the patient, and she seemed to understand.

Patient was taken to the operating room; under general anesthesia, left breast was prepped and draped in a sterile fashion. Left infra-areolar incision was made, mass was dissected free of surrounding tissue. Hemostasis was obtained, wound was closed with interrupted 0-Vicryl, 4-0 Vicryl subcuticular to the skin. Patient tolerated the procedure well and was taken to the recovery room in stable condition.

Adam Westy, MD

GODFREY REGIONAL HOSPITAL
123 Main Street • Aldon, FL 77714 • (407) 555-1234

Answers

OPERATIVE REPORT

Patient information:

Patient name:
DOB:
MR#:

Preoperative diagnosis:

Full thickness skin graft of right lower leg

Postoperative diagnosis:

Procedure(s) performed:

Full thickness skin graft of the right lower leg

Anesthesia:

Assistant surgeon:

Description of procedure:

44-year-old male presents with an 8 x 8 cm area of full thickness skin loss as the result of a motorcycle accident approximately eight weeks ago. The wound is now recommended for debridement and grafting. The options, risks, alternative treatments and exact nature of the procedure were described in detail to the patient and the patient seemed to understand the procedure well.

Patient was taken to the operating room, where under adequate IV analgesia the donor site and recipient site were anesthetized with 1% Xylocaine. The area was lightly debrided. Using air-driven Dermatome, a split thickness skin graft of 5:1000 inch was harvested from the left posterior thigh and meshed to the ratio of 1 1/2 to 1, placed over the defect, and stabilized in place with Proximate. After hemostasis was complete, nylon net was placed over the graft and stapled to the skin. The patient returned to the recovery room in stable condition.

Adm Westg MD

GODFREY REGIONAL HOSPITAL
123 Main Street • Aldon, FL 77714 • (407) 555-1234

Answers

EXERCISE 3

OPERATIVE REPORT

Patient information:
Patient name: DOB: MR#:

Preoperative diagnosis:

Postoperative diagnosis:

Procedure(s) performed:

Anesthesia:

Assistant surgeon:

Description of procedure:

Patient is a 6-year-old who cut his hand on some broken glass when he ended up pushed against a window.

He has a V-shaped laceration that is about 2 cm in length and a small one about 1 cm on the ulnar side of the hand. There is normal movement and no sign of any other injury.

The wound is infiltrated with 1% Lidocaine buffered with sodium bicarb and cleaned. The larger laceration is closed with four 4-0 Ethilon sutures and the smaller one with two 4-0 Ethilon sutures, dressed with antibiotic ointment, Telfa and gauze.

Follow-up for suture removal in ten days.

Robert Rai MD

GODFREY REGIONAL HOSPITAL
123 Main Street • Aldon, FL 77714 • (407) 555-1234

Answers

OPERATIVE REPORT

Patient information:
Patient name: DOB: MR#:

Preoperative diagnosis:

Gangrene of distal right ring finger

Postoperative diagnosis:

Procedure(s) performed:

Amputation of right distal ring finger with wide flap advancement

Anesthesia:

Assistant surgeon:

Description of procedure:

A 52-year-old white female sustained a crushing injury to the right distal ring finger, which subsequently developed gangrene. The injury progressed to the point that amputation and revision were recommended. The options, risks and alternative treatments were explained in detail to the patient in addition to the exact nature of the procedure. She indicated that she understood.

Under adequate Xylocaine block anesthesia, the right hand was prepped and draped in a sterile fashion. The gangrenous finger was debrided beyond the DIP joint proximally. The extensor and flexor mechanisms were approximated with #3-0 Vicryl. Wide flap advancement was performed and the wound was closed with #4-0 Nylon. Tourniquet was let down and sterile pressure dressing was applied. The patient was returned to the recovery room in stable condition.

[signature]

GODFREY REGIONAL HOSPITAL
123 Main Street ¥ Aldon, FL 77714 ¥ (407) 555-1234

Answers

OPERATIVE REPORT

Patient information:

Patient name:
DOB:
MR#:

Preoperative diagnosis:

Left carpal tunnel syndrome

Postoperative diagnosis:

Left carpal tunnel syndrome

Procedure(s) performed:

Left carpal tunnel release

Anesthesia:

Assistant surgeon:

Description of procedure:

A 32-year-old female presented with numbness and tingling of the left hand and was diagnosed with left carpal tunnel syndrome. Patient was taken to the operating room. With adequate Xylocaine block anesthesia the left hand was prepped and draped in a sterile fashion. An incision was made in the volar aspect of the wrist through the skin and subcutaneous tissue. The carpal ligament was divided through its entire length staying on the ulnar side of the median nerve. After hemostasis was complete, the wound was closed with #4-0 Nylon vertical mattress sutures. The patient tolerated the procedure well and was sent to the recovery room in stable condition.

Adm Westy MD

GODFREY REGIONAL HOSPITAL
123 Main Street • Aldon, FL 77714 • (407) 555-1234

Answers

OPERATIVE REPORT

| **Patient information:** |
| Patient name:
DOB:
MR#: |

Preoperative diagnosis:

Left subacromial impingement, partial rotator cuff tear

Postoperative diagnosis:

Same

Procedure(s) performed:

Diagnostic shoulder arthroscopy and subacromial decompression

Anesthesia:

Assistant surgeon:

Description of procedure:

After the usual preoperative evaluation and consent, the patient was brought to the OR and satisfactory anesthetic was induced. She was placed in the beach chair position and the left shoulder was prepped and draped in the usual sterile fashion with DuraPrep. We used a total of 3 arthroscopic portals – posterior, anterior and lateral. Diagnostic arthroscope was carried out and revealed extensive partial-thickness tearing of the rotator cuff tendon. This was debrided using a 5.5 mm full radius resector through the anterior portal. She also had partial thickness tearing of the subscapularis adjacent to the biceps tendon, although the biceps tendon was intact. The labrum appeared to be intact circumferentially and her articular surfaced appeared intact as well.

There was extensive bursitis in the subacromial space. Although we attempted to maintain the CA ligament at its origin from the distal acromion, this was largely released in the process of performing the acromioplasty and subacromial decompression.

At the completion of the procedure, we removed the instruments from the portals of the shoulder and we closed the portals in running intradermal fashion. There were no apparent complications.

GODFREY REGIONAL HOSPITAL
123 Main Street • Aldon, FL 77714 • (407) 555-1234

Answers

OPERATIVE REPORT

Patient information:

Patient name:
DOB:
MR#:

Preoperative diagnosis:

Retained four deep pins right hand

Postoperative diagnosis:

Same

Procedure(s) performed:

Exploration and removal of pins right hand

Anesthesia:

Assistant surgeon:

Description of procedure:

This is a 17-year-old male who fractured his hand approximately two months ago. It was felt that fracture had healed sufficiently to remove these pins. The patient was brought to the OR and given adequate general anesthesia. He had a tourniquet placed on the right arm, and it was blown up to 250. DuraPrep was used to cleanse the hand and sterile draping was performed. The hand was studied closely using an operating microscope, and four separate incisions were made. The pins were moved with a bit of digging about the incision sites.
Nylon 4-0 was utilized to close all four wounds. Dressings were placed over each site and the patient left the Recovery Room in good condition, having tolerated the procedure well.

GODFREY REGIONAL HOSPITAL
123 Main Street ¥ Aldon, FL 77714 ¥ (407) 555-1234

Answers

OPERATIVE REPORT

Patient information:

Patient name:
DOB:
MR#:

Preoperative diagnosis:

Suspected medial meniscus tear

Postoperative diagnosis:

Grade III chondromalacia patella
Medical meniscus tear with grade IV chondral
Flap, acute, right knee
Lateral meniscus tear, right knee

Procedure(s) performed:

Right knee arthroscopy, partial medial and lateral meniscectomy
Chondroplasty with microfracture, medial femoral condyle
Chondromalacia patella chrondroplasty, right knee

Anesthesia:

Assistant surgeon:

Description of procedure:

Patient was prepped and draped in the usual sterile fashion. After undergoing general anesthesia the leg was exsanguinated and tourniquet applied. Anterolateral and anteromedial portals were made and scope was placed in the anterolateral portal. This gave good visualization of the patellofemoral joint. Scope revealed extensive Grade III chondromalacia patella that was not associated with her current injury. This was debrided with a full radius shave and then treated with chrondroplasty with Oratek device. The medial compartment was entered revealing a middle medial meniscus tear, flap type that was resected with a full radius shaver. There was also a full thickness acute chrondral injury to the medial femoral condyle with a large chondral flap. This was resected with a shaver. A microfracture was then performed. Lateral compartment was entered and the lateral meniscus was found to have a tear at the posterior horn. This was resected as well with a full radius shaver. Articular cartilage was completely normal. Lateral gutter was intact. The knee was thoroughly irrigated, endoscopic equipment was removed, Marcaine and Epinephrine were injected and sterile dressings were applied. Patient was taken to the recovery room without complication.

[signature]

GODFREY REGIONAL HOSPITAL
123 Main Street ¥ Aldon, FL 77714 ¥ (407) 555-1234

Answers

OPERATIVE REPORT

Patient information:

Patient name:
DOB:
MR#:

Preoperative diagnosis:

Sick sinus syndrome, failing pacemaker generator due to end of life battery

Postoperative diagnosis:

Replacement of end of life battery

Procedure(s) performed:

Removal of existing pacemaker generator and insertion of new dual chamber pacemaker

Anesthesia:

Assistant surgeon:

Description of procedure:

Patient was brought to the operating room and placed supine on the fluoroscopy table. The skin of the left subclavicular area was draped in the sterile fashion. Local anesthesia with Lidocaine was administered. The old incisional scar was incised. Using blunt and sharp dissection the existing generator was exposed and removed. It was a CPI model 950 Vigor, serial number 9973947. Chronic pacing thresholds, atrium capture at 1.3 volts, P waves 5.7, lead impedance 4580; ventricular, capture thresholds 0.6 volts, R waves 18.9. Next a pacesetter integrity AFX DR dual chamber pacemaker was implanted, serial number 9937495. The pouch was irrigated with 1.0 grams of Nafcillin. Then the subcutaneous tissue was closed with running suture of 3-0 Vicyrl and skin closed with clips.

Ruth Brady MD

GODFREY REGIONAL HOSPITAL
123 Main Street ¥ Aldon, FL 77714 ¥ (407) 555-1234

Answers

OPERATIVE REPORT

Patient information:
Patient name: DOB: MR#:

Preoperative diagnosis:
Port-A-Cath removal

Postoperative diagnosis:
Same

Procedure(s) performed:
Removal of Port-A-Cath

Anesthesia:

Assistant surgeon:

Description of procedure:
Patient presents having completed her IV antibiotics. Patient was placed in the Trendelenburg position. Her right upper chest was prepped and draped sterilely. We anesthetized the skin and subcutaneous tissue with Lidocaine. We incised the skin, dissected down to the catheter. The catheter was removed and the skin was closed with interrupted 4-0 Biosyn suture. We placed a sterile dressing. *Rachel Perez MD*

GODFREY REGIONAL HOSPITAL
123 Main Street ¥ Aldon, FL 77714 ¥ (407) 555-1234

Answers

OPERATIVE REPORT

Patient information:	
Patient name: DOB: MR#:	

Preoperative diagnosis:

Lung mass

Postoperative diagnosis:

Lung mass

Procedure(s) performed:

Bronchoscopy with biopsy(ies)

Anesthesia:

Assistant surgeon:

Description of procedure:

Patient was brought to the endoscopy area. Upon introduction of the bronchoscope, a large amount of mucus was removed from the tracheal lumen. Findings were consistent with severe emphysema. The right side was inspected first. As soon as large amounts of mucus were suctioned with the middle lobe, a large endobronchial lesion was seen. Numerous bronchioalveolar lavage specimens were retrieved for cytologic purposes. Brushings were obtained from these areas as well. The left side was also inspected, however, no evidence of any malignancies or lesions was found.

The patient tolerated the procedure well without complications.

Adm Westg MD

GODFREY REGIONAL HOSPITAL
123 Main Street ¥ Aldon, FL 77714 ¥ (407) 555-1234

Answers

OPERATIVE REPORT

Patient information:

Patient name:
DOB:
MR#:

Preoperative diagnosis:

Thrombosed external hemorrhoids with prolapse

Postoperative diagnosis:

Procedure(s) performed:

Internal and external hemorrhoidectomy

Anesthesia:

Assistant surgeon:

Description of procedure:

Patient presents as a 48-year-old male who has a long history of hemorrhoids. He now presents with acute thrombosis with severe prolapse and surgery is recommended. The options, risks, alternative treatments and exact nature of the procedure were described to the patient and the patient seemed to understand.

The patient was taken to the operating room, under adequate general anesthesia, the patient was placed in the jackknife position. The anus was prepped and draped in a sterile fashion. The anus was dilated. There was severe prolapse with dark mucosa and multiple areas indicating hemorrhage. Point suture of 2-9 Chromic was placed above the hemorrhoid and submucosal dissections were performed. The suture was run over the area of submucosal dissection. After hemostasis was complete, the anus was again dilated and Gelfoam and Nupercaine pack was placed. The area was then infiltrated with Marcaine. The patient appeared to have tolerated the procedure well and went to the recovery room in stable

Rachel Perez MD

GODFREY REGIONAL HOSPITAL
123 Main Street • Aldon, FL 77714 • (407) 555-1234

Answers

OPERATIVE REPORT

Patient information:

Patient name:
DOB:
MR#:

Preoperative diagnosis:

Yearly check-up.

PMH: Diverticular disease

Postoperative diagnosis:

Procedure(s) performed:

Proctosigmoscopy

Anesthesia:

Assistant surgeon:

Description of procedure:

After informed consent and description of possible risks and benefits of the procedure, the patient was positioned in the left lateral decubitus position. Digital examination of the prostate was completed. Scope was inserted to the depth of 50 cm. The last 10 cm or more were marked with numerous diverticula. There was spasm noted as well. The patient began to experience pain, at which point the decision was made to terminate the procedure, not scoping to completion. The scope was withdrawn in a circumferential manner without difficulty. Multiple diverticula were seen.

GODFREY REGIONAL HOSPITAL
123 Main Street • Aldon, FL 77714 • (407) 555-1234

Answers

OPERATIVE REPORT

Patient information:

Patient name:
DOB:
MR#:

Preoperative diagnosis:

Mucous bloody stools

Postoperative diagnosis:

Diverticula

Procedure(s) performed:

Colonoscopy

Anesthesia:

Assistant surgeon:

Description of procedure:

Patient presents with change in bowel habits, intermittent rectal bleeding and some mucus. The procedure was described in detail to the patient and he seemed to understand the risks, alternative treatments.

The patient was taken to the endoscopy suite and in the left lateral position, the long colonoscope was inserted without incident. The perirectal area was normal. The rectal ampulla was normal. There were scattered diverticula of the left colon. The left colon, transverse colon and right colon were otherwise normal. The colonoscope was removed and the patient returned to the recovery room in satisfactory condition.

Rachel Perez MD

GODFREY REGIONAL HOSPITAL
123 Main Street • Aldon, FL 77714 • (407) 555-1234

Answers

OPERATIVE REPORT

Patient information:

Patient name:
DOB:
MR#:

Preoperative diagnosis:

SHORT STAY REPORT

Chronic adenotonsillitis
Bilateral chronic serous otitis media

Postoperative diagnosis:

Procedure(s) performed:

Tonsillectomy and adenoidectomy
Bilateral P. E. tube placement

Anesthesia:

General

Assistant surgeon:

Description of procedure:

9-year-old male with chronic adenotonsillitis along with bilateral chronic serous otitis media. The patient was taken to the operating room, where, under adequate general anesthesia, mouth gag inserted, the right tonsil was grasped, anterior and posterior pillars were incised. The tonsil was dissected free of surrounding tissue, removed with a snare. Identical procedure was then performed on the left side as well. Large amount of adenoid tissue was removed and after appropriate hemostasis, the pharynx was irrigated.

Operating otoscope was then placed in the right external ear canal, where a single myringotomy was made. PE tube was placed without incident and the identical procedure was then performed on the left. After the PE tubes were placed, the

Rachel Perez MD

GODFREY REGIONAL HOSPITAL
123 Main Street • Aldon, FL 77714 • (407) 555-1234

Answers

OPERATIVE REPORT

Patient information:
Patient name: DOB: MR#:

Preoperative diagnosis:
History of colon cancer, multiple colon polyps

Postoperative diagnosis:
Same

Procedure(s) performed:
Colonoscopy with polypectomy X 5

Anesthesia:

Assistant surgeon:

Description of procedure:
This 78-year-old female presents with colon polyps and a previous history of colon carcinoma. Patient was taken to the endoscopy suite and in the left lateral position, the long colonoscope was inserted without difficulty. The perirectal area was normal. Rectal ampulla was normal. The left colon showed a few diverticula. The right colon had multiple polyps, 5 of which were removed with hot forceps. The patient tolerated the procedure well and went to the recovery room in stable condition.

Rachel Perez, MD

GODFREY REGIONAL HOSPITAL
123 Main Street • Aldon, FL 77714 • (407) 555-1234

Answers

OPERATIVE REPORT

Patient information:
Patient name: DOB: MR#:

Preoperative diagnosis:
Esophagitis with stricture

Postoperative diagnosis:
Same along with gastritis

Procedure(s) performed:
Upper GI endoscopy with biopsy

Anesthesia:

Assistant surgeon:

Description of procedure:
33-year-old male with a long history of gastroesophageal reflux, history of strictures, recommended for GI endoscopy. The patient was taken to the endoscopy suite, and under topical anesthesia, the endoscope was inserted without difficulty. The proximal and midesophagus were normal. The distal esophagus showed signs of reflux with circumferential stricture. Upon entering the stomach it was filled with bile. No proximal lesions. The antrum was biopsied with Helicobacter. Pyloric channel and duodenum were clean. J-maneuver revealed no fundic abnormalities. The endoscope was withdrawn and the patient was then dilated with a #42 French with Hurst dilators. The patient tolerated the procedure well and returned to the recovery room in stable condition.

Rachel Perez MD

GODFREY REGIONAL HOSPITAL
123 Main Street • Aldon, FL 77714 • (407) 555-1234

Answers

OPERATIVE REPORT

Patient information:

Patient name:
DOB:
MR#:

Preoperative diagnosis:

Cholecystitis

Postoperative diagnosis:

Cholecystitis

Procedure(s) performed:

Laparoscopic cholecystectomy

Anesthesia:

Assistant surgeon:

Description of procedure:

Patient was put on the table in supine position. The area of the abdomen was prepped and draped in the usual fashion. Patient was adequately anesthetized with general anesthesia. Incision was made in the umbilical area. Dissection was carried down to the fascia. Peritoneum was opened and trocar was inserted. The abdomen was inflated and under direct visualization a 10 mm trocar was inserted in the epigastric area and 12 mm trocar inserted laterally. The gallbladder was retracted from the fundus and the neck.

Dissection was carried out until we could identify the cystic duct which was clipped proximally. The operative cholangiogram showed air in the jejunum. No sign of any defect. The cystic duct was clipped twice distally and cut. The cystic artery was identified and transected, clipped twice distally and one proximally, and cut. The gallbladder was dissected from the liver bed and inserted into the endoscopy bag and retrieved through the umbilical incision. Abdomen was deflated after adequate irrigation and suction were achieved. The fascia was closed by interrupted 0-Vicryl suture and the skin using 4-0 Vicryl subcuticular sutures.

Patient tolerated the procedure well.

Adam Westby, MD

GODFREY REGIONAL HOSPITAL
123 Main Street • Aldon, FL 77714 • (407) 555-1234

Answers

OPERATIVE REPORT

Patient information:
Patient name: DOB: MR#:

Preoperative diagnosis:
Hematuria, likely secondary to prostatic hypertrophy

Postoperative diagnosis:

Procedure(s) performed:
Flexible cystourethroscopy

Anesthesia:

Assistant surgeon:

Description of procedure:
With the patient placed supine and the genitalia prepped and draped in the usual fashion, the lubricated scope was passed per urethra. Anterior and membranous urethra were normal. Prostatic urethra was markedly elongated at 5 cm utilizing the graduations of the scope. No bladder neck contracture. Prostatic urethral mucosa is markedly hypervascular and bleeds with instrumentation. Bladder is entered and is 3+-4+ trabeculated. No definite bladder diverticula. No tumors or suspicious lesions. No stones, orifices or normal morphology on the backside of the intravesical part of the prostate. The patient tolerated the procedure well and was returned to the recovery room in satisfactory condition.

Rachel Perez MD

GODFREY REGIONAL HOSPITAL
123 Main Street • Aldon, FL 77714 • (407) 555-1234

Answers

OPERATIVE REPORT

Patient information:

Patient name:
DOB:
MR#:

Preoperative diagnosis:

Desired sterilization, multiparity

Postoperative diagnosis:

Procedure(s) performed:

Laparoscopic tubal ligation

Anesthesia:

Assistant surgeon:

Description of procedure:

This 24-year-old multigravida female desired tubal sterilization. The patient was taken to the operating room, where, under adequate general anesthesia, the abdomen and perineum were prepped and draped in a sterile fashion. The stomach and bladder were drained. An infraumbilical incision was made and the Veress needle was used for institution of pneumoperitoneum. A 10-mm and 5-mm port was placed. Both tubes were electrocoagulated and divided under direct vision. After hemostasis was assured, the wounds were closed with 2-0 Vicryl and 4-0 Vicryl subcuticular. Skin incisions were infiltrated with Marcaine. The patient went to the recovery room in stable condition.

Patrick Chung MD

GODFREY REGIONAL HOSPITAL
123 Main Street • Aldon, FL 77714 • (407) 555-1234

Answers

OPERATIVE REPORT

Patient information:
Patient name: DOB: MR#:

Preoperative diagnosis:
Carcinoma of the bladder Urinary retention

Postoperative diagnosis:
Same

Procedure(s) performed:
Cystoscopy, insertion of indwelling Foley catheter

Anesthesia:

Assistant surgeon:

Description of procedure:

Patient placed in the lithotomy position and the genitalia prepped and draped in a routine manner after the old Foley catheter was removed. Flexible cystoscope was inserted and bladder mucosa showed some mild inflammatory change but no evidence of any recurrent bladder tumors, stones or other significant changes. No evidence of any vaginal or urethral abnormalities. At the conclusion, a new #18 French foley catheter was inserted.

There was no blood loss or complications with the patient in good condition.

Adm Westg MD

GODFREY REGIONAL HOSPITAL
123 Main Street • Aldon, FL 77714 • (407) 555-1234

Answers

OPERATIVE REPORT

Patient information:
Patient name: DOB: MR#:

Preoperative diagnosis:
Menorrhagia with resultant anemia

Postoperative diagnosis:
Same

Procedure(s) performed:
Fractional D & C

Anesthesia:

Assistant surgeon:

Description of procedure:

With the patient under general anesthesia the patient was placed in the dorsal lithotomy position. The perineum was prepped and draped in the usual fashion. Bimanual exam revealed the uterus to be globular, about six weeks size, anteflexed and mobile. Adnexae were negative.

Self-retaining vaginal speculum was placed and the cervix was grasped with the single-toothed tenaculum and endocervical curettings were done and sent labeled appropriately.

The patient was having some bleeding at the time of the D & C prior to the manipulation of the cervix. The cervix was then dilated and the endouterine cavity was curetted in a systematic fashion and small amounts of tissue were obtained but only from the anterior uterine wall and from the fundus of the uterus.

No uterine polyps were obtained. The tissue obtained from the uterine cavity was sent labeled appropriately and the procedure was then terminated after rectal exam added no new information.

Adhn Westy MD

GODFREY REGIONAL HOSPITAL
123 Main Street • Aldon, FL 77714 • (407) 555-1234

Answers

OPERATIVE REPORT

Patient information:

Patient name:
DOB:
MR#:

Preoperative diagnosis:

Phimosis

Postoperative diagnosis:

Same

Procedure(s) performed:

Circumcision

Anesthesia:

Assistant surgeon:

Description of procedure:

The patient was a 2-year-old with phimosis, presents for elective circumcision. Options were discussed with the family including risks and benefits.

The patient was taken to the operating room and underwent general endotracheal anesthesia, prepped and draped in the usual sterile fashion. The foreskin was marked proximally and distally, incised with the 15 blade and removed in a sleeve fashion with Mets. Bleeders were coagulated and the foreskin was closed with interrupted chromics. Dressing was applied and block placed.

The patient was taken to the recovery room in stable condition.

Adam Westy MD

GODFREY REGIONAL HOSPITAL
123 Main Street • Aldon, FL 77714 • (407) 555-1234

Answers

OPERATIVE REPORT

Patient information:

Patient name:
DOB:
MR#:

Preoperative diagnosis:

Cataract, left eye

Postoperative diagnosis:

Same

Procedure(s) performed:

Extracapsular cataract with IOL

Anesthesia:

Assistant surgeon:

Description of procedure:

The patient was given a retrobulbar injection, consisting of 3 cc of 50/50 mixture of 2% Lidocaine with 0.5% Marcaine. He was also given a modified Van Lint block consisting of 3 cc of a similar mixture. He was then prepped and draped in the usual manner. A wire lid speculum and 4-0 silk bridle suture was placed. A conjunctival peritomy was performed superiorly. Light cautery was used to achieve hemostasis. A groove was made in the limbus superiorly. A crescent blade was used to dissect down into clear cornea. A side port incision was made at 2 o'clock. The anterior chamber was entered with a 3-mm keratome. A capsulorrhexis was done. Hydrodissection of the lens nucleus was done. Phacoemulsufication of the nucleus was then accomplished. The irrigation and aspiration unit was used to aspirate residual cortex. A 19 diopter AMO model S14ONB foldable silicone lens was placed in the unfolder and injected into the eye, where it was positioned in the capsule bag with the haptics at 3 and 9 o'clock. The wound was checked for watertightness. The conjunctiva was brought down over the wound. A subconjunctival injection with Celestone and Gentamicin was given in the inferior cul-de-sac. Maxitrol Ointment and a light pressure was placed.

The patient tolerated the procedure well and there were no complications.

Linda Patrick MD

GODFREY REGIONAL HOSPITAL
123 Main Street • Aldon, FL 77714 • (407) 555-1234

Answers

OPERATIVE REPORT

Patient information:

Patient name: Date:
DOB: Surgeon:
MR#:   Anesthetist:

Preoperative diagnosis:

Thickened endometrium by way of ultrasound

Postoperative diagnosis:

1. Same with path pending suggestive of either an endometrial polyp or a small submucous fibroid
2. Lesions to the right infraclavicular area, right cheek, and right parascapular area

Procedure(s) performed:

OPERATION:
1. Excision of lesions to the right clavicular area, right preauricular area, and right parascapular area
2. Cystoscopy and D&C
FINDINGS: Six 2-mm raised lesions to the right infraclavicular area. Approximately 5-mm lesion to the right preauricular area. Approximately 1.2-cm lesion to the right parascapular area. The general bimanual exam was negative.

Anesthesia:

Assistant surgeon:

Description of procedure:

In lithotomy position under general anesthesia, the patient is appropriately prepped and draped. The bimanual exam is done, which reveals the uterus to be retroverted, retroflexed. There appear to be no adnexal masses. Subsequently, a weighted vaginal speculum is introduced into the vagina. The anterior lip of the cervix is picked up with a tenaculum. The uterus sounded to a depth of approximately 9 cm. The uterus, as mentioned, is noted to be retroverted. The hysteroscope is introduced into the endometrial canal and advanced. There is noted to be somewhat of a polypoid lesion on the mid anterior uterine wall just past the cervix. The rest of the intrauterine cavity appears to be negative. Subsequently, the cervix is then further dilated with Hegar's dilator sufficient enough to admit the uterine curette, the uterine cavity is curetted with a sharp curette, and the mass to the anterior portion of the uterus is removed with a curettage and sent to Pathology. The uterine cavity is checked for other masses and none are noted. The hysteroscope is reintroduced. There appear to be no further lesions noted in the uterine cavity. The tissue was then sent to Pathology. Tenaculum and speculum are removed.

Attention is carried to the lesions to the infraclavicular area, right preauricular area, and the right parascapular area. These areas are all cleaned with Betadine and subsequently curetted off and cauterized with electrocautery. Hemostasis is to be noted quite adequate.

The patient tolerated the procedure well and left operating room in good condition. Estimated blood loss is minimal.

GODFREY REGIONAL HOSPITAL
123 Main Street • Aldon, FL 77714 • (407) 555-1234

Rachel Perez MD

Answers

OPERATIVE REPORT

Patient information:	
Patient name: DOB: MR#:	Date: Surgeon: Anesthetist:

Preoperative diagnosis:

Cutaneous wound fistula with probable suture abscesses

Postoperative diagnosis:

Cutaneous wound fistula with probable suture abscesses

Procedure(s) performed:

Right subcostal wound exploration; removal of suture abscess; scar revision

INDICATIONS: The patient is a 70-year-old Native American gentleman who underwent an emergency cholecystectomy via a right subcostal incision late last year in Texas. The patient has had problems with the incision itself for many months since then, and suture material has been removed from the wound on several occasions by both the patient and his primary care provider, a PA-C. The area has never healed and there have been two persistent fistulas now for many months, which have resisted topical therapy. The patient was referred for surgical evaluation at which time he was advised that a wound exploration, removal of the offending suture material, and scar revision would be the most appropriate treatment. He was given a description of this procedure and various other alternatives and ultimately agreed to proceed. He was given a description of the potential perioperative complications including persistence or recurrence of the fistulous problem. The patient gave his full informed consent.

EBL: Less than 20 cc

Anesthesia:

General endotracheal anesthesia by CRNA

Assistant surgeon:

Description of procedure:

The patient was identified and taken to the operating suite where he received a gram of intravenous Ancef. A general endotracheal anesthetic was then induced and the patient positioned appropriately for abdominal surgery. The abdomen was then prepped and draped in the usual sterile fashion.

The medial portion of the previous incision was opened to include the two cutaneous fistulae. The suture was immediately apparent. This was grasped and divided at the deepest level. The granulomatous reaction in the adjacent fascia was then debrided sharply. Hemostasis was achieved with electrocautery. The wound edges at the skin level were then freshened using a sharp blade. Hemostasis was achieved with electrocautery. The wound was then irrigated with Bacitracin solution. With hemostasis assured, closure was performed in a single layer using titanium skin clips. Sterile bandage and dressing were then placed.

The patient's anesthetic was then reversed. He was uneventfully extubated and taken from the operative suite to the postanesthetic care unit in stable cardiovascular condition.

FINDINGS: The findings at the time of surgery include the presence of a typical suture abscess present with the suture of the anterior fascial closure of this right Kocher incision. The suture had not degraded; it appeared to be a braided-type material. This was removed with no disruption of the fascial closure and the wound closed in a single layer with titanium skin clips. There was no sign of any active infection. The skin of the wound had a probable yeast superficial infection.

COMPLICATIONS: None

Adm Westy, MD

GODFREY REGIONAL HOSPITAL
123 Main Street • Aldon, FL 77714 • (407) 555-1234

Answers

OPERATIVE REPORT

Patient information:

Patient name:
DOB:
MR#:

Date:
Surgeon:
Anesthetist:

Preoperative diagnosis:

Bloody nipple discharge, right nipple, 8 o'clock radius

Postoperative diagnosis:

Same

Procedure(s) performed:

Duct exploration and excision
SPECIMEN: Breast tissue, frozen section benign papilloma and fibrocystic changes
CONDITION: Stable
PROGNOSIS: Excellent
INDICATIONS: The patient presented with bloody nipple discharge, Hemoccult-positive on testing in the office. I had asked her not to express this, and we scheduled her for nipple duct exploration.

Anesthesia:

Assistant surgeon:

Description of procedure:

She was brought to the operating room and placed in the supine position. After appropriate anesthesia was achieved, she was prepped and draped over the right breast. Curvilinear incision was made in the areolar border through a field of injected lidocaine with epinephrine. I elevated an areolar flap until the ductal tissues were encountered and an enlarged blue-black looking duct was encountered. It was circumferentially dissected; actually, it was opened and I was able to pass a lacrimal duct cannula into the duct, and held that in place with a hemostat. I then took the duct down off of the back of the nipple. I then further excised ductal tissue off the back of the nipple as a separate specimen. I then elevated flaps circumferentially and excised the underlying breast tissue in that quadrant. It was oriented with sutures for the pathologist. I then sent it to Pathology for sectioning. Excision was done with the Bovie; controlled bleeding was done with the Bovie. The patient tolerated the procedure without apparent difficulty. The wound was marked with clips circumferentially. I then closed the subcutaneous tissues with 3-0 Vicryl and the skin with 5-0 Prolene, followed by a sterile dressing.

With the patient still under sedation I went to Pathology, reviewed the specimen with the pathologist and the frozen section, which just came back benign. There was a papilloma present. There were fibrocystic changes present. We then released the patient from the OR. She is in stable condition.

Adm Westg MD

GODFREY REGIONAL HOSPITAL
123 Main Street • Aldon, FL 77714 • (407) 555-1234

Answers

OPERATIVE REPORT

Patient information:

Patient name:
DOB:
MR#:

Date:
Surgeon:
Anesthetist:

Preoperative diagnosis:

SUBJECTIVE:
The patient is a 5-year-old boy brought to the OR today for light sedation and treatment of molluscum contagiosum by cryotherapy. The patient has a history of molluscum, and two attempts at treatment in the clinic have taken place. The patient has not tolerated these procedures well at all and has required people to try to hold him down. In discussion with the family, they elected to use some light sedation for treatment of all the lesions at one time.

Postoperative diagnosis:

Procedure(s) performed:

Cryotherapy, attempts at curetting molluscum contagiosum skin lesions. The patient was brought to the operating area by his father. The patient was given light MEC for sedation. Once fully sedated, the lesions were exposed. Curettage was attempted but the lesions were not easily removed. Cryotherapy was then used to treat each of the lesions through two freeze/thaw cycles. Total time probably 5 minutes. Sedation was removed and the patient was awakened. He tolerated it all very well.

Anesthesia:

Assistant surgeon:

Description of procedure:

ASSESSMENT:
Cryotherapy of molluscum contagiosum. Scars of the lesions were discussed with the father. They are encouraged to use some Bacitracin on the lesions. They are encouraged to return with any signs of infection. Father was given a Rx for Atarax 25 mg up to qid as needed for itch. I also encouraged them to use ibuprofen or Tylenol as needed for pain. They are to return to the clinic for recheck in one week.

NOTE:
The patient was admitted through Outpatient Day Surgery.

Adm Westg MD

GODFREY REGIONAL HOSPITAL
123 Main Street • Aldon, FL 77714 • (407) 555-1234

Answers

OPERATIVE REPORT

Patient information:

Patient name:	Date:
DOB:	Surgeon:
MR#:	Anesthetist:

Preoperative diagnosis:

Internal derangement, right knee

Postoperative diagnosis:

1. Grade 3 to grade 4 chondromalacia, medial femoral condyle, right knee
2. Grade 2 to grade 3 chondromalacia, femoral groove, right knee

Procedure(s) performed:

Diagnostic arthroscopy of chondroplasty, medial femoral condyle and femoral groove, right knee

Anesthesia:

Assistant surgeon:

Description of procedure:

The patient was brought to the operating room and general anesthetic was induced. The right lower extremity was exsanguinated and tourniquet inflated to 300 mm Hg for 35 minutes. The leg was placed in a leg holder, prepped with Betadine, and draped in a sterile fashion. The inlet cannula was inserted through the superior and medial portions and the otoscope into the inferolateral portal. Suprapatellar pouch was well visualized for inferior pathology. Along the medial parapatellar region, there was plica evident, and this was trimmed down with a Striker shaver. The patellofemoral joint showed central chondromalacia of grade 2 variety of the patella, and this was trimmed down lightly with a shaver and also with the thermal probe. In the femoral groove there was significant chondromalacia of grade 3 and a few small areas of grade 4 chondromalacia, and this was also trimmed down with the shaver and the thermal probe. Within the medial compartment there were significant and major changes on the medial femoral condyle with loss of cartilage over large areas of about 2 × 3 cm with grade 3 chondromalacia changes. The medial meniscus was entirely intact, and the tibial plateau appeared excellent with only a grade 1 chondromalacia changes. Within the notch a synovectomy was performed, and the underlying anterior cruciate ligament was normal. In the lateral compartment, the lateral meniscus was intact and there was no chondromalacia laterally.

We used the thermal probe in the femoral groove and the medial femoral condyle to shave down some of the loose cartilage. Some loose debris within the joint was also evacuated. At the conclusion of this, we drained the knee of all fluid and injected the knee with 80 mg of Kenalog. The arthroscopy portals were closed with interrupted 3-0 nylon sutures, and gauze dressings and an Ace wrap were applied. The tourniquet was released. Good circulation returned to the leg.

The patient tolerated the procedure well. She went to the recovery room in excellent condition and will be dismissed as an outpatient today with plans for follow-up at the office in 2 weeks for suture removal.

DISCHARGE MEDICATIONS: Darvocet N-100, #25 tablets

GODFREY REGIONAL HOSPITAL
123 Main Street • Aldon, FL 77714 • (407) 555-1234

Answers

OPERATIVE REPORT

Patient information:	
Patient name: DOB: MR#:	Date: Surgeon: Anesthetist:

Preoperative diagnosis:

Loose ulnar collateral ligament of metacarpophalangeal joint, right thumb

Postoperative diagnosis:

Same

Procedure(s) performed:

Excision of bone fragment with repair of ulnar collateral ligament, metacarpophalangeal joint right thumb; application of short-arm thumb spica cast

Anesthesia:

Assistant surgeon:

Description of procedure:

The patient was placed supine on the operating room table and a satisfactory general anesthetic was given. Preoperative intravenous cephalosporin antibiotic was given. Pneumatic tourniquet was placed about the right arm. The right hand, wrist, forearm, and elbow to the tourniquet level were prepped with DuraPrep, and the right hand was draped in the usual sterile fashion. Tourniquet was inflated to 250 mm of mercury. Skin incision was made at the ulnar base of the thumb overlying the metacarpophalangeal joint. The incision was carried through subcutaneous tissue. Hemostasis was achieved as necessary. Full-thickness skin flaps were raised. The conjoined tendon was elevated, and the small displaced bony fragment off the ulnar base of the proximal phalanx was noted to not be healed. It was easily moveable adjacent to the proximal phalanx of the thumb. It was very difficult to rotate this piece into appropriate position and the decision was made to simply remove this small fragment and to repair the ulnar ligament. The wound was irrigated with normal saline antibiotic solution. A 2-0 Prolene suture was weaved into the ulnar collateral ligament and conjoined tendon and placed via a Keith needle drilled from the normal ligament attachment site across the proximal phalanx out its radial side and radial aspect of the thumb. Each end of the Prolene suture was placed in two different drill holes. Attention was turned to the ulnar collateral ligament and the Prolene was then tied over a plastic button at the radial aspect of the thumb over dressings to protect the skin. A good tight repair was obtained, and there was no laxity to stress testing of the ulnar collateral ligament. The wound was irrigated with normal saline antibiotic solution. The skin was reapproximated with interrupted vertical mattress sutures of 3-0 Ethilon. Dry sterile dressings were applied, followed by sterile circumferential cast padding. Tourniquet was deflated. All drapes were removed, including the tourniquet. A well-padded short-arm thumb spica cast was then applied. The patient tolerated the procedure well. There were no complications. She was awakened in the operating room and was transported to the recovery room in stable condition.

Patrick Chung MD

GODFREY REGIONAL HOSPITAL
123 Main Street • Aldon, FL 77714 • (407) 555-1234

Answers

OPERATIVE REPORT

Patient information:

Patient name: Date:
DOB: Surgeon:
MR#:   Anesthetist:

Preoperative diagnosis:

1. Chronic ulcer, left foot
2. Dislocated second digit, left foot
3. Plantar flexed, second metatarsal, left foot

Postoperative diagnosis:

1. Chronic ulcer, left foot
2. Dislocated second digit, left foot
3. Plantar flexed, second metatarsal, left foot

Procedure(s) performed:

1. Amputation, second digit, left foot
2. Plantar condylectomy, second metatarsal, left foot
3. Application of Apligraf skin graft, second MPJ, left foot

Anesthesia:

Assistant surgeon:

Description of procedure:

COMPLICATIONS: None
PATHOLOGY:
1. Skin for ulcer for biopsy, left foot
2. Second digit, left foot

Under local and IV sedation the patient was prepped and draped in the usual aseptic manner. Martin's bandage was applied at the level of the left malleolus. Attention was directed to the dorsum of the left forefoot where a linear incision was made. The incision was continued circumferentially about the second digit on the left foot. The incision was deepened with care taken to clamp and ligate all superficial bleeders as they were encountered, and all neurovascular and tendinous structures were carefully identified and retracted. All soft tissue from the second digit was released away from the metatarsal where it was articulated near the dorsal neck, and the second digit was removed. Next a plastic condylectomy was performed on the second metatarsal on the left foot. All bony tissue was rasped smooth. The wound was flushed with copious amounts of sterile saline and closed in layers with subcutaneous reapproximation with 3-0 Polysorb simple interrupted sutures followed by skin reapproximation with 4-0 nylon simple interrupted sutures.

Next, attention was directed to the plantar aspect of the left foot, and the ulcer at the second MPJ was circumscribed and removed in toto. There was a subdermal bursa that was removed. The wound was flushed again. The tourniquet was let down, and it was noted that there was good bleeding tissue through the ulcer site. Next, the Apligraf skin graft was prepared and cut to size and stitched in place with 4-0 nylon simple interrupted sutures. I applied sterile Vaseline gauze over the incision line, followed by a sterile gauze bandage for compression and hemostasis. The patient tolerated the procedure and anesthesia well and was transported to the recovery room with vital signs stable and in good condition.

Patrick Chug MD

GODFREY REGIONAL HOSPITAL
123 Main Street • Aldon, FL 77714 • (407) 555-1234

Answers

OPERATIVE REPORT

Patient information:

Patient name:
DOB:
MR#:

Date:
Surgeon:
Anesthetist:

Preoperative diagnosis:

Subluxation with contracted toe; 2nd metatarsophalangeal joint, right and left feet

Postoperative diagnosis:

Same

Procedure(s) performed:

Extensor tendon lengthening with capsulotomy, 2nd metatarsophalangeal joint, right and left feet

Anesthesia:

Assistant surgeon:

Description of procedure:

V-lock cuffs were placed above both ankles for hemostasis and the patient was prepped and draped in the usual aseptic manner. With IV sedation, 2% Xylocaine hydrochloride plain was used to infiltrate the operative area on the right forefoot. A series of triangle-shaped skin incisions were made dorsally over the 2nd metatarsophalangeal joint and over the previous skin incision that was hypertrophic and adhesed. The skin and subcutaneous tissues were undermined and carefully retracted. The incision was then deepened to the level of the extensor digitorum longus tendon, which was identified and retracted from the wound. This tendon was found to be quite thickened and fibrotic from previous surgery. The tendon was then lengthened in a Z-plasty fashion. Incision was further deepened to the level of the capsule over the 2nd metatarsophalangeal joint, and the capsule was incised both dorsally and medially, as well as laterally, and a 2nd toe was then plantar flexed. Upon loading of the right foot, the 2nd toe was found to be much more normally positioned and in line with the adjacent toes. There appeared to be good soft tissue release dorsally over the metatarsophalangeal joint, and a subluxation was significantly reduced. While maintaining the 2nd toe in a straight and somewhat plantar flexed position, the capsular structures were then repaired with interrupted sutures of 3-0 Vicryl. Extensor tendon was then repaired with 3-0 Vicryl, and subcutaneous tissue over the tendon was repaired with a continuous strand of 3-0 Vicryl. Skin margins were then approximated with interrupted horizontal mattress sutures of 4-0 nylon. The right foot was loaded, finding the 2nd toe remaining in a normal position with significant reduction of the preoperative deformity and the dorsal skin incision free of suture tension and tightness. Celestone Solu span 5 cc was then deposited in the operative area. Adaptic was applied to the skin incision and a mild compression dressing was then placed around the right foot, maintaining the 2nd toe in a straight and slightly plantar flexed position. The tourniquet was released and returned blood flow was found to be normal.

The immediate postoperative condition of the patient was excellent and she was returned to her room.

GODFREY REGIONAL HOSPITAL
123 Main Street • Aldon, FL 77714 • (407) 555-1234

Answers

EXERCISE 33

OPERATIVE REPORT

Patient information:	
Patient name: DOB: MR#:	Date: Surgeon: Anesthetist:

Preoperative diagnosis:

Impingement, right shoulder, with tear, rotator cuff

Postoperative diagnosis:

Impingement, right shoulder, with undersurface fraying, rotator cuff and inflammation, right glenohumeral joint

Procedure(s) performed:

Arthroscopy, right shoulder with Depo-Medrol injection, right glenohumeral joint, arthroscopic subacromial decompression, placement of infusion catheter

Anesthesia:

Assistant surgeon:

Description of procedure:

The patient was placed supine on the operating room table and a satisfactory general anesthetic was given. Preoperative intravenous cephalosporin antibiotic was given. Bilateral pneumatic compression sleeves were on the calves and were operative throughout the procedure. The patient was placed in the modified beach chair position. The left shoulder was widely prepped sterilely with DuraPrep times two including the lateral neck, anterior, lateral, posterior torso, axilla, and arm down to the hand. The right shoulder was draped in the usual sterile fashion. The scope cannula was introduced via a standard posterior portal and into the glenohumeral joint, followed by the arthroscope. Inflow to the shoulder through the cannula from the arthroscopy pump at a setting of 70 mm Hg. The shoulder was distended with normal saline in this fashion. Outflow from the cannula to suction. A flow of irrigation was maintained for purposes of visualization and removal of debris.

The biceps tendon was intact without evidence of stretching or tearing of its fibers or hemorrhage on its surface. Its attachment to the superior glenoid was intact. The anterior and posterior labral structures were intact without evidence of degeneration or displacement or separation from the glenoid. The articular surfaces of the humeral head and glenoid were intact without evidence of fibrillation, cartilaginous cracking, or breakdown. The anterior ligamentous structures were intact without evidence of stretching or tearing or hemorrhage on their surface. The anterior, posterior, and inferior recesses were of normal size and showed no evidence of intrasubstance pathology or loose body. The rotator cuff was scrutinized and showed some fibrillation at the watershed area but showed no evidence of tearing. There was quite a bit of synovitis involving the glenohumeral joint as a whole. The rotator cuff was visualized through the attachment site and showed no evidence of intrasubstance tear or detachment. A total of 80 mg Depo-Medrol with some Marcaine was then injected through the arthroscope cannula into the glenohumeral joint.

The arthroscope was withdrawn and redirected into the subacromial space. A standard lateral portal was made, followed by a rotary shaver with attached suction. The bursal tissue was excised as well as tissue on the undersurface of the acromion. There was obvious impingement in the subacromial space through range of motion of the shoulder.

A rotary burr with attached suction was used to perform a generous anterior inferior acromioplasty to the level of the acromioclavicular joint. The undersurface of the distal clavicle was slightly prominent and this required resection as well. Debris produced was removed via suction attached to the rotary burr. After the acromioplasty, the shoulder was placed through a range of motion and there was no further evidence of impingement.

An 18-gauge spinal needle was placed percutaneously through the deltoid muscle into the subacromial space, followed by placement through the needle of an epidural type catheter. The catheter remained in the subacromial space as the needle was withdrawn. The catheter was taped to the patient using sterile tape. A total of 30 cc of a combination of 0.5% Marcaine with epinephrine plus 5 mg morphine sulfate was injected into the subacromial space via the arthroscope cannula. The cannula was removed. Each portal was closed with a single simple suture of 3-0 Ethilon. The end of the epidural type catheter was connected to an infusion pump filled with 100 cc of 2% lidocaine without epinephrine at a delivery rate of 2 cc per hour. Dry sterile dressings were applied to the incision and catheter sites and held in place during removal of the drapes. Dressings were taped into place. Sling was applied.

The patient tolerated the procedure well. There were no complications. She was awakened in the operating room and transported to the recovery room in stable condition.

Patrick Chung md

GODFREY REGIONAL HOSPITAL
123 Main Street • Aldon, FL 77714 • (407) 555-1234

Answers

OPERATIVE REPORT

Patient information:

Patient name:	Date:
DOB:	Surgeon:
MR#:	Anesthetist:

Preoperative diagnosis:

Primary hyperparathyroidism secondary to parathyroid adenoma

INDICATIONS:
The patient had presented to her local physician with an elevated calcium level. She had seen Dr. Smith, endocrinologist, and was found to have elevated PTH as well as elevated calcium, and sestamibi scan was consistent with an adenoma of the inferior pole position. The patient was sent to my office for evaluation of surgical excision. The patient underwent injection with sestamibi again here at our facility. She did have images done again, which were consistent with adenoma of the right inferior pole position.

Postoperative diagnosis:

Same

Procedure(s) performed:

Excision of parathyroid adenoma with guided techniques

Anesthesia:

Assistant surgeon:

Description of procedure:

The patient was then brought to the operating room and placed under sedation. She was prepped and draped over the neck, and after this was completed and sedation was adequate, the neck was investigated with the navigator probe. I used a small calumniated probe. There was an area just lateral and slightly below the level of the cricoid. At this point, I did get the highest reading, which was around 417 counts. This was just static counts, not a 10-second count. The standard background seemed to be around 300 to 350. I thought this was most likely the position. I went ahead and planned my incision transversely and made a skin incision through a field of injected anesthetic, elevated platysma flaps for just about a centimeter, placed a self-retaining retractor, and divided the straps in the midline after injection of further lidocaine.

I then began my dissection, exposing the thyroid. There was a nodule on the thyroid that I did remove, feeling it was probably thyroid. It was on the inferior aspect and did come back as thyroid. Attempts to rotate the parathyroid adenoma initially were unsuccessful. The patient became uncomfortable. I went ahead and had the Anesthesia Department put her under general anesthesia and extended my incision. With the incision then larger, I was able to immediately get the probe deeper in the neck and identified the position of the adenoma. This was located in the tracheo-esophageal groove, not consistent with an inferior pole gland but with a superior pole gland that had become heavy and fallen posteriorly into the tracheo-esophageal groove. This was lying adjacent to the inferior thyroid artery where it crosses the recurrent laryngeal nerve. Blunt dissection was used to deliver this gland out of this position. It was teased up and its vascular pedicle was clipped carefully times two, and it was excised. We were careful to stay well away from and preserve the recurrent laryngeal nerve and the inferior thyroid artery in the process. The majority of the case was done with blunt dissection. We did occasionally use the Bovie to divide areolar tissue superficially in the neck. We did divide the middle thyroid vein between clips during the dissection process so that we could better expose the tracheo-esophageal groove.

After removing the gland from the neck and placing it on the tip of the probe, it had about 50% background count. The area of the excision of the gland also had decreased counts by about 50% after its removal. There were no other hot zones. Everything had essentially the same counts in that area, in all four quadrants of the thyroid.

At this point, the wound was irrigated. There was no bleeding. I closed the strap muscles with 3-0 Vicryl, the platysma with 3-0 Vicryl, and the skin with Prolene. The specimen was evaluated by Pathology and confirmed to be parathyroid. With the findings histologically, surgical findings, and radiographic findings as well as nuclear findings, I feel like this was the offending gland.

At this point, the procedure was terminated. The patient is stable in recovery.   *Maurice Deaters, MD*

GODFREY REGIONAL HOSPITAL
123 Main Street • Aldon, FL 77714 • (407) 555-1234

Answers

EXERCISE 35

OPERATIVE REPORT

Patient information:	
Patient name:	Date:
DOB:	Surgeon:
MR#:	Anesthetist:

Preoperative diagnosis:

Traumatic external nasal and internal nasal septal deviation. Deficient nasal tip support. Nasal obstruction.

INDICATION:

69-year-old male who sustained nasal trauma several years ago. Subsequent to that he was left with nasal obstruction. This was never treated. Now present is significant nasal septal deviation with absent nasal tip support.

Postoperative diagnosis:

Same

Procedure(s) performed:

Septoplasty. Columella reconstruction with cartilage graft.

Anesthesia:

Assistant surgeon:

Description of procedure:

After consent was obtained, the patient was taken to the operating room and placed on the operating table in supine position. After an adequate level of general endotracheal anesthesia was obtained, the patient was draped in the appropriate manner for nasal surgery. The patient's nose was prepped with Betadine prep and then draped in a sterile manner. Patient's nose was packed with cotton pledgets soaked with 4% cocaine. After several minutes, an intranasal injection of 1% Xylocaine to 1:100,000 units epinephrine was made. In addition, infiltration was also done in the columella. Nasal hairs were trimmed. Then utilizing a right hemitransfixion incision, bilateral mucoperichondrial and mucoperiosteal flaps were elevated. There was a significant amount of scarring around the cartilaginous septum. There were several fractures in the septum. Portions of the cartilaginous septum were missing. As such, under dissection there were several tears in the mucoperichondrium. Remnants of the cartilaginous septum were removed except for a dorsal strip. Portions of the bony septum were then removed. Spurs off the maxillary crest were also removed. The tears in the mucoperichondrium were reapproximated as best as possible with 4-0 chromic sutures. Attention was then focused on the columella. Utilizing an interior columella incision, the excess tissue at the base of the columella was excised. Excessive scar tissue was excised. Subsequently, a tip support was reconstructed with cartilaginous graft obtained from removed cartilaginous septum remnants. The medial crura were reapproximated with the cartilage graft. The incision was closed with interrupted 4-0 chromic sutures. A hemitransfixion incision was then closed with 4-0 chromic sutures. Sinolastic splints were then placed on both sides of the nasal septum and secured with nylon sutures. The nose was then packed bilaterally with Merocel sponge coated with Bacitracin ointment–infiltrated local solution. Nasal dressings were applied. The patient tolerated the procedure well. There was no break in technique. The patient was extubated and taken to postanesthesia care in good condition.

Fluids administered: 50 cc of RL

Blood loss: Less than 50 cc

Preoperative medication: 12 mg Decadron and 1 gram Ancef IV

Maurice Doater, MD

GODFREY REGIONAL HOSPITAL
123 Main Street • Aldon, FL 77714 • (407) 555-1234

Answers

OPERATIVE REPORT

Patient information:

Patient name:
DOB:
MR#:

Preoperative diagnosis:

Right parotid tumor versus postauricular cyst

CLINICAL NOTE:
The patient is a 62-year-old white male who has a 2-cm right postauricular mass that is soft with underlying deep parotid tissue surrounding it being much harder, measuring approximately 3.5 cm in diameter on palpation. The patient has no other palpable adenopathy in the neck. Operative findings, including frozen section, showed this to be consistent with benign lipoma. The lipoma involved the superficial portion of the parotid gland, comprising the inferior half of the parotid, from the earlobe down. It appeared to be herniating through the parotid fascia and superior region of the sternocleidomastoid muscle, causing the appearance of a postauricular cyst.

Postoperative diagnosis:

Right parotid tumor, consistent with lipoma

Procedure(s) performed:

Right superficial parotidectomy with facial nerve preservation/dissection

Description of procedure:

The patient was brought to the operating room and placed on the operating table in supine position. General endotracheal anesthesia was performed. A modified Blair incision was made from the right preauricular region, around the earlobe, and onto the neck, two fingerbreadths below the inferior border of the mandible. This was injected subcutaneously with injectable saline with 1:100,000 parts epinephrine. The patient was prepped and draped in a sterile fashion. Using a 15-blade scalpel, incision was made through skin and subcutaneous tissue. Initially, dissection was performed around the cystic area, which appeared to be a lipoma, and it was found to involve the superficial portion of the parotid gland. The entire incision was opened, with hemostasis being obtained with bipolar cautery. A subcutaneous flap was elevated anteriorly and the flap was reflected anteriorly. Dissection was made along the pretracheal pointer, but not completely down to the stylomastoid foramen, using tangential dissection along the reposed pathway of the main trunk of the facial nerve. Using meticulous dissection and bipolar cautery, the entire area of the pretracheal pointer, down onto the anterior border of the sternocleidomastoid muscle, was dissected and exposed, exposing the tumor. The tumor easily peeled off the sternocleidomastoid muscle and levator scapulae muscle. Dissection was then carried through the superficial parotid fascia anteriorly, along the palpable margin of the tumor. Using standard cross-clamp technique, followed by sharp incision, stepwise dissection was performed circumferentially around the tumor. Along the deep portion of the tumor, the above standard technique was used. The tumor involved the superficial lobe of the parotid, just lateral to the branch of the facial nerve. Only the small branch of the marginal mandibular branch of the facial nerve was visualized, with the remainder of the facial nerve, including the main trunk and pes anserinus lying within the soft tissue deep to the plane of dissection. The tumor was removed and sent to Pathology for frozen and permanent section. Frozen section revealed this to be lipoma with no malignant cells seen. An adjacent parotid lymph node was dissected in the superior margin of the surgical field and sent for frozen and permanent section. This also came back benign. No other masses were seen within the right parotid gland or neck.

Meticulous hemostasis was obtained with 3-0 silk sutures and bipolar cautery. The wound was copiously irrigated with normal saline and blotted dry. A 7-mm Jackson-Pratt drain was placed through a postauricular stab incision through the skin and sutured with 3-0 nylon purse-string sutures. This was placed just lateral to the area of dissection in the surgical field. The soft tissue of the parotid fascia was re-approximated to the anterior border of the sternocleidomastoid muscle. The deep soft tissue of the earlobe was re-approximated to the parotid fascia with interrupted 3-0 chromic sutures. The neck incision was closed with inverted interrupted 3-0 chromic sutures along the deep subcutaneous layer and around the region of the earlobe. Excess skin was excised posteriorly from the skin flap. The preauricular portion of the incision was closed in a similar fashion along the deep subcutaneous layer. Running interlocking 5-0 nylon sutures were used to close the skin in the preauricular and neck regions, followed by interrupted 5-0 nylon sutures around the earlobe. A Jackson-Pratt drain was placed to self-suction. The wound was dressed with Bacitracin ointment, followed by light Telfa occlusive dressing.

The patient was awakened from general anesthesia, extubated, and brought to the recovery room in stable condition, having tolerated the procedure well. In the recovery room, facial nerve function was intact bilaterally and symmetrically. No facial nerve function deficits were seen.

ESTIMATED BLOOD LOSS: Less than 25 cc

GODFREY REGIONAL HOSPITAL
123 Main Street • Aldon, FL 77714 • (407) 555-1234

Answers

EXERCISE 37

OPERATIVE REPORT

Patient information:	
Patient name: DOB: MR#:	

Preoperative diagnosis:

Right hepatic cyst

INDICATIONS FOR OPERATION:
This is a 57-year-old male with a history of a GI bleed who for several months has had right upper quadrant abdominal pain. His studies are significant for a large hepatic cyst. His symptoms are not consistent with pain from gallbladder disease. An elective hepatic cystectomy is scheduled.

Postoperative diagnosis:

Right hepatic cyst

FINDINGS:
Large hepatic cyst adjacent to the abdominal wall. A large portion of this cyst wall is removed and the fluid aspirated away. It was slightly bile-tinged but not frankly bilious. Specimen in the hepatic cyst wall was sent for pathology.

Procedure(s) performed:

Laparoscopic hepatic cystectomy

Anesthesia:

Assistant surgeon:

Description of procedure:

The patient was brought to the operating room and placed in a supine position on the operating room table. General endotracheal anesthesia was induced and the patient's abdomen was prepped and draped in the usual sterile fashion. The patient was given IV cefotetan preoperatively. An infraumbilical incision was created, and the underlying tissue was dissected to the fascia, which was divided in the midline sharply. Stay sutures of 0 Vicryl were placed in the edges of the fascia. The laparoscope was then inserted into the abdomen via the balloon tip 10-mm port. The abdomen was insufflated with CO_2 and laparoscope was inserted. Three additional 5-mm ports, two in the upper midline and one in the right lower quadrant, were placed. The liver was retracted to the left and superiorly. The large hepatic cyst was visualized. It seemed to be embedded in the abdominal wall. Its inferior portion was bluntly dissected free, as was its superior portion. The harmonic scalpel was then used to incise the cyst. The fluid was suctioned away. A large portion of this cyst wall, beginning at the anterior and superior portions and running inferiorly and posteriorly, created a large oval hole in this cyst. The oval hole was approximately 7 cm in diameter. This cyst was then removed through the infraumbilical port. Hemostasis was achieved. The abdomen was copiously irrigated, and all trocars were removed under direct visualization. The 10-mm port was closed with the previously placed stay sutures and an additional 0 Vicryl suture. All skin incisions were closed with 4-0 Monocryl subcuticular stitches.
Sterile dressings were applied, and the patient was awakened and taken to the PACU in good condition.

Patk Adam MD

GODFREY REGIONAL HOSPITAL
123 Main Street • Aldon, FL 77714 • (407) 555-1234

Answers

OPERATIVE REPORT

Patient information:

Patient name:
DOB:
MR#:

Date:
Surgeon:
Anesthetist:

Preoperative diagnosis:

Symptomatic uterine prolapse, declines pessary

CLINICAL NOTE: The patient is a very alert 93-year-old white female, para 0-0-1-0, with a long history of symptomatic uterine prolapse. In 1990, a pessary was placed with adequate relief. As she has gotten older, she has opted not to continue with the pessary and is now symptomatic with her prolapse. The cervix and anterior wall prolapse passed the introitus. She was counseled regarding the surgical procedure and was agreeable to proceed. She is not sexually active. She is aware of potential surgical risks including blood loss, infection, and urinary dysfunction. Overall she has a good understanding. Medical clearance was obtained from hospitalist.

Her preop lab studies included a normal CHEM-7. CBC reported an H&H of 13 and 40, platelets 255,000, white count 7.4. Her ECG showed a sinus rhythm with a rate of 74, 1st-degree AV block, and left bundle branch block. X-ray showed no evidence of acute infiltrates. The lung spaces were clear. Osteoporosis was noted in the thoracic vertebrae. Pulmonary vasculature was normal. Some granulomatous type calcifications were seen bilaterally.

Postoperative diagnosis:

Symptomatic uterine prolapse, declines pessary

Procedure(s) performed:

LeFort procedure

Anesthesia:

Spinal

Assistant surgeon:

Description of procedure:

OPERATIVE NOTE:
The patient was transferred to the operating room and onto the table where a spinal anesthetic was placed by the anesthesiologist. She was then positioned in the lithotomy position in the stirrups. The abdomen, vulva, and vagina were prepped with Betadine. A Foley catheter was placed to bag drainage. The cervix was extending outside the vagina. The cervix was grasped with a tenaculum. The anterior incision was made approximately 2 cm from the cervix and anteriorly up to approximately 5 cm from the urethral meatus. The denuded strip was approximately 2 to 3 cm in width. The denuded strip was grasped with a clamp. A posterior incision was made the same way. The procedure was then completed by suturing the anterior vaginal mucosa to the posterior vaginal mucosa and then by successive suturing to elevate the uterus and anterior bladder wall. The vaginal epithelium was then closed with a continuous suture of Vicryl. The procedure was terminated.

The patient was returned to the recovery room in satisfactory condition. Blood loss was about 30 cc. She did quite well. She will be maintained in the hospital for a 23-hour stay and then returned to the nursing home tomorrow.

Rachel Perez, MD

GODFREY REGIONAL HOSPITAL
123 Main Street • Aldon, FL 77714 • (407) 555-1234

Answers

EXERCISE 39

OPERATIVE REPORT

Patient information:

Patient name:
DOB:
MR#:

Date:
Surgeon:
Anesthetist:

Preoperative diagnosis:

1. Recurrent urinary retention
2. Enlarged prostate with bladder outlet obstruction
3. Generalized debilitation due to pancreatitis

Postoperative diagnosis:

1. Recurrent urinary retention
2. Enlarged prostate with bladder outlet obstruction
3. Generalized debilitation due to pancreatitis

FINDINGS: The anterior urethra was normal. Membranous urethra was normal. The prostatic urethra revealed enlargement of the prostate causing bladder outlet obstruction.

Examination of the bladder revealed some areas of acute cystitis secondary to recent Foley catheterization, and there were some changes of chronic bladder outlet obstruction with trabeculation of the bladder, but there were no stones, tumors, diverticula, or ulcerations seen.

Procedure(s) performed:

1. Flexible cystourethroscopy   2. Percutaneous cystostomy insertion

Anesthesia:

Assistant surgeon:

Description of procedure:

With the patient in the supine position, the lower midline abdomen and the penis and genitalia were prepped and draped in sterile fashion. The lower midline abdomen, two fingerbreadths above the symphysis pubis, was the site for this cystostomy catheter insertion. This area was infiltrated subcutaneously with 1% plain Xylocaine and infiltration continued inward to the level of the rectus fascia.

A small stab incision was made in this site with an 11-blade knife. Flexible cystourethroscopy was then performed, with the above findings noted. The bladder was distended with the irrigation fluid until the bladder was palpable in the suprapubic area. The cystostomy trocar was then advanced through the stab incision just above the symphysis pubis and passed in all the way through the anterior bladder wall and into the lumen of the bladder under direct vision with the cystoscope in place. The 12 French cystostomy catheter was advanced through the sheath after removing the trocar, and the sheath was then removed, leaving the catheter in place. The balloon of the catheter was inflated with 10 cc of sterile water.

The cystostomy catheter was then attached to a sterile drainage bag. A single stitch of 3-0 nylon was used to tighten the stab incision at the site of the cystostomy catheter. The cystoscope was removed.

The patient tolerated the procedure well and was taken to the day surgery unit in satisfactory condition.

Rachel Perez MD

GODFREY REGIONAL HOSPITAL
123 Main Street • Aldon, FL 77714 • (407) 555-1234

Answers

OPERATIVE REPORT

Patient information:

Patient name:	Date:
DOB:	Surgeon:
MR#:	Anesthetist:

Preoperative diagnosis:

Internal disk disruption at L4-L5 and lumbar disk bulge at L3-L4

Postoperative diagnosis:

Internal disk disruption at L4-L5 and lumbar disk bulge at L3-L4

Procedure(s) performed:

Nucleoplasty at L3-L4 and right L4-L5 IDET

Description of procedure:

PREOPERATIVE INFORMATION: All risks and benefits of the procedure were explained to the patient to include paralysis, nerve injury, worsening of the symptoms, failure of the procedure, bleeding, and infection. The patient understands all of these risks and the patient wishes to proceed. The patient is given 1 gram of vancomycin IV piggyback prior to taking him into the operating room.

DESCRIPTION OF PROCEDURE:
The patient is placed prone on the spinal table in the operative suite, and the patient is sterilely prepped and draped. After localization of the skin at the L3-L4 level, coming in from the right side, a 17-gauge introducer needle is passed into the L3-L4 disk and confirmed on two planes by fluoroscopy, after which the Per-D catheter is passed into the L3-L4 disk, and at this level a total of 8 channels are created at the 2, 4, 6, 8, and 10 o'clock positions along with two additional channels. At each of these channels, coblation is performed during entry into the disk and coagulation is performed during exit from the disk.

The patient experienced muscle spasms during creation of several of these channels, and during the muscle spasm episodes, the coblation was discontinued. Each of the muscle spasms was during coblation and not coagulation. At each time that the patient had muscle spasms, the tip of the needle was confirmed on fluoroscopy. The patient tolerated this procedure well without complications.

The IDET procedure was then set up at the L4-L5 level and initial attempt was made from the right side after entering into the L4-L5 disk with a 17-gauge needle that is part of the IDET kit. The IDET catheter kinked during passage into the L4-L5 disk from the right side, and therefore, the needle and the catheter were removed and the L4-L5 disk was entered from the left side. After the disk was entered with 17-gauge needle, the intradiskal catheter was passed into the L4-L5 disk without complications and was seen to wrap completely around the posterior lateral aspect of the right L4-L5 disk without paresthesias and without complications.

At this level, the catheter tip temperature was set at 65 degrees centigrade, after which it was increased by 1 degree centigrade to a total of 90 degrees centigrade where it was maintained for 4 minutes. There were no paresthesias and there was no radiculopathy during this procedure.

The patient tolerated this without complications.

POSTOPERATIVE DISCUSSION: The patient is given 40 tablets of Lortab 10/650 for postop pain control. The patient states that he must travel tonight and states that he is going to go ahead and put a bed in the back of his car and he will go in the supine position. The patient states that he needs to go because there is no one to take care of him here, and therefore, I have cautioned him against this trip. But he is determined to go, and therefore, I have given him his pain medication that he can take on an as-needed basis. Instructions for him I have given to him on two separate sheets—one for recovery from nucleoplasty and one for recovery from IDET. The patient is to wear a back brace for the first week during recovery in which he is to not perform any strenuous exercises. He is to slowly increase his activity over the next 2 to 3 weeks after his recovery. The patient is to call the pain clinic if he has any problems at all or any signs of an infection. The patient will start his physical therapy sometime around 3 to 4 weeks, depending on his recovery process.

Adm Westg MD

GODFREY REGIONAL HOSPITAL
123 Main Street • Aldon, FL 77714 • (407) 555-1234

Answers

OPERATIVE REPORT

Patient information:	
Patient name: DOB: MR#:	Date: Surgeon: Anesthetist:

Preoperative diagnosis:

Post lumbar laminectomy pain syndrome

Postoperative diagnosis:

Post lumbar laminectomy pain syndrome

Procedure(s) performed:

1. Implantation of constant flow aero pump. The pump chosen is a 50 cc pump with a 1 cc per day delivery rate.
2. Implantation of intrathecal aero catheter with tunneling
3. Intrathecal myelogram with interpretation
4. Intraoperative use of fluoroscopy
5. Pump refill with total of 50 cc of morphine sulfate, concentration 0.5 mg/cc to deliver 0.5 mg of morphine per day
6. Pump re-bolus with 0.5 mg of morphine sulfate using a special aero type of intrathecal bolus injection needle

Anesthesia:

General endotracheal

Description of procedure:

COMPLICATIONS: None

BLOOD LOSS: Less than 25 cc

DESCRIPTION OF PROCEDURE:

After informed consent, and after detailed description of the procedure and its rationale, including complications, benefits, alternatives, and risks, the patient understands and wishes to proceed. The patient was placed on standard monitors with oxygen supplementation and positioned prone on the fluoro table. Mid to lower back area was then prepped with Betadine and draped in the usual sterile fashion. After general anesthesia was administered, he was positioned in the left lateral decubitus, and the right lower back, right flank, and right lower abdominal area were prepped with Betadine and draped in the usual sterile fashion.

Initially, incision was made in the lower lumbar region, along the previous scar. Dissection was carried down to the fascia plane under continuous fluoroscopy, and the 17-gauge intra-thecal needle was used to access the intra-thecal space. At the level of L3, L4, the intra-thecal space was identified and brisk CSF backflow was noted. Under continuous fluoroscopy, the titanium alloy catheter was threaded in a cephalad direction to the lower border of T11. At this time, the distal end of the catheter was accessed and approximately 5 cc of Isovue 200 was injected with visualization of the intrathecal myelographic effect, which was seen to extend from the upper border of T9 to the lower border of L4. A picture was saved for the records. Subsequently, the intrathecal needle was removed and the catheter was secured with pursestring sutures using 4-0 Prolene, and the catheter was secured to the underlying catheter using 2-0 silk at three different points. Subsequently, attention was directed to the right lower abdominal area where a transverse incision was made about the level of the umbilicus, and the tissues were dissected down to the fascia where a pocket was created to accommodate the pump reservoir. The catheter was tunneled from the lumbar region to the site of the pump reservoir. The pump was secured to the underlying fascia using three different points with 0 Prolene sutures. The intrathecal catheter was connected to the pump catheter in the usual manner and a test flow was carried out to verify adequate CSF backflow without any obstruction or leak. The pump was then filled with a total of 50 ccs first delivery of morphine sulfate, concentration 0.5 mg/cc. A special bolus injection needle was introduced and the position appropriately verified, and a total of 0.5 mg of morphine was given as a direct intrathecal bolus.

Both wounds were thoroughly irrigated with Bacitracin-containing irrigant. Verifying adequate hemostasis, the wounds were closed in two layers using 3-0 Vicryl sutures for subcutaneous closure, interrupted. Staples were used for the skin. The patient tolerated the procedure well without complication and was transferred to the recovery room in stable condition. The patient received 2 grams of Ancef preoperatively and will be continued on Ancef IV throughout his hospitalization. He will be admitted to the observation suite. Postoperatively, he was examined and he was found to be hemodynamically and neurologically stable.

PLAN:
1. Admit to the observation suite.
2. Follow up and re-assess.

Adm Westy MD

GODFREY REGIONAL HOSPITAL
123 Main Street • Aldon, FL 77714 • (407) 555-1234

Answers

OPERATIVE REPORT

Patient information:

Patient name:
DOB:
MR#:

Date:
Surgeon:
Anesthetist:

Preoperative diagnosis:

1. Status post implantation of programmable Medtronic pump
2. End of battery life

Postoperative diagnosis:

1. Status post implantation of programmable Medtronic pump
2. End of battery life

Procedure(s) performed:

1. Explantation of Medtronic pump
2. Revision of the implant pocket
3. Implantation of constant-flow aeropump type of pump implanted with 30 cc reservoir with 0.5 cc per day delivery rate
4. Pump refill with a total of 18 cc, the first delivery of morphine sulfate concentration, 10 mg per cc with clonidine concentration 100 micrograms per cc, a total of only 18 cc was used to fill the pump reservoir.
5. Pump bolus with 0.5 mg of morphine sulfate as a direct intrathecal bolus by the implanted catheter for anesthesia/pain management.

Anesthesia:

Endotracheal anesthesia

Assistant surgeon:

Description of procedure:

BLOOD LOSS: Less than 10 cc

COMPLICATIONS: None

INSTRUMENT AND LAP COUNT: Correct

DESCRIPTION OF PROCEDURE:
Following informed consent, and after detailed description of the procedure, complications, and risks, the patient understands and accepts the risks and complications and wishes to proceed. The patient was cleared by primary care physician. The patient was taken to the operating suite and positioned supine on the fluoroscopy table. The existing Medtronic pump was prepped with Betadine and draped in the usual sterile fashion. Incision was made along the previous scar and the tissues were dissected down to the fascial plane. The anchoring sutures of the existing pump were released. It was evident at that point that the previous Medtronic pump was implanted subcutaneously and it was not anchored to the underlying fascia. We then proceeded to dissect the capsule out. The floor of the capsule was completely removed. Subsequently, the subcutaneous tissues were dissected down to the fascial plane. The fascia was exposed. At this point, three 0-Proline sutures were used to anchor the aeropump to the underlying fascia at three different rings. The aeropump catheter was then connected to the existing intrathecal catheter using a special metallic connector. A test flow was then carried out using a special aero intrathecal bolus injection needle with visualization of CSF backflow without any obstruction or leakage. Subsequently, a total of 0.5 mg of morphine sulfate was given as a direct intrathecal bolus. The pump reservoir was then filled with a total of 18 cc of morphine sulfate, concentration at 10 mg per cc, with clonidine concentration 100 mcg per cc. The wound was thoroughly irrigated. Adequate hemostasis was then achieved. Wound was then closed in two layers using 3-0 Vicryl interrupted subcutaneous closure and staples of the skin. Betadine ointment, Telfa, and sterile dressing were applied.

The patient was taken to the recovery room in stable condition. The patient received antibiotic prophylaxis preoperatively and will be continued on oral antibiotics as an outpatient. He will be released today once he is assessed to be hemodynamically and neurologically stable, which he is at this time. The patient will be seen in follow-up in the office for further care.

Ahn Westy MD

GODFREY REGIONAL HOSPITAL
123 Main Street • Aldon, FL 77714 • (407) 555-1234

Answers

OPERATIVE REPORT

Patient information:

Patient name: Date:
DOB: Surgeon:
MR#:   Anesthetist:

Preoperative diagnosis:

Watery eyes since birth

Postoperative diagnosis:

Same

Procedure(s) performed:

Bilateral tear duct probing
HISTORY:
This young child has had watery eyes since birth. Massage and antibiotics controlled it somewhat, but eyes continued to be sticky, so it was elected to syringe and probe his ducts.

Anesthesia:

Assistant surgeon:

Description of procedure:

Under general anesthesia, the left eye was started and the lower canaliculus was dilated, but we were unable to pass along the duct into the lacrimal sac. So going through the upper canaliculus, which was narrow at the junction of the upper and lower canaliculi, I was able to enter the sac. Syringed and probed with a #2 probe. On the right, the inferior duct was opened into the lacrimal sac and syringed and probed with a #2. I discussed with the parents afterwards that the right eye looked like it was going to be okay, but the left one may well need tubes in the future. Patient is to be seen in a week in the office.

Linda Patrick MD

GODFREY REGIONAL HOSPITAL
123 Main Street • Aldon, FL 77714 • (407) 555-1234

Answers

OPERATIVE REPORT

Patient information:

Patient name: Date:
DOB: Surgeon:
MR#:   Anesthetist:

Preoperative diagnosis:

Lower lid ectropion and punctual stenosis, bilateral

Postoperative diagnosis:

Procedure(s) performed:

Bilateral punctoplasty also with a bilateral ectropion repair via a medial spindle procedure, also known as a lower lid shortening procedure

Anesthesia:

Assistant surgeon:

Description of procedure:

The family was informed of the risks and benefits of the procedure, and informed consent was placed in the chart. The patient was brought back to the operating room. Vital signs were noted to be stable. The patient is given local anesthesia using a 50/50 mixture of 0.75% Marcaine, 2% lidocaine with epinephrine, and Wydase. 0.5 cc of the solution was injected into the lower lids of both eyes. The patient was prepped and draped in a sterile fashion. Using a long Vannas scissors, a 1-snip punctoplasty was performed in both lower canaliculi. I then turned my attention to the lower lid. I removed a wedge of conjunctiva as well as underlying muscle and re-approximated the wedge using interrupted 8-0 Vicryl sutures. This turned the lower lid in nicely, medially. Both eyes were done in the exact same manner.

Patient tolerated the procedure well. Estimated blood loss was less than 5 ccs. Patient is to use TobraDex drops 4 times a day for approximately 1 week and follow up in 1 month or sooner if she is having problems. No complications.

Linda Patrick MD

GODFREY REGIONAL HOSPITAL
123 Main Street • Aldon, FL 77714 • (407) 555-1234

Answers

OPERATIVE REPORT

Patient information:

Patient name:
DOB:
MR#:

Preoperative diagnosis:

Left tympanic membrane perforation

CLINICAL NOTE:
The patient is a 79-year-old white male with left tympanic membrane perforation involving the inferior half of the tympanic membrane, central in location. He is being brought to the operating room for repair of the tympanic membrane perforation.

Postoperative diagnosis:

Left tympanic membrane perforation

Procedure(s) performed:

Left tympanoplasty. Temporalis fascia graft. Split-thickness skin graft taken from left postauricular ear to reconstruct tympanic membrane perforation.
ESTIMATED BLOOD LOS: Negligible

Anesthesia:

General

Assistant surgeon:

SURGEON: Faisal Mahmood, MD

Description of procedure:

The patient was brought to the operating room and placed on the operating table in a supine position. General endotracheal anesthesia was performed. The left ear was injected with 1% lidocaine with 1:100,000 parts epinephrine in the bony cartilaginous junction endaurally and postauricularly. The left ear was prepped and draped in a sterile fashion.

Using a microscope for visualization, the left middle ear was examined. There was some erosion of the manubrium of the malleus, but ossicles appeared to be intact on visualization of the stapes superstructure. Using an otic pick and microcup forceps, the tympanic membrane perforation was de-epithelialized around its circumference. There were no middle ear adhesions seen.

Left superior postauricular incision was made with a 15-blade scalpel and dissection was carried down to the temporalis fascia using Bovie cautery. Temporalis fascia was harvested in a standard fashion and placed in a fascia press and allowed to dry. Using a 15-blade scalpel, a split-thickness skin graft was taken from behind the left ear. The donor site was cauterized for hemostasis. A skin graft was also placed in a fascia press and allowed to air dry.

The left middle ear was then packed with a layer of Gelfilm along the medial wall of the middle ear, followed by Gelfoam, impregnated with 1:100,000 parts epinephrine squeeze-dried, up to the level of the tympanic membrane perforation. Temporalis fascia graft was cut to size and placed as an underlay graft. Split-thickness skin graft was placed lateral to the tympanic membrane perforation and directly over the underlay graft, followed by an overlay graft of larger temporalis fascia. A second layer of Gelfilm was placed lateral to the overlay graft, followed by Gelfoam impregnated with Cortisporin otic suspension to completely fill the ear canal. A cotton ball dressing with Bacitracin ointment was placed in the left ear. A postauricular incision was closed with inverted interrupted 4-0 chromic sutures for the subcutaneous layer, followed by interrupted 5-0 nylon sutures for the skin. A mastoid pressure dressing was placed.

The patient was awakened from general anesthesia, extubated, and brought to the recovery room in stable condition, having tolerated the procedure well.

James Ellicott MD

GODFREY REGIONAL HOSPITAL
123 Main Street • Aldon, FL 77714 • (407) 555-1234

Answers

CRITICAL THINKING EXERCISES

The following operative reports have already been assigned CPT and ICD-9-CM codes. Review the code(s) assigned and determine the following:

1. Incorrect Assignment of CPT and/or ICD-9-CM codes
2. Incorrect Order of CPT and/or ICD-9-CM codes
3. Incorrect Use of Modifier Code(s)

After determining what is incorrect about the code assignments, indicate the coding rules that specify how these services should be correctly coded.

CRITICAL THINKING EXERCISE 1

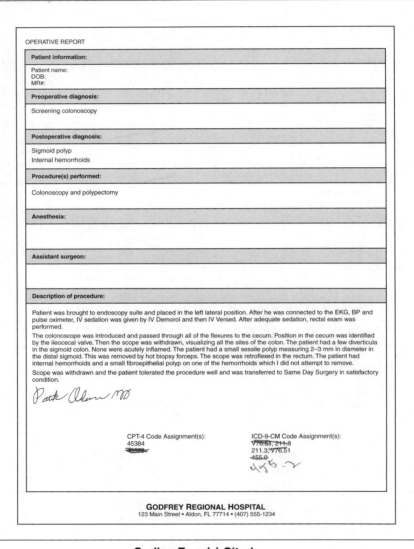

OPERATIVE REPORT

Patient information:

Patient name:
DOB:
MR#:

Preoperative diagnosis:

Screening colonoscopy

Postoperative diagnosis:

Sigmoid polyp
Internal hemorrhoids

Procedure(s) performed:

Colonoscopy and polypectomy

Anesthesia:

Assistant surgeon:

Description of procedure:

Patient was brought to endoscopy suite and placed in the left lateral position. After he was connected to the EKG, BP and pulse oximeter, IV sedation was given by IV Demorol and then IV Versed. After adequate sedation, rectal exam was performed.

The colonoscope was introduced and passed through all of the flexures to the cecum. Position in the cecum was identified by the ileocecal valve. Then the scope was withdrawn, visualizing all the sites of the colon. The patient had a few diverticula in the sigmoid colon. None were acutely inflamed. The patient had a small sessile polyp measuring 2–3 mm in diameter in the distal sigmoid. This was removed by hot biopsy forceps. The scope was retroflexed in the rectum. The patient had internal hemorrhoids and a small fibroepithelial polyp on one of the hemorrhoids which I did not attempt to remove.

Scope was withdrawn and the patient tolerated the procedure well and was transferred to Same Day Surgery in satisfactory condition.

Patke Adams MD

CPT-4 Code Assignment(s):
45384
~~45378~~

ICD-9-CM Code Assignment(s):
~~V76.51, 211.3~~
211.3, V76.51
~~455.0~~
V76.2

GODFREY REGIONAL HOSPITAL
123 Main Street • Aldon, FL 77714 • (407) 555-1234

Coding Error(s) Cited

OPERATIVE REPORT

Patient information:
Patient name: DOB: MR#:

Preoperative diagnosis:
Hematochezia and chronic pyrosis

Postoperative diagnosis:
Same

Procedure(s) performed:
Colonoscopy with pedicle cauterization of AV malformations Upper endoscopy with CLOtest

Anesthesia:

Assistant surgeon:

Description of procedure:

After obtaining informed consent, the patient was brought to the OR and placed in the left lateral position. IV line and IV sedation were given. The colonoscopy was done followed by the upper endoscopy. Digital rectal exam was done and scope was introduced and advanced all the way to the cecum identified by the ileocecal valve and appendical orifice. There were several AV malformations, which were electrocauterized. There were several, of which at least 6 were electrocauterized. The rest of the colon mucosa appeared healthy. No ulcers, no masses, no polyps were seen. Retroflexion was done in the rectum which revealed external hemorrhoids and the scope was straightened and pulled out.

The upper endoscopy was introduced following spraying the mouth with Cetacaine. The EGD scope was introduced in the mouth and guided into the esophagus. Esophagus appeared normal, no signs of inflammation. He has a hiatal hernia extending from 38 to 40 cm. The scope was then advanced into the stomach, where no ulcers or masses were observed. Pylorus appeared normal and the scope was then pushed into the duodenum. The duodenal bulb was severely erythematous. CLOtest biopsy was taken. Retroflexion was done, scope was dropped down into the fundus which also appeared normal. The scope was straightened out and pulled back into the GE junction. Excess air was sucked out. The scope was removed and the patient tolerated the procedure well.

Patrk Adam MD

CPT-4 Code Assignment(s):
43239
45383-51

ICD-9-CM Code Assignment(s):
578.1, 787.2
578.1, 787.1

GODFREY REGIONAL HOSPITAL
123 Main Street • Aldon, FL 77714 • (407) 555-1234

Coding Error(s) Cited

OPERATIVE REPORT

Patient information:

Patient name:
DOB:
MR#:

Preoperative diagnosis:

Chronic adenotonsillitis and serous otitis media left ear, plugged tube right

Postoperative diagnosis:

Same

Procedure(s) performed:

T & A
Clean and replace right tube
Insert tympanostomy tube left

Anesthesia:

Assistant surgeon:

Description of procedure:

This 7-year-old child has had several bouts of severe tonsillitis. He has been on numerous antibiotics without the ability to clear. He has also had a recent bout of otitis with drainage from the right ear.

The patient was placed under general endotracheal anesthesia and the ears examined bilaterally. There was a moderate amount of debris obstructing the tube I previously placed in the right ear. The tube was carefully removed, the area cleaned, and a new tube placed. The left ear was examined, strands of serous fluid were present in the middle ear. The tube had extruded and could not be located. A myringotomy was performed, fluid aspirated and a modified T-grommet tube inserted. Following this, the nasopharynx was examined with hypertrophic adenoidal tissue noted. This was carefully removed with a curette and punch. The tonsils were enlarged as well, and a tonsillectomy was performed using Bovie technique. One cc of

Adm Westg MD

CPT-4 Code Assignment(s):	ICD-9-CM Code Assignment(s):
42820	474.00
69436-50	382.9
69424-RT	382.9

GODFREY REGIONAL HOSPITAL
123 Main Street • Aldon, FL 77714 • (407) 555-1234

Coding Error(s) Cited

OPERATIVE REPORT

Patient information:

Patient name:
DOB:
MR#:

Preoperative diagnosis:

Rectal bleeding

Postoperative diagnosis:

Same
Plus anal fissure

Procedure(s) performed:

Examination under anesthesia with left lateral internal sphincterotomy

Anesthesia:

Assistant surgeon:

Description of procedure:

This 57-year-old female has had several significant episodes of rectal bleeding. By examination, she has no hemorrhoids, but does have history of an anal fissure.

After adequate preparation, Xylocaine was used to infiltrate a perianal block. Exam of the anal canal does not show any significant internal hemorrhoids. She does, however, have a posterior anal fissure. The left lateral mucosa over the internal sphincter was incised and hemostasis was controlled. The direct visualization, the sphincter was completely divided. The mucous membrane was then oversewn in a running locking fashion with 4-0 Vicryl.

The patient was taken to the recovery room in satisfactory condition.

Patk Adam MD

CPT-4 Code Assignment(s):   ICD-9-CM Code Assignment(s):
57410   569.3
52277-51   565.0

GODFREY REGIONAL HOSPITAL
123 Main Street • Aldon, FL 77714 • (407) 555-1234

Coding Error(s) Cited

OPERATIVE REPORT

Patient information:

Patient name:
DOB:
MR#:

Preoperative diagnosis:

Lateral forearm laceration
Elbow laceration

Postoperative diagnosis:

Same

Procedure(s) performed:

Laceration repairs forearm and elbow

Anesthesia:

Assistant surgeon:

Description of procedure:

This 69-year-old female fell approximately 1 hour ago while at home, suffering a significant laceration on the lateral forearm. Over the proximal elbow, is a small laceration as well.

Both locations were anesthetized with 9 ccs of 1% Lidocaine. With adequate anesthesia, the elbow laceration is examined and closed with Steri-Strips only. Next the forearm wound is examined which goes into the deep tissue. The deep layers are closed with 3-0 Dexon in a running stitch closing the deep layer. Then the skin in closed using 5-0 Ethilon. The forearm laceration was approximately 11 cm in length closure.

Robert Rai MD

CPT-4 Code Assignment(s):	ICD-9-CM Code Assignment(s):
12034	881.01
12001-51	881.00

GODFREY REGIONAL HOSPITAL
123 Main Street • Aldon, FL 77714 • (407) 555-1234

Coding Error(s) Cited

OPERATIVE REPORT

Patient information:

Patient name:
DOB:
MR#:

Preoperative diagnosis:

Mass right breast

Postoperative diagnosis:

Infiltrating ductal carcinoma, breast, right

Procedure(s) performed:

Excisional breast biopsy, right breast
followed by lumpectomy and axillary
node dissection

Anesthesia:

Assistant surgeon:

Description of procedure:

Patient was placed on the operating table in the supine position. The right breast and axilla were prepped with DuraPrep and draped in the usual manner. The patient had a palpable mass in the right upper breast correlating with a previous mammogram. A transverse incision was made and deepened through subcutaneous tissue. The mass was felt and excision was carried out around the entire lesion and then sent to pathology.

The results were infiltrating ductal carcinoma with adequate margin. The decision to proceed with a lumpectomy had already been discussed with the patient prior to the procedure in these circumstances. The skin was then marked and an elliptical incision made 2 cm from each edge of the previous incision. The incision was carried down to the pectoralis fascia. A lumpectomy was performed and we proceeded with axillary node dissection deepened through the subcutaneous tissue. The axilla was entered and a few palpable nodes were noted to be enlarged and suspicious. Dissection was completed and submitted for pathology. A Jackson-Pratt was placed in the wound and secured with 2-0 silk.

After irrigation, the incisions were closed with interrupted 2-0 Vicryl. Another layer of running 3-0 Vicryl on the dermis and the skin with subcuticular 4-0 Dexon were used. Neosporin and dressing were applied. The breast was covered with an Ace bandage on the chest for compression. Blood loss was about 100 cc. The patient tolerated the procedure well.

John Werty MD

CPT-4 Code Assignment(s):	ICD-9-CM Code Assignment(s):
19160-RT	174.9
19120-51-RT	174.9

GODFREY REGIONAL HOSPITAL
123 Main Street • Aldon, FL 77714 • (407) 555-1234

Coding Error(s) Cited

OPERATIVE REPORT

Patient information:

Patient name:
DOB:
MR#:

Preoperative diagnosis:

Left knee medial collateral ligament tear
ACL cruciate ligament tear

Postoperative diagnosis:

Same

Procedure(s) performed:

Diagnostic arthroscopy
Debridement, ACL stump
Repair, lateral meniscus

Anesthesia:

Assistant surgeon:

Description of procedure:

Patient was taken to OR, placed in the supine position and turned in the left lateral decubitus position. Patient's left lower extremity was prepped and draped in the normal fashion. The knee was then insufflated with fluid, a large trocar was placed in the medial suprapatellar pouch, two parapatellar ports, one lateral and one medial were made. Visualization of the joint began at the suprapatellar pouch, where no significant abnormalities were found. Exam of the medial gutter revealed no loose bodies. Exam of the medial joint line revealed the meniscus intact.

Examination of the notch revealed the ACL completely avulsed. The remaining tendon was debrided using the automated shaver. Attention was then turned to the posterior horn of the meniscus which was torn in its periphery. Exam of the lateral gutter revealed no loose bodies or abnormalities.

Attention was then turned to the lateral meniscus, where, using a meniscal shaver, the tear was debrided. Using the arthroscope, the posterior horn of the lateral meniscus was then sutured with two mattress-like sutures. The sutures were then tied over the posterolateral capsule and visualization with the scope revealed the meniscus to be stable and in excellent position.

The wound was thoroughly irrigated and the subcutaneous tissue closed with 3-0 Vicryl and the skin with running 3-0 nylon. The knee was irrigated with copious fluid and the patient was taken to the recovery room in stable condition. Instrument, sponge and needle counts were correct.

CPT-4 Code Assignment(s):	ICD-9-CM Code Assignment(s):
29870	884.2, 844.0, 836.2
29877-59-RT	884.2, 844.0, 836.2
29883-59-RT	884.2, 844.0, 836.2

GODFREY REGIONAL HOSPITAL
123 Main Street • Aldon, FL 77714 • (407) 555-1234

Coding Error(s) Cited

OPERATIVE REPORT

Patient information:

Patient name:
DOB:
MR#:

Preoperative diagnosis:

Chronic nasogastric tube feeding
Dysphagia

Postoperative diagnosis:

Same

Procedure(s) performed:

Esophagogastroduodenoscopy with
percutaneous feeding gastrostomy
tube placement

Anesthesia:

Assistant surgeon:

Description of procedure:

The endoscope was advanced into the esophagus which appeared normal. Fundus and body of the stomach were normal as well as the antrum. Pylorus was normal as well as the first and second portion of the duodenum. A guide wire was inserted through a catheter which was snared by the endoscope and brought out through the mouth. The gastrostomy tube was then threaded over the guide wire. The patient was then re-endoscoped for position and it was adequate.

Patk Adam MD

CPT-4 Code Assignment(s):
43246
43235-51

ICD-9-CM Code Assignment(s):
787.2

GODFREY REGIONAL HOSPITAL
123 Main Street • Aldon, FL 77714 • (407) 555-1234

Coding Error(s) Cited

OPERATIVE REPORT

Patient information:

Patient name:
DOB:
MR#:

Preoperative diagnosis:

Scalp Lesion

Postoperative diagnosis:

Squamous cell carcinoma of scalp

Procedure(s) performed:

Excision of squamous cell ca of the scalp

Anesthesia:

Assistant surgeon:

Description of procedure:

The patient was brought to the OR and placed in the supine position. The scalp area was examined and a 3 X 3 cm mass was located at the top of the occiput area. In addition, a small .5 X .5 cm lesion was seen in the paranasal area as well.

The scalp area was prepared with Betadine solution and draped in the usual sterile fashion. The lesion was then sharply excised around its circumference. The lesion was sent to pathology and read as squamous cell carcinoma with clear margins. Hemostasis was obtained using the electrocautery device as well as 3-0 silk ligatures.

The paranasal lesion was examined and determined it should also be removed at this time. After appropriate anesthetic agent was injected into the area, the lesion was removed in toto. The area was closed with 4-0 Vicryl.

The patient was taken to the recovery room in satisfactory condition.

Adm Westg MD

CPT-4 Code Assignment(s):
11604

ICD-9-CM Code Assignment(s):
173.9

GODFREY REGIONAL HOSPITAL
123 Main Street • Aldon, FL 77714 • (407) 555-1234

Coding Error(s) Cited

OPERATIVE REPORT

Patient information:

Patient name:
DOB:
MR#:

Preoperative diagnosis:

Pelvic pain, vulvar lesion

Postoperative diagnosis:

Pelvic pain, vulvar lesion with extensive adhesions

Procedure(s) performed:

Laparoscopic and extensive lysis of adhesions and simple vulvectomy

Anesthesia:

Assistant surgeon:

Description of procedure:

Patient was taken to the operating room after an adequate level of general endotracheal anesthesia, placed in the dorsal lithotomy position, prepped and draped in the usual manner. A vaginal speculum was placed in the vagina. The cervix was grasped with a single tooth tenaculum and a uterine manipulator placed. A subumbilical incision was made and a blunt cannula placed through a 9.9 flow demand of CO_2 with a maximum pressure of 15 mmHg. A second port as well as a left lateral port was also placed. The patient had obvious pelvic infection in the past. There are adhesions from the uterus to the uterovesical fold. There are adhesions from both ovaries to the cul-de-sac. There are adhesions of the rectosigmoid on the left side. The examination revealed a normal liver and appendix. The adhesions in the cul-de-sac and uterus were taken down. The left side had the ovary imbedded into the side wall and the tube had no fimbria. Thus, at the end of the procedure we had freed up both ovaries and tubes, however, there were no openings to the tubes present. The scope was removed and the incision was closed with 2-0 Vicryl.

Attention was now directed to the lesion on the vulvar where the lesion was removed along with a small portion of the vulvar.

Adm Westg MD

CPT-4 Code Assignment(s):   ICD-9-CM Code Assignment(s):
56620   184.4
58660   625.9

GODFREY REGIONAL HOSPITAL
123 Main Street • Aldon, FL 77714 • (407) 555-1234

Coding Error(s) Cited

14 Coding Complexities of Surgical Procedures

EXERCISES 1-40

Identify and assign the appropriate CPT codes for the following medical records.

EXERCISE 1

OPERATIVE REPORT

Patient information:	
Patient name: DOB: MR#:	Date: Surgeon: Anesthetist:

Preoperative diagnosis:

Mass right breast

Postoperative diagnosis:

Same

Procedure(s) performed:

Ultrasound-guided needle localization of right breast lesion. Excision biopsy of lesion of right breast following ultrasound localization. Frozen-section exam, all revealing benign fibroadenoma of the right breast.

Anesthesia:

Assistant surgeon:

Description of procedure:

The patient was admitted this morning for surgery. She had recently been evaluated and found to have a right breast lump. Ultrasound suggested a solid mass, and excision was recommended. We obtained an informed consent and she was admitted this morning for the same. I explained to her that the procedure was to be done with needle localization so that the exact lump palpated was the one that was removed. On admission this morning, an IV line was started in the ED. She was then taken to the x-ray suite where under ultrasound guidance the lump was localized with the needle. She was then brought up for surgery. Preoperatively, she received 1 gram of Ancef IV. Surgery was to be done with local plus IV sedation monitored anesthesia. In surgery, she was appropriately positioned. The right breast area was cleaned with DuraPrep and draped, and the entry point was at the 3-4 o'clock position. The incision site was then infiltrated with my usual anesthetic mix. Once this took, a small incision was then made just abutting to the entry point of needle. Entering the breast substance, hemostasis was achieved. The needle was localized and then followed to its termination. Prior to termination, the area in question was identified; a generous excision margin was now achieved and encompassed the needle and the node in question. All of this was taken in one piece and submitted for radiologic evaluation. This confirmed that the area in question had been removed. Subsequently, frozen section was then done, which showed benign fibroadenoma. At this junction the operation was terminated, and hemostasis was achieved. The breast was then reconstructed in layers: subcu with 2-0 chromic, skin with 3-0 nylon. Appropriate dressings were applied. I will be visiting with the patient's mother, and patient was advised as to our findings and the successful outcome with benign results. Upon discharge, she will see me in the office a week from today. Sponge and instrument counts were correct on two occasions.

GODFREY REGIONAL HOSPITAL
123 Main Street • Aldon, FL 77714 • (407) 555-1234

Ahn Westy, MD

Answers

OPERATIVE REPORT

Patient information:

Patient name: Date:
DOB: Surgeon:
MR#:   Anesthetist:

Preoperative diagnosis:

Right lower eyelid, right upper arm, right forearm, upper back skin lesions, and left hand wound

Postoperative diagnosis:

Right lower eyelid, right upper arm, right forearm, upper back skin lesions, and left hand wound

Procedure(s) performed:

OPERATIVE PROCEDURE:
Excision of right lower eyelid, right upper arm, right forearm, upper back skin lesions, and debridement of left hand wound
INDICATIONS FOR PROCEDURE:
The patient is a 68-year-old white female who is on chronic steroids and has all the stigmata of chronic steroid use. She is also a kidney transplant patient on immunosuppression. She has a history of multiple skin cancers and now presents with four lesions that are suspicious for skin cancers. She wishes to have these excised. The patient also suffered a traumatic injury to the dorsum of her left hand within the last week; the wound has some necrotic tissue within it and needs debridement.

Anesthesia:

Assistant surgeon:

Description of procedure:

The patient was brought to the operating room and placed supine on the operating room table. The patient's right forearm, upper arm, left hand, and face were prepped and draped in the usual sterile fashion.

After adequate IV sedation, the skin lesions on the right lower eyelid, right upper arm, and right forearm were anesthetized with 1% lidocaine with epinephrine. The wound over the left hand was anesthetized with 1% lidocaine plain. After adequate local anesthesia was achieved, the skin lesion from the right lower eyelid was excised using curved iris scissors. The wound edges were closed with simple stitches using 6-0 fast-absorbing catgut sutures.

Next, the lesions on the upper arm and forearm were excised using a 15 blade scalpel, which was used to form a fusiform incision around the lesions, providing a 3-mm border. The lesion was then sent to Pathology for permanent sections. The wound edges were undermined and then closed with 3-0 nylon sutures using horizontal mattress stitches.

These wounds were then cleaned, covered with antibiotic ointment and gauze on the arm; and the lesion on the right lower eyelid was covered with bacitracin ophthalmic ointment.

The lesion on the left hand, dorsal surface, was debrided sharply with a 15 blade scalpel. All necrotic tissue was removed sharply. The wound was then irrigated, hemostasis was achieved with electrocautery, and the wound was then covered with Silvadene and a sterile gauze dressing.

At the end of the procedure, the patient was sat up on the operating room table. The lesion on the patient's upper back below her neck was prepped and draped in the usual sterile fashion. It was then anesthetized with 1% lidocaine with epinephrine. The lesion was then excised using a fusiform incision, and this lesion, too, was sent to Pathology for analysis. The wound edges were then undermined and closed with interrupted 3-0 nylon sutures using horizontal mattress stitches. The patient tolerated the procedure well. Her wounds were cleaned, covered with antibiotic ointment and gauze, and she was then taken to PACU for recovery in stable condition.

Maurice Doater, MD

GODFREY REGIONAL HOSPITAL
123 Main Street • Aldon, FL 77714 • (407) 555-1234

Answers

EXERCISE 3

OPERATIVE REPORT

Patient information:

Patient name: Date:
DOB: Surgeon:
MR#:   Anesthetist:

Preoperative diagnosis:

Possible basal cell carcinoma of the right upper lid

Postoperative diagnosis:

Pending surgical pathology

Procedure(s) performed:

Anesthesia:

Lid block using 2% lidocaine with epinephrine

Assistant surgeon:

Description of procedure:

After written informed consent was obtained, the patient was brought to the operating room where she was prepped and draped in the usual sterile fashion. The area of the right upper lid neoplasm was marked in a wedge shape, and the lid block consisting of 2 ccs of 2% lidocaine with epinephrine was given to the right upper lid.

Next a wedge resection was performed using Westcott scissors. Next the bleeding vessels were cauterized. Three 4-0 Vicryl sutures were used to close the tarsus so that they opposed each other. Then 2 6-0 silk sutures were passed through the anterior and posterior lid margin to oppose the lid margins together. 6-0 Vicryl sutures were used to close the orbicularis oculi layer superior to the tarsus.

Then interrupted 6-0 nylon sutures were used to close the skin incision, taking care to tag the silk sutures around the nylon sutures. At the end of the case, the wedge defect had been closed and the lid margins were nicely opposed to each other without any notching of the lid margin.

Bacitracin ointment was applied to the wound and a patch was placed. The patient was taken to the recovery room in excellent condition.

COMPLICATIONS: None

Adm Westg MD

GODFREY REGIONAL HOSPITAL
123 Main Street • Aldon, FL 77714 • (407) 555-1234

Answers

OPERATIVE REPORT

Patient information:

Patient name:
DOB:
MR#:

Date:
Surgeon:
Anesthetist:

Preoperative diagnosis:

Gynecomastia, right breast

Postoperative diagnosis:

Same

Procedure(s) performed:

OPERATION: Excision gynecomastia right breast with frozen section

INDICATIONS: Patient was admitted for the operation. In the distant past we had excised the gynecomastia of the left breast. No cause could be found for this. He saw me a few weeks ago, having developed another gynecomastia in the right breast and he wanted it removed, so he was brought in this morning for surgery. On admission, he received 1 gram of Ancef on call to surgery. He was then brought to surgery. The procedure was to be done under local with monitored anesthesia.

Anesthesia:

Assistant surgeon:

Description of procedure:

In surgery with an IV line in place, he received IV anesthetics for sedation. Then the right breast, right chest wall was cleaned with DuraPrep and draped and the operation started. The right breast was markedly enlarged, consistent with gynecomastia, and benign. My incision was going to be a circumareolar incision. The area of my planned incision was then marked out with a marking pen, infiltrated with my usual anesthetic mix for an appropriate distance until adequate analgesia/ anesthesia was obtained. The incision was then made. The areolar complex was immobilized and elevated. Then the margins of the breast around the areola were now dissected circumferentially until all breast tissue was marked out. It was then dissected out from the pectoralis muscle until all of the tissue was removed. The breast was then removed in toto and submitted for frozen section exam that confirmed that this was a benign gynecomastia. The empty space resulting was now cleaned. Hemostasis was achieved using the cautery as needed. A small Penrose drain was then inserted prior to closure. The breast was then closed in layers: subcu 2-0 chromic, skin with 3-0 nylon and appropriate pressure dressings were applied. The patient is to see me again on Friday. At that time I will decide whether it would be appropriate to remove the drain or not.

I talked with the patient in the recovery room post recovery, and advised him as to findings and as to when I will be seeing him. He will be discharged on pain meds and I will see him on Friday.

GODFREY REGIONAL HOSPITAL
123 Main Street • Aldon, FL 77714 • (407) 555-1234

Answers

Chapter **14** Coding Complexities of Surgical Procedures

EXERCISE 5

OPERATIVE REPORT

Patient information:	
Patient name:	Date:
DOB:	Surgeon:
MR#:	Anesthetist:

Preoperative diagnosis:

1. Traumatic amputation, tip left 3rd toe
2. Open fracture, distal phalanx, left second toe

Postoperative diagnosis:

Same

Procedure(s) performed:

Irrigation and debridement of wounds with revision of amputation, left third toe

Anesthesia:

Assistant surgeon:

Description of procedure:

The patient was placed supine on the operating room table and a satisfactory general anesthetic was given. The patient was given preoperative Kefzol intravenously in the emergency room. No pneumatic tourniquet was used. The left foot, ankle, and lower leg were prepped sterilely with DuraPrep and the left foot was draped in the usual sterile fashion. 2.5 liters of normal saline antibiotic solution were then used to irrigate out the second and third toes to very healthy and clean tissue. Any debris was removed before and during the irrigation. A spike of bone was protruding from the amputation site of the third toe. This was cleared to soft tissue when resected back beneath the tissue. The toe was not shortened further to provide a closure of the amputation site. Rather, the amputation site was discussed with the patient in the emergency room, and will remain open to allow for granulation. The tip of the second toe was not completely amputated and was actually a flap or open Bookman type of laceration with underlying fracture of the distal phalanx. This was tacked closed loosely with a single simple suture of 3-0 Ethilon. The wounds were irrigated again with 0.5 liters of normal saline antibiotic solution. Neosporin ointment was copiously applied as well as dry sterile dressings and sterile Kerlix wrap.

The patient tolerated the procedure well. There were no complications. He was awakened in the operating room and transported to the recovery room in stable condition.

GODFREY REGIONAL HOSPITAL
123 Main Street • Aldon, FL 77714 • (407) 555-1234

Answers

EMERGENCY ROOM RECORD

Name:		Age:	ER physician:
		DOB:	

Allergies/type of reaction:	Usual medications/dosages:

Triage/presenting complaint:

CC: 44-year-old with simple laceration

Initial assessment:

REVIEW OF SYSTEMS: Patient denies fever

HISTORY: 44-year-old presented to the ED who sustained a laceration immediately prior to arriving to the ED. Patient sustained laceration after being cut by a sharp edge of a can. Laceration is located on the eyebrow.

Time	T	P	R	BP	Other:					

Medication orders:

Lab work:

X-ray:

Physician's report:

EXAM:
General: WD, well nourished and in NAD. Vital signs normal.
Respiratory: Respirations unlabored with symmetric chest expansion.
        Lungs sound equal and clear bilaterally.
CV: Regular rate and rhythm.
Skin: Laceration, 2 cm, left eyebrow, extending through the dermis and into the subcutaneous tissue. Wound was closed with the placement of Steri-strips to the area.

Diagnosis:	Physician sign/date
The patient was discharged from the ED with treatment instructions.	*Robert Rai MD*
Discharge Transfer Admit Good Satisfactory Other:	

GODFREY REGIONAL HOSPITAL
123 Main Street • Aldon, FL 77714 • (407) 555-1234

Answers

EXERCISE 7

OPERATIVE REPORT

Patient information:	
Patient name: DOB: MR#:	Date: Surgeon: Anesthetist:

Preoperative diagnosis:

Complex open wounds to the left ring and small fingers with open fractures of these fingers; simple laceration to the long finger

Postoperative diagnosis:

1. 1 cm dorsal laceration, left long finger
2. 3 cm complex laceration, left ring finger
3. Extensor tendon laceration, left ring finger
4. Intra-articular fracture of proximal phalanx of the left ring finger
5. Intra-articular fracture of the middle phalanx of the left ring finger
6. Complex laceration, approximately 2 cm, left small finger
7. Extensor tendon laceration, left small finger
8. Osteochondral fracture of the proximal phalanx of left small finger

Procedure(s) performed:

1. Debridement and irrigation of open left ring finger proximal phalanx fracture, ring finger middle phalanx fracture, small finger proximal phalanx fracture
2. Open reduction and internal fixation of proximal phalanx fracture of the ring finger and middle phalanx fracture of the ring finger
3. Excision of osteochondral fragment of small finger
4. Extensor tendon repair of the ring finger
5. Extensor tendon repair of the small finger
6. Laceration repair of long, ring, and small fingers
7. Intraoperative use of fluoroscopy
8. Short-arm splinting

Anesthesia:

Assistant surgeon:

Description of procedure:

The patient was taken to the operating room where, after general anesthesia was administered, the left upper extremity was prepped and draped in a sterile fashion. Copious amounts of antibiotic irrigation were used to irrigate all the open fractures. There was a complex intra-articular injury to the PIP joint of the ring finger, and a smaller injury with some small osteochondral fragments at the proximal interphalangeal joint of the small finger. Any loose bony fragments and debris were debrided. Once this was completed, along with debriding the skin edges, attention was turned to the fractures.

The small finger PIP joint had some very small osteochondral fragments that were unable to be affixed in any fashion and these were excised. The majority of the joint here was intact. The ring finger had a complex intra-articular injury with fractures involving the joint surfaces of the proximal and middle phalanges. These were affixed using the mini-frag set 1.5-mm screws and K-wires. Care was taken to seat the K-wire used on the proximal phalanx articular surface beneath the articular surface. Once fixation here was achieved, I was pleased with the articular congruity and the range of motion able to be achieved. The extensor tendons were then repaired. The small finger extensor tendon had a laceration that was somewhat complex, but a good repair was able to be achieved. 4-0 Ethibond mattress and figure-of-eight sutures were used here. The finger was able to be flexed down to 90 degrees without undue tension. The ring finger had a more complex injury to the extensor tendon with some missing tissue, especially along the radial aspect. Despite this, adequate repair was able to be achieved. The central slip was repaired back down to bone through bony drill holes, and the remainder of the tendon was repaired with horizontal mattress and figure-of-eight 4-0 Ethibond sutures. The finger here was able to be flexed to about 30 degrees before some tension was noted. At this point the wound was irrigated out again and the complex lacerations were closed with 4-0 nylon sutures. Sterile bulky hand dressing and short-arm splint were applied. Fluoroscopy was used throughout the case, and fixation of the fractures and permanent pictures were saved on this. The patient was awakened and taken to the recovery room in stable condition. There were no complications. On admission to the recovery room, his fingers were pink with good color and capillary refill.

[signature] MD

GODFREY REGIONAL HOSPITAL
123 Main Street • Aldon, FL 77714 • (407) 555-1234

Answers

OPERATIVE REPORT

Patient information:

Patient name:
DOB:
MR#:

Date:
Surgeon:
Anesthetist:

Preoperative diagnosis:

1. Torn calcaneal fibular ligament, left
2. Attenuated anterior talofibular ligament, left

Postoperative diagnosis:

Same

Procedure(s) performed:

1. Primary repair of calcaneal fibular ligament
2. Primary repair of anterior talofibular ligament left

Anesthesia:

Local with MAC

Assistant surgeon:

Description of procedure:

HEMOSTASIS: Pneumatic ankle tourniquet on the left

ESTIMATED BLOOD LOSS: Less than 1 cc

Under mild sedation, the patient was brought into the operating room and placed on the operating table in a supine position. A pneumatic ankle tourniquet was then placed about the patient's ankle. Following IV sedation, local anesthesia was obtained about the left ankle. The foot was then scrubbed, prepped, and draped in the usual aseptic manner. An Esmarch bandage was then utilized to exsanguinate the patient's left foot and a pneumatic ankle tourniquet was then inflated. Attention was then directed to the lateral aspect of the left foot where a 5-cm curvilinear incision was made, beginning at the anterior distal end of the fibula and curving distal to the plantar aspect of the fibula overlying the calcaneal fibular ligament. Dissection was continued using sharp and blunt dissection down to the level of the ankle capsule where identification of the torn calcaneal fibular ligament was then made. A curvilinear capsulotomy was performed over the dorsal aspect of the anterior talofibular ligament and the calcaneal fibular ligament. Attention was directed to the distal aspect of the fibula where, utilizing a #64 blade, the periosteum was then released from the fibula and the overlying bone was then scraped utilizing a rongeur. Utilizing double 0 Panacryl, a total of 7 sutures were then placed within the distal aspect of the anterior talofibular ligament and calcaneal fibular ligament and attached to the distal aspect of the fibula beneath the periosteum. The overlying periosteum was then further imbricated into the superior portion of the inferior extensor retinaculum. At this time, an anterior drawer sign was no longer positive. The area was flushed with copious amounts of sterile normal saline solution, and the subcuticular tissues were reapproximated and coapted utilizing 4-0 Vicryl, and the skin was reapproximated and coapted utilizing 5-0 Vicryl subcuticular suture technique. Upon completion of the procedure, a total of 1 cc of Decadron phosphate was infiltrated about the incision site. A postoperative block consisting of 0.5% Marcaine plain was also injected. The incision was dressed with Mastisol and Steri-strips and covered with a sterile compressive dressing consisting of 4 × 4s and Kling, and the pneumatic ankle tourniquet was then deflated and a prompt hyperresponse was noted to all digits of the left foot. A mono-valved B-K cast was then applied.

The patient tolerated the procedure and anesthesia well. She was transferred to recovery with vital signs stable and vascular status intact to all of the left foot. Following a period of postoperative monitoring, patient will be discharged home with written and oral postoperative instructions. Patient has instructions to stay nonweight bearing times a period of weeks and will reappoint in my office within a period of one week for follow-up.

GODFREY REGIONAL HOSPITAL
123 Main Street • Aldon, FL 77714 • (407) 555-1234

Answers

EXERCISE 9

OPERATIVE REPORT

Patient information:	
Patient name: DOB: MR#:	Date: Surgeon: Anesthetist:

Preoperative diagnosis:

Right knee medial and lateral meniscal tear

Postoperative diagnosis:

Right knee medial and lateral meniscal tear

Procedure(s) performed:

Right knee diagnostic arthroscopy, partial lateral meniscectomy, and partial medial posterior horn meniscectomy

Anesthesia:

Spinal

Assistant surgeon:

Description of procedure:

ESTIMATED BLOOD LOSS: Minimal

TOTAL TOURNIQUET TIME: Zero

IV FLUID: 1500 cc of crystalloid

INDICATIONS AND/OR FINDINGS: The patient tolerated the procedure well and transferred back to recovery room with noted stable vital signs.

OPERATIVE TECHNIQUE:

The patient was brought to the operating room and transferred onto the operating table. Spinal anesthesia was then induced. Once an adequate level of anesthetic was achieved, the right lower extremity was prepped and draped in the usual sterile fashion. Antibiotic was given preoperatively for prophylaxis. Anterior lateral portal was established for outflow. Inferior lateral portal was established for inflow and camera portal site. Diagnostic arthroscopy began first in the suprapatellar pouch proceeding toward the medial lateral compartment, in viewing the arthritis in the patella femoral surface, as well as defibrillation of the articular surface. There is also no evidence of loose body noted. The medial compartment was then entered as the knee was placed in a valgus position. We noted that there is a small tear in the posterior medial horn of the medial meniscus. This was subsequently evaluated under a probe as we established a working port on the inferior medial port. A small trimmer was used to trim back the medial horn to a stable edge. Of note, we did appreciate some arthritis on the medial compartment. The articular surface appears to be minimally denuded. The intercondylar notch was evaluated. The anterior cruciate ligament appears to be intact. Some moderate amount of fibrotic tissue was debrided, and synovitis was noted in the soft tissue and fibrous tissue region in this area.

Adequate debridement with an arthroscopic incisor was performed for better visualization as we removed the infrapatellar fat pad. The leg was taken to a lateral figure-of-four position to open up and get better visualization into the lateral joint line. Upon entering into the lateral compartment, we noted an extensive amount of defibrillation of the articular surface, as well as denution in both the lateral femoral condyle and the lateral tibia plateau down to its articular surface of pink denuded bone. There is also noticeable meniscal tear on the anterior horn, tracking back to the posterior lateral horn of the lateral meniscus. This was subsequently trimmed using multiple arthroscopic incisors, as well as the arthroscopic trimmer. We trimmed the lateral meniscus back to a stable rim. The knee was taken to full range of motion and noted to be quite smooth. There was no evidence of mechanical catching or locking any further. The knee was irrigated out profusely. Intraoperative x-ray was obtained using the arthroscopic camera. The portal site was then subsequently removed and closed in the routine fashion. Sensorcaine was used to inject the portal sites for postoperative pain management. Compressive dressing was then applied.

The patient was then awakened and transferred back to recovery room with noted stable vital signs.

Patrick Chung MD

GODFREY REGIONAL HOSPITAL
123 Main Street • Aldon, FL 77714 • (407) 555-1234

Answers

OPERATIVE REPORT

Patient information:	
Patient name: DOB: MR#:	Date: Surgeon: Anesthetist:

Preoperative diagnosis:

Hallux limitus

Postoperative diagnosis:

Hallux limitus

Procedure(s) performed:

1. Distal L osteotomy with pin fixation
2. Cheilectomy

Anesthesia:

Assistant surgeon:

Description of procedure:

Patient was brought back to the operating room, properly identified, and placed on the OR table in the supine position. Following IV sedation, the foot was anesthetized with 10 cc of 50/50 mixture of 2% lidocaine plain and 0.5% Marcaine plain in a Mayo H block fashion around the right first ray. The foot was then prepped and draped in the usual sterile aseptic technique.

Utilizing an Esmarch dressing, the foot was exsanguinated, and the previously well-padded ankle tourniquet was inflated to 250 mm of mercury. Attention was then directed to the first dorsal aspect of the first metatarsal-phalangeal joint where a 10-cm curvilinear incision was made. The incision site was deepened down to the joint capsule and care was taken to protect the neurovascular structures. The joint capsule was noted and a linear capsulotomy was performed. The joint capsule was then freed from the metatarsal head dorsally and medially. Next, utilizing a sagittal saw, the medial eminence of the first metatarsal was introduced in the surgical field and resected from the surgical site in total. Next, the dorsal eminence was introduced into the surgical field, and utilizing the sagittal saw, the dorsal eminence was resected from the surgical site in toto. Next, attention was directed to the lateral aspect of the first metatarsal into the first interspace where the intermetatarsal ligament, the abductor tendon, and the sesamoid ligaments were freed from their attachments. Attention was then directed back to the medial aspect of the first metatarsal head where a 0.045 K-wire was introduced, running from medial to lateral with light plantar flexion as a guide. Next utilizing a sagittal saw, the distal L osteotomy cut was performed with the plantar cut first and the dorsal cut second. Next, the K wire guide was removed from the surgical site in toto and the metatarsal head was put into proper position. Next utilizing thesagittal saw, a 3-mm wedge of bone was resected from the dorsal arm of the osteotomy cut and removed from the surgical site en toto. Next, the distal metatarsal osteotomy was positioned in its proper position, slightly laterally and impacted on the metatarsal. Next, a 0.045 K wire was used to secure the osteotomy in place. The wire was then bent and cut. Attention was then directed to the redundant bone on the metatarsal. Utilizing the sagittal saw, the redundant bone was removed from the surgical site en toto. Next the joint itself was inspected and noted to have large yellow cartilaginous deficits and two large red, denuded areas of bone. The denuded bone and the yellow cartilaginous deficits were drilled with 0.045 K wire to promote blood flow to the cartilaginous caps. Next, the surgical site was copiously irrigated with normal saline. The joint capsule was reapproximated with 3-0 Vicryl. The skin tissue was then reapproximated with 4-0 Proline. The foot was then dressed with adaptic fluffs and Kling and Coban.

The patient tolerated the procedure well and anesthesia well and left the OR with vital signs stable and vascular status intact.

GODFREY REGIONAL HOSPITAL
123 Main Street • Aldon, FL 77714 • (407) 555-1234

Answers

EXERCISE 11

OPERATIVE REPORT

Patient information:	
Patient name: DOB: MR#:	Date: Surgeon: Anesthetist:

Preoperative diagnosis:

1) Subluxation, 2nd metatarsophalangeal joint, right foot
2) Hammer toe deformity, 2nd toe, right foot

Postoperative diagnosis:

Same

Procedure(s) performed:

1) Osteoplasty, 2nd metatarsal head, right foot
2) Arthroplasty proximal interphalangeal joint, 2nd toe, right foot

Anesthesia:

Assistant surgeon:

Description of procedure:

A V-lock cuff was placed above the right ankle for hemostasis, and the patient was prepped and draped in usual aseptic manner. With IV sedation, 2% Xylocaine hydrochloride plain was used to infiltrate the operative area on the right forefoot. A dorsolongitudinal skin incision, approximately 4 cm in length, was made extending from mid shaft of the 2nd metatarsal proximally to the base of the proximal phalanx of the 2nd toe distally. The skin and subcutaneous tissues were underscored and retracted. The incision was then deepened medial to the extensor digital and longus tendon and carried down to the level of the metatarsal head. The capsular and ligamentous structures then separated from the 2nd metatarsal head and the 2nd toe plantar flexed, thereby bringing the 2nd metatarsal head into view. Utilizing a power saw and beginning at the surgical neck of the metatarsal head, a cut was made perpendicular to the shaft approximately one half the width of the metatarsal head and then beveled at a 45-degree angle to include the plantar condyles. The severed bone was then dissected out by sharp dissection, and all rough edges were rasped smooth. The wound was then copiously flushed with normal saline solution. The right foot was loaded, finding good release of subluxation occurring at the level of the 2nd metatarsophalangeal joint but with considerable contractures still occurring at the proximal phalangeal joint of the 2nd toe. Therefore, two longitudinal ellipsing skin incisions were made directly over the head of the proximal phalanx of the 2nd toe. The created skin wedge was then sharply dissected. The skin and subcutaneous tissues were underscored and retracted. A transverse incision was then made through the capsule and extensor tendon complex at the proximal interphalangeal joint. The medial and lateral collateral ligaments were incised and the head of the proximal phalanx was delivered. Utilizing a power saw, the head of the proximal phalanx was then resected, and all bony edges were rasped smooth. The wound was then copiously flushed with normal saline solution. The right foot was loaded, finding a much more normally positioned 2nd toe with full reduction of the preoperative deformity. At the level of the 2nd metatarsophalangeal joint, the ligamentous and capsular structures were repaired with interrupted sutures of 2-0 Vicryl. Superficial tissues were then closed with 3-0 Vicryl, and the skin margins were approximated with interrupted horizontal mattress sutures of 4-0 nylon. Attention was then directed to the 2nd toe where the extensor tendon and collateral ligaments were repaired with interrupted sutures of 3-0 Vicryl. Skin margins were then approximated with interrupted horizontal mattress sutures of 4-0 nylon. Before bandaging, the right foot was again loaded, finding a normally positioned 2nd toe. Celestone Solu span 1 cc was then deposited in the operative sites. Adaptic was applied to both skin incisions and a mild compression dressing was then placed around the right foot, maintaining the 2nd toe in a straight and slightly plantar flexed position. The tourniquet was released and return blood flow was found to be normal.

The immediate postoperative condition of the patient was excellent, and she was returned to her room.

Patrick Chung, MD

GODFREY REGIONAL HOSPITAL
123 Main Street • Aldon, FL 77714 • (407) 555-1234

Answers

OPERATIVE REPORT

Patient information:	
Patient name: DOB: MR#:	Date: Surgeon: Anesthetist:

Preoperative diagnosis:

Internal derangement of the right knee with complex tear of the posterior horn of medial meniscus and associated extensive medial femoral condylar osteochondral defect with chondromalacia and early degenerative osteoarthrosis

Postoperative diagnosis:

Same

Procedure(s) performed:

Right knee arthroscopy, arthroscopic partial medial meniscectomy, and arthroscopic abrasion arthroplasty of medial femoral condylar osteochondral defect

Anesthesia:

Spinal

Assistant surgeon:

Description of procedure:

The patient was brought to the operating room and placed under spinal anesthesia without episode. He was then turned to the supine position. Tourniquet was applied high on the proximal aspect of the right thigh. The right lower extremity was then thoroughly prepped and draped in the usual sterile fashion, with the right lower extremity draped as a sterile field from the tourniquet level distally. Venous blood was exsanguinated with a sterile Ace bandage and the tourniquet inflated to 300 mm of mercury pressure. A short anteromedial portal incision was created with a #11 blade, measuring approximately 1 cm in length. The arthroscope and sharp obturator were then advanced through the skin and the capsule and into the joint. The obturator was removed. Upon removal of the obturator, moderate sized interarticular effusion was evacuated through the arthroscope and fluids submitted to the laboratory for synovial fluid studies. The arthroscope and camera were then advanced into the joint. A second superolateral stab wound was created for admission of a large trocar and inflow cannula and the sterile tubing connected to an arthroscopic pump. Arthroscopic examination of the knee was carried out sequentially. Arthroscopic examination was accompanied by several Polaroid films documenting findings throughout the procedure. Arthroscopic examination confirmed the preoperative MRI findings of a complex multiplanar tear involving the posterior horn of the medial meniscus. This tear was too extensive and fragmented for repair.

In addition to the expected tear of the medial meniscus, a substantial defect of the weightbearing surface of the medial femoral condyle was demonstrated; again, this was accompanied by cracking and fragmentation of the margins of the articular cartilage in the area of the lesion.

A second stab wound was created for admission of the arthroscopic surgical equipment, and utilizing a 5-0 shaver, as well as a 4-0 shaver, arthroscopic debridement of the torn portion of the medial meniscus was carried out. This was supplemented with hand instruments to attain a clean margin at the level of resection of the posterior horn tear. Following debridement and rejection of the complex medial meniscus tear of the posterior margin, arthroscopic abrasion arthroplasty of the osteochondral defect over the medial femoral condyle was carried out until a smooth margin was created. The base of the lesion was then drilled multiply, utilizing a small smooth Steinmann pin to reach the osteochondral area for hopeful production of fibrocartilage patching the defect. Copious and repetitive irrigation of the joint was carried out to evacuate arthroscopic debris of meniscal fragments, as well as the osteochondral lesion. This was continued until the irrigation was returning clear. At this point the joint was evacuated, and the arthroscopic instrumentation was withdrawn. The arthroscopic incisions were closed with interrupted sutures of 4-0 nylon. The joint was injected with a solution of 0.5% Marcaine with epinephrine. Sterile Adaptic gauze, sterile 4 × 4s, and sterile soft roll were applied with an Ace bandage, and on release of tourniquet, good distal circulation was noted with good distal pulses at the posterior tibial and dorsalis pedis levels.

The patient subsequently was removed from the operating room and returned to the medical-surgical unit in good condition, having tolerated the procedure without apparent incident. All needle and sponge counts were correct at the termination of the procedure.

Patrick Chung mD

GODFREY REGIONAL HOSPITAL
123 Main Street • Aldon, FL 77714 • (407) 555-1234

Answers

EXERCISE 13

OPERATIVE REPORT

Patient information:	
Patient name: DOB: MR#:	Date: Surgeon: Anesthetist:

Preoperative diagnosis:

Gout versus osteomyelitis

Postoperative diagnosis:

Same

Procedure(s) performed:

Bone biopsy with arthroplasty of interphalangeal joint, right hallux

Anesthesia:

Assistant surgeon:

Description of procedure:

HEMOSTASIS: None
MATERIALS: 3-0 and 4-0 PDS and 5-0 nylon
COMPLICATIONS: None
DESCRIPTION OF PROCEDURE:
The patient was taken to the OR by OR staff, and the patient was placed on the operating room table in the supine position. Once given a small amount of IV sedation, a ring block of the hallux was made using approximately 12 cc of 1% lidocaine plain. The foot was then prepped and draped using sterile technique.
Attention was then directed to the dorsal hallux and the area of the interphalangeal joint where anesthesia was tested and then a linear incision was made using a #15 blade. Using both blunt and sharp dissection, the incision was deepened to the level of the interphalangeal joint. It became evident at this point that there was a large amount of gouty tophi in the area. As much of this was removed as possible and the area flushed throughout the procedure.

The most distal aspect of the proximal phalanx was identified. The head of the proximal phalanx, however, appeared completely eroded and impregnated with gouty tophi. There were no clinical signs of any purulence in the area. The bone proximal to the head of the phalanx was hard to touch and appeared intact. The most distal aspect of the head of the proximal phalanx was resected using a bone saw and sent to Pathology for gross anatomy and culture. The incision was again flushed with copious amounts of sterile saline, and any large gouty tophi were excised at this time and sent to Pathology as well.

At this time, fluoro scan imaging was taken of the foot to ensure that a clean surface had been created with this cut. I was satisfied with the amount of bone resection and satisfied with the sample taken for the biopsy. The incision was again flushed with copious amounts of sterile saline and closed using 3-0 and 4-0 PDS for deep closure and 5-0 nylon for skin closure.

The patient tolerated the surgery well with vital signs stable and no complications. He will follow up in my office in one week.

GODFREY REGIONAL HOSPITAL
123 Main Street • Aldon, FL 77714 • (407) 555-1234

Answers

OPERATIVE REPORT

Patient information:

Patient name:
DOB:
MR#:

Date:
Surgeon:
Anesthetist:

Preoperative diagnosis:

1) Underlapping second digit, left foot
2) Hallux valgus with bunion, right foot

3) Hammertoe, 2nd through 4th digits of right foot

Postoperative diagnosis:

Same

Procedure(s) performed:

1) Syndactylization of digits 2 and 3 on the left foot
2) Bunionectomy, right foot
3) First metatarsal osteotomy with screw fixation, right foot

4) Arthroplasty, 2nd PIPJ, right foot
5) Arthroplasty, 3rd PIPJ, right foot with K-wire fixation
6) Arthroplasty, 4th PIPJ, right foot with K-wire fixation

Description of procedure:

The patient was placed in the supine position on the operating table. A tourniquet was applied to the level of the left malleolus. Attention was directed to the second and third digits on the left foot. Incision was made to remove interdigital skin. The skin was resected in toto. The wound was flushed with copious amounts of sterile saline and closed in a single layer. Skin was reapproximated with 4-0 nylon simple interrupted sutures. Xeroform gauze was applied plus a sterile gauze bandage for compression and hemostasis. The tourniquet was let down and blood flow returned immediately.

Attention was then directed to the right foot where a 6-cm curvilinear incision was made, coursing medial and parallel to the extensor hallucis longus tendon. Incision was deepened, with care taken to clamp and ligate all superficial bleeders as they were encountered. All neurovascular and tendinous structures were carefully identified and retracted. An inverted L-capsulotomy was performed. Hypertrophic bone was delivered from the wound and resected in toto from the dorsomedial and medial aspects of the first metatarsal head. The wound was flushed with copious amounts of sterile saline.

Attention was directed to the proximal aspect of the incision where a periosteal incision was made at the base of the first metatarsal down to bone. All periosteal structures were reflected from bone, and a base wedge osteotomy was performed, with the base of the osteotomy lateral and the apex proximal and medial. The resultant wedge of bone was removed. This was closed and fixated with two compression screws. The wound was flushed with copious amounts of sterile saline and then closed in layers with periosteal reapproximation using 2-0 Polysorb simple interrupted sutures. This was followed by subcutaneous reapproximation with 3-0 Polysorb simple interrupted sutures, followed by skin reapproximation with 4-0 nylon simple interrupted sutures.

Attention was then directed to the second digit on the right foot where a 3-cm linear incision was made over the PIPJ. Incision was carried down to the level of the joint where transverse tenotomy was performed. All tendinous and capsular structures were reflected from the head of the proximal phalanx and were delivered from the wound. The head of the proximal phalanx was resected in toto with care taken to rasp smooth all bony edges. The wound was flushed with copious amounts of sterile saline. The wound was closed with tendon reapproximation using 3-0 Polysorb simple interrupted sutures, followed by skin reapproximation with 4-0 nylon simple interrupted sutures.

Attention was directed to the third digit on the right foot where a 3-cm linear incision was made, coursing proximal and distal over the PIP joint. Transverse tenotomy was performed. All tendinous and capsular structures were reflected from the head of the proximal phalanx. The head of the proximal phalanx was delivered from the wound and resected in toto. Care was taken to rasp smooth all raw bony edges. The third digit was then closed and fixated with a single 0.045-inch K-wire. Tendon reapproximation was achieved with 3-0 Polysorb simple interrupted sutures, followed by skin reapproximation with 4-0 nylon simple interrupted sutures.

Attention was directed to the fourth digit of the right foot where the same exact procedure was performed as on the third, up to and including wound closure.

Dexamethasone phosphate was instilled into each surgical site. This was followed by Xeroform gauze, followed by sterile gauze bandage for compression and hemostasis. All digits were splinted in rectus position.

The tourniquet was let down and blood flow returned immediately to all digits on the right foot.

The patient tolerated the procedure and anesthesia well and was transported to the recovery room with vital signs stable and in good condition.

GODFREY REGIONAL HOSPITAL
123 Main Street • Aldon, FL 77714 • (407) 555-1234

Answers

EXERCISE 15

OPERATIVE REPORT

Patient information:	
Patient name: DOB: MR#:	Date: Surgeon: Anesthetist:

Preoperative diagnosis:

Nasal septal deformity with nasal obstruction due to extensive nasal polyposis, chronic bilateral ethmoid sinusitis. Polypoid degeneration in the middle turbinates bilaterally. Chronic left maxillary sinusitis.
CLINICAL NOTE:
The patient is a 75-year-old white male with severe left nasal septal deviation. He has extensive bilateral nasal polyps and chronic sinusitis. He does not respond to conservative medical treatment. He is being brought to the operating room for these operative procedures. Operative findings showed extensive polyposis filling the left nasal cavities bilaterally and into the ethmoid sinuses bilaterally. The left ostial medial complex was obstructed both by the nasal septal spur from the deviation and by a myosteoma found in the left maxillary sinus. Both middle turbinates showed extensive polypoid degeneration.

Postoperative diagnosis:

Nasal septal deformity with nasal obstruction due to extensive nasal polyposis, chronic bilateral ethmoid sinusitis. Polypoid degeneration in the middle turbinates bilaterally. Myosteoma of the left maxillary sinus.

Procedure(s) performed:

Septoplasty, endoscopic bilateral total ethmoidectomies, left middle meatal antrostomy with removal of left maxillary sinus myosteoma, bilateral turbinate resection. Bilateral extensive nasal polypectomies.

Anesthesia:

General

Description of procedure:

The patient was brought to the operating room and placed on the operating table in supine position. General endotracheal anesthesia was performed. He received Ancef 1 gram IV perioperatively. Nose was prepped and draped after being injected with 12 cc 1% lidocaine with 1:100,000 parts epinephrine into the nasal septal mucosa, middle turbinates, and lateral nasal mucosa bilaterally. Nose was vasoconstricted with topical Afrin.

Left hemitransfixion incision was made on the nasal septum and elevated with Freer elevator to expose the deviated cartilage and bone. The inferior half of the cartilaginous septum was removed, preserving the nasal spine and caudal septum. This was removed off the maxillary crest. The bony cartilaginous septum was separated with a Freer elevator, and the mucoperiosteum was elevated off the bony septum bilaterally. Using open Jansen-Middleton rongeurs, the mid inferior portions of the bony septum were removed. Further removal with Takahashi forceps of the vomer bone was performed.

Using a 3-mm osteotome and mallet, the maxillary crest bone that was deviated severely into the left nasal cavity was removed along the anterior and mid portions of the septum. This completed removal of the deviated bone and cartilage. The left hemitransfixion incision was closed with interrupted 4-0 chromic sutures.

Using straight and biting Blakesley forceps, polyps were removed from the left nasal cavity. Left total ethmoidectomy was performed with the same instruments. The degenerated middle turbinate due to polyposis was removed with same instrumentation as well. After completion of total ethmoidectomy and middle turbinectomy and nasal polypectomy, a Bolger probe was used to bluntly enter the left maxillary sinus. Antrostomy was made with the biting forceps to approximately 1 cm in diameter. Using curved suction and cochlea curets, the myosteoma was removed. Specimen was taken through the Lukens trap and sent to Microbiology for fungal culture. A large curved suction was placed in maxillary sinus and irrigated copiously with normal saline and suctioned through a Frazier suction positioned in the posterior nasal pharynx. Approximately 150 cc was irrigated through the left maxillary sinus until effluent was clear.

Total ethmoidectomy, polypectomy, and middle turbinectomy were performed in similar fashion in the right nasal cavity. After this was completed, Silastic sheeting was cut to size and placed on both sides in the nasal septum and sutured into place with 3-0 silk mattress sutures. MeroGel was placed in the posterior ethmoid cavities bilaterally, followed by small Merocel nasal tampons. 10-cm flat nasal tampons impregnated with Bacitracin ointment were placed at the floor of the left and right nasal airways. I sutured the tampons tight across the columella of the nose. Nasal dripper pad was placed. Oropharynx was suctioned. There was adequate hemostasis present.

The patient was awakened from general anesthesia, extubated, and brought to the recovery room in stable condition, having tolerated the procedure well.
ESTIMATED BLOOD LOSS: 200 cc

Maurice Doater, MD

GODFREY REGIONAL HOSPITAL
123 Main Street • Aldon, FL 77714 • (407) 555-1234

Answers

OPERATIVE REPORT

Patient information:

Patient name:	Date:
DOB:	Surgeon:
MR#:	Anesthetist:

Preoperative diagnosis:

1. Traumatic nasoseptal deformity
2. Septal perforation
3. Nasal obstruction

INDICATION:
55-year-old male with prior history of nasal trauma. He also underwent some sort of nasal surgery. Subsequent to that, he was left with a septal perforation and continued to have nasal obstruction. Examination reveals a significant septal deformity around the perforation with the anterior perforation of approximately 2–3 cm in size.

Postoperative diagnosis:

Same

Procedure(s) performed:

1. Septoplasty utilizing an external columella approach
2. Columella reconstruction utilizing cartilage graft
3. Repair of nasoseptal perforation

Anesthesia:

Assistant surgeon:

Description of procedure:

After consent was obtained, the patient was taken to the operating room and was placed on the operating room table in a supine position. After an adequate level of IV sedation was obtained, the patient was draped in an appropriate manner for nasal surgery. The patient's nose was prepped with Betadine prep and then draped in a sterile manner. The nose was packed with cotton pledgets soaked with 4% cocaine. After several minutes, intranasal and external nasal injection of 1% Xylocaine with 1:100,000 units epinephrine was made. Nasal hairs were trimmed. Then utilizing the columella incision, the skin and subcutaneous tissue were elevated off the lower lateral cartilages. The soft tissue between the lower lateral cartilage and the medial crura of the lower lateral cartilages was removed. Subsequently, the septum was isolated and bilateral mucoperichondrial and mucoperiosteal flaps were elevated. The perforation was encountered and the edges freshened. The cartilaginous septum was then removed in its entirety except for a dorsal strip. Subsequently, the deviated portion of the bony septum, as well as the maxillary crest, was removed. Subsequently, the perforation was closed on both sides with interrupted 4-0 chromic sutures. The septal cartilage that was removed was then shaved to straighten the cartilage out. This was then brought anteriorly between the perforation repair and the lower lateral cartilage to restore nasal tip support. This was secured between the medial crura with 4-0 clear nylon sutures. A quilting suture of 4-0 plain gut was then performed. The columella incision was closed with interrupted 6-0 nylon sutures. Sinolastic splints were then placed on both sides of the nasal septum and secured with nylon suture. The nose was then packed bilaterally with Merocel sponges coated with Bacitracin ointment and inflated with local solution. Nasal dressing was applied.

The patient tolerated the procedure well; there was no break in technique. The patient was awakened and taken to the recovery room in good condition.

Fluids administered: 1000 cc RL

Estimated blood loss: less than 25 cc

Preoperative medication: 12 mg Decadron and 1 gram Ancef IV

Maurice Doater, MD

GODFREY REGIONAL HOSPITAL
123 Main Street • Aldon, FL 77714 • (407) 555-1234

Answers

EXERCISE 17

OPERATIVE REPORT

Patient information:	
Patient name: DOB: MR#:	Date: Surgeon: Anesthetist:

Preoperative diagnosis:

1. Nasal polyposis
2. Chronic sinusitis

Postoperative diagnosis:

1. Nasal polyposis
2. Chronic sinusitis

Procedure(s) performed:

Functional endoscopic sinus surgery with bilateral Caldwell-Luc nasal antral windows; endoscopic anterior and posterior ethmoidectomies

Description of procedure:

The patient was brought to the operating room and placed in the supine position, and general endotracheal anesthesia was obtained without difficulty. The table was turned 180 degrees. The nose was examined. I Neo-Synephrinized his nose and injected his nasal polyps with 1% Xylocaine with 1:100,000 epinephrine after waiting about 10–15 minutes. We then started using the shaver and an endoscope to remove the polyps that were massive in nature and extended from anterior to posterior and inferior to superior inside the patient's nose. He has had previous nasal polypectomy and anterior and posterior ethmoidectomies, Caldwell-Luc and nasal antral windows in the past. There was complete obliteration of all anatomy due to the polyposis. I could identify, however, his nasal septum and it was hypersensitive—that is, swollen and very easy to bruise and start bleeding. In fact, all the structures in his nose were extremely vascular despite Neo-Synephrine and 1% Xylocaine with 1:100,000 epinephrine. I shaved the polyps out of the left side, following them from inferior to superior and identifying polyps medial to the middle turbinate and superior to the middle turbinate. They were lateral to the turbinate, inside the middle meatus, and I followed them into the anterior and posterior ethmoid air cells where I cleaned these areas out. Inspissated mucous was noted in the frontal sinus recess as well as in the anterior and posterior ethmoid air cells, and a large amount of inspissated mucous was in the left maxillary sinus. I enlarged the maxillary sinus opening endoscopically and could not get all the inspissated mucous out from this direction. I therefore injected the upper canine fossa area and used cautery to cut down to the maxillary sinus opening where I identified the anterior maxillary sinus wall. I decided to make a more medial approach to my opening and, therefore, used a Kerrison rongeur to chisel my way into the maxillary sinus, removing that anterior half-dime-sized plate of bone (less than 1 cm in size). I identified massive polyposis and inspissated mucous inside the maxillary sinus. I cleaned it out completely and identified the nasal antral window enlarging it slightly. I packed this area, the maxillary sinus as well as the nasal area, and all the meatus with Neosporin-impregnated Nu-Gauze. I closed the initial incision with interrupted 2-0 chromic. I also packed the nose on that side with Merocel splint impregnated with Neosporin and injected with 1% Xylocaine with 1:100,000 epinephrine. I then turned my attention to the right side where an identical situation occurred and only more bleeding was encountered than on the left side. I removed massive polyposis on the right side and, again, I identified the nasal antral window on the right side. It was stenosed and I enlarged it, again removing inspissated mucous there and from the frontal sinus recess. A lot of bleeding from the anterior ethmoid artery was noted. It was very difficult to control. The septum appeared to be pretty much in the midline, and I decided not to do anything with it. The turbinates were of normal size. He had been on prednisone preoperatively, and I decided not to do anything with the turbinates. After packing the right maxillary sinus after having performed the Caldwell-Luc in an identical fashion to that on the left side, I packed it with Neosporin-impregnated Nu-Gauze and packed the inferior middle meatus with Nu-Gauze. I placed a Merocel splint inside the nasal airway. It should be noted that an anterior-posterior ethmoidectomy was performed on the right, just merely following the massive polyposis into the anterior posterior ethmoid air cells. Previous surgery had been done on this area, removing the uncinate process so access was relatively easy.

Once I found that the patient was no longer bleeding, I awakened him and he was extubated and taken to the recovery room in stable condition.

PATHOLOGY:

1. Bilateral nasal polyps
2. Contents of both maxillary sinuses

Maurice Doater, MD

GODFREY REGIONAL HOSPITAL
123 Main Street • Aldon, FL 77714 • (407) 555-1234

Answers

OPERATIVE REPORT

Patient information:

Patient name: Date:
DOB: Surgeon:
MR#:   Anesthetist:

Preoperative diagnosis:

Left vocal cord polyp and possible right vocal cord polyp

Postoperative diagnosis:

Polyps of both left and right vocal cords consistent with papillomas, pathology pending

Procedure(s) performed:

Microdirect laryngoscopy with CO2 laser excision of polyps/papilloma

Anesthesia:

Assistant surgeon:

Description of procedure:

The patient was taken to the operating room and placed in the usual supine position. After induction of general anesthesia via endotracheal intubation, the patient was prepped and draped in the usual fashion for a clean uncontaminated procedure. All precautions, set-up, and preparation of the patient for use with the CO2 laser were taken prior to initiation of the procedure.

The anterior commissure laryngoscope was entered into the oral cavity and passed down to the level of the vocal cords. It was placed into position using the Lewy suspension. The polyp on the left vocal cord was immediately visible. There was a small polyp on the left false vocal cord as well. The right true vocal cord had a small polyp in the very anterior-most region near the anterior commissure. A biopsy of these was taken and sent to Pathology. Grossly, these definitely appeared to be papillomas.

CO2 laser was used to carefully excise the papillomas without injuring the vocal cords themselves. Hemostasis was achieved with

Afrin-soaked cottonoids.

The patient tolerated the above procedures well. There were no complications. The patient was subsequently moved directly to the recovery room in stable condition.

COUNTS: Instrument count correct at the end of the procedure

Maurice Doater, MD

GODFREY REGIONAL HOSPITAL
123 Main Street • Aldon, FL 77714 • (407) 555-1234

Answers

EXERCISE 19

OPERATIVE REPORT

Patient information:	
Patient name:	Date:
DOB:	Surgeon:
MR#:	Anesthetist:

Preoperative diagnosis:	
1. Left septal deviation	4. Nasal polyposis
2. Bilateral turbinate hypertrophy	5. Nasal airway obstruction
3. Chronic pansinusitis	

Postoperative diagnosis:	
1. Left septal deviation	4. Nasal polyposis
2. Bilateral turbinate hypertrophy	5. Nasal airway obstruction
3. Chronic pansinusitis	

Procedure(s) performed:	
1. Functional endoscopy	4. Endoscopic maxillary sinus antrostomies, bilateral
2. Nasal polypectomy	5. Bilateral endoscopic anterior ethmoidectomies
3. Bilateral inferior turbinectomy	

Description of procedure:

The patient was brought to the operating room and placed in the supine position. General endotracheal anesthesia was obtained without difficulty. The patient was prepped and draped in the usual standard fashion. The table was turned 180 degrees and the nose was Afrinized and cocainized. Examination of the nasal septum revealed an overall bending of the nasal septum that corresponded to what was seen on the CT scan. This was from right to left with what looked like bilateral middle turbinate impactions. Massive nasal mucosal fullness of both bilateral inferior turbinates and bilateral middle turbinates, obliteration of the middle meatus bilaterally due to mucosal thickening, and polyposis were seen. More polyposis was seen endoscopically on the right than left. We endoscopically scoped the inferior, middle, and superior meatus on the right side. We were unable to get a scope between the turbinates and septum, as there was such a deviation of the septum. We endoscopically started removing polyposis, starting from around the anterior aspect of the inferior portion of the middle turbinate all the way posterior into the nasopharyngeal area. This corresponded to the polyposis seen on CT scan. We then removed the mucosa overlying the uncinate process and part of that uncinate process, getting into the infundibulum and the anterior ethmoid air cells that were seen to be mucosally compromised. This again corresponded to what was seen on the CT scan. The maxillary sinus opening was noted to be obliterated. It was found with a seeking olive-tipped sucker. Once identified, the maxillary sinus opening was opened larger with an oscillating endoscopic shaver. This same shaver was utilized in the removal of excess mucosa and of the polyposis. Once I had enlarged the maxillary sinus opening to about a square centimeter, I noted there was diseased mucosa within the confines of the maxillary sinus cavity along with some fluid material. I did not enter the maxillary sinus cavity to any degree. I just suctioned out all the fluid with the olive-tipped seeker and turned my attention to other matters. Once I had removed the anterior ethmoid air cells, I then started to decrease the mucosal fullness on the inferior aspect of the middle turbinate as well as using the Don Dennis depolarizer to reduce the mucosal hypertrophy inferior turbinate. Once I was satisfied that I had opened the airway as much as possible endoscopically, I then used a long nasal speculum to fracture medially the deviated septum anteriorly and posteriorly that was so posteriorly deviated back to the left. This was fractured back to the midline so as to even up the nasal passages in terms of airflow and volume.

We then turned our attention to the right side that was more diseased; inferior and middle turbinate hypertrophy was noted. The middle meatus mucosa was noted to be significant, which corresponded also to what was seen on the CT scan. This area was scoped through the inferior, middle, and superior meatus. Endoscopically, using the shaver, we removed the polyposis noted in the middle meatus and on the inferior surface of the nasal turbinate all the way back into the nasopharyngeal area. All this polyposis was removed with the shaver. Entering into the anterior ethmoid air cells, this was done following the polyposis into the anterior ethmoid air cells. Some of the uncinate bone was likewise removed on the left side. The maxillary sinus opening was noted to be obliterated. There were actually two entries into the maxillary sinus. We took the more posterior and inferior sinus ostium. Immediately when we opened the sinus up, purulent material bubbled out of the maxillary sinus as if it were under pressure. The polyposis surrounding the ostium was removed with the shaver and the ostium itself was enlarged to about 1 square centimeter, as was the case on the opposite side. The Don Dennis depolarizer was utilized to shrink and fulgurate the inferior turbinate on the right side. The shaver was utilized to reduce the fullness of the mucosa on the middle turbinate. We outwardly fractured the impacted middle turbinate on the right side that was impacted into the nasal septum so it again gained more volume and airflow in the right nasal airway. When I was satisfied that I had cleared the airway to my satisfaction, I packed the anterior ethmoid air cell area with Neosporin-impregnated Nu-Gauze. This was done on both sides to about an equal degree. The inferior nasal airway bilaterally was packed with Neosporin-impregnated Merocel injected with 1% Xylocaine with 1:100,000 epinephrine. About 200 cc blood loss ensued during the case.

The patient was awakened, extubated, and brought to the recovery room in stable condition.

PATHOLOGY:
Contents of left and right middle meatus in separate containers

Maurice Doater, MD

GODFREY REGIONAL HOSPITAL
123 Main Street • Aldon, FL 77714 • (407) 555-1234

Answers

OPERATIVE REPORT

Patient information:	
Patient name: DOB: MR#:	Date: Surgeon: Anesthetist:

Preoperative diagnosis:

Chronic dacryocystitis with infection and tearing
INDICATIONS:
This elderly patient, who is 90 years old, has had chronic tearing and mattering on her right side. She normally has a very large cystic area that is very painful and expresses greenish-yellow purulent material. She currently is on Cipro 500 mg twice a day and is doing better than she ever has. It is elected to try and probe this and see if anything can be passed through, and if nothing can, then to incise and drain and pack the area to let it heal secondarily. A consent was signed.

Postoperative diagnosis:

Same

Procedure(s) performed:

Incision and drainage of a chronic dacryocystitis of the right eyelid

Anesthesia:

Local with moderate anesthesia care

Assistant surgeon:

Description of procedure:

The patient was taken to the operating room and prepped and draped. Large amounts of green purulent material were expressed from the right tear sac and this was sent for culture and sensitivity. I expressed until no further mucus was coming from the sac. IV sedation was given and a 2-cc volume of the standard mixture was injected in the upper and lower lid medially as well as the tear sac area near the nose. The patient was prepped with Betadine and draped. A 0 and a 1 Bowman probe were passed through the lower and the upper puncta. I used a 15 blade scalpel to cut down over the tear sac. I used a Westcott scissors to dissect as much of the tear sac to the bone as I could. Then the tear sac wall was incised. Irrigation was done and nothing passed beyond that tear sac obstruction. I did attempt to probe into the nose before cutting the tear sac and this was unsuccessful as far as any passage of irrigation. Cautery was used. Gentamicin-soaked packing was placed after the area was copiously irrigated with gentamicin. Both upper and lower puncta were cauterized completely shut in order to eliminate any inflow into the area. It is thought that with no inflow and outflow, this cyst will not reform. Antibiotic ointment was placed.

The patient tolerated the procedure well. She will be followed in the outpatient clinic in one day's time when her packing will be removed. She will continue on Cipro as well as triple antibiotic ointment to the area until it has healed in secondarily. I did close above and below with some 6-0 Vicryl in order to lessen the area that has to heal in secondarily as the initial incision was made approximately 10 millimeters. The patient was transferred in good condition.

ESTIMATED BLOOD LOSS: Less than 5 ccs
COMPLICATIONS: None

Maurice Doater, MD

GODFREY REGIONAL HOSPITAL
123 Main Street • Aldon, FL 77714 • (407) 555-1234

Answers

OPERATIVE REPORT

Patient information:	
Patient name:	Date:
DOB:	Surgeon:
MR#:	Anesthetist:

Preoperative diagnosis:

1) Recurrent and chronic ethmoid maxillary sinusitis. 2) Right concha bullosa.
INDICATION:
58-year-old female with chronic postnasal drainage from recurrent and chronic ethmoid and maxillary sinusitis. This was confirmed on CT scan. The patient is admitted now for surgical treatment.

Postoperative diagnosis:

Same

Procedure(s) performed:

1) Bilateral endoscopic antral ethmoidectomy. 2) Bilateral endoscopic maxillary antrostomy. 3) Right endoscopic resection of concha bullosa.

Anesthesia:

Assistant surgeon:

Description of procedure:

After consent was obtained, patient was taken to the operating room and placed on the operating room table in the supine position. After an adequate level of IV sedation was obtained, the patient was positioned and draped for sinus surgery. The patient's nose was packed with cotton pledgets soaked with 4% cocaine. After several minutes, 1% Xylocaine with 1:100,000 units epinephrine was infiltrated into the inferior turbinates bilaterally, middle turbinates bilaterally, and into the lateral wall of the nasal cavity bilaterally just anterior to the medial meatus. Attention was first focused on the right side.

Utilizing a 5" sinuscope and the microdebrider, the right concha bullosa was resected in its lateral portion. Subsequently, the uncinate process was infiltrated with local solution. Attention then was focused on the left side where the middle turbinate was medialized and the uncinate process was also injected with local solution. Attention was then refocused on the right side. Utilizing a sickle knife, biting forceps, and microdebrider, the uncinate process was removed. Subsequently, the anterior wall of the ethmoid bulla was removed with the sickle knife and microdebrider; the frontal recess area was examined and was found to be clear of obstruction. Essentially no work was done there. The hypertrophic mucosa and the anterior ethmoid cells were then cleared with the microdebrider. Attention was now focused on the maxillary sinus ostia, which was obstructed by hypertrophic mucosa. This was cleared from the ostia, and the ostia were widened in the posterior inferior direction. Retained secretions were suctioned. The right middle meatus was then packed with cotton pledgets soaked with 1:30,000 units of epinephrine. Attention was then focused on the left side. Again utilizing the sickle knife, biting forceps, and microdebrider, the uncinate process was removed. Subsequently, the anterior wall of the ethmoid bulla was also resected with sickle knife and microdebrider. The third frontal recess was examined and was found to be clear. Hypertrophic mucosa in the anterior ethmoid air cells was then cleared with a microdebrider. Attention was then focused on the maxillary sinus ostia, which were cleared of obstructive mucosa. The ostia were widened in a posterior inferior direction. Retained secretions were suctioned. The middle meatus was then packed with cotton pledgets soaked with the epinephrine solution. Re-inspection showed no active bleeding. FloSeal was coated into the ethmoid area bilaterally. Bacitracin ointment was applied. The middle meatus was then packed with the Merocel sponge coated Bacitracin ointment infiltrated in local solution. Nasal dressing was then applied. The patient tolerated the procedure well; there was no break in technique. Patient was awakened and taken to the recovery room in good condition.

Fluids administered: 800 cc of RL

Blood loss: Less than 10 cc

Preoperative medications: 12.5 mg Decadron IV

Maurice Doater, MD

GODFREY REGIONAL HOSPITAL
123 Main Street • Aldon, FL 77714 • (407) 555-1234

Answers

OPERATIVE REPORT

Patient information:

Patient name:
DOB:
MR#:

Preoperative diagnosis:

Recurrent squamous cell carcinoma of the oral cavity
CLINICAL NOTE:
The patient is an 82-year-old white female who several years ago underwent wide local resection of left anterior and lateral tongue and floor of mouth, squamous cell carcinoma. She had full-course radiation therapy postoperatively. She has been doing well, when on routine follow-up visit, was found to have recurrent squamous cell carcinoma that was biopsied in the office and confirmed the diagnosis. She is being brought to the operating room for resection/ablation.

Postoperative diagnosis:

Recurrent squamous cell carcinoma of the oral cavity

Procedure(s) performed:

Laser ablation of recurrent squamous cell carcinoma of the left anterior floor of mouth/mandibular alveolar mucosa/and left anterior tongue.

Anesthesia:

Assistant surgeon:

Description of procedure:

The patient was brought in the operating room and placed on the operating room table in a supine position. General anesthesia was administered endotracheally with a special laser tube. The left anterior tongue, floor of mouth, and alveolar area of tumor were seen and examined circumferentially. With margins this was marked with Bovie cautery prior to injecting with 1% lidocaine with 1:100,000 epinephrine. Using a hand-held laser set at 15 watts, super pulse power was utilized around the circumference of the lesion, and dysplasia was circumscribed with the laser as well. The central tumor and dysplastic tissue were then ablated and vaporized with the laser. Specimens were sent from the left anterior tongue, anterior and posterior alveolar mucosal margins, and left floor of mouth deep margins from the patient after ablation of the tumor. All these returned back negative for residual squamous cell carcinoma except the posterior alveolar margin that showed one small foci of carcinoma. This area was further ablated with the laser to destroy any residual tumor. There is adequate hemostasis obtained. There was meticulous hemostasis throughout the procedure.

The patient was then awakened from general anesthesia, extubated, and brought to the recovery room in stable condition, having tolerated the procedure well.
ESTIMATED BLOOD LOSS:
Less than 5 cc

Patk Adam MD

GODFREY REGIONAL HOSPITAL
123 Main Street • Aldon, FL 77714 • (407) 555-1234

Answers

OPERATIVE REPORT

Patient information:	

Patient name:
DOB:
MR#:

Preoperative diagnosis:	

Abdominal pain, possible peptic ulcer disease
INDICATIONS FOR SURGERY:
This 66-year-old male has been having symptoms of reflux, also epigastric pain and bloating. Recent upper GI was performed, which showed irregularity in the duodenal bulb, and he is referred for upper endoscopy.

Postoperative diagnosis:	

Duodenitis, gastritis, hiatal hernia, proximal gastric polyp
FINDINGS:
The esophagus does not appear acutely inflamed. The Z line is distinct 43 cm from the incisors. There is a small hiatal hernia but again no acute inflammation is seen. No evidence of stricturing or narrowing. The stomach shows some mild hyperemia in the region of the antrum and pylorus but no definite ulcers. The duodenum demonstrates inflammation and some mild erosions of the mucosa. No definite ulceration is noted in the duodenal bulb. The second portion of the duodenum appears unremarkable. There is a 5-mm benign-appearing gastric polyp noted in the proximal stomach that was removed.

Procedure(s) performed:	

Esophagogastroduodenoscopy with biopsy and removal of gastric polyp

Anesthesia:	

Assistant surgeon:	

Description of procedure:	

The patient is taken to the operating room, given intravenous sedation, and the throat is topically anesthetized. The esophagus is intubated with the Olympus gastroscope and this is carefully advanced under direct visualization through the esophagus, stomach, and then the duodenum, where the first and second portions are carefully examined and the pyloric region is also carefully and clearly examined. Examination of the stomach is then performed, including retroflex examination of the fundus. Biopsies of the antrum are taken, and also a small polyp in the proximal stomach is removed with the biopsy forceps. There did not appear to be any excessive bleeding from the biopsy sites or polyp removal site.

The gastroesophageal junction is carefully examined, and then the scope is fully withdrawn with the esophagus being again examined.

The scope was removed and the patient was taken from the procedure room in satisfactory condition. Estimated blood loss is minimal. Complications none. Prognosis good.

COMMENT:
Operative findings were discussed with the patient. He will be notified when the pathology report returns. I suggested that he consider a two-week course of an acid-blocking medication in an effort to clear his duodenitis, and if biopsies show H. pylori, he may need additional medication.

Patk Adam MD

GODFREY REGIONAL HOSPITAL
123 Main Street • Aldon, FL 77714 • (407) 555-1234

Answers

OPERATIVE REPORT

Patient information:

Patient name:
DOB:
MR#:

Preoperative diagnosis:

1. Bleeding per rectum
2. Increasing bowel movements

Postoperative diagnosis:

1. Spastic colon
2. Polyp in the colon
3. AV malformation
4. Minimal colitis
5. Minimal diverticulosis
6. Internal hemorrhoids

Procedure(s) performed:

Colonoscopy, polypectomy, cauterization of AV malformation and biopsy for colitis

Anesthesia:

RN sedation

Assistant surgeon:

Description of procedure:

The patient was brought to the endoscopy suite and placed in the left lateral position. After he was connected to the ECG, blood pressure and pulse oximeter were found to be within reasonable normal limits. IV sedation was given initially by IV Demerol and then IV Versed. After adequate sedation was obtained, Xylocaine cream was used in the perirectal area. Rectal examination was performed and was found to be normal.

The colonoscope was introduced and passed through all of the flexures into the cecum. Slight sigmoid pressure had to be exerted to go around the hepatic flexure. Then the scope was carefully withdrawn, visualizing all the sites of the colon. The patient did have very occasional diverticulosis. He had one polyp in the splenic flexure that was about 1 to 2 mm, was sessile, and was removed. He also had minimal AL malformation, solitary AV malformation. This was cauterized. The patient had minimal colitis. The patient did have a mild to moderate amount of spastic colon while I was intubating the scope, and required 1 mg of glucagon intravenous to be given slowly, which was done. The patient did, on retroflexion of the scope in the rectum, have minimal hemorrhoids. Then the scope was withdrawn.

The patient tolerated the procedure well and was transferred to the same-day surgery unit in a stable condition.

GODFREY REGIONAL HOSPITAL
123 Main Street • Aldon, FL 77714 • (407) 555-1234

Answers

Chapter **14** **Coding Complexities of Surgical Procedures**

OPERATIVE REPORT

Patient information:

Patient name:
DOB:
MR#:

Date:
Surgeon:
Anesthetist:

Preoperative diagnosis:

Pelvic pain; dysmenorrhea; known endometriosis; failure of hormone therapy

Postoperative diagnosis:

Same with mild endometriosis; red, black, and clear (predominantly red) on both ovaries, both pelvic sidewalls (right greater than left), and a small amount in cul-de-sac

Procedure(s) performed:

Laser laparoscopy

Anesthesia:

Assistant surgeon:

Description of procedure:

The patient is brought to the operating room and placed under general anesthesia by endotracheal tube, prepped and draped in the usual sterile fashion, and placed in the lithotomy position. The bladder was drained with a small Foley, which was left in place. Hulka tenaculum was placed in the cervix. Examination under anesthesia revealed the uterus to be midline and midposition with no adnexal masses. Attention was turned to the upper abdomen after regowning and gloving.

Vertical incision was made through the patient's old laparoscopy incision and carried down through the subcu to the fascia. The fascia was delivered with hemostats and incised with a knife. The Veress needle was used in a modified procedure to inflate the abdomen. Then the Hasson cannula was placed. Next, the abdomen was inflated with CO_2. The laparoscope was introduced and upper abdomen was visualized and was normal. Lower abdomen showed the endometriosis.

Laser was used and the endometriosis was removed under direct visualization without subsequent bleeding. CO_2 gas was released through the umbilical cannula, which was then removed. Both incisions were closed with Dermabond. Hulka tenaculum was removed from the cervix without subsequent bleeding. Needle and sponge counts were reported as correct by the circulating nurse.

General anesthesia was reversed and the patient was sent to the recovery room in stable condition.

ESTIMATED BLOOD LOSS: Less than 10 cc

COMPLICATIONS: None

COUNTS: All counts correct

DISPOSITION: Patient to recovery room in stable condition

Rachel Perez MD

GODFREY REGIONAL HOSPITAL
123 Main Street • Aldon, FL 77714 • (407) 555-1234

Answers

OPERATIVE REPORT

Patient information:

Patient name:
DOB:
MR#:

Date:
Surgeon:
Anesthetist:

Preoperative diagnosis:

1. Weight loss
2. Elevated CA-125

Postoperative diagnosis:

Same

FINDINGS: As determined by exam under anesthesia, the patient has an essentially normal pelvic exam with possible fundal fibroid and retroverted uterus. On laparoscopy, she had a normal upper abdomen and pelvis except for some blebs or cysts at the distal end of each tube bilaterally. Additionally, there were several adhesions of the left ovary and these were cut and biopsied. There was some brownish discoloration of the anterior peritoneum in typical area of biopsy. Additionally, up under the diaphragm near the liver were some fatty deposits, and these were biopsied and felt to be benign. Frozen-section report on all specimens was benign and peritoneal fluid was also sent. A small left functional cyst was biopsied and also reported as benign.

Procedure(s) performed:

Diagnostic scope with multiple biopsies

Anesthesia:

Assistant surgeon:

Description of procedure:

TECHNIQUE:
Following satisfactory and suitable anesthesia, she was placed in the lithotomy position and exam was performed. She was then prepped and draped in the usual fashion for this position. A dilator was used as a manipulator, and the uterus was sounded to 9 cm. Surgeon changed gloves, and laparoscopic portion was commenced. Initially, a Veress needle was used, but I could not maintain appropriate pressure, so the 12-mm trocar was then inserted and the scope passed to ensure proper location and lack of injury. CO_2 was then insufflated to a pressure of 12 mm, and an additional 5-mm suprapubic puncture was made. Examination of the upper abdomen and pelvis was performed and biopsies of both tubal cyst areas were performed. These were multiple little blebs of approximately 3–4 mm at the greatest dimension. The left ovary was then biopsied and the adhesions cut and a specimen taken as well. The peritoneal discolorations were documented on film and then biopsied in typical area. The upper abdomen biopsy was taken under the diaphragm as mentioned above.

Irrigation was used, and a specimen was sent for cytology. Following this, hemostasis was noted and the CO_2 gas was allowed to escape after initial frozen-section reports came back as negative. The instruments were removed and the incision sewn with 4-0 undyed Vicryl in a subcuticular fashion with a deep stitch being placed in the 12-mm site. An additional right-sided 5-mm mid-abdominal puncture had been made to allow us to get the subdiaphragmatic biopsy. This was also closed with 4-0 undyed Vicryl. Vaginal instruments were removed after sterile dressings were placed.

The patient was transferred to the recovery room in good condition.

Rachel Perez, MD

GODFREY REGIONAL HOSPITAL
123 Main Street • Aldon, FL 77714 • (407) 555-1234

Answers

Chapter **14** **Coding Complexities of Surgical Procedures**

OPERATIVE REPORT

Patient information:	
Patient name:	Date:
DOB:	Surgeon:
MR#:	Anesthetist:

Preoperative diagnosis:

Menorrhagia

Postoperative diagnosis:

Menorrhagia

Procedure(s) performed:

Evaluation under anesthesia, hysteroscopy, dilatation and curettage, endometrial ablation

Anesthesia:

General endotracheal

Assistant surgeon:

Description of procedure:

The patient was taken to the operating room. After an adequate level of general endotracheal anesthesia, the patient was placed in a modified lithotomy position in Allen stirrups. Evaluation under anesthesia revealed the uterus upper limits of normal, a multiparous cervix. No adnexal masses. A weighted vaginal speculum was placed in the vagina. Cervix was grasped with single-tooth tenaculum and dilated to a #6 Hegar dilator. Using a Stortz hysteroscope of 30 degrees and D5W, a hysteroscopy was performed, which revealed a fluffy appearance to the uterus consistent with menorrhagia and a proliferative endometrium. The ostia were noted to be normal. There were no submucous myomata. At this time the hysteroscope was removed. A dilation and curettage was performed with moderate amount of tissue. Then using an Ethicon endometrial ablation apparatus, the catheter was primed to 2150 mm Hg and placed into the uterus that had been sounded to 8 cm. Using D5W, the catheter was then primed to 180 mm Hg and the cycle was turned on. There was an endometrial ablation of the cavity of 8 minutes at 87 degrees Celsius. After this, it was removed after it had cooled down. The uterus took approximately 10 cc of D5W to fill. Single-tooth tenaculum was removed, as was the weighted vaginal speculum.

Using a medium-sized sharp curet, the endometrial cavity was curetted and curettings were sent to Pathology.

Hysteroscope was reintroduced. The appearance of the cavity was much smoother.

At this point the procedure was terminated. A single-tooth tenaculum and bivalve speculum were removed from the cervix and vagina, respectively.

The patient tolerated the procedure well and was sent to the recovery room in stable condition.

Adn Wetg MD

GODFREY REGIONAL HOSPITAL
123 Main Street • Aldon, FL 77714 • (407) 555-1234

Answers

OPERATIVE REPORT

Patient information:

Patient name:
DOB:
MR#:

Date:
Surgeon:
Anesthetist:

Preoperative diagnosis:

Pelvic pain, ovarian cyst

Postoperative diagnosis:

Pelvic pain with adhesions and right ovarian cyst

Procedure(s) performed:

Laparoscopy, lysis of adhesions, and right ovarian cystectomy

Anesthesia:

Assistant surgeon:

Description of procedure:

The patient was taken to the operating room here after an adequate level of general endotracheal anesthesia, and placed in a modified lithotomy position in Allen stirrups. A Foley was placed, and the patient was draped and prepped in the usual sterile fashion. A 45-degree side-open vaginal speculum was placed in the vagina. The cervix was grasped with a single-tooth tenaculum and a Hulka uterine manipulator. A subumbilical incision was made with a 15-blade, taken down through the subcutaneous tissue to the fascia, and the fascia was scored and taken transversely. Rectus muscle split. Peritoneum opened. Stay sutures of 2-0 Vicryl on a UR6 placed in the fascia. A blunt origin cannula was placed through which a 9.9 flow demand of CO_2 with a maximum pressure of 15 mm Hg was inserted. A second suprapubic port, as well as a left lateral port, was placed. It should be noted that there are adhesions from the omentum to the anterior abdominal wall as well as to the uterus. Also on the left-hand side, the sigmoid colon was adhered to the sidewall. This was taken down by blunt dissection and also with a laparoscopic cutting shears 5 mm. The previous tubal was noted, and at this point, the adhesions were freed up and the left ovary was noted to be normal. The right ovary had two ovarian cysts and the cyst walls were opened and marsupialized. Thus at the end of the procedure, there was no endometriosis. There were no adhesions left. All the adhesions had been freed up. The previous tubal ligation had been noted to be normal. And all adhesions had been taken down from the omentum to the anterior abdominal wall as well as to the left lateral pelvic sidewall, and the two ovarian cysts on the right side had been marsupialized. All scopes were taken out under direct visualization. The previous subumbilical incision was closed with 2-0 Vicryl. The subcu was injected with 0.5% Marcaine and the skin was re-approximated with 3-0 Monocryl.

Estimated blood loss: Scant

Fluid received: Ringer's lactate

Pathology: None

The patient tolerated the procedure well and left for the recovery room in satisfactory condition.

Adm Westy, MD

GODFREY REGIONAL HOSPITAL
123 Main Street • Aldon, FL 77714 • (407) 555-1234

Answers

EXERCISE 29

OPERATIVE REPORT

Patient information:	
Patient name:	Date:
DOB:	Surgeon:
MR#:	Anesthetist:

Preoperative diagnosis:

1) Right labial mass; 2) Vulvar and vaginal condyloma; 3) HIV positive

Postoperative diagnosis:

Same

FINDINGS: A 2×2 cm firm mass involving the right labia. Upon removal of this, it appeared as a large condyloma. Multiple condylomata of the vulvar, perianal, and vaginal areas are noted.

SPECIMENS: Right labial mass

Procedure(s) performed:

Incision of vaginal mass and laser vaporization of condyloma

Anesthesia:

Assistant surgeon:

Description of procedure:

The patient was taken to the operating room and placed in the supine position. Her legs were placed in candy-cane stirrups, and she was prepped and draped in a sterile fashion. Spinal anesthesia was found to be adequate.

The knife was used to make an incision over the right labial mass, which was excised using Metzenbaum scissors and Bovie. The deep tissues were closed with interrupted figure-of-eight sutures of #3 Vicryl and a subcuticular stitch of 3-0 Vicryl was used to close the epithelium. The laser was then used to vaporize the condyloma; it was set on 15 watts of power and test-fired. Vaporization was then performed at the various vulvar and intravaginal regions. Silvadene cream was then applied to the areas.

The patient tolerated the procedure well and went to the recovery room.

She was given a prescription for Vicodin 5/500 #40 to take one po q4h prn for pain, Silvadene cream to use twice a day, and EMLA cream to use prn for vulvar pain. She is to follow up in the office in one week. *Rachel Perez* MD

GODFREY REGIONAL HOSPITAL
123 Main Street • Aldon, FL 77714 • (407) 555-1234

Answers

OPERATIVE REPORT

Patient information:		
Patient name: DOB: MR#:		Date: Surgeon: Anesthetist:

Preoperative diagnosis:

Status post bladder neck suspension with vesical sling with erosion

Postoperative diagnosis:

Erosion of vesical sling

Procedure(s) performed:

Removal of eroded bladder neck vesical sling

Anesthesia:

General

Assistant surgeon:

Description of procedure:

The patient was placed on the operating table in the lithotomy position after general anesthesia was given. External genitalia and vagina were prepped and draped in the usual sterile manner. Foley catheter was inserted in the bladder and left indwelling throughout the procedure. The labia were retracted laterally. The weighted speculum was placed on the posterior vaginal wall.

A small incision on the anterior vaginal wall was performed with the cautery over the eroded sling. The synthetic sling was grasped at a right angle and pulled, and the lateral sutures were cut and the sling removed. We were able to pull the suture on the left side completely; however, we were able to pull it partially on the right side. Surgical field was irrigated thoroughly with large amount of antibiotic solution.

The small vaginal incision was left open in order to let it granulate, since the opening was very small and because of infection evidence.

The patient tolerated the procedure well. She was sent to the recovery room in satisfactory condition, and she will be discharged home when discharge criteria are met and after her Foley catheter is removed.

DISCHARGE MEDICATIONS: Levaquin 500 mg one tablet daily for 10 days. She will be advised to have follow-up in the office in 4–6 weeks or as needed.

GODFREY REGIONAL HOSPITAL
123 Main Street • Aldon, FL 77714 • (407) 555-1234

Rachel Perez MD

Answers

OPERATIVE REPORT

Patient information:	
Patient name: DOB: MR#:	Date: Surgeon: Anesthetist:

Preoperative diagnosis:

Cancer of the prostate, status post seed implant for prostate cancer, and hematuria

INDICATION FOR PROCEDURE: This patient had a seed implant for prostate cancer in 1997. Recently, the patient has been having blood in the urine. Sometimes it is significant. IVP is negative. The patient also has urgency and urgency incontinence.

Postoperative diagnosis:

Cancer of the prostate, status post seed implant and prostatic urethral stone and bladder stones

Procedure(s) performed:

Cystoscopy, stone extraction, and bilateral retrograde pyelogram

Anesthesia:

Assistant surgeon:

Description of procedure:

The patient was brought to the operating room and spinal anesthesia was given. The patient was placed in lithotomy position. Genitalia were prepped and draped. The cystoscope was introduced. Anterior urethra was normal. Posterior urethra was found to be nonobstructive. But there is evidence of bleeding from this area, especially in the posterior aspect of the prostatic urethra. The prostatic urethra had been resected before. There is no significant obstruction of the prostatic urethra. Bladder neck was found to be open. There are stones stuck in the prostatic urethra. I pushed it back with the cystoscope into the bladder. There were three stones. One of the stones was in the bladder. The stones measure about 1/2 cm. The stones were removed by irrigation. The bladder was examined with a right-angle lens as well as the regular lens. Both ureteric orifices were normal. There is no stone or tumor in the bladder. Then the retrograde was performed by inserting a catheter bilaterally; retrograde is negative. Then the scope was removed, a Foley catheter was inserted, and the patient was sent to the recovery room in good condition.

The patient tolerated the procedure and there was no change in vital signs.

The patient will go home today and we will be removing the catheter tomorrow morning at the office.

GODFREY REGIONAL HOSPITAL
123 Main Street • Aldon, FL 77714 • (407) 555-1234

Rachel Perez MD

Answers

EXERCISE 32

OPERATIVE REPORT

Patient information:

Patient name: Date:
DOB: Surgeon:
MR#:   Anesthetist:

Preoperative diagnosis:

Postoperative diagnosis:

Procedure(s) performed:

Spinal cord stimulator trial; intraoperative screening of the cord lead placement

Anesthesia:

Assistant surgeon:

Description of procedure:

The patient had an IV started and received 1 gram of Ancef IV prior to the procedure. The patient was taken to the operating room and placed prone on the spinal table with a couple of pillows under her hips. The lumbar area was prepped and draped in the usual sterile fashion, and the L2-3 interspace was identified and marked under fluoroscopy. The T9-10 vertebrae were also identified and marked, and a temporary plan to place the tip of the needle around the T9-10 level was made before proceeding with the procedure. The L2-3 interspace was infiltrated with about 6 to 8 cc of 1% lidocaine on the right side. A 17-gauge Tuohy needle was inserted under direct fluoroscopic control into the interspace and advanced gradually until the epidural space was identified using a loss-of-resistance technique. Once the epidural space was identified, an introducer was passed through the needle and advanced a few cm into the epidural space without any resistance. The cord lead was then inserted through the needle and advanced under direct fluoroscopic control gradually into the epidural space and advanced gradually until the tip of the needle was at the T9-10 interspace level. Positioning of the lead was confirmed, both in the AP and the oblique views, and the positioning of the needle was confirmed to be in the posterior epidural space just to the right side of the midline.

The cord lead was then connected to the screener and a trial screening was conducted using various lead settings. The patient had a good coverage of the lower back as well as the right lower extremity and was very satisfied with the type of pain relief that she received with this screening.

The epidural needle was then gradually withdrawn into the subcutaneous tissues, and positioning of the lead was once again confirmed to be in the T9-10 level. The lead was then taped in place using Steri-Strips, and the stylet was then removed. The cord lead was then connected to extension lead, and gauze dressing was then placed over the leads.

The patient was then taken to the recovery area and final stimulator settings were then performed in the recovery area.

The patient had a good response to the stimulation and had good coverage over the area of her pain.

The patient tolerated the procedure well and had very minimal blood loss. The patient was given her discharge instructions and discharged home after the usual discharge criteria were met.

FOLLOW-UP PLAN:
The patient will follow up in the pain clinic in two weeks or so, at which time we will evaluate the patient further, and if she has good control of her pain with this modality, we will go ahead and implant the lead and the generator. Until such time, the patient will take Keflex 500 mg po q8h along with methadone 2.5 mg po q4 to 6 hours prn for breakthrough pain. Patient will also take Soma to treat any muscle spasms.

Ahn Westy, MD

GODFREY REGIONAL HOSPITAL
123 Main Street • Aldon, FL 77714 • (407) 555-1234

Answers

PAIN MANAGEMENT REPORT

Patient information:	
Patient name: DOB: MR#:	Date: Surgeon: Anesthetist:

Preoperative diagnosis:

Postoperative diagnosis:

Procedure(s) performed:

Trigger point injections

Anesthesia:

Assistant surgeon:

Description of procedure:

The patient is a 59-year-old lady who comes in for trigger point injections for treatment of myofascial pain syndrome. She states that she is having some increased pain in the right side of her lower lumbar upper sacral area. She has been to the tanning bed and she is sunburned on the back.

PROCEDURE: Risks, benefits, and options were discussed, and written consent was obtained. Vital signs stable, afebrile. The patient is placed sitting on the examination table. Palpation of the right longissimus muscles in the lumbar area and also the multifidus muscle reveals a total of eight trigger points. These trigger points were marked, skin prepped with alcohol. 1 cc of 0.25% Marcaine with 3 mg of Kenalog was injected into each trigger point. The patient tolerated the procedure well and left the clinic in stable condition.

ASSESSMENT AND PLAN:
1. Chronic low back pain, status post back surgery, failed back syndrome
2. Patient is status post three caudal epidural injections. The patient is on medications for chronic pain. She is currently taking MS Contin 15 mg q12 hours.
3. Myofascial pain syndrome. The patient received trigger point injections as above. The patient will return to the clinic in approximately one or two weeks for possible repeat trigger point injections.

Thank you for allowing us to participate in this patient's care.

Adm Westg MD

GODFREY REGIONAL HOSPITAL
123 Main Street • Aldon, FL 77714 • (407) 555-1234

Answers

OPERATIVE REPORT

Patient information:

Patient name:	Date:
DOB:	Surgeon:
MR#:	Anesthetist:

Preoperative diagnosis:

Primary open-angle glaucoma, left eye

Postoperative diagnosis:

Primary open-angle glaucoma, left eye

Procedure(s) performed:

Trabeculectomy, left eye

Anesthesia:

Assistant surgeon:

Description of procedure:

The eye was dilated with three drops of Cyclogyl along with drops of Ocufen and Ocuflox. In the surgery room, I added a drop of Neo-Synephrine 10%. Betadine was applied to the lid, lashes, and conjunctiva. She was sedated per Vanlint and peribulbar block of the usual anesthetic mixture minus Wydase, administered by me. This was followed with a full Betadine prep and the usual sterile drape. 50 mg of cefazolin was injected into the subconjunctiva and/or applied to the ocular surface. A traction suture was placed under the superior rectus tendon about 12 mm superior to the limbus. A limbus-based conjunctival incision was cut approximately 9–10 mm superior to the limbus, and the conjunctiva was turned back to the limbus. This proceeded very easily. A pledget soaked in 5-FU was applied to the planned trabeculectomy site. This was allowed to touch the tendinous layer over the trabeculectomy site, but not at the conjunctiva wound margin. This was held in place for three minutes and then the dissection bed was thoroughly irrigated. A 4-mm rectangular trabeculectomy flap was cut using a guarded diamond blade at a depth of 0.25 mm. The dissection was carried forward into the clear cornea.

Paracentesis was cut at 1:30 and the chamber was filled with viscoelastic. The incision was cut with a 3.0-mm diamond keratome. The trabeculectomy was then fashioned using a series of 5 overlapping punches with a Kelly punch, 3 radial oriented and 2 circumferentially oriented. Corresponding peripheral iridectomy was cut. The trabeculectomy flap was sutured down with 2 interrupted 10-0 nylons, which clearly allowed filtration. The conjunctiva and tendons were then closed with running sutures of 10-0 nylon. They were closed in two separate layers. 0.1 cc of 5-FU was injected subconjunctivally and internasally. The eye was dressed with a collagen shield soaked in Ocuflox, and Maxitrol was applied to the lid, which was closed with a Steri strip, followed by a sterile pad and metal shield.

She tolerated the procedure extremely well. At the close of the case, filtration was clearly established with irrigation in the paracentesis. The eye would hold soft to normal pressure as estimated digitally. Conjunctiva was intact and the suture line was secure. The cornea and chamber were clear. A modest amount of viscoelastic was left in the chamber.

Linda Patrick MD

GODFREY REGIONAL HOSPITAL
123 Main Street • Aldon, FL 77714 • (407) 555-1234

Answers

EXERCISE 35

OPERATIVE REPORT

Patient information:
Patient name: DOB: MR#:

Preoperative diagnosis:

51-year-old female with severe mental retardation. She has bilateral ear disease with cerumen impactions unable to be cleaned at the clinic.
1) Mental retardation.
2) Bilateral cerumen impaction.

Postoperative diagnosis:

Same

Procedure(s) performed:

Bilateral microscopic ear examination and removal of bilateral cerumen impactions

Anesthesia:

Assistant surgeon:

Description of procedure:

After consent was obtained, the patient was taken to the operating room and placed on the operating room table in the supine position. After an adequate level of IV sedation was obtained, the patient was draped in the appropriate manner for ear cleaning. Attention was first focused on the right ear.

Utilizing the ear speculum and ear microscope, the external canal was cleared of firm cerumen. Subsequent examination showed narrow ear canals. There was no swelling or tenderness. The tympanic membrane was sclerotic and intact. There was no granulation tissue or discharge. There were similar findings in the left ear, and similar procedure was then performed on the left ear. There was a small patch of some granulation on the posterior aspect of the tympanic membrane. Cortisporin otic suspension and cotton ball were placed in the left ear. The patient tolerated the procedure well, there was no break in technique, and the patient was awakened and taken to the recovery room in good condition.

GODFREY REGIONAL HOSPITAL
123 Main Street • Aldon, FL 77714 • (407) 555-1234

James Elliott MD

Answers

PAIN MANAGEMENT REPORT

Patient information:

Patient name:
DOB:
MR#:

Date:
Surgeon:
Anesthetist:

Preoperative diagnosis:

Postoperative diagnosis:

Procedure(s) performed:

Left lumbar facet denervation with pulse radiofrequency

Anesthesia:

Assistant surgeon:

Description of procedure:

The patient follows up at the pain clinic for radiofrequency pulse denervation of her left lumbar facet nerve. All risks and benefits of the procedure are explained to the patient and the patient wishes to proceed.

After sterile prep and drape and localization of the skin using a 20-gauge SMK spinal needle, the needle was advanced down into the medial portion of the left L2 transverse process, corresponding to the left L1-L2 facet nerve after a stimulation test that was positive for pain but negative for radiculopathy, was performed. This area was pulsed for a total of 120 seconds at 42–44 degrees Celsius heat and the patient tolerated the procedure well.

The exact same procedure was carried out at the left L2-L3 facet nerve.

The exact same procedure was carried out at the left L3-L4 facet nerve.

The exact same procedure was carried out at the left L4-L5 facet nerve.

The exact same procedure was carried out at the left L5-S1 facet nerve. A negative motor stimulation test was performed.

ASSESSMENT: Lumbar facet disease with chronic low back pain.

PLAN: The plan will be for the patient to follow up in the pain clinic in one week, and we will see how she is doing after the completion of her lumbar facet pulse denervation. She is to continue with all her current medications.

Rachel Perez MD

GODFREY REGIONAL HOSPITAL
123 Main Street • Aldon, FL 77714 • (407) 555-1234

Answers

Chapter **14** **Coding Complexities of Surgical Procedures**

EXERCISE 37

OPERATIVE REPORT

Patient information:	
Patient name: DOB: MR#:	Date: Surgeon: Anesthetist:

Postoperative diagnosis:

DIAGNOSES:
1. Chronic, intractable, excruciating low back pain with lower extremity pain, which resists treatment. The patient had a successful trial of morphine pump to control the pain using a continuous morphine drip.
2. Post hemilaminectomy pain syndrome associated with neuropathic pain in the bilateral lower extremities

Procedure(s) performed:

1. Placement of intrathecal subarachnoid implantable non-programmable catheter
2. Thoracic myelogram
3. Placement of non-programmable Arrow implantable morphine pump

Anesthesia:

Using MAC/fentanyl and propofol drip accompanied with local infiltration of the wounds with bupivacaine 0.25% with epinephrine and spinal anesthesia for the rest of the case with MAC

Description of procedure:

ESTIMATED BLOOD LOSS: Minimal, 5 to 10 ml blood
DESCRIPTION OF THE PROCEDURE:
The patient signed an informed consent after full discussion and explanation with the patient and his friend about the procedure, rationale, side effects, complications, limitations, risks, and alternatives. The patient received 2 mg Ancef intraoperatively intravenously, and he will receive another 1 mg in the PACU.

The patient was brought to the operating room and positioned in the left lateral decubitus. The sites of the wound incisions in the back and in the right lower abdominal wall were marked. The patient was then prepped and draped in sterile technique, which was maintained all through. The back and the right side of the abdomen were prepared in routine sterile fashion. The L2-L3 vertebral spine was identified and infiltrated using bupivacaine 0.25% with epinephrine. The percutaneous 17-gauge Tuohy needle was inserted at the level of L2/3. The bevel was cephalad. The dura was punctured at about 5 cm deep from the skin. After free flow, an intrathecal special catheter was threaded through the needle with bevel directed cephalad. The tip of the catheter was placed around T12 and was threaded up in the subarachnoid space, about 10 to 12 cm. A C-arm fluoroscope with a TV monitor was used. The contrast material, Isovue 266 about 1.25 ml, was injected and was given a good intrathecal spread with myelogram picture without any pathological findings. A midline skin incision was made and carried out through subcutaneous tissue to the dorsal fascia. A clear flow was tested again. No blood but clear cerebral spinal fluid. With the needle in place, purse-string stitches were placed using 3-0 Prolene. The catheter stylet was removed. Then 3-0 Prolene ties sutured the anchor to the underlying fascia using 3-0 Prolene and secured the catheter.

At the same time, another physician, at the other side of the table, created a pocket in the lower part of the right abdominal quadrant of the abdominal wall to hold the Arrow pump, and a transverse skin incision about 3 to 4 inches was made through the subcutaneous tissue to the external oblique fascia. The other surgeon used the previously marked pocket site, which was in between the costal margin and the iliac crest region, using cautery to desiccate down through the subcutaneous tissue to the level about the fascia and the pocket, adequate to accommodate the pump. The other physician created a pocket there.

Meticulous hemostasis was used on the abdominal wall and back where the catheter was placed. Using the tunneling device provided, a subcutaneous tunnel was created between the posterior incision and the abdominal incision. The tubing that connected to the catheter with reservoir was brought through the tunnel. Of course, we provided titanium connector to connect them. Sutures secured the connection. The Arrow pump with capacity of 30 ml and 0.5 ml per day perfusion rate was prepped at the back table by emptying its water content and was refilled with 18 ml of the preservative-free Duramorph 1 mg/ml concentration. The extension tubing was connected as mentioned above to the Arrow pump after tying the catheter. The morphine pump was secured in place. Subcutaneously, the Arrow pump was placed into the pocket and secured to the underlying fascia using an 0 Prolene suture. Hemostasis was adequately achieved throughout the procedure using electrocautery. Hemostasis was meticulously performed. At this time, using a special needle to prime the catheter, 0.5 ml and another 0.5 ml which equals 0.5 ml Duramorph were used to prime the catheter and to give bolus intrathecally to the patient. The wounds were copiously irrigated with Bacitracin solution and closed in layers in routine fashion using 3-0 Vicryl for the subcutaneous tissue. The skin was closed using 2-0 nylon sutures with continuous stitches. After the sterile dressing was applied, the instrument, needle, and sponge counts were correct after being counted by scrub nurse and both surgeons.

The patient is transferred to the PACU in stable condition with no complications and absolute pain-free status. The patient will remain in the recovery room or in the same-day surgery unit for a few hours and will be discharged home per criteria to follow as outpatient with the surgeon.

Rachel Perez MD

GODFREY REGIONAL HOSPITAL
123 Main Street • Aldon, FL 77714 • (407) 555-1234

Answers

OPERATIVE REPORT

Patient information:

Patient name:	Date:
DOB:	Surgeon:
MR#:	Anesthetist:

Preoperative diagnosis:

Chronic back pain, status post back injury and multiple herniated disks and back surgery

Postoperative diagnosis:

Chronic back pain, status post back injury and multiple herniated disks and back surgery

Procedure(s) performed:

Insertion of morphine pump in conjunction with another surgeon

Anesthesia:

Assistant surgeon:

Description of procedure:

After the patient was given sedation by anesthesiologist, he was put with his left side down, and the abdomen and back were prepped with Betadine and then sterile towel-draped. After the other surgeon did his incision in the back and inserted the epidural catheter, I did an incision in the left upper outer quadrant area, about 3.5 inches, and then I dissected down and created a pocket about 5 inches below that and then subcutaneous over the fascia, and hemostasis was done with cautery. I flushed the wound with Kantrex antibiotics. Then I inserted the pump and sutured it in four places with nylon 0 to the deep fascia to keep it in place. Then we ran a tunnel between this wound and the spine wound, and we tied the spinal catheter to the abdominal wound. Then we connected the catheter from the pump and spinal catheter together with a special device. We made a loop of them, about 3 inches to 4 inches, to be lying without tension, and the loop of the catheter behind the pump, and the pump was filled first before with morphine, and after we inserted the catheters together, we inserted 1 cc of morphine to the pump as requested by the representative of the pump. Then the wound was again irrigated with Kantrex antibiotics; we closed the subcutaneous tissue with chromic 3-0 and silk with nylon 3-0 as well, and the patient lost maybe 4–5 cc of blood and tolerated the procedure.

The other surgeon finished his wound and the patient tolerated the procedure and went to the recovery room. The patient received Ancef before and during the procedure by IV.

Rachel Perez MD

GODFREY REGIONAL HOSPITAL
123 Main Street • Aldon, FL 77714 • (407) 555-1234

Answers

EXERCISE 39

OPERATIVE REPORT

Patient information:

Patient name:
DOB:
MR#:

Date:
Surgeon:
Anesthetist:

Preoperative diagnosis:

Anisometropia, status post inaccurate intraocular lens implantation one month ago

Postoperative diagnosis:

Same

Procedure(s) performed:

Intraocular lens exchange, posterior chamber—left eye
ESTIMATED BLOOD LOSS: Less than 0.1 cc
COMPLICATIONS: None
INDICATIONS FOR SURGERY: This 76-year-old patient had an inaccurate intraocular lens calculation that resulted in four diopters of anisometropia. This is not tolerable to the patient as she likes to get up in the evening without needing her glasses. The risks and benefits of the exchange were discussed. A consent was signed. Her physical was updated.

Anesthesia:

Local retrobulbar with modified lid block

Assistant surgeon:

Description of procedure:

The patient was taken to the operating room and given IV sedation. She was given a four-cc volume of the standard mixture as a retrobulbar block with a modified lid block. The surgeon massaged the eye for four minutes. The patient was prepped and draped. The eyelashes were taped off the field. A speculum was placed. A peritomy was made superiorly. Cautery was used. A 5.2 millimeter incision was made 1.5 millimeters from the limbus. This was tunneled into clear cornea superiorly. The chamber was entered. Viscoat on a cannula was used to dissect the capsular bag away from the intraocular lens. The intraocular lens was then dialed out of the bag. The wound was expanded to 5.2 millimeters. The implant was removed with a forceps. Part of the wound was closed with a 10-0 nylon suture. A 17 diopter AMQSI40NB was inserted into the capsular bag and dialed into the 3 and 9 o'clock positions. The residual Viscoat was removed in its entirety using an automated irrigation aspiration set-up. Miochol was used to bring the pupil to a small round size. The wound was sutured with a second 10-0 nylon suture. The conjunctiva was sutured with 8-0 Vicryl. The patient received an inferior injection of Kenalog and gentamicin. TobraDex ointment was placed. The eye was patched.

The patient tolerated the procedure well. There were no complications. She will receive a Diamox sequel x one. She will leave her eye patched until the morning and then she will start her TobraDex four times a day. I will see her tomorrow.

Linda Patrick, MD

GODFREY REGIONAL HOSPITAL
123 Main Street • Aldon, FL 77714 • (407) 555-1234

Answers

OPERATIVE REPORT

Patient information:

Patient name:
DOB:
MR#:

Preoperative diagnosis:

CC: Here to have wax cleaned from left ear
ROS: Negative ear pains, positive decreased authority acuity, Negative chills, fever
PMH/SH: Unremarkable

Postoperative diagnosis:

Cerumen Impaction, Ear

Procedure(s) performed:

Cerumen was removed from both ears. Patient tolerated the procedure well.

Anesthesia:

Assistant surgeon:

Description of procedure:

EXAM:
HEENT: Left Ear, Canal with large amount of dry cerumen. Right ear, normal. Nose, normal external appearance.
Septum midline and intact. Pharynx normal in appearance.
Respiratory: No respiratory distress. Lungs clear.
CV: Unremarkable
Skin: Warm, dry, with normal turgor
Neuro: Oriented to person, time, and place

James Ellicott, MD

GODFREY REGIONAL HOSPITAL
123 Main Street • Aldon, FL 77714 • (407) 555-1234

Answers

15 Radiology Services

EXERCISES 1-20

Assign the appropriate CPT codes for the following. Also assign any modifier code(s) that may be applicable as well. Identify additional information that is needed to most correctly assign the codes necessary for coding or billing.

1. 3-View x-ray forearm

   CPT code(s) assignment: _____

   Modifier code(s) assignment (if applicable): _____

   Additional information/clarification needed (if applicable):

   _____

2. CT scan, abdomen

   CPT code(s) assignment: _____

   Modifier code(s) assignment (if applicable): _____

   Additional information/clarification needed (if applicable):

   _____

3. Chest x-ray

   CPT code(s) assignment: _____

   Modifier code(s) assignment (if applicable): _____

   Additional information/clarification needed (if applicable):

   _____

4. 3-View wrist, left

   CPT code(s) assignment: _____

   Modifier code(s) assignment (if applicable): _____

   Additional information/clarification needed (if applicable):

   _____

5. Pelvic ultrasound, complete

   CPT code(s) assignment: _____

   Modifier code(s) assignment (if applicable): _____

   Additional information/clarification needed (if applicable):

   _____

6. Total body bone scan

   CPT code(s) assignment: _____

   Modifier code(s) assignment (if applicable): _____

   Additional information/clarification needed (if applicable):

   _____

7. MRI brain, w/without contrast

   CPT code(s) assignment: _____

   Modifier code(s) assignment (if applicable): _____

   Additional information/clarification needed (if applicable):

   _____

8. Screening mammogram

   CPT code(s) assignment: _____

   Modifier code(s) assignment (if applicable): _____

   Additional information/clarification needed (if applicable):

   _____

9. CTA, pelvis, with contrast

   CPT code(s) assignment: _____

   Modifier code(s) assignment (if applicable): _____

   Additional information/clarification needed (if applicable):

   _____

10. KUB

    CPT code(s) assignment: _____

    Modifier code(s) assignment (if applicable): _____

    Additional information/clarification needed (if applicable):

    _____

11. Thoracic spine, 3-view

    CPT code(s) assignment: _____

    Modifier code(s) assignment (if applicable): _____

    Additional information/clarification needed (if applicable):

    _____

12. Tibia/fibula, right, 2 V

    CPT code(s) assignment: _____

    Modifier code(s) assignment (if applicable): _____

    Additional information/clarification needed (if applicable):

    _____

13. Abdominal aortography, radiologic S&I

    CPT code(s) assignment: _____

    Modifier code(s) assignment (if applicable): _____

    Additional information/clarification needed (if applicable):

    _____

14. Breast ultrasound, right and left

    CPT code(s) assignment: _____

    Modifier code(s) assignment (if applicable): _____

    Additional information/clarification needed (if applicable):

    _____

15. Ultrasonic guidance for needle placement for biopsy

    CPT code(s) assignment: _____

    Modifier code(s) assignment (if applicable): _____

    Additional information/clarification needed (if applicable):

    _____

16. Radiation treatment planning, simple

    CPT code(s) assignment: _____

    Modifier code(s) assignment (if applicable): _____

    Additional information/clarification needed (if applicable):

    _____

17. Radiation treatment delivery, single treatment area, 8 MeV

    CPT code(s) assignment: _____

    Modifier code(s) assignment (if applicable): _____

    Additional information/clarification needed (if applicable):

    _____

18. Thoracic myelography, rad supervision and interpretation

    CPT code(s) assignment: _____

    Modifier code(s) assignment (if applicable): _____

    Additional information/clarification needed (if applicable):

    _____

19. CT C spine, without contrast

    CPT code(s) assignment: _____

    Modifier code(s) assignment (if applicable): _____

    Additional information/clarification needed (if applicable):

    _____

20. Bilateral ribs

    CPT code(s) assignment: _____

    Modifier code(s) assignment (if applicable): _____

    Additional information/clarification needed (if applicable):

    _____

Assign the appropriate ICD-9-CM and CPT codes for the following radiology reports.

EXERCISE 21

RADIOLOGY REPORT

MR#:
DOB:
Dr.

Clinical summary:

PATIENT NAME:
Bridget Nash
HISTORY:
Fall, left lower leg pain
LEFT TIB-FIB: 01/01/XX
There is an obliquely oriented distal tibial diaphyseal with one cortical width posterior displacement of the distal fracture fragment. The fracture does not involve the epiphyseal plate distally. The fibula appears intact.

Abdomen:

Conclusion:

IMPRESSION:
Minimally displaced fracture of the left distal tibia

Ddt/mm

D:
T:

_____
, M.D.   Date

GODFREY REGIONAL HOSPITAL
123 Main Street • Aldon, FL 77714 • (407) 555-1234

Answers

RADIOLOGY REPORT

MR#:
DOB:
Dr.

Clinical summary:

PATIENT NAME:
Mary Nomme
HISTORY:
Cramping, uterine bleeding

Abdomen:

PELVIC ULTRASOUND: 01/02/XX
Transabdominal imaging was performed. The uterus is midline in position measuring 7.9 x 3.9 x 3.4 cm. The echotexture is homogeneous. Normal endometrial stripe measuring 5.1 mm. A small amount of free cul-de-sac fluid was appreciated. The right ovary measures 3.0 x 2.5 x 2.3 cm and the left measures 2.8 x 2.6 x 2.4 cm. Both ovaries demonstrate normal echotexture and normal color flow.

Conclusion:

IMPRESSION:
Normal pelvic ultrasound

A normal examination does not exclude the possibility of ectopic pregnancy and if this is suspected clinically, correlation with Beta HCG would be recommended.

Ddt/mm

D:
T:

_____
, M.D.   Date

GODFREY REGIONAL HOSPITAL
123 Main Street • Aldon, FL 77714 • (407) 555-1234

Answers

EXERCISE 23

RADIOLOGY REPORT

MR#:
DOB:
Dr.

Clinical summary:

PATIENT NAME:
Jason Rice

HISTORY:
Patient fell, pain in mid back, rule out rib fracture

Abdomen:

Conclusion:

CHEST PA AND LATERAL: 03/01/XX
PA and lateral chest showing normal heart size with no vascular congestion. Status post cardiac surgery. Suspected subtle bibasilar atelectasis and/or infiltrate with subtle densities compared with prior views. No abnormal pleural fluid. Peripheral lung fields otherwise clear.

IMPRESSION:
Normal chest with subtle bibasilar atelectasis and/or infiltrate

Ddt/mm

D:
T:

_____
, M.D.   Date

GODFREY REGIONAL HOSPITAL
123 Main Street • Aldon, FL 77714 • (407) 555-1234

Answers

RADIOLOGY REPORT

MR#:
DOB:
Dr.

Clinical summary:

PATIENT NAME:
Robert Hanes
HISTORY:
MVA, chest pain

Abdomen:

Conclusion:

LEFT RIBS:
Three views of the left ribs with no fracture identified. No underlying pleural or parenchymal opacity identified.

IMPRESSION:
Negative left ribs

Ddt/mm

D:
T:

_____
                    , M.D.   Date

GODFREY REGIONAL HOSPITAL
123 Main Street • Aldon, FL 77714 • (407) 555-1234

Answers

RADIOLOGY REPORT

MR#:
DOB:
Dr.

Clinical summary:

PATIENT NAME:
Laura Siesmore
HISTORY:
MVA with head injury

Abdomen:

Conclusion:

SKULL SERIES: 05/01/XX
Four views of the skull with no depressed fracture identified. CT would provide adequate assessment in the setting of significant trauma.

Ddt/mm

D:
T:

_____
, M.D.   Date

GODFREY REGIONAL HOSPITAL
123 Main Street • Aldon, FL 77714 • (407) 555-1234

Answers

RADIOLOGY REPORT

MR#:
DOB:
Dr.

Clinical summary:

PATIENT NAME:
Michael Anderson
HISTORY:
Fall from building, lower back pain

Abdomen:

Conclusion:

CERVICAL SPINE: 01/02/XX
Three views of the cervical spine with odontoid partially obscured. Otherwise, no fracture or focal malalignment identified. Normal prevertebral soft tissues.

IMPRESSION:
No fracture or focal malalignment seen.

Ddt/mm

D:
T:

_____
, M.D.   Date

GODFREY REGIONAL HOSPITAL
123 Main Street • Aldon, FL 77714 • (407) 555-1234

Answers

RADIOLOGY REPORT

MR#:
DOB:
Dr.

Clinical summary:

PATIENT NAME:
Richard Melmer
HISTORY:
Injury to right 2nd finger

Abdomen:

Conclusion:

RIGHT SECOND FINGER: 01/15/XX
The osseous structures are normally mineralized. No acute fractures, dislocations or destructive changes seen. Soft tissue swelling apparent dorsally over the PIP joint.

IMPRESSION:
No acute osseous findings involving the right second finger

Ddt/mm

D:
T:

_____
, M.D.   Date

GODFREY REGIONAL HOSPITAL
123 Main Street • Aldon, FL 77714 • (407) 555-1234

Answers

RADIOLOGY REPORT

MR#:
DOB:
Dr.

Clinical summary:

PATIENT NAME:
Jane Geigenbaum

HISTORY:
Twisted ankle while walking the dog

Abdomen:

Conclusion:

LEFT ANKLE: 02/01/XX
The osseous structures are normally mineralized. No acute fractures or dislocations are seen. The ankle mortise is intact.

IMPRESSION:
Negative for fracture

Ddt/mm

D:
T:

_____, M.D.   Date

GODFREY REGIONAL HOSPITAL
123 Main Street • Aldon, FL 77714 • (407) 555-1234

Answers

EXERCISE 29

RADIOLOGY REPORT

MR#:
DOB:
Dr.

Clinical summary:

PATIENT NAME:
Casey Robinson
HISTORY:
Fever, rule out pneumonia

Abdomen:

Conclusion:

PA AND LATERAL CHEST: 04/08/XX
Deep inspiration. No infiltrate seen in either lung. Infiltrate present previously in the right upper lobe has resolved since film of 02/01/XX.

Normal chest.

Ddt/mm

D:
T:

_____
, M.D.   Date

GODFREY REGIONAL HOSPITAL
123 Main Street • Aldon, FL 77714 • (407) 555-1234

Answers

RADIOLOGY REPORT

MR#:
DOB:
Dr.

Clinical summary:

PATIENT NAME:
Chad Lorris
HISTORY:
Right upper quadrant abdominal pain

Abdomen:

TWO VIEW ABDOMEN: 03/01/XX
FINDINGS:
Two views of the abdomen reveal a non-specific bowel gas pattern. There is no evidence of small bowel obstruction, nor evidence of free air. The solid organs are unremarkable. No calcifications are seen to suggest renal/ureteral calculus. The lung bases are clear. The lumbar spine and pelvis are within normal limits for age.

Conclusion:

IMPRESSION:
Normal two view abdomen
No acute findings
Clips in the right upper quadrant from previous cholecystectomy

Ddt/mm

D:
T:

_____
, M.D.   Date

GODFREY REGIONAL HOSPITAL
123 Main Street • Aldon, FL 77714 • (407) 555-1234

Answers

RADIOLOGY REPORT

MR#:
DOB:
Dr.

Clinical summary:

DIAGNOSIS:
Pain—no injury, chronic sinusitis

PART TO BE EXAMINED:
Right shoulder, sinus CT

Abdomen:

Conclusion:

CT PARANASAL SINUSES:
Coronal images without contrast obtained. Paranasal sinuses well pneumatized and clear. No abnormality in the posterior nasopharyngeal area. No abnormality in the area of the nares other than very slight deviation of the nasal septum.

TWO VIEWS RIGHT SHOULDER:
There is a 1 1/2 centimeter by 1 centimeter separate calcification projecting along the superior lateral aspect of the head of the right humerus, which may be secondary to previous tendinitis. Correlate clinically.

Ddt/mm

D:
T:

_____
Lisa Valhas, M.D.   Date

GODFREY REGIONAL HOSPITAL
123 Main Street • Aldon, FL 77714 • (407) 555-1234

Answers

RADIOLOGY REPORT

MR#:
DOB:
Dr.

Clinical summary:

UGI/AIR CONTRAST WITH SBFT

REASON FOR EXAM:
Abdominal pain

Abdomen:

Conclusion:

Patient ingested gas crystals, then barium. Multiple spot and overhead images were obtained of the upper GI tract. Patient ingested two more cups of barium, and the small bowel was followed through to the terminal ileum.

The stomach is normal in shape, size, and contour. Gastric rugae are moderately thickened throughout in a diffuse pattern. On one view, there is slight narrowing of the distal body where it becomes confluent with the antrum, but it completely remits on another overhead image. The duodenal bulb maintains a normal arrowhead configuration. The most proximal second part of the sweep has mild thickening of the duodenal folds, and they are spiculated and irregular, involving several centimeters of the second part of the sweep. Multiple images were obtained of the duodenum, and the second part maintains its irregular narrowing. This is suggestive of duodenitis; other entities can cause this appearance, including pancreatic head changes.

Looking back on a prior CAT scan, there was some fluid in the duodenum as it coursed around the pancreatic head. The uncinate process was sharp; however, given this focus of fluid in the second part of the duodenum and the upper GI and small bowel follow-through today, would recommend the patient return for CAT scan of the abdomen with thin cuts through the pancreas with optimal duodenal opacification. An ERCP may be indicated. The body of the pancreas appears normal, but a thin-sliced CT will better delineate the head from the duodenal sweep. There was not a clear delineation of a pancreatic head mass but further studies are warranted.

Back to the barium study, the jejunal loops are normal. The ileal loops are normal.

Ddt/mm

D:
T:

_____
Lisa Valhas, M.D.   Date

GODFREY REGIONAL HOSPITAL
123 Main Street • Aldon, FL 77714 • (407) 555-1234

Answers

RADIOLOGY REPORT

MR#:
DOB:
Dr.

Clinical summary:

CLINICAL INFORMATION:
Chest pain

Abdomen:

Conclusion:

MYOVIEW STRESS TEST:
The patient achieved maximum heart rate of 147 per minute.
Rest imaging was performed utilizing 9.8 mCi of stress-imaging 32.9 mCi Tc 99m tetrofosmin. Gated imaging demonstrates a left ventricular ejection fraction of 36%. End-systolic and end-diastolic images show decreased contractility.

On stress imaging there is symmetric perfusion of the left ventricle. There is no evidence of infarct or ischemia.

CONCLUSION:
Decreased ejection fraction at 36%. No evidence of infarct or ischemia.

Ddt/mm

D:
T:

_____
Lisa Valhas, M.D.   Date

GODFREY MEDICAL ASSOCIATES
1532 Third Avenue, Suite 120 • Aldon, FL 77713 • (407) 555-4000

Answers

RADIOLOGY REPORT

MR#:
DOB:
Dr.

Clinical summary:

Abdomen:

RETROGRADE PYELOGRAPHY RIGHT:
Preliminary film of the abdomen revealed a catheter in place in the right renal pelvis. Following injection of contrast into the renal pelvis, the pyelocaliceal system and ureter were visualized, revealing no evidence of obstructive uropathy or filling defects. Upright view showed contrast urine level in the urinary bladder, with emptying of the pyelocaliceal system and ureter to a high degree.

Conclusion:

IMPRESSION:
Normal retrograde pyelography on the right. Findings are compared with previous IVP. A total of 5 films were obtained for this examination.

Ddt/mm

D:
T:

_____
Lisa Valhas, M.D.   Date

GODFREY REGIONAL HOSPITAL
123 Main Street • Aldon, FL 77714 • (407) 555-1234

Answers

RADIOLOGY REPORT

MR#:
DOB:
Dr.

Clinical summary:

DIAGNOSIS:
Injury

PART TO BE EXAMINED:
Right shoulder

Abdomen:

Conclusion:

RIGHT SHOULDER, TWO VIEWS:
0.4-cm area of calcification projected adjacent to the lateral aspect of the humeral head on the AP view. This is likely due to tendinous disease, or less likely, small avulsion fracture. Also, there is prominence of the inferior surface of the acromion that could be due to injury or anatomic variation. This projects into the upper aspect of the space between the acromion and humeral head. Evaluate further with MRI if indicated.

Ddt/mm

D:
T:

_____
Lisa Valhas, M.D.   Date

GODFREY MEDICAL ASSOCIATES
1532 Third Avenue, Suite 120 • Aldon, FL 77713 • (407) 555-4000

Answers

RADIOLOGY REPORT

MR#:
DOB:
Dr.

Clinical summary:

DIAGNOSIS:
Pain, heel

PART TO BE EXAMINED:
Rt. heel

Abdomen:

Conclusion:

TWO VIEWS RIGHT HEEL:
Moderate size spur planter aspect os calcis.

Ddt/mm

D:
T:

_____
Lisa Valhas, M.D.   Date

GODFREY MEDICAL ASSOCIATES
1532 Third Avenue, Suite 120 • Aldon, FL 77713 • (407) 555-4000

Answers

EXERCISE 37

RADIOLOGY REPORT

MR#:
DOB:
Dr.

Clinical summary:

DIAGNOSIS:
GB disease

PART TO BE EXAMINED:
Abdominal ultrasound

Abdomen:

Conclusion:

ABDOMINAL ULTRASOUND:
Gallbladder normal with no biliary ductal dilatation. Liver, spleen, and kidneys are normal. The pancreas was not optimally visualized, but no definite pancreatic abnormality. Abdominal aorta normal size. No ascites.

Ddt/mm

D:
T:

_____
Lisa Valhas, M.D.   Date

GODFREY REGIONAL HOSPITAL
123 Main Street • Aldon, FL 77714 • (407) 555-1234

Answers

RADIOLOGY REPORT

MR#:
DOB:
Dr.

Clinical summary:

DIAGNOSIS:
UTI

PART TO BE EXAMINED:
VCUG

Abdomen:

Conclusion:

VOIDING CYSTOURETHROGRAM:
Scout film unremarkable. Following injection of contrast into the urinary bladder, urinary bladder is well distended, smooth in outline without filling defect. There is reflux up to the pelvic portion of the left ureter. There is complete emptying of the urinary bladder after voiding with no contrast remaining in the left ureter.

Ddt/mm

D:
T:

_____
Lisa Valhas, M.D.   Date

GODFREY REGIONAL HOSPITAL
123 Main Street • Aldon, FL 77714 • (407) 555-1234

Answers

RADIOLOGY REPORT

MR#:
DOB:
Dr.

Clinical summary:

DIAGNOSIS:
Chronic sinusitis

PART TO BE EXAMINED:
Sinus CT

Abdomen:

Conclusion:

CT PARANASAL SINUSES:
Coronal images without contrast obtained. The lower half or so of the right maxillary sinus is opacified and this is apparently secondary to mucous membrane thickening. Small amount of mucous membrane in the right ethmoidal sinus. Paranasal sinuses otherwise clear. No abnormality in the posterior nasopharyngeal area. A slight deviation of the nasal septum with slight prominence of the inferonasal turbinates bilaterally.

Ddt/mm

D:
T:

_____
Lisa Valhas, M.D.   Date

GODFREY REGIONAL HOSPITAL
123 Main Street • Aldon, FL 77714 • (407) 555-1234

Answers

RADIOLOGY REPORT

MR#:
DOB:
Dr.

Clinical summary:

DIAGNOSIS:
Epigastric and RUQ pain

PART TO BE EXAMINED:
UGI, gallbladder US

Abdomen:

Conclusion:

UPPER GI SERIES:
Moderate amount of gastroesophageal reflux without associated hiatal hernia. Stomach normal. Mild duodenitis in first and second portions of the duodenum with no ulceration or mass. Proximal jejunum normal.

ABDOMINAL ULTRASOUND:
Gallbladder of normal size and with no evidence of calculus. There is a very small polyp along the inner wall of the gallbladder, which is most likely of no clinical significance. No biliary ductal dilatation. Liver, pancreas, and spleen normal. Kidneys are normal except for a 5-cm benign cyst, upper aspect of the left kidney. Abdominal aorta normal size. No ascites.

Ddt/mm

D:
T:

_____
Lisa Valhas, M.D.   Date

GODFREY REGIONAL HOSPITAL
123 Main Street • Aldon, FL 77714 • (407) 555-1234

Answers

16 Pathology Services

Identify the appropriate CPT codes for the following pathology services.

                                    CPT Code

1. Phenobarbital
   level   _____

2. Heavy metal screen   _____

3. Urinalysis, automated
   w/o microscopy   _____

4. Potassium   _____

5. PSA   _____

6. Amylase and lipase   _____

7. Troponin   _____

8. Digoxin level   _____

9. 3-hour glucose
   tolerance test   _____

10. TSH   _____

Identify the appropriate CPT codes for the following surgical pathology reports.

EXERCISE 11

SURGICAL PATHOLOGY REPORT

Name:_____ Hosp. No.:_____ Path. No.:_____
Date:_____Room:_____Age:_____Sex:_____Surgeon:_____ M.D.
Operation:_____
Material submitted: <u>Gallbladder</u>_____
Pre-op diagnosis:_____
Post-op diagnosis:_____
Previous material:_____Pertinent history:_____

Diagnosis:

Maria Colley M.D.
Surgical Pathologist

Gross description:

There is a single calculus that is yellow to brown 0.7 cm mulberry in type. The previously opened gallbladder consists of two portions, one showing abundant fat and multiple staples. The other portion is the portion of the fundus that was previously opened presently measuring 6.0 x 3.5 x 1.2 cm, the remaining portion measuring 6.0 x 3.0 x 1.5 cm. Representative portion of soft tissue embedded.

Micro description:

MICROSCOPIC DIAGNOSES:
1. Chronic cholecystitis—no evidence of malignancy these sections.
2. Cholelithiasis.

GODFREY CLINICAL LABORATORIES
465 Dogwood Court • Aldon, FL 77712 • (407) 555-9876

Answers

EXERCISE 12

SURGICAL PATHOLOGY REPORT

Name:_____ Hosp. No.:_____ Path. No.:_____
Date:_____ Room:_____ Age:_____ Sex:_____ Surgeon:_____ M.D.
Operation:_____
Material submitted: Right breast mass_____
Pre-op diagnosis:_____
Post-op diagnosis:_____
Previous material:_____Pertinent history:_____

Diagnosis:

Right breast mass

Maria Colley M.D.
Surgical Pathologist

Gross description:

The specimen is received in the fresh state (frozen), labeled with the patient's name and accession number as "RIGHT BREAST MASS" and consists of an irregular portion of fibroadipose breast tissue, 3.0 x 1.5 x 1 cm in greatest dimensions. No specimen radiograph is received. No skin is received. There is a sharply circumscribed rubbery mass 1 x 0.5 x 0.5 cm in greatest dimensions with a gray-tan, slightly bulging cut surface. The entire margin is inked in black. Representative sections submitted in 3 cassettes.

Micro description:

FROZEN SECTION DIAGNOSIS:
Right breast biopsy hyalinized fibroadenoma.

GODFREY CLINICAL LABORATORIES
465 Dogwood Court • Aldon, FL 77712 • (407) 555-9876

Answers

SURGICAL PATHOLOGY REPORT

Name:_____ Hosp. No.:_____ Path. No.:_____
Date:_____Room:_____Age:_____Sex:_____Surgeon:_____ M.D.
Operation:_____
Material submitted: <u>Lipoma and sac of hernia</u>_____
Pre-op diagnosis:_____
Post-op diagnosis:_____
Previous material:_____Pertinent history: <u>Recurrent right inguinal hernia</u>_____

Diagnosis:

PREVIOUS OPERATION:
Repair of right inguinal hernia.

CLINICAL DIAGNOSIS:
Repair of right inguinal hernia.

Maria Colby M.D.
Surgical Pathologist

Gross description:

PATHOLOGICAL REPORT:
Specimen received in 1 container in formalin and is labeled lipoma and sac. Specimen consists of two fragments of fat and soft tissue that measure 4 x 3 x 0.6 cm in aggregate. Representative sections submitted in 1 cassette.

Micro description:

MICROSCOPIC DIAGNOSIS:
Lipomatous adipose tissue and hernia sac.

GODFREY CLINICAL LABORATORIES
465 Dogwood Court • Aldon, FL 77712 • (407) 555-9876

Answers

SURGICAL PATHOLOGY REPORT

Name:_____Hosp. No.:_____Path. No.:_____
Date:_____Room:_____Age: _____Sex: _____Surgeon: _____M.D._____
Operation:_____
Material submitted: _Spleen_____
Pre-op diagnosis:_____
Post-op diagnosis:_____
Previous material:_____Pertinent history: _Thrombocytopenia_____

Diagnosis:

SPLEEN:
Benign splenic tissue demonstrating mild sinus congestion together with small aggregates of foamy histiocytes.

No evidence of malignancy.

Maria Colby _____ M.D.
Surgical Pathologist

Gross description:

The specimen is labeled "spleen." Received in formalin is an 80 g spleen measuring 10.0 x 7.0 x 2.5 cm. The external capsule appears discretely lobulated and wrinkled purple-gray, without evidence of lacerations or discolorations. A small amount of attached fatty tissue is present throughout the hilum. Upon sectioning, the parenchyma appears glistening dark red, with pinpoint bulging follicles and unremarkable trabecular architecture. No areas suggestive of infarction or hemorrhage are grossly noted. Representative sections are submitted in four cassettes (A–D).

Micro description:

Sections from the spleen reveal somewhat attenuated white pulp regions with only a rare small germinal center found. The sinuses are slightly congested, with slight infiltration of neutrophils. Occasional plasma cells are also found. Small collections of two and three foamy histiocytes are found in some areas. A rare megakaryocyte is also present. There is no evidence of capsular fibrosis, granuloma formation, or malignancy in the tissue submitted.

GODFREY CLINICAL LABORATORIES
465 Dogwood Court • Aldon, FL 77712 • (407) 555-9876

Answers

SURGICAL PATHOLOGY REPORT

Name: _____ Hosp. No.: _____ Path. No.: _____

Date: _____ Room: _____ Age: _____ Sex: _____ Surgeon: _____ M.D.

Operation: _____

Material submitted: A. Right spermatic cord lipoma.   B. Right inguinal node. _____

Pre-op diagnosis: _____

Post-op diagnosis: _____

Previous material: _____ Pertinent history: _____

Diagnosis:

Not given.

Maria Colley M.D.
Surgical Pathologist

Gross description:

A. Received is a fragment of fibromembranous and fatty tissue which measures 4.4 x 3.0 x 2.0 cm. On cut section most of the tissue appears to be fat which is circumscribed and appears to be partially encapsulated. One representative section is submitted.

B. Received is a fragment of yellow fatty tissue measuring 1.5 x 1.4 x 0.8 cm. On cut section all of the tissue appears to be fat, and it appears to be partially encapsulated. No evident lymph node structure is identified grossly. Representative section is submitted.

Micro description:

MICROSCOPIC DIAGNOSES:

A. Hernia sac and lipoma.

B. Lymph node showing extensive fatty replacement.

GODFREY CLINICAL LABORATORIES
465 Dogwood Court • Aldon, FL 77712 • (407) 555-9876

Answers

17 Medicine Services

EXERCISES 1-20

Identify the appropriate CPT codes for the following medicine services.

CPT Code(s)

1. Allergy tests, percutaneous, 14 tests _____

2. CPAP ventilation _____

3. PUVA light therapy _____

4. IV chemotherapy infusion of 50 mg methotrexate over 1½ hours _____

5. Ophthalmologic examination under anesthesia, complete _____

6. ESRD services, 1 full month _____

7. Administration of tetanus toxoid _____

8. Intramuscular injection of penicillin _____

9. Psychotherapy, 45 minutes, behavior-modifying _____

10. Gastric intubation _____

In the following cases, assign the CPT codes necessary to correctly code for the services.

CPT Code(s)

11. Patient undergoes a cardiac catheterization with three stent placements in the right coronary artery _____

12. Patient receives evaluation and treatment for swallowing dysfunction for feeding _____

13. Patient receives battery of hearing evaluation and tests including the following:
    ■ Speech audiometry threshold
    ■ Acoustic reflex testing

    Followed by hearing aid examination and selection for bilateral hearing loss _____

14. Tilt table evaluation _____

15. Allergy immunotherapy provided for the following (extract not provided):
    ■ Ragweed pollen, dust, mites (one injection)
    ■ Tomatoes, peanuts (one injection) _____

16. Electromyography, by needle, two extremities _____

17. Child with accidental ingestion of iron treated with gastric lavage _____

18. Neurologist tests a patient by EMG and nerve conduction velocity for comparison of unaffected side for a total of three motor nerves and two sensory nerves _____

19. Medical testimony _____

20. Neurophysiologic testing, intraoperative, 2 hours _____

Assign appropriate codes for the following cardiac catheterization scenarios.

EXERCISE 21

OPERATIVE REPORT

Patient information:
Patient name: DOB: MR#:

Preoperative diagnosis:
Chest Pain

Postoperative diagnosis:
ASHD right coronary

Procedure(s) performed:
Heart cath

Anesthesia:

Assistant surgeon:

Description of procedure:
Access was via the left femoral vein Imaging was obtained of the pulmonary, coronary and left and right ventricles Obstruction was noted in the right coronary vessels X3 and the left circumflex X4 PTCA (angioplasty) was performed X 3 in the right coronary vessel, two of which required the placement of an intracoronary stent. The left circumflex received four (4) angioplasties only.

Ruth Brody M

GODFREY REGIONAL HOSPITAL
123 Main Street • Aldon, FL 77714 • (407) 555-1234

Answers

OPERATIVE REPORT

Patient information:
Patient name: DOB: MR#:

Preoperative diagnosis:
Chest pain

Postoperative diagnosis:
Same

Procedure(s) performed:
Heart cath

Anesthesia:

Assistant surgeon:

Description of procedure:
Access was via the left femoral artery Imaging was obtained on the pulmonary and coronary vessels as well as the aorta and left ventricle and atrium As the vessels were patent, no further procedures were necessary.

Ruth Brady MD

GODFREY REGIONAL HOSPITAL
123 Main Street • Aldon, FL 77714 • (407) 555-1234

Answers

OPERATIVE REPORT

Patient information:
Patient name: DOB: MR#:

Preoperative diagnosis:
Chest pain

Postoperative diagnosis:
ASHD descending, coronary, circumflex

Procedure(s) performed:
Heart cath

Anesthesia:

Assistant surgeon:

Description of procedure:

Access via the left femoral artery
Imaging was obtained of the left and right ventricles, the aorta and coronary arteries. Obstructions were identified in the circumflex, the descending and the coronary vessel appeared clear.

Angioplasties X 3 were performed in the left circumflex, followed by stent placement; however, neither were successful and atherectomy was performed to the three (3) obstructed areas in the left circumflex. Angioplasties X 2 were performed in the left descending, one followed by stent placement.

Ruth Brody MD

GODFREY REGIONAL HOSPITAL
123 Main Street • Aldon, FL 77714 • (407) 555-1234

Answers

OPERATIVE REPORT

Patient information:
Patient name: DOB: MR#:

Preoperative diagnosis:
Chest pain

Postoperative diagnosis:
ASHD right coronary, descending, Circumflex

Procedure(s) performed:
Heart cath

Anesthesia:

Assistant surgeon:

Description of procedure:
Access was via the right femoral vein Imaging was obtained of the left ventricle and left atrium, the coronary vessels and the pulmonary vessel. Angioplasties were performed as follows: 3 angioplasties to the right coronary 2 angioplasties to the left circumflex 3 angioplasties to the left descending

GODFREY REGIONAL HOSPITAL
123 Main Street • Aldon, FL 77714 • (407) 555-1234

Answers

OPERATIVE REPORT

Patient information:
Patient name: DOB: MR#:

Preoperative diagnosis:
Chest pain

Postoperative diagnosis:
Chest pain

Procedure(s) performed:
Heart cath

Anesthesia:

Assistant surgeon:

Description of procedure:
Access was via the left femoral artery and vein Imaging was obtained of the following: Left and right atrium Pulmonary vessel Coronary vessel Aorta   *Ruth Brady MD*

GODFREY REGIONAL HOSPITAL
123 Main Street • Aldon, FL 77714 • (407) 555-1234

Answers

EXERCISE 26

OPERATIVE REPORT—CARDIAC CATHETERIZATION REPORT

Patient information:

Patient name:
DOB:
MR#:

Preoperative diagnosis:

Postoperative diagnosis:

Procedure(s) performed:

Left heart catheterization, selective left and right coronary angiography, and left ventriculography.

Anesthesia:

Assistant surgeon:

Description of procedure:

INDICATIONS:
The patient is a 54-year-old white male with a history of coronary artery disease, status post inferior MI and multiple interventions to the right coronary artery with last in August 2002 being cutting balloon atherectomy and brachytherapy to the right coronary artery for in-stent restenosis. The patient presents with chest discomfort and abnormal stress suggestive of inferior ischemia. This is a small defect and with the patient's body habitus, artifact cannot be ruled out.
Due to this, the patient presents for cardiac catheterization.
Risks and benefits of the procedure were explained to patient. He wished to proceed. Informed consent was obtained.
PROCEDURE/TECHNIQUE:
The patient was brought to the cardiac catheterization laboratory in a fasting state, where he was prepped and draped in a sterile fashion. The right groin was anesthetized with 1% Xylocaine. The patient was given Versed and fentanyl for conscious sedation. Using a modified Seldinger technique, the right femoral artery was cannulated, and a 6 French intravascular sheath was inserted, aspirated and flushed. A wire was used to advance a 6 French multipurpose catheter under fluoroscopic guidance, into the ascending aorta. This catheter was used to enter the left ventricle and perform left heart recordings. Subsequently, left ventriculography was performed in the 30-degree RAO projection using hand injection of contrast through the multipurpose catheter. The catheter was then re-flushed and used to perform transaortic valve pullback gradient measurements. This catheter was aspirated, flushed, and filled with contrast and used to engage the left and right coronary arteries, to perform left and right coronary angiograms in multiple views. The catheter was removed and an angiogram was obtained through the right femoral artery sheath of the access site. This revealed good sheath placement and the Angio-Seal system was utilized for sheath removal and hemostasis. At the conclusion of the procedure, all catheters and sheaths were withdrawn, and pressure was held over the puncture site until hemostasis was obtained. The patient tolerated the procedure well, without apparent complications, and he was transferred to the recovery room in a stable condition for further observation. A total of 70 cc of contrast was used during the case.

FINDINGS:
1. Left heart catheterization hemodynamics: Left ventricular pressure 126/18, aortic pressure 124/58, mean 81, no significant aortic gradient.
2. Left ventriculography: Mild global LV dysfunction without significant regional wall motion abnormalities. The overall left ventricular systolic function was mildly reduced with an EP (ejection fraction) of 50%. No mitral regurgitation was noted.
3. Left main coronary angiography: The left main has a long distal 40% to 50% stenosis. This does not appear obstructive.
4. Left anterior descending angiography: The left anterior descending has mild diffuse luminal irregularities. There is a moderate-sized first diagonal with a 30% proximal lesion and a moderate-sized vessel.
5. Left circumflex angiography: The left circumflex supplies a moderate-sized first obtuse marginal, a tiny second obtuse marginal and a small third obtuse marginal. The first obtuse marginal has a 30% proximal stenosis. The mid left circumflex before the third obtuse marginal has a 60% lesion.
6. Right coronary artery angiography: The right coronary artery is large and dominant. There is a long mid and mid-to-distal stenting which is patent. There is a moderate-sized PDA and posterolateral branch without significant disease. There are luminal irregularities in the proximal and mid right coronary artery, including the proximal portion of the mid right coronary artery stents. This is minimal restenosis. The site of previous brachytherapy is widely patent with no evidence of restenosis or obstructive disease.

IMPRESSION:
1. Chest pain with abnormal stress.
2. Nonobstructive coronary disease with moderate left main stenosis.
3. Patent right coronary artery at site of previous brachytherapy.
4. Diabetes mellitus.
5. Hypertension.
6. Obesity.
7. Gastroesophageal reflux disease.

RECOMMENDATIONS:
1. Medical therapy.
2. Discharge home.
3. Follow with personal physician in four to six weeks.

Ruth Brady MD

GODFREY REGIONAL HOSPITAL
123 Main Street • Aldon, FL 77714 • (407) 555-1234

Answers

OPERATIVE REPORT—CARDIAC CATHETERIZATION REPORT

Patient information:

Patient name:
DOB:
MR#:

Preoperative diagnosis:

Postoperative diagnosis:

Procedure(s) performed:

Left heart catheterization, selective left and right coronary angiography, left ventriculography, saphenous vein graft angiography.

Anesthesia:

Assistant surgeon:

Description of procedure:

INDICATION:
The patient is a 60-year-old gentleman with known coronary artery disease, status post coronary artery bypass surgery. He recently underwent angioplasty and stent placement via the right saphenous vein graft to the PLV/PDA bifurcation. The true distal right was stented from the vein graft into the distal right, across the PDA and the PDA was dilated with a balloon with a "kissing balloon" technique utilized at the end of the procedure. The patient was discharged the following day, but returned with recurrent chest pain and underwent repeat catheterization because of his recurrent chest pain and known coronary artery disease.

PROCEDURE AND TECHNIQUE:
The risks and benefits were explained to the patient; with full understanding he wished to proceed. Informed consent was obtained. The patient was taken to the catheterization laboratory in a fasting state. The right groin was prepped and draped in a sterile fashion. One percent Xylocaine was used for local anesthesia. Versed 1 mg and 25 mcg of fentanyl were given for conscious sedation. A 6 French intravascular sheath was placed in the right femoral artery using modified Seldinger technique. A 6 French multipurpose catheter was advanced over guide wire under fluoroscopy into the descending aorta. This catheter was aspirated, flushed, filled with contrast and used to engage the saphenous vein graft and left coronary system. Angiograms were obtained in multiple views. This catheter was then flushed and used in the left ventricle. Left ventriculography was performed after left heart measurements were obtained. The catheter was flushed and used to perform transaortic valve pullback and aortic measurements. This catheter was removed. The patient was transferred to the recovery room in stable condition for sheath removal and further observation. Total contrast 80 cc.

FINDINGS:
1. Hemodynamics: Aortic pressure 105/52, LV pressure 106/13. No significant aortic gradient.
2. Left ventriculography: Moderate anterior and anterolateral wall hypokinesis with overall ejection fraction estimated at 45%. No mitral regurgitation noted.
3. Saphenous vein graft angiography: Saphenous vein graft to the right coronary artery has a mid stent which has mild in-stent restenosis and no significant obstructive disease. The distal right coronary artery has a widely patent stent from the vein graft into the continuation of the right coronary artery and posterolateral branch. This goes across the PDA bifurcation with good filling of the PDA and no evidence of impingement of flow. Multiple views were obtained which revealed it to be patent without significant stenosis. There was moderate disease in the distal posterolateral branch and PDA. Saphenous vein graft to the diagonal was occluded. The saphenous vein graft to the obtuse marginal is patent and fills a small obtuse marginal system.
4. Left coronary angiography: The circumflex system is 100% occluded, filling only a diffusely diseased small marginal. The LAD system has a proximal stent into a second diagonal that is patent. The true LAD is occluded in the mid portion and fills via the IMA graft. The LIMA was not injected, but known to be patent four days ago with severe distal LAD disease.

IMPRESSION:
1. Recurrent chest pain.
2. Coronary artery disease, status post coronary bypass surgery and percutaneous coronary intervention.
3. Small vessel coronary artery disease.
4. Patent posterolateral branch, PDA (posterior descending artery) stent from May 24, 2004.
5. Dilated cardiomyopathy with EP (ejection fraction) 45%.

GODFREY REGIONAL HOSPITAL
123 Main Street • Aldon, FL 77714 • (407) 555-1234

Answers

EXERCISE 28

OPERATIVE REPORT—CARDIAC CATHETERIZATION REPORT

Patient information:

Patient name:
DOB:
MR#:

Preoperative diagnosis:

Postoperative diagnosis:

Procedure(s) performed:

Anesthesia:

Assistant surgeon:

Description of procedure:

PROCEDURE:
After informed consent, the patient was taken to the Cardiac Catheterization Lab, right groin was prepped and draped in the usual fashion under sterile condition.
Under local anesthesia and conscious sedation with IV Midazolam and Fentanyl, right femoral arterial access was secured using the Seldinger technique, a 6 French sheath was inserted in the femoral artery and flushed in the usual fashion.
Using 6 French right and left Judkin's #4 catheters and angled pigtail catheters, coronary angiography, left ventriculography, and bilateral renal angiograms were performed without any complications.
At the end of the procedure, the catheters were removed, sheath removed from the right femoral artery and pressure was applied at the insertion site for 20 minutes, no hematomas were noted, good pulses were noted bilaterally.
I. Ventriculography: Using an angled pigtail catheter, ventriculography was performed in the RAO projection, showing normal LV systolic function, estimated ejection fraction equal 60%, no MR was noted.
II. Coronary angiography: 1. The left main is free of significant disease.
2. The left anterior descending shows some luminal irregularities, no occlusive lesions are noted.
3. The circumflex artery is a small vessel with no significant lesions.
4. The right coronary artery is dominant; no lesions are noted in the RCA or in the PDA.
III. Hemodynamics: LV pressure 119/15, aortic pressure 119/60. There was no gradient noted on pull back across the aortic valve.
IV. Renal angiograms: Selective right and left renal angiography was performed using the right Judkin's catheter #4, no evidence of occlusive disease in both renal arteries.
V. IMPRESSION:
1. Normal left ventricular systolic function.
2. No evidence of occlusive coronary artery disease.
3. No evidence of renal artery stenosis.

Recommend medical therapy. Follow-up with primary care physician.

Ruth Brady MD

GODFREY REGIONAL HOSPITAL
123 Main Street • Aldon, FL 77714 • (407) 555-1234

Answers

OPERATIVE REPORT—CARDIAC CATHETERIZATION REPORT

Patient information:

Patient name:
DOB:
MR#:

Preoperative diagnosis:

Postoperative diagnosis:

Procedure(s) performed:

Left heart catheterization, diagnostic coronary arteriography, left ventricular angiography, aortic root aortography, abdominal aortography, selective left subclavian angiography, interpretation of angiographic films, cardiac fluoroscopy

Anesthesia:

Assistant surgeon:

Description of procedure:

INDICATIONS:
Unstable angina.
Congestive heart failure.
Status post 4-vessel coronary artery bypass surgery.

PREMEDICATIONS: Versed 2 mg.

CATHETERS USED:
6 French JL4, 6 French JR4,6 French pigtail, 6 French left bypass catheter and 6 French right bypass catheter.

PROCEDURE:
The patient was explained about the risks and benefits of cardiac catheterization with coronary arteriography and a written informed consent was obtained. Thereafter, the patient was taken to the Cardiac Catheterization Laboratory where both groins were thoroughly prepped in the usual fashion.

Under strict aseptic precautions, under local anesthesia, the right femoral artery was cannulated with modified Seldinger technique. All catheters were advanced under fluoroscopic guidance over the guide wire. Subsequently, the left and right coronary arteries were selectively cannulated and coronary angiography was performed. Thereafter, a pigtail catheter was introduced into the left ventricle and left ventricle filling pressures were noted followed by performance of the left ventricle angiography in the RAO 30-degree position.

After the performance of the angiography, the pigtail catheter was withdrawn from the left ventricle into the aorta and pullback pressures were noted across the aortic valve. During the whole procedure, intravenous Heparin was used as per protocol. The patient tolerated the procedure well.

After the completion of the native coronary angiography using several catheters the saphenous venous grafts were cannulated. Subsequently, selective granulation of the left subclavian artery was made and angiography was performed visualizing the left internal mammary artery. Patient tolerated the procedure well.

LEFT VENTRICLE ANGIOGRAPHY IN THE RAO PROJECTION:
1. Reveals a totally akinetic anterior apical and infraapical walls with left ventricular aneurysm formation.
2. The left ventricular ejection fraction is approximately 30–35%.
3. Minimal mitral regurgitation was noted.

LEFT MAIN CORONARY ARTERY:
Patent and divides into left anterior descending artery and circumflex vessels.

LEFT ANTERIOR DESCENDING ARTERY:
Is totally occluded in its proximal portion.

CIRCUMFLEX VESSEL
Reveals 70% narrowing in its proximal portion and gives rise to two obtuse marginal branches.
The first obtuse marginal branch is a moderate size vessel and reveals subtotal occlusion at its origin.

RIGHT CORONARY ARTERY:
Dominant and is totally occluded.

BYPASS GRAFT:
1. The saphenous venous graft to the left anterior descending artery is patent with good vessel runoff.
2. The saphenous venous graft to the diagonal branch could not be cannulated and probably occluded.
3. The saphenous venous graft to the obtuse marginal branch appears normal.

AORTOGRAPHY REVEALS:
1. A normal size aortic root.
2. Three saphenous venous grafts were visualized.

ABDOMINAL AORTOGRAPHY:
Reveals a torturous abdominal aorta with atherosclerotic plaque.

DIAGNOSES:
1. Atherosclerotic heart disease.
2. Severe triple vessel coronary artery disease.
3. 3 out of 4 saphenous venous grafts patent.
4. Left ventricular dysfunction with an LV ejection fraction of 30–35%.

Ruth Brady MD

GODFREY REGIONAL HOSPITAL
123 Main Street • Aldon, FL 77714 • (407) 555-1234

Answers

EXERCISE 30

OPERATIVE REPORT—CARDIAC CATHETERIZATION REPORT

Patient information:

Patient name:
DOB:
MR#:

Preoperative diagnosis:

Postoperative diagnosis:

Procedure(s) performed:

Left heart cath with coronary angiography, left ventriculography

Anesthesia:

Assistant surgeon:

Description of procedure:

The right femoral artery was accessed via the modified Seldinger technique and a 6 French arterial sheath was placed. After initial difficulty with engagement of the coronary catheter, the catheter was inserted, coronary angiography was performed and then the catheter was passed into the left ventricle where ventriculography was performed.
Upon completion, the pigtail catheter was repositioned whereby ascending aortic angiography was performed.

FINDINGS:
Left Main Coronary Artery
The left main coronary artery has significant disease present. The right coronary artery also shows evidence of significant disease within the right coronary ostium as evidenced by significant ventricularization and dropping of arterial pressures.

Venticulography
Ventriculography reveals overall normal left ventricle function without evidence of abnormality.

Ascending Aortography
Reveals essentially tri-leaflet aortic valve which is somewhat calcified, but without evidence of aortic valve insufficiency.

GODFREY REGIONAL HOSPITAL
123 Main Street • Aldon, FL 77714 • (407) 555-1234

Answers

18 HCPCS Codes

Chapter 18 HCPCS Codes

EXERCISES 1-10

Determine the appropriate HCPCS code(s) for the following.

HCPCS Code(s)

1. Indwelling Foley catheter _____

2. Surgical tray _____

3. Topical dental fluoride application, adult _____

4. Breast pump _____

5. Injection, testosterone cypionate, 1 cc, 400 mg _____

6. Injection heparin sodium, 2500 units _____

7. Injection, cyclophosphamide, 1½ grams _____

8. Screening Pap smear _____

9. Catheterization for collection of specimen, single patient _____

10. Hearing aid, behind-ear monaural _____

Identify and assign the appropriate CPT, HCPCS, and modifer codes for the following medical charts.

OFFICE NOTE

Chief complaint: _____

Date: _____

Vital signs: BP_____ P_____ R_____

History:

Jason is a 27-year-old man who comes in because of persistent bleeding from his gums. He had four wisdom teeth removed earlier today by his dentist: two on the lower jaw and two on the upper jaw. This was done because of significant pain the patient was experiencing.

Interestingly, the reason why Jason is bleeding so much is because he is on Coumadin. His last INR was 2.9. His anticoagulation is secondary to aortic valve replacement secondary to endocarditis, which was performed a few years ago. He follows up with another physician for this purpose and he has been doing very well since.

Exam:

He appears as a healthy young man, in no distress, afebrile; BP is 138/98.

HEENT: no pallor or jaundice. Hydration is well maintained. Oral examination reveals soaked gauze that patient was holding between his teeth. When these were removed, there were obviously four opened sockets with very soft clot in the bottom ones and oozing from the upper ones. Otherwise, there were no abnormalities.

NECK: supple without lymphadenopathies.

CHEST: lungs—CTA. Heart regular rate and rhythm. 2-3/6 systolic ejection murmur and a click are heard, no gallops or tachycardia.

LOWER EXTREMITIES: no edema.

NEUROLOGICAL: intact.

Diagnosis/assessment:

IMPRESSION: Persistent slow bleed SP teeth extraction times four secondary to anticoagulation.

PLAN: We will recheck his PT and INR. If it is certainly above 2.7 or 2.8, we may need to give him some vitamin K today until the clots are formed and oozing from the sockets is decreased. Then he should restart his Coumadin. Will await the test results to make any further decisions. This was explained to the patient.

ADDENDUM: The patient's PT and INR were a little bit higher, although not super-therapeutic. His INR was 3.06. At this time, we have suggested the following:
A. Vitamin K 5 mg IM now.
B. Hold Coumadin tomorrow morning.
C. Continue to apply pressure to the sockets.
D. If he continues to have problems with oozing and bleeding the following day, he needs to still hold his Coumadin and come back here to have everything rechecked. He showed understanding and agreement.

Steny Kractt, MD

Patient name: _____

Date of service: _____

GODFREY MEDICAL ASSOCIATES
1532 Third Avenue, Suite 120 • Aldon, FL 77713 • (407) 555-4000

Answers

EXERCISE 12

OFFICE NOTE

Date:	Vital signs:	T	R
Chief complaint:		P	BP

S: 28-year-old gentleman presents with a severe sore throat; is unable to even swallow Tylenol at this time because his throat is so sore. He has had fever and chills today.

Physical examination:

O: On exam, his temp is 98.2. Pulse is 95. Respirations are 20. Blood pressure is 144/23. He is lying on the cot in the exam room with his coat over his shoulders and a blanket over that. He is in moderate distress from his sore throat and he has a muffled sounding voice. His TMs are nondistended and nonerythematous. Conjunctivae are noninjected. Pupils are equal, round, and reactive. Nasopharynx: noncongested with septum midline. Posterior pharynx is very erythematous with large tonsillar hypertrophy and white and yellow exudate seen in the tonsillar crypts. Neck reveals lymphadenopathy along the cervical chain. Lung sounds are clear. Heart is regular rate and rhythm without murmur.

Assessment:

A: Acute tonsillitis/pharyngitis.

Plan:

P: Patient is given Bicillin CR 1.2 milliunits IM. He will rest and take Tylenol as needed for fever, drink plenty of fluids, and follow up if worsening occurs over the course of the next 24 hours or if not improving in the next two days.

Willen Olst MD

	Patient name:
	DOB:
	MR/Chart #:

GODFREY REGIONAL OUTPATIENT CLINIC
3122 Shannon Avenue • Aldon, FL 77712 • (407) 555-7654

Answers

Copyright © 2010, 2006, 2003, 2001 by Saunders, an imprint of Elsevier Inc.
CPT only Copyright © American Medical Association.
All rights reserved.

365
Chapter **18** HCPCS Codes

OFFICE NOTE

| Date: | Vital signs: | T | R |
| Chief complaint: | | P | BP |

SUBJECTIVE: This 43-year-old woman new patient presents complaining of a migraine headache. The patient states that she woke up a little after midnight and started vomiting. She has not been able to keep anything down and rates her pain as an 8 on a 1–10 scale. The pain is behind her right eye and she has photophobia. These are her typical migraine headache problems. Patient has been seen multiple times over the last couple of months for these types of migraine headaches.

Past medical history—Migraine headaches.

Current medications—See nurse's list.

Allergies—See list.

Physical examination:

OBJECTIVE: Temperature 99.1, pulse 64, respiratory 12, BP 116/82.

Shows patient to be alert. HEENT shows pupils equal, round, and reactive to light and accommodation extraocular motion intact. Patient has normal nasal and oral mucosa. Neck is supple without adenopathy. Lungs are clear. Heart is regular rate and rhythm. Abdomen is soft with positive bowel sounds. She is tender diffusely. Extremities show full range of motion. Neurologically, the cranial nerves are grossly intact. The patient has good strength and sensation in all extremities. Normal gait. Glasgow Coma Scale of 15.

Assessment:

Migraine headache.

Plan:

The patient had a saline-lock IV started and was given 10 mg of IV Reglan and 6 mg of IV morphine. She did require another 2 mg of IV morphine, but her headache was much improved. She felt that she could go home and sleep. She was instructed to return if her headache worsened or if she developed any new symptoms.

Felix Wandin MD

	Patient name:
	DOB:
	MR/Chart #:

GODFREY REGIONAL OUTPATIENT CLINIC
3122 Shannon Avenue • Aldon, FL 77712 • (407) 555-7654

Answers

EXERCISE 14

OFFICE NOTE

Date:	Vital signs:	T		R	
Chief complaint: Back pain. Passed out.		P		BP	

S: This is a 73-year-old woman who has had back pain since September, and it has been very bad the last couple of days. She woke up this morning with severe back pain, tried going down some stairs, and she got lightheaded. Her husband feels she may have passed out doing this. Therefore they called an ambulance. She does not have chest pain, trouble breathing, or other neurological symptoms. She had fallen off a step in September, and she had had a sort of constant pain in the low back since then, but it has recently been worse as noted above for the past couple of days. She doesn't have pain that goes into her legs, numbness in the legs, or bladder dysfunction. She has been taking ibuprofen, two twice a day. She had had a headache also from the fall. Medical history includes atrial fibrillation and depression. She is on Lanoxin and Effexor also. She doesn't have allergies. No heart disease other than atrial fibrillation. No diabetes or high blood pressure. Review of systems is otherwise negative.

Examination:

O: On exam, her vital signs are stable. She is alert and orientated. She has good carotid upstrokes. Lungs are clear. Heart sounds fairly regular, and I don't hear any murmurs. Abdomen is nontender. She has a little bit of tenderness over her right greater trochanter. She says she has pain in this area when she lies on that side. There is a little bit of lower back palpatory tenderness. Straight leg raising is negative. Motor and sensory is intact. Pulses are good. Reflexes are normal. X-rays of her back show anterior slippage of L4 on 5 but no compression fractures.

Impression:

A: Vasovagal episode secondary to acute back pain.

Plan:

P: Discussion. She has a little slippage of the spine vertebrae that is probably causing her back problems. I am not sure how long this slippage has been there. She was given Toradol, 60 mg IM, that gave her some relief, so she was dispensed with Toradol, 10 mg q6h prn pain #30. She should follow up with her physician regarding her back problems.

Willden Olst MD

	Patient name:
	DOB:
	MR/Chart #:

GODFREY REGIONAL OUTPATIENT CLINIC
3122 Shannon Avenue • Aldon, FL 77712 • (407) 555-7654

Answers

EMERGENCY ROOM RECORD

Name:		Age:	ER physician:
		DOB:	

Allergies/type of reaction:	Usual medications/dosages:

| Triage/presenting complaint: | HISTORY: This 86-year-old woman was seen in this ER five days ago with a fractured right radius. Her splint has become loose and is irritating her arm. Her |

medications are as listed. There is no allergy to medicine. The splint was removed. There is ecchymosis of the distal forearm. The skin is intact.

Initial assessment:

Time	T	P	R	BP	Other:					

Medication orders:

Lab work:

X-ray:

Physician's report:

TREATMENT COURSE: A fiberglass short-arm splint was reapplied.

Diagnosis:	Physician sign/date

Fracture, right radius.

DISPOSITION: She is to keep the splint clean and dry. If she develops increased pain or any other problem, she is to go to the emergency room; otherwise, she plans to follow up with her regular physician next week after returning home.

Nancy Cauley MD

Discharge	Transfer	Admit	Good	Satisfactory	Other:

GODFREY REGIONAL HOSPITAL
123 Main Street • Aldon, FL 77714 • (407) 555-1234

Answers

EXERCISE 16

OPERATIVE REPORT

Patient information:	
Patient name: DOB: MR#:	Date: Surgeon: Anesthetist:

Preoperative diagnosis:

Severe retracted rotator cuff tear (acute), chronic impingement, acromioclavicular arthritis, right shoulder

Postoperative diagnosis:

Severe retracted rotator cuff tear, chronic impingement, acromioclavicular arthritis, right shoulder

Procedure(s) performed:

Neer anterior acromioplasty and coracoacromial ligament release, acromioclavicular joint debridement with excision of distal tip of clavicle, repair of chronic avulsion and rotator cuff tendon with transosseous sutures, and interrupted and inverted suture repair of right shoulder.

Description of procedure:

After informed consent and complete discussion of the alternatives and complications with no guarantees, implied or given, the patient was taken to the operating room. After an adequate level of an intravenous sedation had been obtained, the patient's lower neck, shoulder, and upper extremity were surgically scrubbed with Betadine soap, prepped with Betadine solution, and draped in the usual sterile fashion utilizing the double Vi-drape technique. Next, the incision was marked along the anterolateral aspect of the shoulder in a longitudinal fashion. 0.1% epinephrine was utilized for hemostasis. Under 3Z\× wide field loupe magnification, an incision was made and the dissection was carried down through the subcutaneous fat and fascia. Hemostasis was obtained with Bovie coagulation. The fascia was divided in a longitudinal fashion overlying the AC joint and anterior aspect of the acromion. The dissection was carried down subperiosteal and anterior to the AC joint and anterolateral acromion. The elongated and beak type III acromion was identified. The anterior acromioplasty was carried out to transform this to a type I acromion. Following this, marked adhesions were noted anteriorly, laterally, and posteriorly. Severe impingement was noted under the undersurface of the AC joint. The AC joint was exposed and the osteotome was utilized to remove the tip of the distal clavicle. This allowed marked improvement in the area beneath the distal clavicle. Wax was placed on the cancellous bone face. Next, attention was turned to the rotator cuff.

The rotator cuff was severely retracted and was noted to be torn from the area adjacent to the subscapularis, well posteriorly into the teres minor. The cuff was freshened at the area of the tear. The cuff was approximately two inches in width. The tear was carefully advanced and mattress sutures of 0 Ethibond were utilized ×6 for the repair. A trough was made in the area of avulsion and soft tissue was removed down to bleeding cancellous bone. A margin of cuff was present on the greater tuberosity area, and this was subsequently utilized for interrupted inverted suture repair with 0 Ethibond, following the passage of the transosseous sutures tied along the lateral aspect of the cortex with the arm abducted. Excellent repair was noted with the transosseous sutures and interrupted inverted sutures of 0 Ethibond. There was no tension on the repair with the arm in the neutral position. The rotator cuff, upon evaluation, revealed thinning under the undersurface. Some horizontal portions of the anterior cuff were debrided. There were obvious degenerative changes within the cuff tissue. Marked bursal inflammation and thickening of the subacromial bursa was noted. Partial bursectomy was performed. Thorough irrigation was carried out with triple antibiotic solution throughout the procedure. 0.5% Marcaine was instilled in the glenohumeral joint, as well as in the subacromial area, for analgesia. The reconstruction of the deltoid was carried out with transosseous and interrupted inverted sutures of 0 Ethibond. The subcutaneous layers were approximated with 3-0 Vicryl in an interrupted and inverted fashion. The skins were reapproximated with subcutaneous 4-0 Prolene.

Sterile dressings were applied to the shoulder, and the patient was immediately placed in a sling and slough. The patient received cephalosporin antibiotics thirty minutes prior to the procedure prophylactically. Irrigation was carried out throughout the procedure with triple antibiotic solution.

The patient tolerated the operative procedure and anesthesia satisfactorily. No breaks in sterile technique occured. No complications occured.

In regard to physical therapy, the patient was instructed preoperatively and expected postoperatively to undergo rotator cuff tear rehabilitation protocol, and the patient voiced understanding of the importance of this to maximize healing potential. This was discussed with the patient at length and in detail. The patient voiced understanding of the above and wished to proceed.

Robert Chung MD

GODFREY REGIONAL HOSPITAL
123 Main Street • Aldon, FL 77714 • (407) 555-1234

Answers

19 Coding From a Reimbursement Perspective

CLAIMS REVIEW EXERCISES 1-20

The following exercises are representative of a portion of the CMS-1500 claim form. Review the following claims and determine the problem with each specific claim that will prevent or delay payment; recommend the corrective actions needed.

EXERCISE 1

14. DATE OF CURRENT: ILLNESS (first symptom) OR INJURY (accident) OR PREGNANCY (LMP)			15. IF PATIENT HAS HAD SAME OR SIMILAR ILLNESS. GIVE FIRST DATE			16. DATES PATIENT UNABLE TO WORK IN CURRENT OCCUPATION		
MM DD YY			MM DD YY			MM DD YY	MM DD YY	
03 01 20XX			03 01 20XX			FROM	TO	

14. DATE OF CURRENT: ILLNESS (first symptom) OR INJURY (accident) OR PREGNANCY (LMP) MM 03 DD 01 YY 20XX

15. IF PATIENT HAS HAD SAME OR SIMILAR ILLNESS. GIVE FIRST DATE MM 03 DD 01 YY 20XX

16. DATES PATIENT UNABLE TO WORK IN CURRENT OCCUPATION FROM MM DD YY TO MM DD YY

17. NAME OF REFERRING PHYSICIAN OR OTHER SOURCE

17a. I.D. NUMBER OR REFERRING PHYSICIAN

18. HOSPITALIZATION DATES RELATED TO CURRENT SERVICES FROM MM DD YY TO MM DD YY

19. RESERVED FOR LOCAL USE

20. OUTSIDE LAB? ☐ YES ☒ NO $ CHARGES

21. DIAGNOSIS OR NATURE OF ILLNESS OR INJURY. (RELATE ITEMS 1,2,3 OR 4 TO ITEM 24E BY LINE)
1. 784.0
2. _____
3. _____
4. _____

22. MEDICAID RESUBMISSION CODE ORIGINAL REF NO.

23. PRIOR AUTHORIZATION NUMBER

24.	DATE(S) OF SERVICE						B Place of Service	C Type of Service	D PROCEDURES, SERVICES, OR SUPPLIES (Explain Unusual Circumstances)		E DIAGNOSIS CODE	F $ CHARGES	G DAYS OR UNITS	H EPSDT Family Plan	I EMG	J COB	K RESERVED FOR LOCAL USE
	From MM DD YY			To MM DD YY					CPT/HCPCS	MODIFIER							
1	03 01 20XX			03 01 20XX			11	1	99214		1,2	125 00	1				
2																	
3																	
4																	
5																	
6																	

Problem(s) identified:

_____

_____

_____

_____

Correction(s) needed:

_____

_____

_____

_____

14. DATE OF CURRENT: ILLNESS (first symptom) OR INJURY (accident) OR PREGNANCY (LMP) MM 02 DD 10 YY 20XX		15. IF PATIENT HAS HAD SAME OR SIMILAR ILLNESS. MM DD YY GIVE FIRST DATE	16. DATES PATIENT UNABLE TO WORK IN CURRENT OCCUPATION MM DD YY MM DD YY FROM TO		
17. NAME OF REFERRING PHYSICIAN OR OTHER SOURCE		17a. I.D. NUMBER OR REFERRING PHYSICIAN	18. HOSPITALIZATION DATES RELATED TO CURRENT SERVICES MM DD YY MM DD YY FROM TO		
19. RESERVED FOR LOCAL USE			20. OUTSIDE LAB? ☐ YES ☒ NO	$ CHARGES	
21. DIAGNOSIS OR NATURE OF ILLNESS OR INJURY. (RELATE ITEMS 1,2,3 OR 4 TO ITEM 24E BY LINE) 1. _____ 2. _____ 3. _____ 4. _____			22. MEDICAID RESUBMISSION CODE	ORIGINAL REF NO.	
			23. PRIOR AUTHORIZATION NUMBER		

24.	A DATE(S) OF SERVICE						B Place of Service	C Type of Service	D PROCEDURES, SERVICES, OR SUPPLIES (Explain Unusual Circumstances) CPT/HCPCS MODIFIER		E DIAGNOSIS CODE	F $ CHARGES		G DAYS OR UNITS	H EPSDT Family Plan	I EMG	J COB	K RESERVED FOR LOCAL USE
	From MM	DD	YY	To MM	DD	YY												
1	02	10	20XX	02	10	20XX	11	1	99214		1	75	00	1				
2																		
3																		
4																		
5																		
6																		

PHYSICIAN OR SUPPLIER INFORMATION

Problem(s) identified:

_____

_____

_____

_____

_____

Correction(s) needed:

_____

_____

_____

_____

_____

EXERCISE 3

<table>
<tr>
<td colspan="2">14. DATE OF CURRENT:
MM   DD   YY
02   11   20XX   ◄   ILLNESS (first symptom) OR
INJURY (accident) OR
PREGNANCY (LMP)</td>
<td colspan="2">15. IF PATIENT HAS HAD SAME OR
SIMILAR ILLNESS.   MM   DD   YY
GIVE FIRST DATE</td>
<td colspan="5">16. DATES PATIENT UNABLE TO WORK IN CURRENT OCCUPATION
MM   DD   YY   MM   DD   YY
FROM   TO</td>
</tr>
<tr>
<td colspan="2">17. NAME OF REFERRING PHYSICIAN OR OTHER SOURCE</td>
<td colspan="2">17a. I.D. NUMBER OR REFERRING PHYSICIAN</td>
<td colspan="5">18. HOSPITALIZATION DATES RELATED TO CURRENT SERVICES
MM   DD   YY   MM   DD   YY
FROM   TO</td>
</tr>
<tr>
<td colspan="4">19. RESERVED FOR LOCAL USE</td>
<td colspan="5">20. OUTSIDE LAB? $ CHARGES
☐ YES   ☒ NO</td>
</tr>
<tr>
<td colspan="4">21. DIAGNOSIS OR NATURE OF ILLNESS OR INJURY. (RELATE ITEMS 1,2,3 OR 4 TO ITEM 24E BY LINE)
1. __599.0__   3. _____

2. __465.9__   4. _____</td>
<td colspan="5">22. MEDICAID RESUBMISSION
CODE   ORIGINAL REF NO.

23. PRIOR AUTHORIZATION NUMBER</td>
</tr>
</table>

24.	A DATE(S) OF SERVICE		B Place of Service	C Type of Service	D PROCEDURES, SERVICES, OR SUPPLIES (Explain Unusual Circumstances) CPT/HCPCS / MODIFIER	E DIAGNOSIS CODE	F $ CHARGES	G DAYS OR UNITS	H EPSDT Family Plan	I EMG	J COB	K RESERVED FOR LOCAL USE
	From MM DD YY	To MM DD YY										
1	02 11 20XX	02 11 20XX	11	1	99213	1	65 00	1				
2												
3												
4												
5												
6												

PHYSICIAN OR SUPPLIER INFORMATION

Problem(s) identified:

_____

_____

_____

_____

_____

Correction(s) needed:

_____

_____

_____

_____

_____

EXERCISE 4

14. DATE OF CURRENT: MM DD YY	ILLNESS (first symptom) OR INJURY (accident) OR PREGNANCY (LMP)	15. IF PATIENT HAS HAD SAME OR SIMILAR ILLNESS. MM DD YY GIVE FIRST DATE	16. DATES PATIENT UNABLE TO WORK IN CURRENT OCCUPATION MM DD YY MM DD YY FROM TO
17. NAME OF REFERRING PHYSICIAN OR OTHER SOURCE		17a. I.D. NUMBER OR REFERRING PHYSICIAN	18. HOSPITALIZATION DATES RELATED TO CURRENT SERVICES MM DD YY MM DD YY FROM TO
19. RESERVED FOR LOCAL USE			20. OUTSIDE LAB? ☐ YES ☐ NO $ CHARGES

21. DIAGNOSIS OR NATURE OF ILLNESS OR INJURY. (RELATE ITEMS 1,2,3 OR 4 TO ITEM 24E BY LINE) →

1. __784.0__   3. _____

2. _____   4. _____

22. MEDICAID RESUBMISSION CODE   ORIGINAL REF NO.

23. PRIOR AUTHORIZATION NUMBER

24.	A DATE(S) OF SERVICE						B Place of Service	C Type of Service	D PROCEDURES, SERVICES, OR SUPPLIES (Explain Unusual Circumstances) CPT/HCPCS MODIFIER		E DIAGNOSIS CODE	F $ CHARGES		G DAYS OR UNITS	H EPSDT Family Plan	I EMG	J COB	K RESERVED FOR LOCAL USE
	From MM	DD	YY	To MM	DD	YY												
1	01	10	20XX	01	10	20XX	11	3	99243		1	175	00	1				
2																		
3																		
4																		
5																		
6																		

PHYSICIAN OR SUPPLIER INFORMATION

Problem(s) identified:

_____

_____

_____

_____

_____

Correction(s) needed:

_____

_____

_____

_____

_____

Chapter **19** **Coding From a Reimbursement Perspective**

EXERCISE 5

14. DATE OF CURRENT: MM DD YY	◀ ILLNESS (first symptom) OR INJURY (accident) OR PREGNANCY (LMP)	15. IF PATIENT HAS HAD SAME OR SIMILAR ILLNESS. MM DD YY GIVE FIRST DATE	16. DATES PATIENT UNABLE TO WORK IN CURRENT OCCUPATION MM DD YY MM DD YY FROM TO
17. NAME OF REFERRING PHYSICIAN OR OTHER SOURCE Tara Johnson, M.D.		**17a. I.D. NUMBER OR REFERRING PHYSICIAN** UPIN #00002	**18. HOSPITALIZATION DATES RELATED TO CURRENT SERVICES** MM DD YY MM DD YY FROM TO
19. RESERVED FOR LOCAL USE			**20. OUTSIDE LAB?** ☐ YES ☐ NO $ CHARGES

21. DIAGNOSIS OR NATURE OF ILLNESS OR INJURY. (RELATE ITEMS 1,2,3 OR 4 TO ITEM 24E BY LINE)	22. MEDICAID RESUBMISSION CODE ORIGINAL REF NO.
1. 599.0 3. 789.0	
2. 465.9 4. _____	23. PRIOR AUTHORIZATION NUMBER

24.	A						B	C	D		E	F		G	H	I	J	K
	DATE(S) OF SERVICE						Place of Service	Type of Service	**PROCEDURES, SERVICES, OR SUPPLIES** (Explain Unusual Circumstances)		DIAGNOSIS CODE	**$ CHARGES**		DAYS OR UNITS	EPSDT Family Plan	EMG	COB	RESERVED FOR LOCAL USE
	From			**To**					CPT/HCPCS	MODIFIER								
	MM	DD	YY	MM	DD	YY												
1	02	10	20XX	02	10	20XX	11	1	99213		1,2,3	75 00		1				
2	02	10	20XX	02	10	20XX	11	1	81000		1,2,3	15 00		1				
3	02	10	20XX	02	10	20XX	11	1	71020		1,2,3	55 00		1				
4																		
5																		
6																		

PHYSICIAN OR SUPPLIER INFORMATION

Problem(s) identified:

_____

_____

_____

_____

_____

Correction(s) needed:

_____

_____

_____

_____

_____

EXERCISE 6

14. DATE OF CURRENT:		ILLNESS (first symptom) OR INJURY (accident) OR PREGNANCY (LMP)	15. IF PATIENT HAS HAD SAME OR SIMILAR ILLNESS. GIVE FIRST DATE	16. DATES PATIENT UNABLE TO WORK IN CURRENT OCCUPATION

14. DATE OF CURRENT: ◄ ILLNESS (first symptom) OR INJURY (accident) OR PREGNANCY (LMP)	15. IF PATIENT HAS HAD SAME OR SIMILAR ILLNESS. GIVE FIRST DATE	16. DATES PATIENT UNABLE TO WORK IN CURRENT OCCUPATION
MM 02 DD 10 YY 20XX	MM DD YY	MM DD YY MM DD YY FROM TO
17. NAME OF REFERRING PHYSICIAN OR OTHER SOURCE	**17a. I.D. NUMBER OR REFERRING PHYSICIAN**	**18. HOSPITALIZATION DATES RELATED TO CURRENT SERVICES** MM DD YY MM DD YY FROM TO
19. RESERVED FOR LOCAL USE		**20. OUTSIDE LAB?** ☐ YES ☐ NO $ CHARGES

21. DIAGNOSIS OR NATURE OF ILLNESS OR INJURY. (RELATE ITEMS 1,2,3 OR 4 TO ITEM 24E BY LINE)

1. __599.0__   3. _____
2. __465.9__   4. _____

22. MEDICAID RESUBMISSION CODE   ORIGINAL REF NO.

23. PRIOR AUTHORIZATION NUMBER

24. A DATE(S) OF SERVICE						B Place of Service	C Type of Service	D PROCEDURES, SERVICES, OR SUPPLIES (Explain Unusual Circumstances)		E DIAGNOSIS CODE	F $ CHARGES	G DAYS OR UNITS	H EPSDT Family Plan	I EMG	J COB	K RESERVED FOR LOCAL USE
From MM	DD	YY	To MM	DD	YY			CPT/HCPCS	MODIFIER							
02	10	20XX	02	10	20XX	11	1	99213		1	75 00					

PHYSICIAN OR SUPPLIER INFORMATION

Problem(s) identified:

_____

_____

_____

_____

Correction(s) needed:

_____

_____

_____

_____

EXERCISE 7

14. DATE OF CURRENT: ILLNESS (first symptom) OR INJURY (accident) OR PREGNANCY (LMP)			15. IF PATIENT HAS HAD SAME OR SIMILAR ILLNESS. GIVE FIRST DATE	16. DATES PATIENT UNABLE TO WORK IN CURRENT OCCUPATION	
MM 02	DD 10	YY 20XX	MM DD YY	FROM MM DD YY	TO MM DD YY

17. NAME OF REFERRING PHYSICIAN OR OTHER SOURCE	17a. I.D. NUMBER OR REFERRING PHYSICIAN	18. HOSPITALIZATION DATES RELATED TO CURRENT SERVICES
		FROM MM DD YY TO MM DD YY

19. RESERVED FOR LOCAL USE	20. OUTSIDE LAB? $ CHARGES
	☐ YES ☐ NO

21. DIAGNOSIS OR NATURE OF ILLNESS OR INJURY. (RELATE ITEMS 1,2,3 OR 4 TO ITEM 24E BY LINE)

1. 786.50   3. _____

2. _____   4. _____

22. MEDICAID RESUBMISSION CODE   ORIGINAL REF NO.

23. PRIOR AUTHORIZATION NUMBER

24. A DATE(S) OF SERVICE						B Place of Service	C Type of Service	D PROCEDURES, SERVICES, OR SUPPLIES (Explain Unusual Circumstances) CPT/HCPCS MODIFIER	E DIAGNOSIS CODE	F $ CHARGES	G DAYS OR UNITS	H EPSDT Family Plan	I EMG	J COB	K RESERVED FOR LOCAL USE
From MM	DD	YY	To MM	DD	YY										
02	10	20XX	02	10	20XX	11	4	71020	1	55 00	1				

PHYSICIAN OR SUPPLIER INFORMATION

Problem(s) identified:

_____

_____

_____

_____

_____

Correction(s) needed:

_____

_____

_____

_____

_____

EXERCISE 8

14. DATE OF CURRENT:	ILLNESS (first symptom) OR	15. IF PATIENT HAS HAD SAME OR	16. DATES PATIENT UNABLE TO WORK IN CURRENT OCCUPATION

14. DATE OF CURRENT: MM DD YY — ILLNESS (first symptom) OR INJURY (accident) OR PREGNANCY (LMP)
01 | 10 | 20XX

15. IF PATIENT HAS HAD SAME OR SIMILAR ILLNESS. MM DD YY GIVE FIRST DATE

16. DATES PATIENT UNABLE TO WORK IN CURRENT OCCUPATION MM DD YY — MM DD YY
FROM — TO

17. NAME OF REFERRING PHYSICIAN OR OTHER SOURCE

17a. I.D. NUMBER OR REFERRING PHYSICIAN

18. HOSPITALIZATION DATES RELATED TO CURRENT SERVICES MM DD YY — MM DD YY
FROM 01 | 10 | 20XX TO 01 | 14 | 20XX

19. RESERVED FOR LOCAL USE

20. OUTSIDE LAB? $ CHARGES
☐ YES ☐ NO

21. DIAGNOSIS OR NATURE OF ILLNESS OR INJURY. (RELATE ITEMS 1,2,3 OR 4 TO ITEM 24E BY LINE)
1. 789.00
2. _____
3. _____
4. _____

22. MEDICAID RESUBMISSION CODE ORIGINAL REF NO.

23. PRIOR AUTHORIZATION NUMBER

24. A DATE(S) OF SERVICE						B Place of Service	C Type of Service	D PROCEDURES, SERVICES, OR SUPPLIES (Explain Unusual Circumstances) CPT/HCPCS	MODIFIER	E DIAGNOSIS CODE	F $ CHARGES	G DAYS OR UNITS	H EPSDT Family Plan	I EMG	J COB	K RESERVED FOR LOCAL USE
From MM	DD	YY	To MM	DD	YY											
02	10	20XX	02	10	20XX	11	1	99213		1	75 00	1				

PHYSICIAN OR SUPPLIER INFORMATION

Problem(s) identified:

_____

_____

_____

_____

Correction(s) needed:

_____

_____

_____

_____

EXERCISE 9

14. DATE OF CURRENT:	ILLNESS (first symptom) OR INJURY (accident) OR PREGNANCY (LMP)	15. IF PATIENT HAS HAD SAME OR SIMILAR ILLNESS. MM DD YY GIVE FIRST DATE	16. DATES PATIENT UNABLE TO WORK IN CURRENT OCCUPATION MM DD YY MM DD YY
MM DD YY 02 10 20XX			FROM TO

17. NAME OF REFERRING PHYSICIAN OR OTHER SOURCE	17a. I.D. NUMBER OR REFERRING PHYSICIAN	18. HOSPITALIZATION DATES RELATED TO CURRENT SERVICES MM DD YY MM DD YY
		FROM TO

19. RESERVED FOR LOCAL USE	20. OUTSIDE LAB? ☐ YES ☐ NO	$ CHARGES

21. DIAGNOSIS OR NATURE OF ILLNESS OR INJURY. (RELATE ITEMS 1,2,3 OR 4 TO ITEM 24E BY LINE)

1. __789.00__   3. _____

2. _____   4. _____

22. MEDICAID RESUBMISSION CODE	ORIGINAL REF NO.

23. PRIOR AUTHORIZATION NUMBER

24.	A					B	C	D		E	F	G	H	I	J	K
	DATE(S) OF SERVICE					Place of Service	Type of Service	PROCEDURES, SERVICES, OR SUPPLIES (Explain Unusual Circumstances)		DIAGNOSIS CODE	$ CHARGES	DAYS OR UNITS	EPSDT Family Plan	EMG	COB	RESERVED FOR LOCAL USE
	From MM	DD	YY	To MM	DD	YY			CPT/HCPCS	MODIFIER							
1	02	10	20XX	02	10	20XX	21	1	99231		1	75 00	1				
2																	
3																	
4																	
5																	
6																	

PHYSICIAN OR SUPPLIER INFORMATION

Problem(s) identified:

_____

_____

_____

_____

Correction(s) needed:

_____

_____

_____

_____

EXERCISE 10

14. DATE OF CURRENT:	ILLNESS (first symptom) OR INJURY (accident) OR PREGNANCY (LMP)	15. IF PATIENT HAS HAD SAME OR SIMILAR ILLNESS. GIVE FIRST DATE	16. DATES PATIENT UNABLE TO WORK IN CURRENT OCCUPATION
MM DD YY 01 10 20XX		MM DD YY	MM DD YY FROM ... TO MM DD YY

17. NAME OF REFERRING PHYSICIAN OR OTHER SOURCE	17a. I.D. NUMBER OR REFERRING PHYSICIAN	18. HOSPITALIZATION DATES RELATED TO CURRENT SERVICES
Josef Hirsch, M.D.	UP# 00002	MM DD YY FROM ... TO MM DD YY

19. RESERVED FOR LOCAL USE	20. OUTSIDE LAB? ☐ YES ☐ NO	$ CHARGES

21. DIAGNOSIS OR NATURE OF ILLNESS OR INJURY. (RELATE ITEMS 1,2,3 OR 4 TO ITEM 24E BY LINE)

1. 786.50   3. _____

2. _____   4. _____

22. MEDICAID RESUBMISSION CODE   ORIGINAL REF NO.

23. PRIOR AUTHORIZATION NUMBER

24.	A DATE(S) OF SERVICE		B Place of Service	C Type of Service	D PROCEDURES, SERVICES, OR SUPPLIES (Explain Unusual Circumstances)		E DIAGNOSIS CODE	F $ CHARGES	G DAYS OR UNITS	H EPSDT Family Plan	I EMG	J COB	K RESERVED FOR LOCAL USE
	From MM DD YY	To MM DD YY			CPT/HCPCS	MODIFIER							
1	01 10 20XX	01 10 20XX	21	9	93010		1	150 00	3				
2													
3													
4													
5													
6													

PHYSICIAN OR SUPPLIER INFORMATION

Problem(s) identified:

_____

_____

_____

_____

_____

Correction(s) needed:

_____

_____

_____

_____

_____

EXERCISE 11

| 14. DATE OF CURRENT: ILLNESS (first symptom) OR
 MM   DD   YY   INJURY (accident) OR
    PREGNANCY (LMP)
 02   10   20XX | 15. IF PATIENT HAS HAD SAME OR
 SIMILAR ILLNESS.   MM   DD   YY
 GIVE FIRST DATE | 16. DATES PATIENT UNABLE TO WORK IN CURRENT OCCUPATION
 MM   DD   YY   MM   DD   YY
 FROM   TO |

| 17. NAME OF REFERRING PHYSICIAN OR OTHER SOURCE | 17a. I.D. NUMBER OR REFERRING PHYSICIAN | 18. HOSPITALIZATION DATES RELATED TO CURRENT SERVICES
 MM   DD   YY   MM   DD   YY
 FROM   TO |

| 19. RESERVED FOR LOCAL USE | 20. OUTSIDE LAB? $ CHARGES
 ☐ YES   ☐ NO |

21. DIAGNOSIS OR NATURE OF ILLNESS OR INJURY. (RELATE ITEMS 1,2,3 OR 4 TO ITEM 24E BY LINE) ⬇

1. __883.0__   3. _____

2. __784.0__   4. _____

22. MEDICAID RESUBMISSION CODE   ORIGINAL REF NO.

23. PRIOR AUTHORIZATION NUMBER

24.	A DATE(S) OF SERVICE						B Place of Service	C Type of Service	D PROCEDURES, SERVICES, OR SUPPLIES (Explain Unusual Circumstances) CPT/HCPCS MODIFIER	E DIAGNOSIS CODE	F $ CHARGES	G DAYS OR UNITS	H EPSDT Family Plan	I EMG	J COB	K RESERVED FOR LOCAL USE
	From MM	DD	YY	To MM	DD	YY										
1	02	10	20XX	02	10	20XX	11	1	99212	2,1	75 00	1				
2	02	10	20XX	02	10	20XX	11	2	12001	2,1	80 00	1				
3																
4																
5																
6																

PHYSICIAN OR SUPPLIER INFORMATION

Problem(s) identified:

_____

_____

_____

_____

_____

Correction(s) needed:

_____

_____

_____

_____

_____

EXERCISE 12

14. DATE OF CURRENT:		ILLNESS (first symptom) OR INJURY (accident) OR PREGNANCY (LMP)	15. IF PATIENT HAS HAD SAME OR SIMILAR ILLNESS. GIVE FIRST DATE		16. DATES PATIENT UNABLE TO WORK IN CURRENT OCCUPATION
MM DD YY			MM DD YY		MM DD YY — MM DD YY
02 10 20XX					FROM — TO

17. NAME OF REFERRING PHYSICIAN OR OTHER SOURCE — Melissa Landry, M.D.

17a. I.D. NUMBER OR REFERRING PHYSICIAN

18. HOSPITALIZATION DATES RELATED TO CURRENT SERVICES — FROM — TO

19. RESERVED FOR LOCAL USE

20. OUTSIDE LAB? ☐ YES ☐ NO $ CHARGES

21. DIAGNOSIS OR NATURE OF ILLNESS OR INJURY. (RELATE ITEMS 1,2,3 OR 4 TO ITEM 24E BY LINE)
1. 784.0
2.
3.
4.

22. MEDICAID RESUBMISSION CODE   ORIGINAL REF NO.

23. PRIOR AUTHORIZATION NUMBER

From MM DD YY	To MM DD YY	B Place of Service	C Type of Service	D CPT/HCPCS MODIFIER	E DIAGNOSIS CODE	F $ CHARGES	G DAYS OR UNITS	H EPSDT Family Plan	I EMG	J COB	K RESERVED FOR LOCAL USE
02 10 20XX	02 10 20XX	11	1	99243	1	150 00	1				

Problem(s) identified:

Correction(s) needed:

EXERCISE 13

14. DATE OF CURRENT: MM DD YY — ILLNESS (first symptom) OR INJURY (accident) OR PREGNANCY (LMP)	15. IF PATIENT HAS HAD SAME OR SIMILAR ILLNESS. GIVE FIRST DATE MM DD YY	16. DATES PATIENT UNABLE TO WORK IN CURRENT OCCUPATION FROM MM DD YY TO MM DD YY
02 20 20XX		
17. NAME OF REFERRING PHYSICIAN OR OTHER SOURCE	17a. I.D. NUMBER OR REFERRING PHYSICIAN	18. HOSPITALIZATION DATES RELATED TO CURRENT SERVICES FROM MM DD YY TO MM DD YY
19. RESERVED FOR LOCAL USE		20. OUTSIDE LAB? ☐ YES ☐ NO — $ CHARGES
21. DIAGNOSIS OR NATURE OF ILLNESS OR INJURY. (RELATE ITEMS 1,2,3 OR 4 TO ITEM 24E BY LINE) 1. 599.0 2. 3. 4.		22. MEDICAID RESUBMISSION CODE — ORIGINAL REF NO.
		23. PRIOR AUTHORIZATION NUMBER

24. A DATE(S) OF SERVICE From MM DD YY	To MM DD YY	B Place of Service	C Type of Service	D PROCEDURES, SERVICES, OR SUPPLIES (Explain Unusual Circumstances) CPT/HCPCS	MODIFIER	E DIAGNOSIS CODE	F $ CHARGES	G DAYS OR UNITS	H EPSDT Family Plan	I EMG	J COB	K RESERVED FOR LOCAL USE
1 02 10 20XX	02 10 20XX	11	1	81000		1	15 00	1				
2												
3												
4												
5												
6												

PHYSICIAN OR SUPPLIER INFORMATION

Problem(s) identified:

Correction(s) needed:

EXERCISE 14

14. DATE OF CURRENT: ILLNESS (first symptom) OR INJURY (accident) OR PREGNANCY (LMP)						15. IF PATIENT HAS HAD SAME OR SIMILAR ILLNESS. GIVE FIRST DATE					16. DATES PATIENT UNABLE TO WORK IN CURRENT OCCUPATION						
MM 02	DD 10	YY 20XX				MM	DD	YY			FROM MM DD YY			TO MM DD YY			

17. NAME OF REFERRING PHYSICIAN OR OTHER SOURCE	17a. I.D. NUMBER OR REFERRING PHYSICIAN	18. HOSPITALIZATION DATES RELATED TO CURRENT SERVICES
Josef Hirsch, M.D.		FROM MM DD YY TO MM DD YY

19. RESERVED FOR LOCAL USE	20. OUTSIDE LAB? $ CHARGES
	☐ YES ☐ NO

21. DIAGNOSIS OR NATURE OF ILLNESS OR INJURY. (RELATE ITEMS 1,2,3 OR 4 TO ITEM 24E BY LINE)	22. MEDICAID RESUBMISSION CODE ORIGINAL REF NO.
1. 786.50 3. _____	
	23. PRIOR AUTHORIZATION NUMBER
2. _____ 4. _____	

24. A DATE(S) OF SERVICE						B Place of Service	C Type of Service	D PROCEDURES, SERVICES, OR SUPPLIES (Explain Unusual Circumstances)		E DIAGNOSIS CODE	F $ CHARGES	G DAYS OR UNITS	H EPSDT Family Plan	I EMG	J COB	K RESERVED FOR LOCAL USE
From MM	DD	YY	To MM	DD	YY			CPT/HCPCS	MODIFIER							
02	10	20XX	02	10	20XX	11	4	71020		1	75 00	1				

PHYSICIAN OR SUPPLIER INFORMATION

Problem(s) identified:

_____

_____

_____

_____

_____

Correction(s) needed:

_____

_____

_____

_____

_____

EXERCISE 15

14. DATE OF CURRENT:	ILLNESS (first symptom) OR INJURY (accident) OR PREGNANCY (LMP)	15. IF PATIENT HAS HAD SAME OR SIMILAR ILLNESS. MM DD YY GIVE FIRST DATE	16. DATES PATIENT UNABLE TO WORK IN CURRENT OCCUPATION
MM DD YY 02 10 20XX			MM DD YY MM DD YY FROM TO

17. NAME OF REFERRING PHYSICIAN OR OTHER SOURCE	17a. I.D. NUMBER OR REFERRING PHYSICIAN	18. HOSPITALIZATION DATES RELATED TO CURRENT SERVICES MM DD YY MM DD YY FROM TO

19. RESERVED FOR LOCAL USE	20. OUTSIDE LAB? ☐ YES ☐ NO	$ CHARGES

21. DIAGNOSIS OR NATURE OF ILLNESS OR INJURY. (RELATE ITEMS 1,2,3 OR 4 TO ITEM 24E BY LINE)

1. V03.7   3. _____
2. 784.0   4. _____

22. MEDICAID RESUBMISSION CODE	ORIGINAL REF NO.

23. PRIOR AUTHORIZATION NUMBER

24.	A DATE(S) OF SERVICE						B Place of Service	C Type of Service	D PROCEDURES, SERVICES, OR SUPPLIES (Explain Unusual Circumstances) CPT/HCPCS — MODIFIER	E DIAGNOSIS CODE	F $ CHARGES	G DAYS OR UNITS	H EPSDT Family Plan	I EMG	J COB	K RESERVED FOR LOCAL USE
	From MM	DD	YY	To MM	DD	YY										
1	02	10	20XX	02	10	20XX	11	9	90703	1,2	15 00	1				
2	02	10	20XX	02	10	20XX	11	1	99212	1,2	75 00	1				
3																
4																
5																
6																

PHYSICIAN OR SUPPLIER INFORMATION

Problem(s) identified:

_____

_____

_____

_____

_____

Correction(s) needed:

_____

_____

_____

_____

_____

14. DATE OF CURRENT:			ILLNESS (first symptom) OR INJURY (accident) OR PREGNANCY (LMP)	15. IF PATIENT HAS HAD SAME OR SIMILAR ILLNESS. GIVE FIRST DATE				16. DATES PATIENT UNABLE TO WORK IN CURRENT OCCUPATION					
MM	DD	YY		MM DD YY				MM DD YY			MM DD YY		
02	10	20XX						FROM			TO		

17. NAME OF REFERRING PHYSICIAN OR OTHER SOURCE	17a. I.D. NUMBER OR REFERRING PHYSICIAN	18. HOSPITALIZATION DATES RELATED TO CURRENT SERVICES
		MM DD YY MM DD YY
Marvin Susimsky, M.D.	UPIN #S12345	FROM TO

19. RESERVED FOR LOCAL USE	20. OUTSIDE LAB?	$ CHARGES
	☐ YES ☐ NO	

21. DIAGNOSIS OR NATURE OF ILLNESS OR INJURY. (RELATE ITEMS 1,2,3 OR 4 TO ITEM 24E BY LINE)

1. __786.50__   3. _____

2. _____   4. _____

22. MEDICAID RESUBMISSION CODE   ORIGINAL REF NO.

23. PRIOR AUTHORIZATION NUMBER

24.	A						B	C	D		E	F		G	H	I	J	K
	DATE(S) OF SERVICE						Place of Service	Type of Service	PROCEDURES, SERVICES, OR SUPPLIES (Explain Unusual Circumstances)		DIAGNOSIS CODE	$ CHARGES		DAYS OR UNITS	EPSDT Family Plan	EMG	COB	RESERVED FOR LOCAL USE
	From MM	DD	YY	To MM	DD	YY			CPT/HCPCS	MODIFIER								
1	02	10	20XX	02	10	20XX	11	9	93000		1	75 00		1				
2	02	10	20XX	02	10	20XX	11	9	93000		1	75 00		1				
3	02	10	20XX	02	10	20XX	11	9	93000		1	75 00		1				
4																		
5																		
6																		

PHYSICIAN OR SUPPLIER INFORMATION

Problem(s) identified:

_____

_____

_____

_____

Correction(s) needed:

_____

_____

_____

_____

EXERCISE 17

14. DATE OF CURRENT: ILLNESS (first symptom) OR INJURY (accident) OR PREGNANCY (LMP)			15. IF PATIENT HAS HAD SAME OR SIMILAR ILLNESS. GIVE FIRST DATE			16. DATES PATIENT UNABLE TO WORK IN CURRENT OCCUPATION		
MM 02	DD 10	YY 20XX	MM	DD	YY	FROM MM DD YY	TO MM DD YY	

17. NAME OF REFERRING PHYSICIAN OR OTHER SOURCE	17a. I.D. NUMBER OR REFERRING PHYSICIAN	18. HOSPITALIZATION DATES RELATED TO CURRENT SERVICES
		FROM MM DD YY TO MM DD YY

19. RESERVED FOR LOCAL USE	20. OUTSIDE LAB? ☐ YES ☐ NO	$ CHARGES

21. DIAGNOSIS OR NATURE OF ILLNESS OR INJURY. (RELATE ITEMS 1,2,3 OR 4 TO ITEM 24E BY LINE)

1. __883.0__   3. _____

2. __784.0__   4. _____

22. MEDICAID RESUBMISSION CODE   ORIGINAL REF NO.

23. PRIOR AUTHORIZATION NUMBER

24. A. DATE(S) OF SERVICE						B. Place of Service	C. Type of Service	D. PROCEDURES, SERVICES, OR SUPPLIES (Explain Unusual Circumstances)		E. DIAGNOSIS CODE	F. $ CHARGES	G. DAYS OR UNITS	H. EPSDT Family Plan	I. EMG	J. COB	K. RESERVED FOR LOCAL USE
From MM	DD	YY	To MM	DD	YY			CPT/HCPCS	MODIFIER							
02	10	20XX	02	10	20XX	11	2	12001		1	80 00	1				
02	10	20XX	02	10	20XX	11	1	99212		2	75 00	1				

PHYSICIAN OR SUPPLIER INFORMATION

Problem(s) identified:

_____

_____

_____

_____

_____

Correction(s) needed:

_____

_____

_____

_____

_____

EXERCISE 18

<table>
<tr><td colspan="3">14. DATE OF CURRENT:
MM   DD   YY</td><td colspan="2">ILLNESS (first symptom) OR
INJURY (accident) OR
PREGNANCY (LMP)</td><td colspan="2">15. IF PATIENT HAS HAD SAME OR
    SIMILAR ILLNESS.   MM   DD   YY
GIVE FIRST DATE</td><td colspan="4">16. DATES PATIENT UNABLE TO WORK IN CURRENT OCCUPATION
MM   DD   YY   MM   DD   YY</td></tr>
<tr><td colspan="3">02   10   20XX</td><td colspan="2"></td><td colspan="2"></td><td colspan="4">FROM   TO</td></tr>
</table>

14. DATE OF CURRENT:	15. IF PATIENT HAS HAD SAME OR SIMILAR ILLNESS	16. DATES PATIENT UNABLE TO WORK IN CURRENT OCCUPATION
MM DD YY ILLNESS (first symptom) OR INJURY (accident) OR PREGNANCY (LMP)	MM DD YY GIVE FIRST DATE	MM DD YY MM DD YY
02 10 20XX		FROM TO

17. NAME OF REFERRING PHYSICIAN OR OTHER SOURCE	17a. I.D. NUMBER OR REFERRING PHYSICIAN	18. HOSPITALIZATION DATES RELATED TO CURRENT SERVICES
Joane Massey, M.D.	UPIN #S12345	MM DD YY MM DD YY FROM TO

19. RESERVED FOR LOCAL USE	20. OUTSIDE LAB? $ CHARGES
	☐ YES ☒ NO

21. DIAGNOSIS OR NATURE OF ILLNESS OR INJURY. (RELATE ITEMS 1,2,3 OR 4 TO ITEM 24E BY LINE)	22. MEDICAID RESUBMISSION CODE ORIGINAL REF NO.
1. 786.50 3. _____	
2. 599.0 4. _____	23. PRIOR AUTHORIZATION NUMBER

24.						A				B	C	D		E	F	G	H	I	J	K
		DATE(S) OF SERVICE								Place of Service	Type of Service	PROCEDURES, SERVICES, OR SUPPLIES (Explain Unusual Circumstances)		DIAGNOSIS CODE	$ CHARGES	DAYS OR UNITS	EPSDT Family Plan	EMG	COB	RESERVED FOR LOCAL USE
	From MM	DD	YY	To MM	DD	YY						CPT/HCPCS	MODIFIER							
1	02	10	20XX	02	10	20XX				11	4	71020		2	75 00	1				
2	02	10	20XX	02	10	20XX				11	5	81000		1	15 00	1				
3																				
4																				
5																				
6																				

PHYSICIAN OR SUPPLIER INFORMATION

Problem(s) identified:

_____

_____

_____

_____

_____

Correction(s) needed:

_____

_____

_____

_____

_____

EXERCISE 19

14. DATE OF CURRENT: MM DD YY	ILLNESS (first symptom) OR INJURY (accident) OR PREGNANCY (LMP)	15. IF PATIENT HAS HAD SAME OR SIMILAR ILLNESS. MM DD YY GIVE FIRST DATE	16. DATES PATIENT UNABLE TO WORK IN CURRENT OCCUPATION
02 10 20XX			MM DD YY MM DD YY FROM TO

17. NAME OF REFERRING PHYSICIAN OR OTHER SOURCE	17a. I.D. NUMBER OR REFERRING PHYSICIAN	18. HOSPITALIZATION DATES RELATED TO CURRENT SERVICES MM DD YY MM DD YY FROM TO

19. RESERVED FOR LOCAL USE	20. OUTSIDE LAB? ☐ YES ☐ NO	$ CHARGES

21. DIAGNOSIS OR NATURE OF ILLNESS OR INJURY. (RELATE ITEMS 1,2,3 OR 4 TO ITEM 24E BY LINE)	22. MEDICAID RESUBMISSION CODE	ORIGINAL REF NO.
1. 789.00 3. 382.9	23. PRIOR AUTHORIZATION NUMBER	
2. 465.9 4. _____		

24.	A DATE(S) OF SERVICE		B Place of Service	C Type of Service	D PROCEDURES, SERVICES, OR SUPPLIES (Explain Unusual Circumstances) CPT/HCPCS MODIFIER	E DIAGNOSIS CODE	F $ CHARGES	G DAYS OR UNITS	H EPSDT Family Plan	I EMG	J COB	K RESERVED FOR LOCAL USE
	From MM DD YY	To MM DD YY										
1	02 10 20XX	02 10 20XX	11	1	99213	1,2	75 00	1				
2												
3												
4												
5												
6												

PHYSICIAN OR SUPPLIER INFORMATION

Problem(s) identified:

_____

_____

_____

_____

_____

Correction(s) needed:

_____

_____

_____

_____

_____

EXERCISE 20

14. DATE OF CURRENT: ILLNESS (first symptom) OR INJURY (accident) OR PREGNANCY (LMP)	15. IF PATIENT HAS HAD SAME OR SIMILAR ILLNESS. GIVE FIRST DATE	16. DATES PATIENT UNABLE TO WORK IN CURRENT OCCUPATION
MM DD YY 02 ¦ 10 ¦ 20XX	MM DD YY	MM DD YY FROM ¦ ¦ TO ¦ ¦
17. NAME OF REFERRING PHYSICIAN OR OTHER SOURCE Ask-A-Nurse	17a. I.D. NUMBER OR REFERRING PHYSICIAN None	18. HOSPITALIZATION DATES RELATED TO CURRENT SERVICES MM DD YY MM DD YY FROM ¦ ¦ TO ¦ ¦

19. RESERVED FOR LOCAL USE	20. OUTSIDE LAB? $ CHARGES
	☐ YES ☐ NO

21. DIAGNOSIS OR NATURE OF ILLNESS OR INJURY. (RELATE ITEMS 1,2,3 OR 4 TO ITEM 24E BY LINE)	22. MEDICAID RESUBMISSION CODE ORIGINAL REF NO.
1. __784.0__ 3. _____	
2. _____ 4. _____	23. PRIOR AUTHORIZATION NUMBER

24.	A DATE(S) OF SERVICE		B Place of Service	C Type of Service	D PROCEDURES, SERVICES, OR SUPPLIES (Explain Unusual Circumstances) CPT/HCPCS MODIFIER	E DIAGNOSIS CODE	F $ CHARGES	G DAYS OR UNITS	H EPSDT Family Plan	I EMG	J COB	K RESERVED FOR LOCAL USE
	From MM DD YY	To MM DD YY										
1	02 ¦ 10 ¦ 20XX	02 ¦ 10 ¦ 20XX	11	3	99243	1	125 ¦ 00	1				
2												
3												
4												
5												
6												

PHYSICIAN OR SUPPLIER INFORMATION

Problem(s) identified:

_____

_____

_____

_____

_____

Correction(s) needed:

_____

_____

_____

_____

_____

EXPLANATION OF BENEFITS EXERCISES 21-40

Review the following Explanation of Benefits and **identify** the problem or reason the services were denied or paid incorrectly. Determine what **corrective action** should be taken to correct the problem with the claim and receive proper payment (e.g., modifier code).

General Health Insurance USA

Provider Name: Dr. Corman

Provider Address:

Provider #:

Explanation of Insurance Benefits

Patient Name: Smith, Barnard

Patient Account #: 621354

Service Dates				Major Medical/Comprehensive					Patient Responsibility				
From	To	Procedure Code	Provider Charge	Allowed Amount	Deductible	% Payment	Payment Amount		Co-Pay	Co-Ins	Total Payment	Claim#	REMARKS (see below)
0210XX	0210XX	71020	75.00								0.00	1234	C

REMARKS:

A: Included in surgical allowance

B: Denied, part of global fee

C: Not covered diagnosis: 784.0

D: Not covered procedure

E: Procedure not covered for diagnosis listed

F: Invalid information provided

EXERCISE 22

General Health Insurance USA

Provider Name: Dr. Corman
Provider Address:
Provider #:

Explanation of Insurance Benefits

Patient Name: Smith, Barnard
Patient Account #: 621354

| Service Dates | | Procedure Code | Provider Charge | Major Medical/Comprehensive | | | | Patient Responsibility | | Total Payment | Claim# | REMARKS (see below) |
From	To			Allowed Amount	Deductible	% Payment	Payment Amount	Co-Pay	Co-Ins			
0210XX	0210XX	69210	75.00	75.00		100	75.00			75.00	12345	
0210XX	0210XX	69212	45.00	0.00		0	0.00			0.00		B

REMARKS:
A: Included in surgical allowance
B: Denied, part of global fee

C: Not covered diagnosis: 784.0
D: Not covered procedure

E: Procedure not covered for diagnosis listed
F: Invalid information provided

General Health Insurance USA

Provider Name: Dr. Corman

Provider Address:

Provider #:

Explanation of Insurance Benefits

Patient Name: Smith, Barnard

Patient Account #: 621354

Service Dates				Major Medical/Comprehensive				Patient Responsibility				
From	To	Procedure Code	Provider Charge	Allowed Amount	Deductible	% Payment	Payment Amount	Co-Pay	Co-Ins	Total Payment	Claim#	REMARKS (see below)
0210XX	0210XX	12001	90.00	0.00			0.00			0.00	12345	E
0210XX	0210XX	99213	75.00	65.00		100	65.00			65.00		

REMARKS:

A: Included in surgical allowance

B: Denied, part of global fee

C: Not covered diagnosis: 784.0

D: Not covered procedure

E: Procedure not covered for diagnosis listed

F: Invalid information provided

EXERCISE 24

General Health Insurance USA

Provider Name: Dr. Corman

Provider Address:

Provider #:

Explanation of Insurance Benefits

Patient Name: Smith, Barnard

Patient Account #: 621354

| Service Dates | | Procedure Code | Provider Charge | Major Medical/Comprehensive | | | Patient Responsibility | | | Total Payment | Claim# | REMARKS (see below) |
From	To			Allowed Amount	Deductible	% Payment	Payment Amount	Co-Pay	Co-Ins			
0210XX	0210XX	0210XX	75.00	0.00			0.00			0.00	12345	F

REMARKS:

A: Included in surgical allowance

B: Denied, part of global fee

C: Not covered diagnosis: 784.0

D: Not covered procedure

E: Procedure not covered for diagnosis listed

F: Invalid information provided

General Health Insurance USA

Provider Name: Dr. Corman

Provider Address:

Provider #:

Explanation of Insurance Benefits

Patient Name: Smith, Barnard

Patient Account #: 621354

| Service Dates | | Procedure Code | Provider Charge | Major Medical/Comprehensive | | | Payment Amount | Patient Responsibility | | Total Payment | Claim# | REMARKS (see below) |
From	To			Allowed Amount	Deductible	% Payment		Co-Pay	Co-Ins			
0210XX	0210XX	81000	15.00	0.00			0.00			0.00	12345	E

REMARKS:

A: Included in surgical allowance
B: Denied, part of global fee

C: Not covered diagnosis: 784.0
D: Not covered procedure

E: Procedure not covered for diagnosis listed
F: Invalid information provided

EXERCISE 26

General Health Insurance USA

Provider Name: Dr. Corman

Provider Address:

Provider #:

Explanation of Insurance Benefits

Patient Name: Smith, Barnard

Patient Account #: 621354

Service Dates		Procedure Code	Provider Charge	Major Medical/Comprehensive				Patient Responsibility		Total Payment	Claim#	REMARKS (see below)
From	To			Allowed Amount	Deductible	% Payment	Payment Amount	Co-Pay	Co-Ins			
0210XX	0210XX	85022	25.00	25.00	25.00		0.00		25.00	0.00	12345	
0210XX	0210XX	36415	10.00	0.00			0.00			0.00	12345	B

REMARKS:

A: Included in surgical allowance

B: Denied, part of global fee

C: Not covered diagnosis: 784.0

D: Not covered procedure

E: Procedure not covered for diagnosis listed

F: Invalid information provided

General Health Insurance USA

Provider Name: Dr. Corman

Provider Address:

Provider #:

Explanation of Insurance Benefits

Patient Name: Smith, Barnard

Patient Account #: 621354

| Service Dates | | Procedure Code | Provider Charge | Major Medical/Comprehensive | | | | Patient Responsibility | | Total Payment | Claim# | REMARKS (see below) |
From	To			Allowed Amount	Deductible	% Payment	Payment Amount	Co-Pay	Co-Ins			
	0210XX	99231	240.00	0.00			0.00			0.00	12345	F

REMARKS:

A: Included in surgical allowance

B: Denied, part of global fee

C: Not covered diagnosis: 784.0

D: Not covered procedure

E: Procedure not covered for diagnosis listed

F: Invalid information provided

General Health Insurance USA
Provider Name: Dr. Corman
Provider Address:
Provider #:

Explanation of Insurance Benefits
Patient Name: Smith, Barnard
Patient Account #: 621354

Service Dates		Procedure Code	Provider Charge	Major Medical/Comprehensive				Patient Responsibility		Total Payment	Claim#	REMARKS (see below)
From	To			Allowed Amount	Deductible	% Payment	Payment Amount	Co-Pay	Co-Ins			
0210XX	0210XX	99210	35.00	0.00			0.00			0.00	12345	D

REMARKS:
A: Included in surgical allowance
B: Denied, part of global fee
C: Not covered diagnosis: 784.0
D: Not covered procedure
E: Procedure not covered for diagnosis listed
F: Invalid information provided

General Health Insurance USA

Provider Name: Dr. Corman

Provider Address:

Provider #:

Explanation of Insurance Benefits

Patient Name: Smith, Barnard

Patient Account #: 621354

| Service Dates | | Procedure Code | Provider Charge | Major Medical/Comprehensive | | | | Patient Responsibility | | Total Payment | Claim# | REMARKS (see below) |
From	To			Allowed Amount	Deductible	% Payment	Payment Amount	Co-Pay	Co-Ins			
0210XX	0210XX	71020	75.00	0.00			0.00			0.00	12345	F

REMARKS:

A: Included in surgical allowance

B: Denied, part of global fee

C: Not covered diagnosis: 784.0

D: Not covered procedure

E: Procedure not covered for diagnosis listed

F: Invalid information provided

EXERCISE 30

General Health Insurance USA

Provider Name: Dr. Corman

Provider Address:

Provider #:

Explanation of Insurance Benefits

Patient Name: Smith, Barnard

Patient Account #: 621354

| Service Dates | | Procedure Code | Provider Charge | Major Medical/Comprehensive | | | Payment Amount | Patient Responsibility | | Total Payment | Claim# | REMARKS (see below) |
From	To			Allowed Amount	Deductible	% Payment		Co-Pay	Co-Ins			
0210XX	0210XX	71020	75.00	0.00			0.00			0.00	12345	F

REMARKS:

A: Included in surgical allowance

B: Denied, part of global fee

C: Not covered diagnosis: 784.0

D: Not covered procedure

E: Procedure not covered for diagnosis listed

F: Invalid information provided

General Health Insurance USA

Provider Name: Dr. Corman

Provider Address:

Provider #:

Explanation of Insurance Benefits

Patient Name: Smith, Barnard

Patient Account #: 621354

Service Dates				Major Medical/Comprehensive				Patient Responsibility				
From	To	Procedure Code	Provider Charge	Allowed Amount	Deductible	% Payment	Payment Amount	Co-Pay	Co-Ins	Total Payment	Claim#	REMARKS (see below)
0210XX	0210XX	99231	75.00	75.00		100	75.00			75.00	12345	
0210XX	0210XX	99231	75.00	0.00		0	0.00			0.00		F
0210XX	0210XX	99231	75.00	0.00		0	0.00			0.00		F

REMARKS:

A: Included in surgical allowance

B: Denied, part of global fee

C: Not covered diagnosis: 784.0

D: Not covered procedure

E: Procedure not covered for diagnosis listed

F: Invalid information provided

EXERCISE 32

General Health Insurance USA

Provider Name: Dr. Corman

Provider Address:

Provider #:

Explanation of Insurance Benefits

Patient Name: Smith, Barnard

Patient Account #: 621354

Service Dates				Major Medical/Comprehensive				Patient Responsibility				
From	To	Procedure Code	Provider Charge	Allowed Amount	Deductible	% Payment	Payment Amount	Co-Pay	Co-Ins	Total Payment	Claim#	REMARKS (see below)
0210XX	0210XX	99213	75.00	0.00			0.00			0.00	12345	F

REMARKS:

A: Included in surgical allowance

B: Denied, part of global fee

C: Not covered diagnosis: 784.0

D: Not covered procedure

E: Procedure not covered for diagnosis listed

F: Invalid information provided

General Health Insurance USA

Provider Name: Dr. Corman

Provider Address:

Provider #:

Explanation of Insurance Benefits

Patient Name: Smith, Barnard

Patient Account #: 621354

| Service Dates | | Procedure Code | Provider Charge | Major Medical/Comprehensive | | % Payment | Payment Amount | Patient Responsibility | | Total Payment | Claim# | REMARKS (see below) |
From	To			Allowed Amount	Deductible			Co-Pay	Co-Ins			
0210XX	0210XX	99243	125.00	0.00			0.00			0.00	12345	A
0210XX	0210XX	45380	450.00	350.00		100	350.00			350.00		

REMARKS:

A: Included in surgical allowance

B: Denied, part of global fee

C: Not covered diagnosis: 784.0

D: Not covered procedure

E: Procedure not covered for diagnosis listed

F: Invalid information provided

EXERCISE 34

General Health Insurance USA

Provider Name: Dr. Corman

Provider Address:

Provider #:

Explanation of Insurance Benefits

Patient Name: Smith, Barnard

Patient Account #: 62135

Service Dates				Major Medical/Comprehensive				Patient Responsibility				
From	To	Procedure Code	Provider Charge	Allowed Amount	Deductible	% Payment	Payment Amount	Co-Pay	Co-Ins	Total Payment	Claim#	REMARKS (see below)
0210XX	0210XX	99213	75.00	0.00			0.00			0.00	12345	B
0210XX	0210XX	69210	25.00	25.00			25.00			25.00		

REMARKS:

A: Included in surgical allowance

B: Denied, part of global fee

C: Not covered diagnosis: 784.0

D: Not covered procedure

E: Procedure not covered for diagnosis listed

F: Invalid information provided

General Health Insurance USA

Provider Name: Dr. Corman

Provider Address:

Provider #:

Explanation of Insurance Benefits

Patient Name: Smith, Barnard

Patient Account #: 62135

| Service Dates | | | | Major Medical/Comprehensive | | | | Patient Responsibility | | | | |
From	To	Procedure Code	Provider Charge	Allowed Amount	Deductible	% Payment	Payment Amount	Co-Pay	Co-Ins	Total Payment	Claim#	REMARKS (see below)
0210XX	0210XX	45830	450.00	350.00		100	350.00			350.00	12345	
0210XX	0210XX	45378	400.00	0.00			0.00			0.00		B

REMARKS:

A: Included in surgical allowance

B: Denied, part of global fee

C: Not covered diagnosis: 784.0

D: Not covered procedure

E: Procedure not covered for diagnosis listed

F: Invalid information provided

EXERCISE 36

General Health Insurance USA

Provider Name: Dr. Corman

Provider Address:

Provider #:

Explanation of Insurance Benefits

Patient Name: Smith, Barnard

Patient Account #: 62135

| Service Dates | | Procedure Code | Provider Charge | Major Medical/Comprehensive | | | | Patient Responsibility | | Total Payment | Claim# | REMARKS (see below) |
From	To			Allowed Amount	Deductible	% Payment	Payment Amount	Co-Pay	Co-Ins			
0210XX	0210XX	12001	120.00	120.00		100	120.00			120.00	1234	
0210XX	0210XX	12001	120.00	0.00		0	0.00			0.00		A
0210XX	0210XX	12011	120.00	0.00		0	0.00			0.00		A

REMARKS:

A: Included in surgical allowance

B: Denied, part of global fee

C: Not covered diagnosis: 784.0

D: Not covered procedure

E: Procedure not covered for diagnosis listed

F: Invalid information provided

General Health Insurance USA

Provider Name: Dr. Corman

Provider Address:

Provider #:

Explanation of Insurance Benefits

Patient Name: Smith, Barnard

Patient Account #: 62135

| Service Dates | | Procedure Code | Provider Charge | Major Medical/Comprehensive | | | | Patient Responsibility | | Total Payment | Claim# | REMARKS (see below) |
From	To			Allowed Amount	Deductible	% Payment	Payment Amount	Co-Pay	Co-Ins			
0210XX	0210XX	81000	15.00	15.00		100	15.00			15.00	12345	
0210XX	0210XX	99000	10.00	0.00		0	0.00			0.00		B

REMARKS:

A: Included in surgical allowance

B: Denied, part of global fee

C: Not covered diagnosis: 784.0

D: Not covered procedure

E: Procedure not covered for diagnosis listed

F: Invalid information provided

EXERCISE 38

General Health Insurance USA

Provider Name: Dr. Corman

Provider Address:

Provider #:

Explanation of Insurance Benefits

Patient Name: Smith, Barnard

Patient Account #: 62135

| Service Dates | | Procedure Code | Provider Charge | Major Medical/Comprehensive | | | Payment Amount | Patient Responsibility | | Total Payment | Claim# | REMARKS (see below) |
From	To			Allowed Amount	Deductible	% Payment		Co-Pay	Co-Ins			
0210XX	0210XX	7102	75.00	0.00			0.00			0.00	1234	F

REMARKS:

A: Included in surgical allowance

B: Denied, part of global fee

C: Not covered diagnosis: 784.0

D: Not covered procedure

E: Procedure not covered for diagnosis listed

F: Invalid information provided

General Health Insurance USA

Provider Name: Dr. Corman

Provider Address:

Provider #:

Explanation of Insurance Benefits

Patient Name: Smith, Barnard

Patient Account #: 62135

Service Dates		Procedure Code	Provider Charge	Major Medical/Comprehensive				Patient Responsibility		Total Payment	Claim#	REMARKS (see below)
From	To			Allowed Amount	Deductible	% Payment	Payment Amount	Co-Pay	Co-Ins			
0210XX	0210XX	93000	75.00	75.00		100	75.00			75.00	12345	
0210XX	0210XX	93000	75.00	0.00		0	0.00			0.00		Dup
0210XX	0210XX	93000	75.00	0.00		0	0.00			0.00		Dup
0210XX	0210XX	93000	75.00	0.00		0	0.00			0.00		Dup

REMARKS:

A: Included in surgical allowance

B: Denied, part of global fee

C: Not covered diagnosis: 784.0

D: Not covered procedure

E: Procedure not covered for diagnosis listed

F: Invalid information provided

EXERCISE 40

General Health Insurance USA

Provider Name: Dr. Corman

Provider Address:

Provider #:

Explanation of Insurance Benefits

Patient Name: Smith, Barnard

Patient Account #: 62135

| Service Dates | | Procedure Code | Provider Charge | Major Medical/Comprehensive | | | | Patient Responsibility | | Total Payment | Claim# | REMARKS (see below) |
From	To			Allowed Amount	Deductible	% Payment	Payment Amount	Co-Pay	Co-Ins			
0210XX	0210XX	71020	45.00	0.00			0.00			0.00		F

REMARKS:

A: Included in surgical allowance

B: Denied, part of global fee

C: Not covered diagnosis: 784.0

D: Not covered procedure

E: Procedure not covered for diagnosis listed

F: Invalid information provided

20 Hospital and Facility Coding

Identify the *principal* diagnosis in the following cases.

1. Chest pain

   R/O MI

   Principal diagnosis: _____   ICD-9-CM code(s): _____

2. Congestive heart failure

   Pneumonia

   Principal diagnosis: _____   ICD-9-CM code(s): _____

3. Abdominal pain

   R/O appendicitis

   R/O cholecystitis

   Principal diagnosis: _____   ICD-9-CM code(s): _____

4. Urinary tract infection

   Urinary retention

   Dysuria

   Principal diagnosis: _____   ICD-9-CM code(s): _____

5. Congestive heart failure

   Urinary tract infection

   Atrial fibrillation

   Coronary artery disease

   Principal diagnosis: _____   ICD-9-CM code(s): _____

6. Nausea with vomiting

   Inability to tolerate po

   Probable gastroenteritis

   Principal diagnosis: _____   ICD-9-CM code(s): _____

7. History of occasional diarrhea

   Colon carcinoma, extensive with metastatic progression

   Dehydration

   Principal diagnosis: _____   ICD-9-CM code(s): _____

8. Multiple myeloma

   Underlying depression

   Hypertension, controlled

   Principal diagnosis: _____   ICD-9-CM code(s): _____

9. Pyelonephritis

   Possible urosepsis

   Principal diagnosis: _____   ICD-9-CM code(s): _____

10. Acute abdominal pain

    Possibility of peptic gastritis

    Principal diagnosis: _____   ICD-9-CM code(s): _____

11. Fever

    Burning with urination

    Type 1 diabetes, controlled

    Principal diagnosis: _____   ICD-9-CM code(s): _____

12. History of low back pain

    Chest pain

    Pleural effusion

    History of Parkinson's disease

    Principal diagnosis: _____   ICD-9-CM code(s): _____

13. Fever

    Upper right quadrant abdominal pain

    Elevated white blood cell count

    Gastroenteritis

    Principal diagnosis: _____   ICD-9-CM code(s): _____

14. Nausea and vomiting due to metastatic colon
    carcinoma and chemotherapy

    Principal diagnosis: _____   ICD-9-CM code(s): _____

15. Fractured left hip

    Laceration left tibia

    Contusion, nose

    Acute alcohol intoxication

    Principal diagnosis: _____   ICD-9-CM code(s): _____

16. Abdominal pain

    Acute cholecystitis

    Cholelithiasis

    Principal diagnosis: _____   ICD-9-CM code(s): _____

17. Fever

    Febrile seizures

    Convulsions

    Principal diagnosis: _____   ICD-9-CM code(s): _____

18. Type 2 diabetes, controlled

    Hypertension, uncontrolled

    Urinary tract infection

    Principal diagnosis: _____   ICD-9-CM code(s): _____

19. Acute abdominal pain

    R/O endometriosis

    R/O tubal pregnancy

    R/O abdominal adhesions

    Principal diagnosis: _____   ICD-9-CM code(s): _____

20. Abdominal pain

    Intrauterine pregnancy

    R/O incomplete abortion

    Principal diagnosis: _____   ICD-9-CM code(s): _____

Review the complete records for each inpatient case. Complete the DRG Coding Worksheet for each case, assigning the appropriate codes (ICD-9-CM and DRG).

EXERCISE 1A

DISCHARGE SUMMARY

Admitted: 04/04/XX
Discharged: 04/08/XX

Rec#: 0112345

Discharge diagnoses:

PRINCIPAL DIAGNOSIS:
  Pyelonephritis
SECONDARY DIAGNOSIS:
  Pregnancy
  Dehydration
  Vomiting

History:

The patient was seen approximately three days prior to admission and diagnosed with pyelonephritis. Outpatient therapy was attempted but the patient was unable to keep the antibiotics down so she was admitted on 04/04/XX with dehydration and pyelonephritis. She was rehydrated with IV fluids, given Rocephin IV and improved over the course of her admission.

Laboratory and radiology studies:

Hospital course:

She was given IV antibiotics until she proved afebrile for more than 24 hours at which time she was discharged on oral antibiotics.

Jay Corman MD

GODFREY REGIONAL HOSPITAL
123 Main Street • Aldon, FL 77714 • (407) 555-1234

Answers

HISTORY AND PHYSICAL EXAMINATION

Admitted: 04/04/XX

Medical record number:

CHIEF COMPLAINT: 24-year-old with pyelonephritis in early pregnancy
This 24-year-old had her last menstrual period in the middle of February. She had a home pregnancy test that was positive approximately one week ago. For about the past two weeks she has been having dysuria, frequency and urgency with some back pain but then she started to get sicker with nausea and vomiting. She had been feeling very hot with shaking chills and had been feeling dizzy. She was seen on an outpatient basis and diagnosed with pyelonephritis. Outpatient versus inpatient treatment was discussed with the patient at that time, and she wished to attempt treatment on an outpatient basis. She called her physician and indicated she was having increasing chills and fever and also dry mouth and the decision was made to admit her for further treatment.

CURRENT MEDICATIONS: No medications. She was on OCPs until two weeks ago when her home pregnancy test was positive.

Past medical history:

She has a history of pyelonephritis with a previous pregnancy and a history of frequent UTIs. The patient also notes a history of panic attacks. ALLERGIES: No known allergies

Family and social history:

Single, divorced mother of one child. HABITS: Smokes cigarettes. Drinks occasionally.

Review of systems:

General – fevers and chills. HEENT no complaints. Cardiac, no complaints. Respiratory no complaints.
GI, no diarrhea or constipation. No blood in her stools or black, tarry stools. Psychologic – patient is quite anxious.

Physical exam:

General, ill-appearing female. Vitals, temperature 99.9, pulse 88, respirations 24, blood pressure 120/80. HEENT exam, PERRL, pharynx with tacky mucous membranes. Neck supple without lymphadenopathy. Heart regular rate and rhythm. Lungs clear to auscultation bilaterally. Abdomen soft, mild tenderness in lower quadrants. Extremities without clubbing, cyanosis or edema.

Laboratory/radiology:

X-ray:

Assessment:

Pyelonephritis and dehydration.

Plan:

Will admit patient, give her IV fluids, IV antibiotics and medication to control her nausea. Will get urine cultures performed outpatient and continue IV antibiotics until she is afebrile for 24 hours or more.

Jay Corm MD

GODFREY REGIONAL HOSPITAL
123 Main Street • Aldon, FL 77714 • (407) 555-1234

Answers

EXERCISE 1C

PROGRESS NOTES

Date:	Vital signs:	T	R
Chief complaint:		P	BP

04/04/XX	Patient complains of nausea and vomiting, abdominal pain. Medicated with Phenergan 25 mg IV. Patient indicates much relief with medications. *Jay Corm mo*
04/05/XX	Patient continues to complain of nausea and vomiting. Emesis X2 with evening meal. Phenergan 25 mg IV given with relief. *Jay Corm mo*
04/06/XX	Improved control of N/V with Phenergan. *Jay Corm mo*
04/07/XX	Continued improved control of N/V. If afebrile throughout day, will d/c tomorrow. *Jay Corm mo*
04/08/XX	Patient much improved. No nausea/vomiting. Afebrile since yesterday. OK to discharge on oral meds. Follow-up OB appointment and ultrasound for dates. *Jay Corm mo*

	Patient name:
	DOB:
	MR/Chart #:

GODFREY REGIONAL OUTPATIENT CLINIC
3122 Shannon Avenue • Aldon, FL 77712 • (407) 555-7654

Answers

HISTORY AND PHYSICAL EXAMINATION

Admitted: 10/10/XX
Medical record number:

CHIEF COMPLAINT: 59-year-old with dehydration and uncontrolled diabetes mellitus.

This 59-year-old was seen on an outpatient basis approximately two weeks ago and diagnosed with diabetes mellitus type II. She was started on Glucophage and she was to see a dietician. Last night she reported nausea and emesis x2. She continues to be quite thirsty and has had polyuria, dry mouth. She started checking her blood sugars with the presentation of these symptoms and she reports her monitor showed a blood glucose greater than 600 this morning.

CURRENT MEDS: Glucophage 500 mg po BID Zestoretic: BID, 20 mg AM/25 mg PM

Past medical history:

Hypertension

Family and social history:

Patient's mother died of congestive heart failure as did her father. Two brothers have died of coronary artery disease. One surviving brother is in good health. Patient does not work, lives with husband in the area. She was a smoker until approximately 6 weeks ago at which time she reports she stopped. No alcohol intake.

Review of systems:

No fever or chills. HEENT, dry mouth. Cardiac, no complaints. Respiratory, no complaints. No other complaints other than those listed in chief complaint.

Physical exam:

Pleasant lady in no acute distress. Vital signs as noted. HEENT, PERLA, TMs clear bilaterally. Neck supple without lymphadenopathy. Lungs are clear to auscultation bilaterally. Abdomen, soft nontender. Reflexes no clubbing, cyanosis or edema.

Laboratory/radiology:

X-ray:

Assessment:

1. Dehydration 2. Uncontrolled diabetes mellitus type II. This is probably due to her dehydration.

Plan:

1. Will rehydrate with IV fluids.
2. Will put on sliding insulin scale to bring her blood sugar under control.

Filia Warden MD

GODFREY REGIONAL HOSPITAL
123 Main Street • Aldon, FL 77714 • (407) 555-1234

Answers

PROGRESS NOTES

Date:	Vital signs:	T	R
Chief complaint:		P	BP

10/10/XX	Patient admitted with uncontrolled Type II DM and dehydration. Will rehydrate and start sliding scale insulin. Patient BS 347 at 1530 Patient BS 345 at 1850 Patient BS 283 at 2300 Reviewed, signed, *Felix Warden* MD
10/11/XX	Patient feeling much better. Blood sugar 183. OK to discharge after diet/diabetes consult with dietician this morning. S) Rested well O) Wt 177, Glucose 183, BP 170/60 A) New onset DM with hyperglycemia P) Doing well, will discharge with follow-up on outpatient basis *Felix Warden* MD

	Patient name:
	DOB:
	MR/Chart #:

GODFREY REGIONAL OUTPATIENT CLINIC
3122 Shannon Avenue • Aldon, FL 77712 • (407) 555-7654

Answers

HISTORY AND PHYSICAL EXAMINATION

Admitted: 05/03/XX
Medical record number:

CHIEF COMPLAINT:
"I could not awaken him" (wife informant)

69-year-old who was brought in because of the above noted problem. He has a history of multiple myeloma and apparently could not be aroused by his wife this morning. Two weeks ago, it was noted he could not void and an indwelling catheter was placed. At this time, blood is noted in the urine.

Past medical history:

No allergies. Medications: baby aspirin, 1 qd, Lasix 20 qd, Dexamethasone 4 mg day, Oxycodone 5 mg q 4 hours breakthrough pain. Previous history of MI approximately 4 years ago. He used to smoke, quit following his MI. History of hypertension, and type II diabetes mellitus.

Family and social history:

Retired. Severely limited over the past several years as a result of his medical problems.

Review of systems:

Physical exam:

Blood pressure 119/68, temp 100.4, pulse 106, respirations 20. He appears pale and pasty. He says he is not having any pain, but, if he moves, he has low back pain. Lungs: he has some scattered expiratory rhonchi. Genitalia: normal. Presently had a Foley in place with dark blood in tubing. Back/extremities: absent of pulses in both feet.
Neuro: his mental status reveals he is oriented to place, but not to time or person.

Laboratory/radiology:

Labs reveal white count 6,800. Hemoglobin and hematocrit 8.9 and 26.3.
He also has an elevated total protein and UA is grossly positive.

X-ray:

Assessment:

1. Decreased level of consciousness, probably secondary to infection	2. Dehydration	4. Hypertension
	3. Progressive multiple myeloma	5. Type II diabetes mellitus

Plan:

Will admit to hospital. Start on Unasyn and follow clinically. Obviously, his long term prognosis is extremely guarded.

Felix Warden MD

GODFREY REGIONAL HOSPITAL
123 Main Street • Aldon, FL 77714 • (407) 555-1234

Answers

PROGRESS NOTES

Date:	Vital signs:	T	R
Chief complaint:		P	BP

05/03/XX	Patient admitted with urinary tract infection which resulted in decreased level of consciousness and dehydration. Will rehydrate and begin Unasyn.
	Felix Warden MD
05/04/XX	Patient continues to have gross hematuria not improving while UTI is beginning to resolve. Will plan on urology consult for possible cysto.
	Felix Warden MD
05/05/XX	Urine continues to be dark red. Couple of small clots passed. Clots continue to clog catheter.
	Felix Warden MD

05/06/XX	S) Patient without complaints
	O) Urine remains red. Requires irrigation at times for clots. Hgb down to 12.1 from 13.9.
	A) UTI
	      Persistent hematuria
	      Anemia from above
	      Bladder outlet obstruction
	      DMII
	      Multiple myeloma
	P) Urology consult

	Felix Warden MD

Patient name:

DOB:

MR/Chart #:

GODFREY REGIONAL OUTPATIENT CLINIC
3122 Shannon Avenue • Aldon, FL 77712 • (407) 555-7654

Answers

HISTORY AND PHYSICAL EXAMINATION

Admitted: 04/10/XX

Medical record number:

Patient presents with chief complaint of pain and redness in the left foot with underlying history of peripheral vascular disease, insulin-dependent diabetes.

SUMMARY: Patient with complex history of slow healing ulcers and pain between the fourth and fifth toe has been followed with debridement and antibiotic coverage. She has been treated with oral antibiotics without success. Cultures which were drawn have now reported Pseudomonas and she was advised to come in for admission and treatment of her foot ulcer.

CURRENT MEDICATIONS: Percocet for pain, Silvadene, Norvasc 5 mg bid, Catapres TTS 2 patch, prednisone 5 mg, Zocor 20 mg day, calcium carbonate and Keflex 500.

Past medical history:

Significant for insulin-dependent diabetes with subsequent diabetic retinopathy. Patient has also had venous thrombosis in the past.

Family and social history:

HABITS: Patient has continued to smoke, having quit once in 1995.

Review of systems:

Physical exam:

She is afebrile with pulse of 110, respirations 20, BP 190/88. HEENT, respirations, cardiac, abdomen all appear normal. Extremities remarkable for erythema on the left foot particularly up to the ankle. Has purulent discharge and open sore between fourth and fifth digit on left toe. Skin otherwise intact on right foot.

Laboratory/radiology:

Glucose, 263, creatinine 0.9, potassium 4.3. Patient's wound culture grew out numerous Pseudomonas sensitivity.

X-ray:

Assessment:

Patient with vascular disease and now deep nonhealing ulcer of the left foot.

Plan:

Initiate broad spectrum IV coverage watching her diabetes status cautiously during treatment.

Ruth Brady M

GODFREY REGIONAL HOSPITAL
123 Main Street • Aldon, FL 77714 • (407) 555-1234

Answers

PROGRESS NOTES

Date:	Vital signs:	T	R
Chief complaint:		P	BP

04/10/XX — Patient complaining of pain. Percocet given with good relief. L foot has edema and redness above toes, more pronounced on outer edge of foot, has healing area on great toe.

Also complains of "boil" under (L) arm which is irritating to her as well. Will inform MD.

Ruth Brady Me

04/11/XX
S) Patient hasn't noticed large change re: foot ulcer. Also complaining of L axillary boil that is tender.
O) Afebrile, vital signs normal
   Boil noted in L axilla
   Chest clear, black edge to foot ulcer
A) Axillary boil
   Foot ulcer
   PVD LLE
P) Will discuss vascular assessment

Ruth Brady Me

04/12/XX — Patient states pain better controlled today. Decreased redness and no drainage to open ulcer between 4th and 5th digits. Will switch to oral antibiotics and discharge.

Ruth Brady Me

Patient name:

DOB:

MR/Chart #:

GODFREY REGIONAL OUTPATIENT CLINIC
3122 Shannon Avenue • Aldon, FL 77712 • (407) 555-7654

Answers

DISCHARGE SUMMARY

Admitted: 05/18/XX
Discharged: 05/19/XX

Discharge diagnoses:

1. Pneumonia
2. Dehydration
3. Dementia
4. Chronic ITP
5. Peripheral vascular disease with AKA right leg
6. History CHF

History:

This is a patient who resides at a nursing home due to his dementia and the numerous medical problems listed above. He had been doing rather poorly the last few weeks reporting intermittent fevers, cough and not eating well.

Laboratory and radiology studies:

Hospital course:

He was initially treated with oral antibiotics, but, in spite of these medications continued to be quite lethargic in his mental status. He had very dry mucous membranes, some rales in the chest bilaterally. His chest x-ray showed questionable infiltrate in the fifth field. He was admitted, treated with IV fluids and IV antibiotics. His dehydration improved, he became much more alert, and his white count has continued to fall.

At the time of discharge, he is in improved condition. He is back to his usual level of alertness.

Stany Kraitt, MD

GODFREY REGIONAL HOSPITAL
123 Main Street • Aldon, FL 77714 • (407) 555-1234

Answers

HISTORY AND PHYSICAL EXAMINATION

Admitted: 05/18/XX

Medical record number:

This gentleman usually resides at a local nursing home and was sent over via ambulance to evaluate change in mental status. The patient had significant respiratory symptoms over the last couple months, having been admitted and treated previously for pneumonia. He has been off his oxygen today, reporting weakness, ashenness and heart rate greater than 160 and irregular.

Past medical history:

Prior hospitalizations and medical problems include ITP, status post CVA with chronic dementia as a result. He has a right AK amputation as a result of his progressive peripheral vascular disease. He is status post appendectomy and renal calculi.

Family and social history:

Review of systems:

Patient does complain of occasional abdominal pain but is not more specific than this. History is difficult due to patient's CVA induced dementia.

Physical exam:

This patient is slightly anxious about being in the hospital. Otherwise, in no acute distress. BP 107/68, pulse of 110, respirations 20, temperature 98.2. Pharynx is clear, mucous membranes are slightly dry. Auscultation of lungs show inspiratory rales bilaterally with fair air flow. Abdomen is protuberant, but no masses or organomegaly.

Laboratory/radiology:

Chest x-ray shows infiltrate, but pneumonia not visualized probably due to dehydration. ECG normal, elevated white count.

X-ray:

Assessment:

1. Acute dyspnea, hypoxia most probably consistent with pneumonia which could not be seen on x-ray due to dehydration
2. Dehydration
3. Chronic ITP on steroids
4. History of chronic constipation
5. Underlying vascular disease
6. Dementia secondary to severe CVA in 1996

Plan:

Patient will be admitted, IV antibiotics, IV hydration. This was discussed with the patient; however, due to his dementia, his understanding is probably poor.

Stony Kratt MD

GODFREY REGIONAL HOSPITAL
123 Main Street • Aldon, FL 77714 • (407) 555-1234

Answers

PROGRESS NOTES

Date:	Vital signs:	T		R	
Chief complaint:		P		BP	

05/18/XX	S)	Patient confused, agitated in the evening
		Apparently not a problem when in nursing home
	O)	Patient afebrile, rales diminishing
	A)	Pneumonia resolving, dementia improving with rehydration
		Patient will require IM antibiotics after discharge
	P)	If symptoms continue to improve, will discharge tomorrow

Steny Kractt, MD

05/19/XX	S)	Patient's dementia continues to improve
		Unsure of baseline, but significantly improved from admission
	O)	Patient afebrile, no rales heard
	A)	Pneumonia resolving
	P)	Discharge patient, with IM antibiotics for 7–10 days post discharge

Steny Kractt, MD

Patient name:

DOB:

MR/Chart #:

GODFREY REGIONAL OUTPATIENT CLINIC
3122 Shannon Avenue • Aldon, FL 77712 • (407) 555-7654

Answers

HISTORY AND PHYSICAL EXAMINATION

Admitted: 03/01/XX

Medical record number:

CHIEF COMPLAINT: Cough and chills

This 80-year-old man reports feeling poorly for the past 2–3 weeks. He developed a cough approximately one week ago which has been non-productive and associated with some fever and chills. He has had no appetite with very little if any oral intake over the past 24–48 hours. No emesis. He was seen in the emergency room where chest x-ray revealed pneumonia.

He will be admitted for IV antibiotics.

CURRENT MEDICATIONS: Pravachol 20 mg po daily.

Past medical history:

He relates having pneumonia as a child at age three and again at age 12.

Family and social history:

Patient is married and lives with his wife. One son and one granddaughter alive and well. Positive for family history of heart disease in father and one brother. HABITS: Patient quit smoking approximately 20 years ago. No alcohol.

Review of systems:

Unremarkable. No problems with ears, nose or throat. No history of heart disease. History of hypertension, well controlled. No problem with edema or neurological problems.

Physical exam:

Blood pressure 126/65, pulse is 87, temperature 97.6, respirations 16. His oxygen saturation on room air was 94%. He appears a little dry. No adenopathy in the neck. Lungs have some rales in the right base. Neck veins are not distended. Heart was regular, no murmurs appreciated. Abdomen is soft and nontender. Extremities show no edema.

Laboratory/radiology:

White count elevated at 20.4, potassium somewhat low.

X-ray:

Assessment:

1. Pneumonia   2. Anorexia   3. Weakness secondary to #1   4. Hypokalemia   5. Hypertension

Plan:

Patient is admitted for IV antibiotics. Encourage oral fluids, replace potassium and see how he progresses. Plan of care was discussed with patient and he understands and agrees.

GODFREY REGIONAL HOSPITAL
123 Main Street • Aldon, FL 77714 • (407) 555-1234

Answers

DISCHARGE SUMMARY

Admitted: 07/11/XX
Discharged: 07/13/XX

Discharge diagnoses:

FINAL DIAGNOSIS:
1. Congestive heart failure with classic PND
2. CAD
3. Atrial fibrillation
4. Hypercholesterolemia
5. Chronic DJD knee, right

History:

62-year-old admitted with chest discomfort. Long-standing history of atrial fibrillation. Awoke feeling short of breath, had some substernal chest pressure. No relief with nitroglycerin. Had been having classic PND for last several days before admission.
Pain abated with oxygen.

Laboratory and radiology studies:

ECG serially showing atrial fibrillation with relative well controlled ventricular rate. White count 8700. H & H 13.2, 39.4. INR 3.3 LDH slightly elevated at 192. Negative serial CPKs and troponin.

Hospital course:

Patient was admitted to hospital and felt to have unstable angina. He had no evidence of myocardial infarction and with diuresis went from an admission weight of 148.2 to a discharge weight of 142.1. His PND, chest pain, etc. all resolved prior to discharge.

DISPOSITION AND PLAN:
Patient was discharged home on a no-added salt diet. Meds: Nitro .4 prn 50; Atenolol 10, Furosemide BID; Lanoxin .25; calcium; Vitamin D; Imdur 60.

Ruth Brady MD

GODFREY REGIONAL HOSPITAL
123 Main Street • Aldon, FL 77714 • (407) 555-1234

Answers

EXERCISE 7B

HISTORY AND PHYSICAL EXAMINATION

Admitted: 07/11/XX

Medical record number:

CHIEF COMPLAINT: Chest pain

62-year-old with long standing afib awoke with shortness of breath and some substernal chest pain during the night. No relief with nitroglycerin. Pain abated in the emergency room with the use of oxygen. He was also given a GI cocktail in the ER without any resolution of symptoms.

CURRENT MEDICATIONS: Atenolol 50 mg once daily, Imdur 60 mg once daily, Zocor 10 mg daily, Furosemide 20 mg daily, aspirin 81 mg daily, calcium with Vitamin D supplement 400 mg twice daily.

Past medical history:

Medical illness includes borderline diabetes mellitus controlled by diet. DJD of right knee. Congestive heart failure. Atrial fibrillation and hypercholesterolemia.
PAST SURGICAL HISTORY: Right knee arthroscopic surgery. Cataract extraction in 1997. ALLERGIES: Sulfa

Family and social history:

Mother died of stroke and father of car accident. Sister recently died of a brain tumor. No surviving siblings. Denies alcohol or tobacco. One to two caffeinated beverages per day. Married and lives with wife in area.

Review of systems:

HEENT wears glasses. Has had cataract surgery on left. Denies asthma, rheumatic fever. No past history of peptic disease or any GI disturbance. Denied any blood in stool.

Physical exam:

Patient resting in CCU bed in no acute distress. Vital signs: pulse 118, respirations 14, BP 126/67. HEENT normal. Neck: soft and supple without lymphadenopathy. Cardiorespiratory: lungs clear to auscultation. Heart, normal S1, S1 without murmurs. Extremities 2+ pitting edema to lower shins bilaterally. Abdomen soft non-tender without mass. Back: no tenderness present.

Laboratory/radiology:

Troponin is 0. LDH 192, glucose 219, BUN 31, creatinine 1.3

EKG: Split t-waves, in V5 and V6. In atrial fibrillation in the upper 80s.

X-ray:

Assessment:

Unstable angina, rule out MI.

Plan:

Admit to CCU and follow closely.

[signature]

GODFREY REGIONAL HOSPITAL
123 Main Street • Aldon, FL 77714 • (407) 555-1234

Answers

HISTORY AND PHYSICAL EXAMINATION

Admitted: 01/01/XX

Medical record number:

CHIEF COMPLAINT: Chest pain

This 58-year-old developed chest pain acutely at approximately 6 PM this evening. Developed some diaphoresis and nausea. Pain radiated to back and left arm. Started on nitroglycerin drop and found to have ST depression. She had taken an aspirin on the way to the hospital.

Past medical history:

Surgeries include tonsillectomy 1935, appendectomy 1975, colonoscopy 1988. She has hypertension, COPD, dependent edema. She has type II diabetes mellitus, controlled with diet and hypocholesterolemia.

Family and social history:

Patient is a widow who lives with her youngest son. Has two brothers who have had CABG and father had CVA.

Review of systems:

Patient wears dentures and glasses. Denies any previous history of angina, chest pain, asthma, rheumatic fever, gastrointestinal. No history peptic disease or bowel problems. Denies blood in stool or black, tarry stools.

Physical exam:

Patient afebrile. Pulse 85, blood pressure 128/78, respirations 12. Weight 159 lbs. HEENT: PERRLA. Extraocular movements intact. Neck soft and supple without lymphadenopathy. Chest clear to auscultation with only occasional basilar rale auscultated. Cardiac exam reveals normal S1, S2 without murmurs, clicks or rubs. No jugular venous distension. Abdomen soft and nontender. Extremities without edema. Neuro testing is grossly normal.

Laboratory/radiology:

Reveals white blood cell count 9,700 with hemoglobin 13. Protime 9.6 with INR of 1 and PTT 26. EKG shows ST depression in leads V4 and V5.

X-ray:

Assessment:

Chest pain, unstable angina.

Plan:

Will admit to CCU. Rule out MI. Given aspirin, beta-blocker. Will continue nitroglycerin.

GODFREY REGIONAL HOSPITAL
123 Main Street • Aldon, FL 77714 • (407) 555-1234

Answers

EXERCISE 9A

DISCHARGE SUMMARY

Admitted: 07/01/XX
Discharged: 07/03/XX

Discharge diagnoses:

ADMITTING DIAGNOSIS:
Left-sided hemorrhagic CVA

DISCHARGE DIAGNOSIS:
1. Left-sided hemorrhagic CVA
2. Hypertension
3. GERD
4. History of delirium

History:

Patient is a DNR/DNI. Admitted, her steroids increased, and initial findings were right arm and leg weakness, positive Babinski on right.

By the time of discharge was using her right hand and able to move her right leg upon command. Other findings were UTI, for which she was placed on Cipro.

Laboratory and radiology studies:

Hospital course:

DISCHARGE PLANNING:
Continue Cipro for UTI for a total of ten doses. Prednisone 40 mg daily for ten days, taper to 30 for five days, then to 20. Cardizem CD 120 daily, Synthroid 0.125, Prilosec 20 daily.

DISCHARGE DIAGNOSIS:
1. Left-sided hemorrhagic CVA with improvement
2. Hyperthyroidism
3. GERD
4. UTI
5. History of tachycardia
6. Polymyalgia
7. DJD

GODFREY REGIONAL HOSPITAL
123 Main Street • Aldon, FL 77714 • (407) 555-1234

Answers

HISTORY AND PHYSICAL EXAMINATION

Admitted: 07/01/XX

Medical record number:

Patient arrives from a local nursing home where she was felt by nursing personnel to have right-sided weakness and initially aphasic. Also thought to be confused and not alert. When seen in the ER, could answer questions but unable to lift her right leg, some motions of her right arm, however unable to squeeze right hand. Found by ER physician to be confused, and difficult to understand. CT revealed large, left hemispheric bleed. Verbal report from radiology is this is a hematoma.

CURRENT MEDICATIONS:
Prilosec 20 qd, Synthroid .125 daily, Propulsid 10 bid, Prednisone 20 daily, Tylenol one gram bid, Cardizem CD 120 daily.

Past medical history:

From old charts. Remarkable for polymyalgia, GERD, hyperthyroid and DJD.

Family and social history:

Review of systems:

Unobtainable from patient.

Physical exam:

Patient is alert but confused. Not dysarthric. PERRL. Extraocular movements are normal. Slight right 7th nerve weakness. Lungs clear. Abdomen soft, nontender without guarding, rebound, masses. Full ROM for left arm and leg. Right arm is 4/5 power and able to squeeze weakly on command. Unable to raise her left leg or move it with positive Babinski on right.

Laboratory/radiology:

X-ray:

Assessment:

Intracranial bleed.

Plan:

Admit and observe.

GODFREY REGIONAL HOSPITAL
123 Main Street • Aldon, FL 77714 • (407) 555-1234

Answers

EXERCISE 10

HISTORY AND PHYSICAL EXAMINATION

Admitted: 03/01/XX

Medical record number:

CHIEF COMPLAINT: Right shoulder pain/fracture

Patient is a 54-year-old female who works as a health care worker. While out exercising last night she fell on her right shoulder. She has a comminuted fracture of the proximal humerus involving the humeral head, extending into the joint space. Admitted for observation and analgesia. CT of shoulder reveals the need for a humeral prosthesis. Some discomfort with deep inspiration. Unclear whether this is in the shoulder or possible right chest wall.

Past medical history:

Cholecystectomy 1986. ORIF left forearm, fracture same forearm age 9. Has some dependent edema and takes Lasix 80 mg qd for it. Does not wear compression stockings as they make her feet feel cold. Also diagnosis of fibromyalgia.

Family and social history:

Mother died age 64 post surgical pulmonary embolus.

Review of systems:

Negative

Physical exam:

Pleasant, uncomfortable, overweight female appearing her stated age and in no distress. HEENT normal, neck supple, thyroid normal. No JVD, carotids normal. Lungs decreased breath sounds at bases. Heart regular rate and rhythm. Abdomen obese. Extremities: normal range of motion of lower extremities. Motor sensory deep tendon reflexes are normal in arm. Trace pretibial edema bilaterally without venostasis changes. Excellent peripheral pulses. X-ray of shoulder and CT show comminuted fracture.

Laboratory/radiology:

X-ray:

Assessment:

Comminuted right proximal humeral fracture involving humeral head

Plan:

Admit for analgesia, IV fluids. Has a little nausea probably from analgesics. Won't have surgery until tomorrow. Preoperative labs, EKG and chest x-ray will be obtained prior to that time.

Maurice Doater MD

GODFREY REGIONAL HOSPITAL
123 Main Street • Aldon, FL 77714 • (407) 555-1234

Answers

HISTORY AND PHYSICAL EXAMINATION

Admitted: 02/01/XX

Medical record number:

CHIEF COMPLAINT: Hip pain

This nice 68-year-old lady is visiting us from up north. She was pulling out a sofa bed and fell fracturing her right hip. She apparently has had some alcohol at the time. Blood alcohol level was 126. She was brought to the emergency room for evaluation.

CURRENT MEDICATIONS: Multiple including Polaramine, quinine, Levoxyl, Cardura, Nephro, Zocor, Norvasc, Pepcid, Prempro. The patient is also on dialysis.

Past medical history:

Chronic renal failure with dialysis, congestive heart failure, status post coronary artery bypass graft. ALLERGIES: Allopurinol, penicillin

Family and social history:

FAMILY HISTORY: Noncontributory. SOCIAL HISTORY: She has been visiting since January. She has been having dialysis done three times per week at the local hospital. She is staying here with another family member.

Review of systems:

Otherwise negative listed above. She has had no chest pain and no shortness of breath.

Physical exam:

General appearance: the patient is alert, oriented times three. Generally she looks quite young. She communicates very well.
Vital signs: Stable; she is afebrile. HEENT: She does have hearing aids and is hard of hearing, however, seems to do an excellent job of understanding me. Neck: No jugular venous distention noted. Heart: Regular rate and rhythm with 3/6 holosystolic murmur. The coronary artery bypass graft scar was noted. Chest: Clear to auscultation bilaterally without any crackles or wheezes. She is in no respiratory distress. Abdomen: Soft. Nontender. Nondistended. Normal active bowel sounds. No masses. Extremities: No edema in the extremities, upper or lower. No varicosities are noted. No evidence of any deep venous thrombosis. The hip is tender. No ecchymosis is noted. The right leg is shorter than the left leg and externally rotated.

Laboratory/radiology:

White count 7.5, hemoglobin 13.5, hematocrit 46.5%, platelets 303,000. She is massively macrocytic at 119. Electrolytes are fairly good, glucose 92, BUN 20, creatinine 3.5, sodium and potassium are within normal limits. Alcohol level 128. ECG: Consistent with left ventricular hypertrophy.

X-ray:

Assessment:

Right hip fracture

Plan:

We will admit her and request the orthopedic surgeon see this patient for surgical intervention. We will manage her medications and arrange for dialysis during her admission.

We will also plan on controlling her pain with pain medications until consultation with the orthopedic surgeon. At that time, care for her fracture will most probably be assumed by Orthopedics.

GODFREY REGIONAL HOSPITAL
123 Main Street • Aldon, FL 77714 • (407) 555-1234

Answers

HISTORY AND PHYSICAL EXAMINATION

Admitted: 03/19/XX

Medical record number:

CHIEF COMPLAINT: Patient is readmitted for recurrent diarrhea.

INTERVAL HISTORY: Patient continues 5-Fluorouracil and Leucovorin given in standard fashion on an adjuvant basis for Stage II adenocarcinoma of the colon. When her diarrhea recurred, she was begun on oral antidiarrheals and these were ineffective.

She is unable to hold down fluids and is having as many as eight to ten bowel movements a day.

There is no formed stool, no blood in the stool, but unfortunately it is not resolving.

Standard protocol calls for admission for intravenous hydration and the use of Octreotide.

Past medical history:

Can be found in previous chart.
PAST SURGICAL HISTORY: Can be found in previous notes

Family and social history:

Previous chart

Review of systems:

Physical exam:

General appearance: Patient is a pleasant ill-appearing white female
Skin: Turgor is decreased significantly
HEENT: Pupils equal, react to light and accommodation
Heart: Regular rate and rhythm
Lungs: Clear
Abdomen: Soft, bowel sounds are present
Extremities: Nontender, nonedematous

Laboratory/radiology:

X-ray:

Assessment:

Gastrointestinal toxicity related to systemic chemotherapy.

Plan:

Will admit the patient and begin her on octreotide.
SHORT-TERM PROGNOSIS: Fair
LONG-TERM PROGNOSIS: Guarded

Felix Wanden MD

GODFREY REGIONAL HOSPITAL
123 Main Street • Aldon, FL 77714 • (407) 555-1234

Answers

HISTORY AND PHYSICAL EXAMINATION

Admitted: 03/31/XX

Medical record number:

The patient is a 95-year-old white female with a past medical history of atrial fibrillation and coronary artery disease. She had an acute episode of vertigo this morning while sitting on the edge of the bed. She had suffered a fall around 4:00 this morning. She also had chest pain which lasted about thirty seconds limited to the anterior chest. It was a dull ache without any radiation. She suffered some abrasions to the right lower extremity.

CURRENT MEDICATONS: Nitroglycerin 0.4 mg per hour, metoprolol 100 mg twice daily, Norpace 100 mg two in the morning, one in the evening, Lasix 20 mg bid, Tagamet 200 mg big, Meclizine 25 mg tid.

Past medical history:

Significant for atrial fibrillation, arteriosclerotic heart disease, legally blind secondary to macular degeneration, hysterectomy, tonsillectomy, coronary implants times four.
ALLERGIES: Penicillin

Family and social history:

Positive for CAD and cancer of the uterus. Does not smoke, alcohol occasionally.

Review of systems:

HEENT: Legally blind secondary to macular degeneration. Cardiovascular: History of angina. Respiratory: Negative. Gastrointestinal: Denies any abdominal pain, occasionally diarrhea. Genitourinary: History of stress incontinence, dysuria, urgency. Neuromuscular: Negative.

Physical exam:

Vital signs: Temperature, BP and respirations normal
HEENT: Atraumatic. Normocephalic. Eyes are status post iridectomy in both eyes. Tympanic membranes are grey. Nares patent. Pharynx shows upper denture without exudates.
Neck: Supple, no lymphadenopathy
Heart: S1 and S2, irregularly irregular
Chest: Bibasilar rales
Abdomen: Soft, nontender. There is an abdominal hernia noted
Extremities: Without cyanosis. One plus ankle edema.

Laboratory/radiology:

Sodium 140, potassium 3.5, chloride 102, BUN 18, creatinine 1, glucose 166. White blood cell count 8.24, hemoglobin 33.3, hematocrit 42%, platelets normal. CT of the head shows no bleed. Urinalysis showed four plus bacteria, nitrate positive. ECG: Shows atrial fibrillation. Precordial lead has poor R-wave progression.

X-ray:

Assessment:

Congestive heart failure. Urinary tract infection. Atrial fibrillation. Coronary artery disease. Legally blind.

Plan:

[signature]

GODFREY REGIONAL OUTPATIENT CLINIC
3122 Shannon Avenue • Aldon, FL 77712 • (407) 555-7654

Answers

PROGRESS NOTES

Date:	Vital signs:	T	R
Chief complaint:		P	BP

03/31/XX	Cardiology consult
	Patient complaining of continued vertigo. Will try Digoxin 0.125 mg
	[signature] Ruth Brady MD
04/01/XX	Cardiology visit
	Patient dizziness +
	Agree to continue Digoxin and discharge tomorrow if still stable at that time.
	[signature] Ruth Brady MD

Patient name:

DOB:

MR/Chart #:

GODFREY REGIONAL OUTPATIENT CLINIC
3122 Shannon Avenue • Aldon, FL 77712 • (407) 555-7654

Answers

HISTORY AND PHYSICAL EXAMINATION

Admitted: 02/10/XX

Medical record number:

REASON FOR ADMISSION: Management of hypertension and headache

PROBLEMS: 1. Uncontrolled hypertension 2. History of supraventricular tachycardia and atrial fib 3. History of diabetes mellitus

CURRENT MEDS: Zestril 10 mg po q day, Verapamil 180 mg po every day, Lasix 40 mg q day, nitroglycerin 0.2 mg patch, Zantac 150 mg po bid.

Patient came to the emergency room with chief complaint of severe headache, uncontrolled hypertension and palpitations. She denies any chest pain at this time.

She is being admitted for better control of her blood pressure as well as workup for headache.

Past medical history:

Family and social history:

Review of systems:

Physical exam:

Blood pressure 210/110, pulse 78 and regular
Respirations 14
Heart: Regular rate and rhythm
Chest: Clear to auscultation
Abdomen: Soft, nontender, nondistended
Extremities: Negative for cyanosis, clubbing or edema
EKG: Done earlier reveals normal sinus rhythm. No evidence of acute ischemia or infarction.

Laboratory/radiology:

X-ray:

Assessment:

Plan:

Patient is being admitted for control of blood pressure. We will increase her Zestril and will also add Norvasc 5 mg po q day.

Also will get a neurological consult for further evaluation and management.

Nancy Cauly MD

GODFREY REGIONAL HOSPITAL
123 Main Street • Aldon, FL 77714 • (407) 555-1234

Answers

EXERCISE 15A

DISCHARGE SUMMARY

Admitted: 12/06/XX
Discharged: 12/10/XX

Discharge diagnoses:

Final Diagnosis:
1. Metastatic breast cancer
2. Dehydration with confusion

History:

This is a 65-year-old woman who developed breast cancer approximately one year ago. She had surgery, chemotherapy, seemed to be doing well, but this fall, developed recurrence. This was present in the neck and liver. She underwent cycles of chemotherapy. Although her nodes in her neck subsided, she has had advancing cancer in the liver and does not seem to be responding to chemotherapy, and in fact, the chemotherapy is making her quite ill. This has been discussed with her family, and because this therapy is not going to cure her and is making her ill, she has decided to forego any more chemotherapy at this time which seems appropriate.

She has had some right flank pain, I presume from the liver metastases. She has had a very poor appetite, poor oral intake, and has become quite dehydrated and confused. She presented to the hospital in an extremely weak and confused condition. She was noted to have hyponatremia with sodium down to 125, extremely dry mucous membranes. White count was elevated to 16.5. Hemoglobin has been right around 10. Initial labs also suggested a urinary tract infection, although the culture did not grow anything.

Laboratory and radiology studies:

Hospital course:

She was admitted and treated with IV fluids, nausea medication and started on Cipro for presumed UTI. Her condition improved so that she became mentally clear. She continues to have poor oral intake and needs a lot of encouragement but is discharged home to be followed by hospice. Her long-term prognosis is poor, probably in the range of months.

Discharge medications include Cipro 500 mg for an additional 7 days. Compazine 10 mg po q 6 h for nausea, Ultram 1–2 tablets tid for pain, Senokot 1–2 tablets prn for constipation. Plan of care was discussed with her and her family and hospice will be following her.

Rachel Perez MD

GODFREY REGIONAL HOSPITAL
123 Main Street • Aldon, FL 77714 • (407) 555-1234

Answers

HISTORY AND PHYSICAL EXAMINATION

Admitted: 12/06/XX

Medical record number:

SOURCE OF HISTORY: Most of history is obtained from the sisters, some from the patient whose reliability is only fair.

HISTORY: Patient is brought in today following a nursing visit in the home finding her moderately confused and dehydrated. Patient was diagnosed with bronchitis and pneumonia about a month and a half ago and has not done real well since then. She has been decreasing her oral intake to just drinking water only and a few bites of something before she stops. Occasional vomiting and just sleeping a lot. Skin and eyes have become more jaundiced over the recent past. She has had low grade temp and chills. She sweats a lot. She has had some gait problems and has fallen several times in the past two weeks.

Patient had history of breast carcinoma of the right breast, status post modified radical mastectomy, four cycles of Adriamycin Cyclophosphamide chemotherapy, 5FU and methotrexate. Prominently known is her excessive liver metastases and an intrathoracic metastases.

Past medical history:

Her current medications are Ultram up to tid prn. Daypro rarely prn. Compazine and Atrivan rarely prn.

Family and social history:

Married for 43 years. She has seven children, six living. She has two brothers and one sister.
The sister is very involved in care and lives only five miles away.

Review of systems:

Significant for occasional diarrhea since she has been on antibiotics, occasional problems swallowing.
Husband has had a cough recently. She has been fairly depressed lately.

Physical exam:

SUBJECTIVE: Shows a pleasant, cooperative woman who is moderately confused but attempts to answer questions as appropriately as she can. She appears a little dazed when aroused from her sleepiness.
HEENT: Pupils equal, round and reactive to light. Fundi appear benign. TMs normal. Mucous membranes are quite tacky and dry.
Skin: Examination of skin shows significant dry patches. She has bruises over the left breast and right humeral area.
Lungs: Auscultation of lungs was difficult. She has only minimal inspiratory effort but no rales or wheezes are heard.
Heart: Regular rate and rhythm without murmurs.
Abdomen: Soft, apparently nontender, significant hepatomegaly 4–5 fingerbreadths below the margin with nodularity.
Chest wall: Shows absent right breast, and left breast without masses.
Extremities: Without edema. Peripheral pulses are palpable.

Laboratory/radiology:

Chest x-ray shows no acute process. CBC shows white count 16.5 with 75 segs, 9 bands and hemoglobin 9.6. Comprehensive panel shows glucose 276, sodium 125 and albumin 1.5. Liver function shows SGOT 343, bilirubin 2.1, alkaline phosphatase 636.

X-ray:

Assessment:

1. Dehydration	3. Hyperglycemia	5. Anemia secondary to above	7. Underlying depression
2. Hyponatremia	4. Breast carcinoma, extensively metastatic, with progression of liver mets	6. Elevated white count	

Plan:

Rachel Perez, MD

GODFREY REGIONAL HOSPITAL
123 Main Street • Aldon, FL 77714 • (407) 555-1234

Answers

HISTORY AND PHYSICAL EXAMINATION

Admitted: 01/16/XX

Medical record number:

This is a 92-year-old widowed woman recently discharged after a stay for weakness thought secondary to exacerbation of polymyalgia rheumatica and depression. History today mostly from the daughter, stated she hasnÖt done well since her discharge home. Over the weekend lost three pounds, was feeling weaker, had increased tachycardia, irregular heartbeat, and complaining of rattling in her chest. She has had cold symptoms for over a week. No chest pain. She has been probably short of breath for ten days to two weeks according to the daughter. She usually can get up to the bathroom with her walker however can barely do this. Has been eating less though no nausea or vomiting.

CURRENT MEDICATIONS: Digoxin 0.125 mg daily. Prevacid 15 mg daily, aspirin one to two daily on prn basis. Furosemide prn basis. Prednisone 10 mg qam, 5 mg qpm. Zoloft 50 mg daily.

Past medical history:

Prior hospitalization for appendectomy, pneumonia, acute peptic ulcer, atrial fib, renal calculi. Hospitalized for severe weakness due to depression in 1996. She is a gravida VI para VI, status post cataract extraction and lens implant.
ALLERGIES: No known allergies

Family and social history:

Widowed 19 years.

Review of systems:

Has been voiding frequently in small amount but no dysuria, has chronic fecal incontinence.
Does have chronic pedal edema.

Physical exam:

Shows an elderly woman lying with her oxygen on. Initial vitals are 140/70 BP, pulse 86, respirations 20. Temperature 98.3. Pupil is distorted from prior surgery. Fundi benign. TMs normal. Pharynx shows dry mucous membranes. Neck supple without adenopathy. Thyromegaly. Back without vertebral or CVA tenderness. Lungs show inspiratory and expiratory wheezes bilaterally. Heart is irregular and slightly tachycardic. Abdomen is obese, but soft nontender without organomegaly. Breast and pelvic exams are not done. Extremities are quite puffy but no pedal edema. Peripheral pulses are palpable.

With attempt at ambulation the patient was noted to have a sat of 83, had been on just room air of 88. With oxygen this came up to 94.

Laboratory/radiology:

WBC 12.4, platelet count is 134,000, 77 segs, 2 bands, glucose 193, rest of Chem 7 is normal.

X-ray:

Chest x-ray showed no definite acute changes.

Assessment:

1. Hypoxia with auscultated broncho-spasm. Probably due to viral versus bacterial respiratory infection.
2. Progressive weakness and debility
3. History of polymyalgia rheumatica
4. History of depression
5. History of peptic ulcer disease
6. Atrial fibrilation
7. Hyperglycemia probably due to increased steroids.

Plan:

Maurice Doater, MD

GODFREY REGIONAL HOSPITAL
123 Main Street ¥ Aldon, FL 77714 ¥ (407) 555-1234

Answers

HISTORY AND PHYSICAL EXAMINATION

Admitted: 01/11/XX

Medical record number:

Patient is a 69-year-old married white man admitted with chief complaint of upper abdominal pain. For the last three evenings he has had some upper abdominal pain worsening to the point of being quite severe. Seems to start on the left mid-epigastric area and radiates across his upper abdomen to the right. He feels bloated so much that even his back feels kind of a fullness sensation. He has no nausea or vomiting, stools have been looser to the point of being watery with diarrheal stools four to five times yesterday. Tried some Prilosec at home without relief. His MS in higher doses only helped slightly. He did have chills two nights ago but not last night, denies note of any fever.

CURRENT MEDICATIONS: Taking Lopressor 50 mg daily, temazepam 30 mg qhs. MC Contin 30 mg once daily, morphine elixir prn basis. He is on course of Decadron 40 mg daily for four days every 2 weeks.

Past medical history:

Prior hospitalizations include episode of transient global amnesia, DVT left arm, multiple myeloma, status post vasectomy, status post fractured right ankle and multiple repairs. Has been hospitalized for UTI. He has history of MI in the past and last work up known 50% proximal LAD lesion. ALLERGIES: Rash to Ciprofloxacin

Family and social history:

Married, lives at home with his wife. Up until fall was working driving big rigs.

Review of systems:

Patient notes he has had a hacky cough last 3–4 days. About 3–4 days ago exposed to Strep. Denies any problem with chest pain or cardiac symptoms.

Physical exam:

Weight 170, temperature 98.3, pulse 86, BP 120/72. Patient is obviously jaundiced and in no acute distress until he gets up to move about. Fundi are benign, TMs are normal, pharynx is clear. Neck supple without adenopathy or thyromegaly. Back without vertebral or CVA tenderness. Lungs clear. Heart regular rate and rhythm without murmurs. Abdomen is distended, tender in the mid-epigastric area and bilaterally upper quadrants without hepatosplenomegaly. Extremities without edema.

Laboratory/radiology:

BUN 29, total protein 8.1, albumin 2.7, SGOT 202, bili 6.3, alk-phos 421, amylase 203. Platelet count is 143,000. Flat and upright abdomen reveals couple of air fluid levels, stool in the right colon. Preliminary report on gallbladder u/s shows slightly dilated common duct at 7.5 mm with dilated intrahepatic duct, thickened gallbladder and gallstones.

X-ray:

Assessment:

1. Common duct stone with cholecystitis and pancreatic. Patient admitted for IV antibiotics.
2. Multiple myeloma refractory but clinically stable

3. History of MI with diffuse LAD lesion
4. Hypertension well controlled

Plan:

Patk Adam MD

GODFREY REGIONAL HOSPITAL
123 Main Street • Aldon, FL 77714 • (407) 555-1234

Answers

HISTORY AND PHYSICAL EXAMINATION

Admitted: 09/07/XX

Medical record number:

Patient is admitted with chief complaint of chest pain. Patient had onset of chest pain starting initially in the left shoulder and went into the shoulder blade and arm. Seemed to move more into his chest over time so at 0330 hours on the morning of admission he decided to come to the hospital. Has a long-standing history of stones with hiatal hernia and first thought that was what was bothering him.

Past medical history:

Current medications are Prilosec and Tagamet. He is on ICN 10 mg tid, DSS bid, Metamucil 1 tbsp bid. Allergies to penicillin. Prior hospitalizations for pneumonias and bronchitis. Status post appendectomy, status post TUR and herniorrhaphy, repair of hip fracture.

Family and social history:

Significant for father dying of CVA, mother dying of CVA but was always an invalid due to her heart. The patient had 3 siblings all died of cancer.

Review of systems:

Wears glasses. Complains of dry mouth recently. Does have occasional edema, no change. He does not drink, smoke, or take caffeine at all. Otherwise, ROS is unremarkable.

Physical exam:

Shows a patient laying in bed in no acute distress. Blood pressure was 110/70 with a pulse of 70.
HEENT: Pupils equal, round, reactive to light. Fundi benign.
Neck: Supple without adenopathy, thyromegaly or JVD
Lungs: Clear
Back: No CVA tenderness
Heart: Regular rate and rhythm, soft diastolic murmur
Abdomen: Soft, nontender
Extremities: Without edema. Peripheral pulses full and symmetric.

Laboratory/radiology:

ECG shows right bundle branch block which is not new. However, there is T-wave blunting and inversion in I and avL which is change as well as deep Q-waves in V1 through V3 which is also new. CBC shows hemoglobin of 11.3, PT PTT are normal. Creatinine elevated at 1.5, BUN 20, LDH 193, troponin 14.8, CK 225.

X-ray:

Assessment:

1. Myocardial infarction   2. History of GERD   3. Recent problem with constipation

Plan:

[signature] M

GODFREY REGIONAL HOSPITAL
123 Main Street • Aldon, FL 77714 • (407) 555-1234

Answers

HISTORY AND PHYSICAL EXAMINATION

Admitted: 09/23/XX

Medical record number:

This is a 49-year-old with a long history of cardiac dysrhythmias who had an episode where she felt unable to get up and go to the bathroom because she felt she was going to fall. She says she just shook, felt very light headed and felt like she was going to faint. This lasted for about an hour and then she called a friend to bring her to the hospital. She had no chest pain or pressure, no shortness of breath, no nausea, no history of upper respiratory infection. Because of this episode and what sounded like a near syncope and the fact she has had cardiac dysrhythmias in the past, she was admitted for telemetry to monitor her rhythm. Has a history of both atrial tachycardias and had an episode of third-degree heart block earlier in the year. She has declined to get a pacemaker.

In the ED she was noted to have atrial fibrillation in her usual rhythm with rates in the 70s and 80s. Occasional PVCs. Cardiac enzymes were normal, although her potassium was somewhat low at 3.3. Troponin was 0, digoxin level 0.7.

CURRENT MEDICATIONS: Digoxin 0.125 mg daily, Prinvil 10 mg po daily, hydrochlorathiazide 25 mg daily, potassium 10 mEq daily.

Past medical history:

Includes cardiac dysrhythmias with syncopal episodes. History of congestive heart failure, hypertension and glaucoma. Blindness in her right eye, history of colon polyps, appendectomy at age 35.
ALLERGIES: None

Family and social history:

Mother died of CVA at age 80, brother as mentioned with Parkinson's.
Non-smoker, non-drinker. Patient lives in an apartment and has brother with Parkinson's.

Review of systems:

Noncontributory

Physical exam:

Fully alert woman who is mentally alert and not distressed at the moment. Blood pressure 180/82, pulse 68, and irregular. She is on telemetry now showing afib with controlled rate. Respirations are 16, and she is afebrile. ENT unremarkable, lungs sound clear without evidence of CHF. Heart has a light systolic murmur. Abdomen was soft with normal bowel sounds and no masses. Good circulation in legs without edema.

Laboratory/radiology:

X-ray:

Assessment:

1. Near syncope rule out cardiac dysrhythmia   2. Congestive heart failure compensated   3. Hypertension compensated

Plan:

Admit patient to telemetry. Will check some cardiac enzymes, keep her on her usual medications and see how she progresses.

Robert Rai MD

GODFREY REGIONAL HOSPITAL
123 Main Street • Aldon, FL 77714 • (407) 555-1234

Answers

HISTORY AND PHYSICAL EXAMINATION

Admitted: 07/21/XX

Medical record number:

Patient is a 53-year-old male who was in his normal state of health until 5 days ago when he vomited 4–5 times. Did feel mildly feverish with some chills on that day. Felt somewhat better over the next day or two but symptoms returned. Over the course of today, nausea was subsequently worsened and even after IV phenergan and fluids in the ER unable to tolerate fluids. Denies any loose stools, no chest pain, no SOB, no cough, no fever. No dysuria although decreased frequency.

CURRENT MEDS: Prozac, Azmacort and Combivent inhalers

Past medical history:

Significant for COPD with chronic bronchitis. History of depression and alcoholism although has not been drinking in the past several years.

Family and social history:

He is a 1 1/2 pack smoker, smoking for the past 35 years.

Review of systems:

Physical exam:

Reveals a pleasant male, no acute distress. Initial BP 171/91, temperature 98.2, pulse 56, respiratory rate 20. HEENT essentially unremarkable. Neck is normal. Chest is clear to auscultation bilaterally. Cardiovascular exam reveals regular rate and rhythm, no murmur, rub, or gallop. Abdominal exam has some minimal epigastric and bilateral upper quadrant discomfort with deep palpation. Abdomen is soft, has no guarding or rebound. Murphy's sign is negative. Extremities without edema and well perfused.

Laboratory/radiology:

Chem. 7 normal. Had a recent abdominal ultrasound that was reported as normal. He had an EKG performed which is reviewed and normal.

X-ray:

Assessment:

Nausea and vomiting with inability to tolerate p.o. No fever, recent normal white count, liver functions and abdominal u/s. The most likely etiology at this point is viral process/gastroenteritis.

Plan:

Prudent to admit him for IV fluid, rehydration and antiemetics.

Willem Obst MD

GODFREY REGIONAL HOSPITAL
123 Main Street • Aldon, FL 77714 • (407) 555-1234

Answers

22 Monitoring and Compliance Process

Change instructions as follows:

Step 1: Review the following 20 medical charts and assign the appropriate E & M and CPT codes.

Step 2: Record the code assignments for these charts on the Chart Review Logsheet.

Step 3: Record the following assignments of CPT codes for these charts by the practice. Note that several of the code assignments may be incorrect.

Chart 1	99214
Chart 2	99213
Chart 3	99215
Chart 4	99221
Chart 5	99212
Chart 6	99204
Chart 7	99212
Chart 8	99282
Chart 9	99212
Chart 10	99212
Chart 11	99215
Chart 12	99242
Chart 13	36558
Chart 14	49520
Chart 15	59514
Chart 16	33208
Chart 17	66984-RT
Chart 18	33208
Chart 19	99329
Chart 20	99215

Step 4: Complete the Chart Audit Logsheet, noting any discrepancies.

Step 5: Complete the calculations from any discrepancies. Your instructor will have the reimbursement amounts for the correct/incorrect procedures.

Step 6: Complete the chart audit process outlined in the textbook.

Step 7: Prepare a chart audit report from your findings.

CHART AUDIT LOGSHEET

Date _____

Practice _____

Date of Service	Physician/ Provider	Patient Name	Chart # Patient #	Code Submitted	Coder Review	Change Up	Change Down	Reason	Calculation + / −

PROGRESS NOTE

Chief complaint: _____

Date: _____

Vital signs: BP _____   P _____   R _____

History:

Patient has had pain over the right breast for the last month now. She was seen initially by Dr. Seers and then reexamined recently. She still has pain at 9 o'clock mark close to the areolar/breast junction.

Family history pertinent for breast cancer in grandmother.

Exam:

Cannot really appreciate any distinct mass although when I squeezed around the periareolar area I was able to express clear glary draining fluid from the nipple. This is typically not the type of appearance one would see with intraductal papilloma. Not clear why this should affect just the right breast. If related to hormone therapy that she has been on for the past several years, it would appear in both breasts. Mammograms have been normal. Ultrasound has suggested cyst but cannot palpate any real distinct mass.

Diagnosis/assessment:

I saw no evidence of any signs of infection. I will treat empirically with Augmentin and will discuss this case further with the general surgeon. Needle localization would not seem useful as we are unable to palpate a mass.

Maurice Doater, MD

Patient name: _____

Date of service: _____

GODFREY MEDICAL ASSOCIATES
1532 Third Avenue, Suite 120 • Aldon, FL 77713 • (407) 555-4000

Answers

PROGRESS NOTE

Chief complaint: __Possible hypertension__

Date: __06/13/XX__

DOB: __2/26/19XX__

Vital signs: BP_____ P_____ R_____

MR/Chart #: __11438__

History:

68-year-old female who does have a history of elevation of blood pressure. Has not had any chest pain, shortness of breath, PND, orthopnea.

She did have a dizzy spell several months ago and had an MRI and ultrasound which were essentially normal.

Exam:

Her blood pressure today was 180/120, and subsequently during her examination, her blood pressure was recorded as 175/110, 180/110, 174/108.

Diagnosis/assessment:

She will be started on Norvasc 10 mg bid and she is to keep a blood pressure diary for the next 2–3 weeks and return at that time for further evaluation.

ASSESSMENT:
Hypertension

Robert Rai MD

Patient name: __Louise Maylor__

Date of service: __06/13/XX__

GODFREY MEDICAL ASSOCIATES
1532 Third Avenue, Suite 120 • Aldon, FL 77713 • (407) 555-4000

Answers

Chapter **22 Monitoring and Compliance Process**

EXERCISE 3

EMERGENCY ROOM RECORD

Name:		Age: 26	ER physician:
Tracey Hockler		DOB: 6/5/19XX	*Nancy Connelly M.D.*

Allergies/type of reaction:	Usual medications/dosages:

Triage/presenting complaint:

Abdominal cramping—pregnant

Initial assessment:

Pregnant 26-year-old female complaining of abdominal cramps

Time	T	P	R	BP	Other:					

Medication orders:

Lab work:

X-Ray:

Physician's report:

26-year-old female presents with abdominal cramping. She is 26–28 weeks pregnant. Upon further investigation, she had a busy day and sat near an air conditioner instead of drinking fluids. She had vomited once. She indicates some pressure in the suprapubic area and a pulling feeling. Physical exam is entirely unremarkable. FHTs were 140.

Mild abdominal cramping, possibility of early Braxton Hick's phenomenon may be present, but not of severity to pursue now.

Diagnosis:	Physician sign/date
Abdominal pain	*Nancy Connelly MD* 9/14/XX

Discharge	Transfer	Admit	Good	Satisfactory	Other:

GODFREY REGIONAL HOSPITAL
123 Main Street • Aldon, FL 77714 • (407) 555-1234

Answers

PROGRESS NOTE

Date: 03/12/XX	**Vital signs:**	T		R	
Chief complaint: Recurrent heartburn		P		BP	

Patient presents with recurrent heartburn for the past 5–10 years. It has worsened however in the past year. Rolaids and other antacids no longer take care of the symptoms. He has been on Prevacid and if he stops, the symptoms get worse. He smokes 1–2 packs per day, drinks 2–3 cans of beer per day. His weight has been stable. No dysphagias, no abdominal discomfort, no SOB, no other problems.

Medications include 30 mg Prevacid on a regular basis. No allergies. Father died of lung cancer, brother died in Vietnam, other brother died in MVA. He has 3 daughters.

Overall weight is stable. Denies chest pain, tightness, heaviness or any other discomfort other than heartburn. No fever, chills, sweats, or cough.

Examination:

Physical exam is height 5' 10", weight 305. Oxygen saturation 90% on room. BP 138/64, respirations 18, pulse 69, temperature 97.3. HEENT normal. Lymph, no cervical lymphadenopathy. Lungs clear, heart regular rate without murmur. Abdomen is obese, bowel sounds normal. Extremities warm without cyanosis, clubbing or edema.

Impression:

Plan:

Will order colonoscopy for persistent and progressive heartburn.

Willen Obst MD

Patient name: Rudy Stinton
DOB: 10/01/19XX
MR/Chart #: 91552

GODFREY REGIONAL OUTPATIENT CLINIC
3122 Shannon Avenue • Aldon, FL 77712 • (407) 555-7654

Answers

Chapter **22** **Monitoring and Compliance Process**

EMERGENCY ROOM RECORD

Name:		Age: 7	ER physician:
Dylan Koldmann		DOB: 8/5/19XX	Nancy Connelly M.D.

Allergies/type of reaction:	Usual medications/dosages:

Triage/presenting complaint:

Injury to hand

Initial assessment:

7-year-old fell off bike, injured hand, unable to flex first digit, R hand

Time	T	P	R	BP	Other:					

Medication orders:

Lab work:

X-Ray:

Physician's report:

7-year-old sustained injury to right hand when fell off bike. Pain over thenar eminence. Able to bend at his wrist and flex at his DIP and PIP joints and every digit of the hand with exception of first digit.

Exam of right hand is significant for mild protrusion but no ecchymosis and minimal edema overlying thenar eminence of the right hand. Good wrist mobility. X-ray significant for what appears to be a Salter-Harris fracture of the first metacarpal. Immobile and follow-up tomorrow with Ortho for possible cast.

Diagnosis:	Physician sign/date
Right 1st metacarpal fracture	Nancy Connelly MD 11/13/XX

Discharge	Transfer	Admit	Good	Satisfactory	Other:

GODFREY REGIONAL HOSPITAL
123 Main Street • Aldon, FL 77714 • (407) 555-1234

Answers

PROGRESS NOTE

Date:	Vital signs:	T		R
Chief complaint: Abdominal pain and vaginal bleeding		P		BP

This 32-year-old female states her last menstrual period ended approximately 20 days ago. She presents today with heavy vaginal bleeding with passage of clots, crampy lower abdominal pain, right quadrant. She has also felt weak.

She is on birth control but states she has only taken 1 tablet.

Gravida 1 Para 1. History of normal vaginal delivery approximately 10 years ago.

Examination:

There is minimal amount of blood in the vaginal vault. No tissue noted. Cervix is normal in appearance. The os is closed. The fundus of the uterus was not well appreciated.

Serum pregnancy testing was negative. The white blood cell count was 11,300 with normal hemoglobin and hematocrit.

Impression:

DIAGNOSIS:
Vaginal bleeding
Possible PID

Plan:

Maurice Doates MD

Patient name:

DOB:

MR/Chart #:

GODFREY REGIONAL OUTPATIENT CLINIC
3122 Shannon Avenue • Aldon, FL 77712 • (407) 555-7654

Answers

EXERCISE 7

PROGRESS NOTE

Date:	Vital signs:	T	R
Chief complaint:		P	BP

68-year-old female patient was seen due to progressively generalized weakness and decrease in mental status. Patient is followed up at home by nursing personnel on weekly visits. There has been no cough, although patient has been complaining of abdominal pain on and off. The patient vomited upon arrival. There was no blood in the vomitus. No chest pain or shortness of breath.

Physical examination:

Exam was entirely within normal limits, except the patient was unable to follow commands and could not recall the current president.

Assessment:

Right lower lobe pneumonia
Rule out sepsis
Hypokalemia
Dehydration

Plan:

The patient at this time has a clinical picture compatible with sepsis. She does have a right lower lobe pneumonia. She has hypokalemia and intravenous potassium will be administered.

Maurice Doates, MD

	Patient name:
	DOB:
	MR/Chart #:

GODFREY REGIONAL OUTPATIENT CLINIC
3122 Shannon Avenue • Aldon, FL 77712 • (407) 555-7654

Answers

PROGRESS NOTE

Chief complaint: _Stepped on nail_

Date: _03/12/XX_

DOB: _2/16/19XX_

Vital signs: BP_____ P_____ R_____

MR/Chart #: _48333_

History:

42-year-old man stepped on a nail three days ago. Believes there may be something in the foot and has developed redness, swelling, and pain in that area.

He does have a past medical history of diabetes mellitus.

Exam:

Puncture wound over mid ball of right foot with redness, increased warmth, and swelling.

Diagnosis/assessment:

Will begin Keflex 500 mg tid for 10 days.
ASSESSMENT:
Cellulitis of right foot

Willem Obst MD

Patient name: _Leroy Patterson_

Date of service: _03/12/XX_

GODFREY MEDICAL ASSOCIATES
1532 Third Avenue, Suite 120 • Aldon, FL 77713 • (407) 555-4000

Answers

PROGRESS NOTE

Date:		Vital signs:	T		R	
Chief complaint:			P		BP	

32-year-old male states he has been having frequent spells where he feels he is going to pass out. Says following a head injury as a child he was placed on Ativan and this seemed to help. Patient states currently he feels as though he is going to pass out. He either wants to see a neurologist immediately or be put back on his Ativan.

Examination:

Exam was unremarkable. PERRLA/EOMI intact. Heart, lungs and abdomen were unremarkable. No family history significant.

Impression:

Patient is also concerned his blood pressure may be high; however, he does not have any history of high blood pressure or hypertension.

Plan:

I do not feel at this time this patient has a history of seizures, but anxiety attacks. I am willing to treat this patient for anxiety, however, if he wishes to be evaluated for seizures, he will need to see a neurologist.

Maurice Doater, MD

Patient name:

DOB:

MR/Chart #:

GODFREY REGIONAL OUTPATIENT CLINIC
3122 Shannon Avenue • Aldon, FL 77712 • (407) 555-7654

Answers

CONSULTATION REPORT
GODFREY REGIONAL OUTPATIENT CLINIC

Patient:
Date of consultation:
Consulting physician:
Referring physician:
Indication for consultation:

History:

This patient is a very pleasant 58-year-old male. He is an extremely hyper, type A personality who spends a great deal of time with his work. Basically, this patient has had hypertension for 30 years. He has been on just about every medication that has ever come out with variable results in management of his hypertension.

He is currently on Minipress 5 mg tid, Catapres 1 mg tid, Lopressor 100 mg tid. Lasix 40 mg a day, and on a 4 g sodium diet.

Exam:

Patient's pulse is 50, regular. Blood pressure 138/70, fundi show very minimal arteriovenous nicking in each eye. There is a bruit noted in the right carotid area. There is an S4 noted. There is a very faint systolic ejection murmur along the left sternal border.

EKG performed shows sinus bradycardia at 50 beats per minute. There are changes consistent with old inferior infarction.

Diagnosis/assessment:

IMPRESSION:
S/P acute inferior wall infarction with residual sinus bradycardia
Long-term chronic hypertension

Will perform a Holter monitor to determine extent of his sinus bradycardia. If his rate drops into the 40s I would then consider atrial pacing and whether there is a need for a permanent atrial pacemaker.

Maurice Doaters, MD

Patient name: _____
Date of service: _____

GODFREY REGIONAL OUTPATIENT CLINIC
3122 Shannon Avenue • Aldon, FL 77712 • (407) 555-7654

Answers

CONSULTATION REPORT
GODFREY REGIONAL OUTPATIENT CLINIC

Patient:
Date of consultation:
Consulting physician:
Referring physician:
Indication for consultation:

History:

The patient received multiple transfusions for his multiple vascular surgeries. There was no history of any jaundice following any of these transfusions, although he relates some jaundice many, many years ago, with the etiology at that time being unclear. He has manifested no symptoms referable to liver disease and generally remains asymptomatic in this regard. There is no history of significant alcohol intake or recent travel, and the only drug one could implicate in his hepatitis is Aldomet, which he has been on for only one year.

Exam:

His physical examination revealed that his liver extended 3 to 4 fingerbreadths below his right costal margin and was firm; however, no other signs of liver disease, namely, spider angiomata or palmar erythema, were present. We have found that his SGOT was elevated at least as far back as February. Several repeat blood tests have shown varying degrees of elevation of the bilirubin and transaminases. Additionally, his globulins have been elevated, and his pro time has been mildly prolonged to approximately 50% of control.

Diagnosis/assessment:

It seems likely that the patient has chronic liver disease from his transfusions in the 1980s, the etiology being hepatitis C. It is unlikely that Aldomet is contributing to his elevated transaminases, as the elevations have been documented prior to the Aldomet usage. The possible chronic liver diseases include chronic persistent hepatitis, chronic active hepatitis, and the possible development of cirrhosis. I am concerned about the development of cirrhosis in view of the prolonged pro time and the elevated globulin level, although one cannot be sure regarding this diagnosis without a liver biopsy.

In view of his mild enzyme elevations and his asymptomatic state in regard to his liver disease, despite a liver biopsy showing chronic active hepatitis, I could not imagine treating him with immunosuppressive therapy in view of his age and general medical condition. Additionally, it is still unknown at this time what the natural history of this disease is, as well as whether there is any significant response to steroid therapy in terms of prognosis. As well, with his mildly prolonged pro time, this would pose a slightly increased risk for the liver biopsy that at this time I do not feel is warranted in view of the unlikelihood of any treatment based on the liver biopsy findings.

We will simply watch him and have repeat liver tests in approximately 3 months. Should the disease progress in any way or he become symptomatic or new data become available on the use of steroids in the treatment of hepatitis C liver disease, then we may reassess the need for liver biopsy at that time.

Patk Adam MD

Patient name: _____

Date of service: _____

GODFREY REGIONAL OUTPATIENT CLINIC
3122 Shannon Avenue • Aldon, FL 77712 • (407) 555-7654

Answers

CONSULTATION REPORT
GODFREY REGIONAL OUTPATIENT CLINIC

Patient:
Date of consultation:
Consulting physician:
Referring physician:
Indication for consultation:

History:

PULMONARY MEDICINE CONSULTATION
This is a 32-year-old East Indian male, lifelong nonsmoker, referred to me. He complains of a less than 2-week history of dry cough associated with dull substernal discomfort and dyspnea, particularly on exertion. Otherwise, he has been remarkably free of any other associated symptoms. In particular, he denies any preceding cold or flu or allergic exposure. He denies any associated fevers, chills, night sweats, or weight loss.

He admits to having childhood asthma, but felt he grew out of this by the time he was a teenager. He has traveled extensively throughout the U.S., including travel to the California deserts and Central Valley. He has not had pneumonia vaccine. He had a TB skin test 10 years ago and a flu vaccine 3 years ago.

PAST MEDICAL HISTORY:
Past medical history is remarkably negative.

Exam:

PHYSICAL EXAMINATION:
Blood pressure 140/80, pulse 85, respiratory rate 22, temperature 99.3. Chest exam is completely normal, with no rales, wheezes, rhonchi, or rubs. Even on forced exhalation there was no cough or prolongation. Cardiac exam showed a regular rate and rhythm with no murmur or gallop.

LABORATORY DATA:
PA chest x-ray is striking for a new interstitial infiltrate seen in both mid-lung zones with some shagging of the cardiac borders, indicating involvement of the lingula and right middle lobe. Surprisingly, the lowest part of the lung fields and the apices appear to be spared.

Spirometry before and after bronchodilator performed in my office shows a vital capacity of 3.79 or 69% after an 11% improvement with bronchodilator. The *FEV1* achieves 3.24 liters or 72% of predicted after 12% improvement with bronchodilator. The FEV1/FVC ratio was mildly increased at 85 instead of predicted 82.

Diagnosis/assessment:

ASSESSMENT AND PLAN:
Differential diagnosis includes the following:
1. Hypersensitivity pneumonia.
2. Mycoplasmal pneumonia.
3. Less likely candidates appear to be Wegener's Granulomatosis, Goodpasture's syndrome, sarcoidosis, alveolar proteinosis, and allergic bronchopulmonary aspergillosis.

Patient name: _____

Date of service: _____

GODFREY REGIONAL OUTPATIENT CLINIC
3122 Shannon Avenue • Aldon, FL 77712 • (407) 555-7654

Answers

OPERATIVE REPORT

Patient information:

Patient name:
DOB:
MR#:

Preoperative diagnosis:

Acquired immune deficiency syndrome.

Postoperative diagnosis:

Acquired immune deficiency syndrome.

Procedure(s) performed:

Insertion of Hickman catheter
ESTIMATED BLOOD LOSS: Approximately 5 cc.
IV FLUIDS: Approximately 250 cc of lactated Ringer's.

Anesthesia:

Local

Assistant surgeon:

Description of procedure:

Patient was brought to the operating room and placed in the supine position. The left shoulder was prepped and draped in the usual sterile manner. Approximately 8 cc of 1% lidocaine without epinephrine was used to infiltrate the skin and subcutaneous tissue in the area of the clavicle. Access was gained to the subclavian vein via the percutaneous approach with good blood return. The double-lumen Hickman catheter was fed over a wire and introduced through the subclavian vein. Position of the tip was confirmed to be in the superior vena cava by fluoroscopy. A subcutaneous tunnel was made from the percutaneous puncture site down to a level of approximately 2 cm medial and 2+ cm caudad of the left nipple.

The Hickman catheter was then brought down the tunnel and brought exteriorly at the level of the exit site with good venous return from all three ports. A stat portable chest x-ray in the recovery room revealed no pneumothorax as well as the catheter tip being in position in the superior vena cava. The wounds were dressed with Telfa and Tegaderm in the operating room. Patient tolerated the procedure well and went to the recovery room in stable condition.

Jay Corm MD

GODFREY REGIONAL HOSPITAL
123 Main Street • Aldon, FL 77714 • (407) 555-1234

Answers

OPERATIVE REPORT

Patient information:
Patient name: DOB: MR#:

Preoperative diagnosis:
Recurrent right inguinal hernia.

Postoperative diagnosis:
Recurrent right inguinal hernia.

Procedure(s) performed:
Right inguinal hernia repair.

Anesthesia:

Assistant surgeon:

Description of procedure:
After the patient was placed supine on the operating table and a proper level of anesthesia was attained, the abdomen was prepped and draped in the usual sterile fashion. A right groin incision was made and carried through the subcutaneous tissue, through Scarpa's fascia, and to the external oblique fascia. The external oblique fascia was opened from the internal inguinal ring to the external inguinal ring. The ilioinguinal nerve was identified and preserved. The cord was mobilized and a defect was found medially. This was a direct inguinal hernia recurrence. The floor was entirely opened up, and a hernia repair was carried out by reapproximating the conjoined tendon down to Cooper's ligament with a running 0 Prolene stitch. This was carried out until a transition suture was placed, and then the conjoined tendon was reapproximated to the shelving edge until the internal inguinal ring was snug. The external oblique was dosed over the cord with a running 3-0 Vicryl suture, the subcutaneous tissue with 3-0 plain, and the skin with a running 4-0 subcuticular Dexon stitch. The patient's wound was dressed, and he was sent to the recovery room in satisfactory condition. *Adm Westy MD*

GODFREY REGIONAL HOSPITAL
123 Main Street • Aldon, FL 77714 • (407) 555-1234

Answers

OPERATIVE REPORT

Patient information:

Patient name:
DOB:
MR#:

Preoperative diagnosis:

1. Intrauterine pregnancy, 40 weeks.
2. Arrest of descent with 3 hours pushing in second stage, failed trial of vacuum.
3. Chorioamnionitis.

Postoperative diagnosis:

Same.

Procedure(s) performed:

Primary low transverse c/section

Anesthesia:

Continuous lumbar epidural.

Assistant surgeon:

Description of procedure:

The patient became exhausted after approximately 3 hours of pushing in the second stage, wide descent of the vertex to +2 in the OT position. She had been on cefotetan since developing a fever during the second stage. After discussion of concerns and alternatives, it was decided to proceed with a trial of vacuum. She had a Foley catheter in place. Fetal heart tones were monitored continuously during the procedure and were stable. With placement of vacuum over the occiput area was absolutely no descent with two attempts at extraction with patient's efforts to push during a contraction. Attempts to continue a vaginal delivery were halted, the Pitocin augmentation was discontinued, and the intrauterine pressure catheter was removed. She was taken to the operating room after full informed consent was obtained. The epidural was adjusted for abdominal surgical analgesia.

The patient was prepped and draped in the usual manner for an abdominal procedure. A low transverse skin incision was made with the scalpel, and through a Pfannenstiel approach the peritoneum exposed and entered relatively high, care being taken to avoid underlying bowel. The incision was extended superiorly and inferiorly, with care being taken to avoid the bladder. Palpation revealed the vertex to be well down into the pelvis. The anterior leaf of the broad ligament was incised and the incision extended laterally in both directions and a bladder flap formed by a combination of sharp and blunt dissection. This was held out of the way with the bladder retractors, and a uterine incision was made in the midline with the scalpel. This was extended in both directions by gentle blunt traction. The vertex was found to be OT, +2 station, and well wedged into the pelvis and was removed from the pelvis with some difficulty. Once it had been elevated, the delivery of the head was accomplished with ease. Because of light meconium the mouth and nares were suctioned on the perineum thoroughly. The shoulders and remainder of the baby were delivered without difficulty, the cord clamped and cut, and the neonate handed off to the waiting pediatrician. A segment of cord was obtained for cord blood gases. The 9 pound 5 ounce female was delivered at 0211 on 3/20/99. Had Apgars of 9 and 9 and UA pH of 7.319.

Rachel Perez MD

GODFREY REGIONAL HOSPITAL
123 Main Street • Aldon, FL 77714 • (407) 555-1234

Answers

OPERATIVE REPORT

Patient information:

Patient name:
DOB:
MR#:

Preoperative diagnosis:

Presyncope with intermittent junctional bradycardia.

Postoperative diagnosis:

Same.

Procedure(s) performed:

Dual-chamber DDD transvenous pacemaker placement.
PACEMAKER GENERATOR: Pacesetter Model 2010T

Anesthesia:

Assistant surgeon:

Description of procedure:

The patient was prepped and draped in the usual manner. Using sedation and 1% Xylocaine anesthesia, an infraclavicular incision was made. The pocket was carried down to the fascia and placed subfascially. Then the subclavian vein was located with a needle and a guide wire placed into the vein. Two introducers were placed over this wire, and the atrial and ventricular leads placed into the superior vena cava. Then the atrial lead was put into place and the leads screwed in. Then the ventricular lead was placed in the ventricular apex.

Thresholds were measured as obtained and were found to be quite adequate. The lead was checked for length on fluoroscopy and then attached into the pocket around a collar with a 2-0 silk suture. Then the leads and generator were connected together and the pacemaker placed into the pocket.

Incision was closed and the patient was taken to the recovery room in excellent condition.

GODFREY REGIONAL HOSPITAL
123 Main Street • Aldon, FL 77714 • (407) 555-1234

Answers

Chapter **22** **Monitoring and Compliance Process**

RADIOLOGY REPORT

MR#:
DOB:
Dr.

Clinical summary:

PREOPERATIVE DIAGNOSIS:
Cataract of right eye.
SURGICAL PROCEDURE:
Extracapsular cataract extraction with lens implant of right eye.

Abdomen:

Conclusion:

PROCEDURE:
The patient was placed in the supine position on the operating room table after having received preoperative sedation and dilating drops to the right eye. An O'Brien akinesia of the right eye was done using 4 cc of a mixture containing two-thirds Marcaine 0.75% and one-third Xylocaine 2% plain. A retrobulbar block was given through the lower lid temporally using 3 cc of the same. Light digital pressure was applied for a few minutes, and satisfactory anesthesia was achieved. The right eye and face were prepped with 0.5% Betadine solution and draped in a sterile fashion.

A lid speculum was inserted into the right eye and 4-0 silk traction sutures passed through the superior and inferior rectus muscles. The Zeiss operating microscope was swung into position. A conjunctival peritomy was opened over the superior 140 at the limbus and episcleral bleeders cauterized. A groove was made in the surgical limbus with a #64 Beaver blade and a 7-0 silk suture passed at 12 o'clock. The anterior chamber was entered at 11 o'clock with a razor blade knife and an irrigating cystitome used to do a 360 anterior capsulotomy. Dissection was completed with scissors, and the lens nucleus was expressed. The 7-0 silk suture was tied and cut, and an additional 8-0 Vicryl was placed 3.5 mm on either side of silk. The Cavitron AIS irrigating-aspirating needle was placed into the anterior chamber, and using BSS (balanced salt solution) for irrigation, the lens cortex was removed and the posterior capsule remained intact. The posterior capsule was polished and the capsular bag filled with Amvisc. The 7-0 silk sutures were removed.

An Iolab intraocular lens, model G157E, power +24.0 diopters, control #011288G157E5902, was inspected under the microscope and appeared to be grossly free of defects. It was grasped with angulated McPherson forceps and placed into the capsular bag. The implant was rotated to the 3 to 9 o'clock position with a Sinskey hook. The Amvisc was replaced with BSS and the pupil constricted with Miochol. The incision was closed securely with nine additional 10-0 nylon sutures. The conjunctiva was drawn over the suture line and coapted at 3 and 9 o'clock with bipolar cautery. Garamycin 20 mg and 20 mg of Kenalog were injected subconjunctivally below, and a patch and Fox shield were put in place. Prior to the patch, a drop of Timoptic was placed on the cornea. The patient tolerated the procedure well and returned to the outpatient surgery area in good condition.

Ddt/mm

D:
T:

Linda Patrick, M.D.

Linda Patrick, M.D.   Date

GODFREY REGIONAL HOSPITAL
123 Main Street • Aldon, FL 77714 • (407) 555-1234

Answers

OPERATIVE REPORT

Patient information:

Patient name:
DOB:
MR#:

Preoperative diagnosis:

Intermittent atrial flutter/fibrillation with severe ventricular bradycardia.

Postoperative diagnosis:

Intermittent atrial flutter/fibrillation with severe ventricular bradycardia.

Procedure(s) performed:

Implantation of permanent transvenous cardiac pacemaker (Medtronic model 5985) single chamber

Anesthesia:

Local, 1% Xylocaine.

Assistant surgeon:

Description of procedure:

FINDINGS (including the condition of all organs examined):
The patient was admitted with episodes of atrial flutter/fibrillation with very slow ventricular response in low 40s. The patient was entirely uncooperative and combative during the course of operation. It took five people to hold him on the cath table. Also, his heart rate was between 140 and 180. He had very small veins in the region of the deltopectoral groove. All these problems led to great difficulty putting this pacemaker in. However, the electrode was finally positioned in the apex of the right ventricle, and I assumed that his threshold was satisfactory; but we could not be entirely sure of this because of his very fast ventricular rate of 140 to 160. It appeared that the threshold was an MA of 0.8, voltage 0.5, with resistance of 610 ohms. R-wave sensitivity was 7.3.

PROCEDURE IN DETAIL:
With the patient in the supine position, the right pectoral region was prepped and draped in the usual fashion. As mentioned above, the patient was entirely combative and uncooperative so that five people had to hold him down. After satisfactory local anesthesia and regional anesthesia were induced, a transverse incision was made and the deltopectoral groove was dissected. One vein appeared to be slightly larger than the rest of the very small venules in this area; and it was cannulated with a cardiac electrode, which with some difficulty was gotten into the apex of the right ventricle under fluoroscopic control. As mentioned above, the patient's threshold appeared to be satisfactory, though this was not entirely certain. Electrode was ligated in place with heavy silk, after which it was attached to the Medtronic pacemaker model 5985. The unit was implanted into the subcutaneous pocket. It should be noted that the patient had practically no subcutaneous fat, so that only a very, very thin layer of subcutaneous tissue and skin overlies the pacemaker. The wound was closed in two layers. Dressings were applied, and the patient was taken back to his room.

Ruth Brady M

GODFREY REGIONAL HOSPITAL
123 Main Street • Aldon, FL 77714 • (407) 555-1234

Answers

DISCHARGE SUMMARY

Admitted:	
Discharged:	

Discharge diagnoses:

Will ask for a follow up in one week. Her underlying problems of dementia and then her more long-standing hypocomplementemic vasculitis are persistent problems for her that will continue to require management.

DISCHARGE MEDICATIONS:
1. Potassium 10 mEq 2 tablets bid (that is up from qd prior to admit).
2. Suiar 10 mg daily.
3. Isosorbide 10 mg tid
4. Lasix 40 mg 1 in the morning
5. Prednisone 15 mg daily.
6. Vitamin D
7. Calcium

History:

Laboratory and radiology studies:

Hospital course:

SUMMARY:
The patient was admitted with dehydration, weakness, and hypokalemia. She was treated with IV fluids, IV potassium, as she was hypokalemic. She improved slowly but steadily on the second hospital day or actually early in the morning of the third hospital day. She actually ended up fluid overloaded just a hit and got some IV Lasix lo which she responded nicely. On the day of discharge, which was the third hospital day, she was able to eat her breakfast without difficulty. While still weak she was able to be up safely with her daughter's help and will be discharged for follow-up as an outpatient. Her progressive dementia may well require min-assisted living type setting or even nursing home some point in the near future.

Joe Palermo

GODFREY REGIONAL HOSPITAL
123 Main Street • Aldon, FL 77714 • (407) 555-1234

Answers

PROGRESS NOTE

Chief complaint: _____

Date: _____

Vital signs: BP_____ P_____ R_____

History:

SUBJECTIVE:
Comes in today for annual exam. Menses are regular without intermenstrual bleeding. Her galactorrhea is unchanged. She continues to take bromocriptine 2.5 mg p.o. b.i.d. She takes chlorthalidone 50 mg daily and also daily potassium supplement. When seen a year ago she felt fatigued. Blood work at that time showed her to be hypokalemic. She resumed a potassium supplement at that time and felt much better. She has no headaches. She had some vaginal itching and discharge off and on during the summer but currently doesn't have any. She has never had a mammogram.

Exam:

OBJECTIVE:
Breasts without masses. There is bilateral galactorrhea. There was no axillary adenopathy. Abdomen soft and nontender. Pelvic: External genitalia are normal. Vagina rugous, with a small amount of yellow discharge. Cervix clean. Uterus anterior, mobile, nontender, normal in size, shape, and consistency. Adnexa clear, nontender. Rectovaginal exam confirms. Pap smear was obtained. Wet smear is unremarkable.

Diagnosis/assessment:

ASSESSMENT:
1. Long history of galactorrhea. Prolactins have been well controlled on Parlodel, as have her menses.
2. Has taken chlorthalidone daily for many years. This is for fluid retention.
PLAN:
1. Parlodel 2.5 mg p.o. b.i.d. is renewed for a year.
2. Chlorthalidone 50 mg daily and potassium supplement one daily are renewed.
3. Serum prolactin and serum potassium levels are obtained.

Willen Olnt MD

Patient name: _____

Date of service: _____

GODFREY MEDICAL ASSOCIATES
1532 Third Avenue, Suite 120 • Aldon, FL 77713 • (407) 555-4000

Answers

23 The Certification Process

Try this mock 50-question examination in preparation for an actual certification examination. You will need to score approximately 70% on the examination; therefore you will need to successfully answer 35 of the 50 questions.

Use this test for timing purposes as well. You should be able to complete this examination in no more than 1 hour and 45 minutes to finish within the time constraints of the real examination.

Keep in mind that the actual certification examinations are approximately 5 hours in length and contain approximately 150 questions. See www.aapc.com and www.ahima.org for details.

MOCK 50-QUESTION CPC EXAMINATION

SECTION I: MEDICAL TERMINOLOGY

1. The medical term "ostomy" indicates:

   a. excision
   b. surgical creation of an opening
   c. removal of
   d. none of the above

2. ORIF refers to:

   a. repair and fixation of a fracture, open
   b. repair of open fracture
   c. repair and reduction of open fracture with fixation
   d. none of the above

3. Phalanges refer to:

   a. fingers
   b. toes
   c. bones of the finger
   d. bones of the fingers or toes

4. Fibula refers to:

   a. lower leg bone
   b. upper leg bone
   c. bone connecting ankle to lower leg bone
   d. none of the above

5. The abbreviation "ca" is most commonly used for:

   a. cause
   b. carcinoma
   c. cancer
   d. both b & c

SECTION II: EVALUATION AND MANAGEMENT CODING

6. Patient schedules and attends an office visit for the purpose of receiving immunizations for school. The correct services would be coded as follows:

   a. office visit only
   b. immunization code only
   c. office visit and immunization code
   d. office visit, immunization code, and supply code

7. Patient presents to the emergency department for evaluation of multiple traumas received in an auto accident. History significant for diabetes mellitus, CHF, and S/P bypass graft; patient presents with chest pain. Examination extended to the chest, abdomen, and injuries received to the left tibia and clavicular areas. ECG indicates chest pain noncardiac in nature, possibly due to anxiety/stress. Treatment is limited to x-rays of the tibia and clavicle, both of which are negative. Sprains/contusions are diagnosed and treated appropriately. Patient is discharged home. E & M services would be coded as follows:

   a. 99283
   b. 99284
   c. 99285
   d. appropriate consult code

8. Patient is seen in the physician's office complaining of chest pain. ECG is performed after a detailed history and examination are performed. Impending myocardial infarction is diagnosed, and the patient is transported to the hospital. On arrival at the hospital, the patient is admitted and a comprehensive history is taken and a physical is performed; the patient is considered unstable and critical. The E & M services would be coded as:

   a. 99284
   b. 99285
   c. 99215
   d. 99223

SECTION III: ICD-9-CM CODING

9. Carcinoma in situ of the cervix, currently being treated. Code:

   _____

   _____

10. Patient with an increased blood pressure recording would be coded as:

    a. need additional information to code
    b. hypertension
    c. increased blood pressure
    d. other diagnosis code not listed

Select the correct diagnosis codes for the following:

11. 54-year-old female patient currently being treated for carcinoma of the liver, metastatic from the cervix. Primary site currently not being treated, no recurrence.

    Code: _____

12. Patient visiting the physician for inoculation of chickenpox because she is pregnant.

    Code: _____

13. Patient is currently 7 months' pregnant. Patient now presents with glucose level indicating gestational diabetes. The patient is examined by the physician, and in addition to the office visit an ultrasound is performed for advanced maternal age.

    Office visit, diagnostic code(s): _____

    Ultrasound, diagnostic code(s): _____

14. Patient seeks additional advice from an ENT after the diagnosis of acute tonsillitis from the general practitioner. The patient's request would be coded as:

    a. office visit, established
    b. office visit, new patient
    c. consultation, outpatient
    d. consultation, confirmatory

15. Patient is inpatient in the critical care unit of the local hospital. The patient has been removed from the critical list; however, surgery and end-stage renal disease necessitate the patient be monitored carefully. Physician spends 45 minutes examining the stable patient, performing a history and physical. E & M services would be coded as:

    a. critical care, first hour
    b. hospital visit code
    c. hospital consultation code
    d. none of the above

SECTION IV: ANESTHESIA CODING

16. Epidural for vaginal delivery for 24-year-old well woman:

    a. 00857
    b. 00850
    c. 00955
    d. none of the above

17. General anesthesia for a 75-year-old man with hypertension and Parkinson's disease for transurethral resection of the prostate:

    a. 00910
    b. 00914
    c. 00914-P2
    d. 00914-P2, 99100

18. Regional anesthesia administered by a surgeon in the performance of repair of a closed hand fracture:

    a. 01830-P1
    b. 01820-P1
    c. 26600-47
    d. 26600-P1

19. Anesthesia is coded as:

    a. time
    b. anesthesia codes from the anesthesia section
    c. physical status modifiers
    d. all the above

20. Anesthesia time begins when the anesthesiologist enters the operating room and ends when he or she leaves the room.

    a. true
    b. false

SECTION V: RADIOLOGY CODING

21. Chest x-ray posteroanterior and lateral would be coded as:

    a. 71010
    b. 71020
    c. 71030
    d. 71050

22. Left and right mammograms for benign fibrocystic breast disease would be coded as:

    a. 77055
    b. 77056
    c. 87092
    d. 77057

23. When professional services only are performed for the fluoroscopy and radiography involved with the insertion of a pacemaker, the following code(s) would be used:

    a. 71090
    b. 71090-26
    c. 71100
    d. 32208

24. MRI of the brain and brainstem, with and without contrast, would be coded as:

    a. 70541
    b. 70551
    c. 70553
    d. 70540

25. A "DEC" view performed in the radiology section refers to:

    a. view of a deceased patient
    b. descending view of the anatomic part
    c. decubitus view
    d. none of the above

SECTION VI: PATHOLOGY CODING

26. Multiple blood tests may be coded as:

    a. individually as outlined
    b. use the organic diseases panel
    c. either of the above when appropriate
    d. none of the above

27. Testing for therapeutic levels of digoxin is coded as:

    a. 80299
    b. 80162
    c. 80101
    d. none of the above

28. Automated hemogram would be coded as:

    a. 85022
    b. 85023
    c. 85021
    d. none of the above

29. Surgical pathology for three specimens of biopsies of the urethra received from the operative suite in one container would be coded as:

    a. 88305-90
    b. 88305
    c. 88305 ×3
    d. none of the above

30. Autopsy is distinguished by gross examination only and gross and microscopic examination.

    a. true
    b. false

SECTION VII: SURGERY CODING

31. Physician performs diagnostic bronchoscopy followed immediately by a radical resection of the lung.

    a. bronchoscopy and resection of the lung
    b. bronchoscopy-51 and resection of the lung
    c. resection of the lung
    d. none of the above

32. Excision of benign lesion, trunk, 0.7 cm with closure.

    a. 11401
    b. 11400
    c. 11401, 12001
    d. none of the above

33. Cast application, long leg cast and repair fracture of leg

    a. 29345
    b. fracture code + 29345
    c. fracture care code only
    d. none of the above

34. Temporary pacemaker implantation for stabilization followed by implantation of permanent ventricular pacemaker with electrodes.

    a. 33208
    b. 33206
    c. 33207, 33210-51
    d. 33207, 33210-59

35. Coronary venous bypass, single-vein graft using arterial grafts.

    a. 33517
    b. 33517, 33533
    c. 33533
    d. none of the above

36. Laparoscopy cholecystectomy.

    a. 47600
    b. 47562
    c. 56340
    d. none of the above

37. Exploratory laparotomy with abdominal hysterectomy with salpingectomy and oophorectomy.

    a. 58150, 49000-51
    b. 58200
    c. 58150
    d. 58150, 58700-51, 58943-51

38. Cochlear implant is performed by the neurovascular surgeon while the mastoidectomy is performed by the otolaryngological surgeon.

    a. 69930
    b. 69930, 69501-51
    c. 69930-62, 69501-62
    d. 69930-62

39. Individual supportive psychotherapy, outpatient, 22 minutes.

    a. 90804
    b. 90806
    c. 90810
    d. none of the above

40. Cardiac catheterization, performed for placement of two stents, right coronary artery.

    a. 93501, 92980
    b. 93501-51, 92980
    c. 92980 ×2, 93501-52
    d. 92980

41. Electrocardiogram performed four times in the same day.

    a. 93000 ×4
    b. 93000, 93000-76, 93000-76, 93000-76
    c. 93000-77, 93000-77, 93000-77, 93000-77
    d. none of the above

42. Postoperative visits during a global period are coded as:

    a. 99024
    b. 99025
    c. the appropriate E & M visit
    d. none of the above

43. Allergy immunotherapy and a problem-focused established office visit.

    a. 95115 and 99212
    b. 95115
    c. 95115 and 99212-25
    d. none of the above

44. Chemotherapy infusion for 4 hours.

    a. 96410 ×4
    b. 96412 ×4
    c. 96413, 96415 ×3
    d. 96413, 96413 ×2

45. All supplies and materials used in the performance of a procedure should be coded as 99070.

    a. true
    b. false

46. Venipuncture charges are coded as follows:

    a. 36415
    b. 99000
    c. not charged in addition to procedures
    d. none of the above

47. Specimen handling costs may be charged when the specimen is being transported out of the physician's office and preparation is required to handle and transfer the specimen.

    a. true
    b. false

48. Pulmonary spirometry.

    a. 94010
    b. 94010-26
    c. 94656
    d. none of the above

49. Ophthalmologists performing ophthalmologic examinations should use the E & M level of service for billing services.

    a. true
    b. false

50. Injection of antibiotics would be coded as:

    a. 96374
    b. 96375
    c. 96372
    d. 96372 + drug code